Volunteer Nomads

A Mother's Memories
of Foreign Service Family Life

NANCY POGUE LaTURNER

Outskirts Press, Inc.
Denver, Colorado

To Fred, Dakota and Tina with all my love

Acknowledgements

I always thought of myself as a woman of few words and, with this memoir in mind, I wondered if it would be possible for me to write a book's worth of words on one subject. I joined National Novel Writing Month to find out. NaNoWriMo challenges writers to produce 50,000 words in one month, and I succeeded! With that strong beginning, I had no trouble continuing for several thousand more. Then I sent all thirty-three chapters to my marvelous friend and editor, Ruth Friesen, who scrutinized every sentence with her discriminating eye for both grammar and content. After making the changes that Ruth suggested, I rounded up a posse of readers. My husband Fred and daughter Tina helped jog my memory of key events. Dave Malitz offered valuable advice on several elements and also found a few pesky typos. Ellen LaPenna provided her expert editorial guidance, and Beth Malitz wowed me by reading the whole book in one day. Throughout the whole process I felt empowered by the support of writing coach and mentor Mark David Gerson who exemplifies what it means to live and write one's own truth. My heartfelt thanks go to all of you.

Author's Note

This book describes events and people in my life as I remember them. Descriptions of places, events, and people are as accurate as my memory. When I wanted to protect the privacy of certain individuals, I changed their names and made note of that in the narrative; the rest is my truth.

"Memory is a complicated thing, a relative to truth, but not its twin."
~ Barbara Kingsolver ~

Contents

PART ONE
NEW MEXICO GENESIS

Tina and Nancy on the farm in New Mexico

April 1974 – March 1975

Destiny Plays at the Cactus

The day that changed our lives forever began like any other. The sun rose in our brilliant azure New Mexico sky. Ordinary spring winds whipped blossoms off native plum trees outside our dining room window. The drudgery of daily chores promised to fill every hour with sameness.

I pushed my thrift-store chair back from the scarred second-hand table and dug deep to summon enough energy to face the sour smell of two-babies-worth of dirty diapers in the wringer washer tub and the chaos in our toddlerized living room. With my back turned to the kitchen counter I ignored the intimidating stack of unopened bills that loomed over the few food stamps we had left. I clutched a clump of short brown

hair in each fist and felt the raggedness of my self-inflicted haircut. If Fred
didn't come home with a job today....

Rather than wallow in the all too familiar poor-me pit, I reached for
yesterday's newspaper, passed along by our neighbors who lived across the
irrigation ditch. Whether Fred had good news to celebrate or bad news
to rise above, we should try to do something fun for a change; I flipped
through the pages of the paper looking for the movie schedule. With
money so tight, we had to be frugal. If there was a good show at the drive-
in we could bundle our babes into the rickety old Plymouth sedan, grab
a brown paper bag full of homemade popcorn and make the twenty-mile
trip from our little place in Los Lunas to the Cactus Drive-In Theatre in
Albuquerque. By the time we hit I-25, we could expect both babies to fall
asleep and snooze in peace for the rest of the night, granting us an evening
out without the expense of a babysitter.

That fateful April day I missed the movie page entirely when an advertisement with a bold black border captured my attention like a 3D image:

"Interested in working overseas? If you have experience in any of
the following fields, call the number listed below. Recruiters will be in
Albuquerque in May."

A thrilling tingle raced round my neck and down my spine. Overseas...
Fred and I had spent many an evening sharing our dreams about seeing
the world together. Inspired by the two years we had lived in Chitose,
Japan, while Fred completed his military service, we had explored as many
avenues for overseas employment as we could find; but it seemed that neither of us had the required education or experience. *This could be it.* The
ad trembling in my hands might hold the key to our future.

When Fred got home that afternoon, he didn't have a chance to report on his job-hunting. Before the screen door banged shut behind him,
I fluttered the newspaper in front of his face.

"Look at this ad -- did you do any of this when you were in the
Army?"

Fred's eyes moved quickly down the list. "Yeah... I did a little on the
Teletype, but it wasn't a big part of my job. Do you think...?"

I pawed through the kitchen junk drawer, found the scissors, and clipped the ad. "There's only one way to find out – call this number."

The sponsor of the advertisement was the U.S. State Department, and Fred's phone call initiated the federal government hiring process. Reams of paperwork challenged Fred's determination. He swore to fill in every single blank; he pledged to do whatever was required to get this job. The alternative was to sell life insurance or manage the Belen Kentucky Fried Chicken. Nightmares about failing to provide for his family plagued him. Images of the Kentucky Colonel spurred him on.

Fred did everything in his power to enhance his application. He rented a typewriter to fill in the forms and also to practice for the typing test. He restyled his appearance from radical hippy to fresh-faced, button-down moderate. I wouldn't miss the beard, but oh how I hated to see those thick black curls fall to the bathroom floor.

The application checklist included an interview, place and time to be set by government officials as soon as Fred submitted his packet of paperwork. Fred wanted to be prepared in case a Secret Service Agent came to our home -- he slapped a thick coat of primer over my artwork in the yard. I had painted a nude blue figure, Picasso-like, larger than life-size. I thought it brought humor to the modesty panel we built to shield our neighbors from the view of our naked bodies tip-toeing from the wood-burning sauna shed to the icy water of our stock tank. Fred wasn't sure a government official would appreciate my sense of humor. Alas, he censored unnecessarily. His interview took place at the nearest federal building, the Los Lunas Post Office, and we never exposed the Secret Service man to the idiosyncrasies of our private life.

After the paperwork and the interview we suffered the waiting game. Fred's experience, education, and Army-related top-secret clearance met the job requirements. He impressed the interviewer with his charming personality. All that remained was the security background investigation.

Some days we talked confidently about The Job in sentences that started, "When…" and other days we shared our worries about the background check, "If…."

There was nothing to be done but wait. We waited.

After four months Fred couldn't stand the suspense any longer. He called Washington. I watched his face as he listened to the State Department official. His expression gave nothing away. As soon as he hung up, I begged for an instant replay.

"Well, first she said not to worry, that my investigation is on schedule." He sighed. "We should hear something definite in six to eight weeks."

I groaned.

As the weeks passed in slow motion, Fred worked the night shift at our local convenience store. I dreaded those long hours when he faced the underbelly of Los Lunas, alone and unarmed in that sleazy dump. I sang both babies to sleep in our scratchy brown upholstered rocking chair, watching cottonwood shadows in the moonlight as I yearned to see our Plymouth's cock-eyed headlights cross the ditch bridge.

Day after day, we imagined how a career in the State Department would change our lives. What would it be like to walk inside the pictures of National Geographic, the magazine that had enthralled us both as children? I predicted that our new friends would be sophisticated American diplomats. Fred looked forward to meeting intriguing foreign characters. Would we become multilingual? And the kids' education – imagine the opportunities at private international schools. No boarding school for our kids, we decided, but maybe we should shoot for high school in the States, to ease their transition into college....

Our dreaming out loud convinced us both that the State Department job was it. It had to be. It was a perfect match: a steady job with good benefits and the possibility of advancement, a chance to explore the world and experience other cultures, a marvelous education for our children. And the clincher – the prospect of early retirement.

And we waited.

The New Beirut

The call came in November 1974, six months after Fred submitted his application, even though it seemed like at least a year had gone by.

Fred mouthed the words "State Department" and held the phone up so I could hear too.

"Congratulations, your application for the position of Communications and Records Officer has been approved and you are assigned to Tehran, Iran."

Fred's polite response didn't register with me. The expression on his face asked, "What did she say?"

The woman's voice chirped with good cheer. "Tehran is a marvelous first assignment. You might not know that Beirut used to be considered the Paris of the Middle East, but since the threat of civil war escalated in Lebanon, everyone has been calling Tehran the new Beirut. I've heard that caviar is so plentiful, you'll be spreading it on bread like peanut butter."

Tehran-Beirut-Paris-Lebanese civil war-Iranian caviar. It was too much to absorb all at once. Fred grabbed my hands and whirled me around the living room in a crazy victory dance. We flopped down on the sway-backed sofa and Fred picked up our tattered National Geographic World Atlas from the coffee table. He opened it to the map of Iran and poked the circled star symbol indicating the capital, Tehran.

"There it is. That's where we're going -- where we'll be for the next two years."

Of course our trip didn't follow a straight line. No, our journey from Los Lunas, New Mexico to Tehran, Iran included some hurdles, a couple of detours and several stops along the way.

A few days after the phone call announcing Fred's assignment we received a hefty packet in the mail giving us guidance on the mechanics of becoming a Foreign Service family. Once we sorted out our belongings into sea freight, airfreight, and storage categories, we had to decide how to get to Washington, DC for Fred's eight-week orientation and training course. We could fly or we could drive. Both choices had advantages and disadvantages, but we chose to drive, in order to have our own car in Washington rather than a rental. With the help of our parents we financed a shiny black 1967 Volkswagen beetle. We loved our new car. It was an incredible improvement over the rattle-trap Plymouth.

On departure day, Fred folded down the back seat of the VW and I spread out two well-worn flannel-lined sleeping bags. First in, our son Dakota, aged 20 months, followed by our daughter Tina, not quite one year old. They babbled, cooed, gnawed on their teething toys, and took frequent naps. The highway hum and car motion lulled them into a relaxed state that allowed Fred and me to have wonderful long conversations. When Tina wanted to nurse, I swung her into the front seat with me. Dakota snacked on unfiltered apple juice and graham crackers in the backseat play-lounge. Even though a road trip with two toddlers might not be everybody's ideal, it worked for us, and the ease of our maiden voyage foretold the spirit of twenty-odd years of travel to come.

Somewhere in East Texas, early in the morning of the third travel day, with the rising sun bright in our eyes, I leaned back to see if the glare bothered the babies. They were fine, but I noticed a small empty space on the sleeping bag. For the past hour I'd had that nagging feeling that I'd forgotten something, and now I knew what it was.

"Oh, dammit, Fred, you have to pull over."

"Why, what's wrong?"

"I don't see Baby-Kinsey. You know how Dakota is about his Baby-Kinsey."

Fred stopped the car on the shoulder and we searched for Dakota's lovey, a baby pillow covered in the soft birds-eye diaper material that he always rubbed across his lips when he was sleepy. I went through everything in the back seat while Fred looked in the suitcases.

"We must have left her in the motel room," I said. "We have to go back."

"Are you sure? We'll have to backtrack eighty miles or more."

Fred closed his eyes for a second, then looked at Dakota and smiled. I nodded. We piled back in the car and Fred made a U-turn.

Our Nation's Capital

There should have been fanfare when we parked in front of the brick apartment building at 3908 Elbert Avenue in Alexandria, VA, our home for the next eight weeks. It was January 9, 1975, Tina's first birthday.

Strapped for cash, we had rented this place sight unseen from an ad in a Washington Post that we had found at a newsstand in Albuquerque. Both the building and the neighborhood suffered from a serious lack of care and upkeep. I didn't want to admit it, but the place was downright ugly. The inside looked even shabbier than the dingy exterior and the miasma of many meals cooked long ago lingered in the air and soured my stomach.

Our apartment was almost a basement apartment -- "almost" because it was not entirely below ground. It had normal sized windows, but the windowsills were at the level of the sidewalk outside. At first I didn't like the idea of living that low, but I soon learned that Dakota and Tina found nothing more entertaining than standing on a chair, eye-to-eye with Nature. I wrestled the window and storm window open, and the kids tossed scraps of bread to scampering squirrels and the hungry cardinals and sparrows that joined the feast.

The rest of the place looked like pictures I had seen of ghetto tenements -- peeling linoleum, chipped paint, cracked Formica, and stained carpeting. I resolved to overlook the shortcomings of our building and ignore the reek of other people's odors, reminding myself that I had to learn to adapt to all sorts of living conditions, short term and long term. Thank goodness we would be here only eight weeks.

When our accumulation of dirty clothes threatened to burst the seams of Fred's threadbare duffle bag, I headed for the laundry facilities in the sub-basement. With Tina in the backpack I held Dakota's hand beside me on the right and dragged the heavy duffle behind me on the other side, thump-thumping down the narrow stairway.

The laundry room lurked at the end of a dimly lit, moldy smelling, twisted passageway. I pulled Dakota close to me, as far as possible from the smears of suspicious substances along the walls. Odd shaped shadows darkened the corners. Loud clanking and hissing noises from the boiler room drove me into a panic. I had watched too many TV news reports about violent crime in the Washington, DC area. I acted on gut instinct, dropped the duffle, swooped Dakota into my arms and fled the film noir murder scene of my anxious imagination.

That evening, Fred rescued our laundry bag and invented a new family activity: do our washing at a public laundromat and have Saturday lunch at Pizza Hut while the clothes flopped around in the dryer. For many years after, when Foreign Service friends craved a MacDonald's hamburger as a taste of home, we four shook our heads and said, "Pizza Hut."

At the end of Fred's first week at the State Department, he came home with a surprise -- a cash advance. He spread eleven $100 bills on the bed and we all danced around the most money we had ever seen in one place. In that moment of joy I knew how it felt to hold a winning lottery ticket.

Fred took the bus every weekday morning to his training classes, while the rest of us watched Captain Kangaroo on the apartment's black and white TV, played in the park or went grocery shopping. The State Department also offered an orientation course for wives (called dependent spouses in governmentese, a term I hated. I couldn't stifle the image of all of us dangling uselessly from the hems of our sponsors' worthy garments). I went to the mandatory security briefing but declined the invitation for the rest of the program. The look on the faces of my children when I picked them up from daycare on that one occasion killed any desire to leave them ever again in the hands of strangers.

The days passed slowly for me. I invented reasons to go to the supermarket or drug store, just to escape our dreary apartment. In February the weather turned exceptionally mild and I took the kids to the park every day. They enjoyed watching older children doing tricks on the monkey bars while the younger crowd dug in the sand box. One boy, Louie, a year or so older than Dakota, showed up every time we visited the park, and eventually his mom and I introduced ourselves.

"Your kids sure don't look alike," said Louie's mom.

Although most people didn't blurt it out like that, their second glances telegraphed the same thought. Sometimes I felt tempted to make a smart remark, but the truth is, I never tired of telling our true story.

"It's 'cause Dakota is adopted. He gets his creamy café au lait complexion from his African-American biological father." Louie's mom raised her eyebrows, so I continued. "He was three days old when we got him, and I didn't know that I was already pregnant with Tina – so they're only eight months apart."

"That's almost like having twins," Louie's mom said. "I don't know how you do it." She pointed at Louie, who was trying to climb over the chain link fence to retrieve his ball. "One is plenty for me!"

Sometimes I wasn't sure how I did it either, especially at that critical hour when both kids acted cranky at the very moment I started to cook dinner. Like mothers everywhere, I invented strategies to keep the kids entertained and me from having a meltdown. Often I would put Tina in the backpack so she could look over my shoulder. Then I installed Dakota on a kitchen chair at the sink and let him play with water. That system never failed.

When we neared the end of our eight-week stay in Washington in March 1975, it was time to prepare for our departure from the States. We received official U.S. government employee passports, travel papers, airline tickets, and dozens of immunizations, some against diseases we thought belonged to the nineteenth century. A few of the shots or vaccinations, for example cholera, small pox, typhoid and yellow fever, weren't painful. Tina merely made a face, and Dakota let out a tiny yelp. The tetanus shots were the worst for the kids, not only because of the sting but also the sore, hot arm and fever over the next twenty-four hours. My least favorite was the gamma globulin, for adults only. It went in via a long needle in one butt cheek and my whole leg burned like fire for the rest of the day. The other shots (rabies, measles-mumps-rubella, Hepatitis B, tuberculosis skin test) were forgettable in comparison.

During our last days Stateside, we turned our car over to State Department's transportation experts for shipment to Tehran. A moving company packed and shipped our airfreight. We called our parents to say goodbye. Finally, we packed our bags and called a taxi.

Plane to Tehran

As we settled into our seats on the plane, the kids looking adorable in their brand new Winnie-The-Pooh travel outfits from Sears, an unbidden terrible image flooded my mind. I could see Dakota's milk and juice bottles sitting all alone on the top shelf of the cleaned-out fridge, back in the vacant apartment, right where I had so carefully put them the night before. Bad mommy, bad bad mommy. It took a few minutes to swallow my pride and summon the courage to beg a bottle from the family seated two rows ahead of us. Dakota beamed when he saw the cute bear-shape, much more fun than his plain old ones. At least I didn't lose face in his eyes. I tucked Baby-Kinsey in beside him for good measure.

Here we go. Tomorrow we'll arrive in Tehran and start to build our new life. I sure hope the kids like traveling by air as much as traveling by car.

Fred and Tina played their favorite game of talking fingers, making up their own language as they went along. Dakota and I made beautiful marks in the coloring book provided by the airline. I silently thanked the State Department for the comfort of full-fare seats for all four of us.

Our flight was PanAm Number One, a route that went around the world. It landed briefly in major airports to drop off and pick up passengers. Through passengers did not deplane. The landing in Istanbul was one of those stops. One problem. The cargo door refused to open. After at least an hour of effort on the part of Turkish ground crew, it did finally open and a collective sigh of relief rippled down the length of the plane. Too soon, that relief. The stewardess announced that take-off would be delayed due to another problem with the cargo door. Now it wouldn't close.

Hours went by. The galley ran out of water and everything else. The toilets threatened to overflow. Even the air seemed stale and over-used. The passengers murmured, frowned, fidgeted. I pulled out a Richard Scarry book to absorb the kids in their much-loved search for Lowly Worm in the complex illustrations. The captain's loud voice blaring over the intercom startled everyone.

"Well, folks, I'm happy to say that the cargo door is now fully functional."

He paused while the passengers cheered.

"Before we prepare for take-off, though, we are going to send you folks into the terminal for a bite to eat while the ground crew cleans and restocks the plane. I need to caution you about some security issues we have here. You will be entering a restricted area, and for your safety armed guards will escort you. Relax, enjoy your meal, stretch your legs, and be ready to re-board in an hour."

I wondered about the security issues. Looking back, I suspect that the lack of welcome to our American flag carrier was due to the U.S. threat to cut off military aid to Turkey in protest of their conflict with Greece over the island of Cyprus. At the time though, our innocence and ignorance of world affairs kept us blissfully in the dark.

We trooped obediently off the plane and across the tarmac. The importance of a meal paled before the ecstasy of freedom from the airplane. I wanted to whirl like a dervish. I'm sure Dakota and Tina did too. But they behaved beautifully, in spite of being in a strange place at 11:00 PM local time, over-tired, bored, hungry, and thirsty. They dutifully ate their watery soup, pushing the gristly bones to the side, and drank the fizzy orange Fanta, even though they had never before tasted a soft drink.

Within the prescribed hour, we marched back to the plane, found our seats, and buckled our seatbelts. I sent positive thoughts to the cargo door as the plane carried us through the dark sky toward Iran. Dakota and Tina fell asleep as soon as the cabin lights dimmed, and we parents plugged into the in-flight feature film, unremembered because we too slept until the bustle of preparations for landing nudged us back to consciousness.

PART TWO
IRAN ODYSSEYS

Nancy visits the bazaar

2

Dressed for the plane to Tehran

March - June 1975

Tehran

The view of Tehran from the air reminded me of Albuquerque. The city spread out at the foot of the mountains. A wide river meandered across rolling desert terrain that stretched in all directions. But I forgot the similarities when the differences bombarded my senses.

The stink of burning coal pinched my nostrils. A film of grime coated every surface, muting the world to shades of gray and black. Stark cement buildings towered beside narrow streets in the nearly deserted business sector where a few people, all dressed in gray or black, loitered listlessly. High brick walls concealed the homes in the neighborhoods we passed. An occasional gray or black car moved slowly down the wider avenues.

Even though we arrived six hours late, Fred's boss Bob Hammond met us at the airport and helped us through customs and the rest of the formalities, making our first arrival at post much less stressful than trying to do it on our own. In our experience that part of the system never broke down. Someone always met newcomers and guided them through the maze of host-country officialdom.

"Take a good look around," Bob told us, "you won't see the city looking this empty until next March. You're lucky to arrive at the beginning of No Ruz, the Iranian New Year. People are mostly off work and away visiting family and friends for the next three weeks. After No Ruz you won't believe how noisy and busy Tehran is."

Bob drove directly to the embassy compound and ushered us into our temporary quarters, a spacious apartment on the third floor of a long building. Five other apartments shared the building along with the Marine Security Detachment's barracks, known as the Marine House. Looking out the front windows, we saw a huge grassy area, bordered on one side by three small houses, and on the other side a row of tall trees. Directly across the grassy field stood the embassy chancery (the office building where the diplomatic delegation works) with a helicopter pad off to the side.

"It's like a park," Fred exclaimed. "Look down there, Nancy. An Olympic-size swimming pool!"

Bob pointed to the left. "See those trees? Well, the compound extends back behind there. The Ambassador's residence, tennis courts, and DCM's (Deputy Charge of Mission) house are all on that side. The property really is beautiful. It covers twenty-two acres."

"Who lives in the cute little houses?" I asked.

"They're reserved for employees in our section because we are on call twenty-four hours a day."

Fred's orientation briefing had prepared us for the schedule. We knew that the communicators took turns being on call for a week at a time. I imagined how convenient it would be to be living right there on the compound.

Bob pointed out the window and continued talking. "It looks like a sweet deal, but some guys say convenience isn't worth the sacrifice of privacy. Living on the compound is like living in a fish bowl."

Visions of Dakota and Tina splashing in the pool and running across the wide expanse of grass inspired me to ask, "Would one of those houses be available to us?"

"Afraid not. No vacancies there for at least nine months. You'll be looking for housing outside, but don't worry, the Housing Section is all set to help you. You have plenty of time -- you're allowed up to three months in temporary quarters."

As Bob was leaving, he said he would take us grocery shopping the next day and bring us to his home for dinner with his family that evening. As soon as the door closed, we rushed to explore the apartment. The kitchen, located three steps up in an alcove, was fully equipped and stocked with a welcome kit of staples and enough food for the next few meals. A short note on the counter explained that the food had been charged to our account at the PX and we could return any unwanted items. It felt good to be looked after this way, welcomed as members of a community rather than strangers in a strange land -- another example of the trustworthy welcome-to-post system.

We moved from room to room, the kids checking the furniture for bounciness while I opened closets and drawers and Fred tested the bathroom. His voice echoed in the cavernous tiled room.

"Come look at this."

Mint green fixtures fought peach and maroon tiles in a color war that made me blink. But that wasn't what interested Fred. He pointed at the fixture next to the toilet.

"Guess what that is."

It was an oval bowl with two faucet handles on the rim and a spray-head-looking-thingie in the bottom. I couldn't imagine what it was. Fred had spent a year in Turkey, so he could tell me all about it. I never did learn to use it properly but I did discover that a bidet makes a perfect place to drain and store kids' bath toys.

The décor in the rest of the apartment was less surprising and more like a modern American hotel. I noticed that the furniture was all Drexel and I reveled in the luxury that everything matched. It needed only a few personal touches to make it homey. I smiled, inside and out, at this vast improvement over the depressing apartment in Virginia.

While I settled our toddlers for a much-needed nap, Fred went out to see what lay beyond the compound walls. The kids' cribs were in the airfreight shipment, not yet delivered, so they had to sleep in the big bed. I cuddled up between them and dozed off.

A loud buzzing noise melded with my dream and I struggled to wake up, disoriented. Fred buzzed the doorbell again. Finally I realized where I was and what was going on. I got up to let him in. Dakota and Tina slept on, and I noticed that Dakota snored lightly, something he had never done before. I touched his forehead to check for fever. *A little on the warm side maybe, but probably nothing to worry about.* I slipped through the half-closed bedroom door and tiptoed to the entry.

"Look what I found." Fred's arms overflowed with newspaper-wrapped bundles. His eyes sparkled. He was close to jumping up and down with excitement. His enthusiasm was contagious.

"Let me see, let me see."

Fred put his packages on the table and unwrapped them one by one.

"Ooh, pistachios. Mmmm, watermelon. What's this, Persian melon? And this other looks good, what…."

"I got lucky and found one tiny shop open. Try a pistachio, they are great. Oh, sorry, you asked about the candy – it's Halvah, you'll love it."

Tina and Dakota peeked around the doorframe. "What dat, Daddy?"

We sampled all of Fred's booty. The melons were juicy, sweet, perfectly ripe. The halvah tasted rich and decadent. The pistachios disappeared in ten minutes. My thumbs ached from opening nut after nut destined for the open mouths of my two begging baby birds. That evening we suffered. Too many pistachios guarantee a tummy ache, although the flavor is probably worth the pain.

Later, in the middle of the night, Dakota woke crying. Over and over he sobbed, "Walk me, Daddy, walk me."

We took turns pacing back and forth, patting his back, trying to comfort him, and begging him to tell us what was the matter. Could he still have gas from the pistachio overdose?

On my umpteenth round of the living room, just at daybreak, I felt Dakota move his arm.

"Look, he's rubbing his ear. I hope it's not an infection. What can we do? Is it way too early to call Bob Hammond?"

Fred said the best idea was to call Post One, the Marine Security Detachment. Someone was always on guard there. The Marine on duty arranged for a car to take us to the Army hospital where Dakota was examined and given an antibiotic for his ear infection.

An uneasy feeling undermined my confidence. What had we gotten ourselves into? Would we be able to keep our children safe while dragging them all around the world? I wanted to share my feelings with Fred, but I didn't want to imply that I was unhappy with our new life. Before I could work out how to begin, Fred offered a bit of wisdom accompanied by a comforting hug.

"We sure didn't get chauffer-driven transportation at dawn to the doctor in Los Lunas. Or free medicine either."

It did help to look on the positive side, but I still had to wonder, what other dangers lurked around us?

Najibey and The Magic Carpet

As the mother of two toddlers, though, I didn't have time to dwell on possible dangers. My daily concerns focused on childcare and homemaking. In those early days, grocery shopping presented a real challenge. Returning home from my first shopping excursion, I faced three flights of stairs to our temporary apartment. I stood at the bottom of the first flight and stared at the combination of four full grocery bags plus two small children.

That's when our neighbor, Helga, came to the rescue. With babies and purchases safely delivered, I invited Helga to stay for a cup of tea. I learned that Helga's husband cooked for the Ambassador, who provided housing for their family in the ground floor apartment of our building. It seemed odd to me that the U.S. Ambassador brought a Swiss chef to Iran -- an addition to my growing list of bewildering aspects of the Foreign Service.

Helga shared her insights about life on the compound as well as life in Tehran. She also introduced me to Najibey, cleaning woman and baby-sitter-extraordinaire.

A few weeks later, with Helga translating, I hired Najibey to baby-sit while Fred and I went to the Persian carpet market on an embassy-sponsored tour. Najibey had been coming to our apartment every day to clean, and she always spent a few minutes interacting with Dakota and Tina, so it wasn't a huge stretch to imagine that they would be happy with her for a couple of hours. On the day of the carpet tour, neither of the kids cried or fussed when Fred and I went out the door, even though they hadn't been with a babysitter since that one sad day back in Washington when I left them at the daycare center to attend a security briefing.

"See how easy that was?" Fred gave me a quick hug. "I don't know what you were so worried about."

"Okay, I'm glad they weren't upset, but I'm still concerned about nap-time. What if…."

Fred gave me another squeeze. "You worry too much. Everything's gonna be fine."

On the main shopping street, dozens of carpet shops tempted buyers with curbside displays of wool and silk rugs in riots of rich colors and in-tricate patterns. The tour guide directed us into the store where our group of embassy couples had an appointment for a private showing.

For a moment I couldn't see in the subtle interior lighting. My com-panions murmured and shuffled in the dark. Dye odors mingled with dust, a slight whiff of musk, and the tannic fragrance of brewing tea. When my eyes adjusted to the gloom, I focused on the wealth of carpets surrounding us. Piled to the ceiling, hundreds of carpets crowded us into a narrow aisle leading to a doorway at the back of the main showroom.

Abdul Abbas, owner of the shop, dressed in the typical Tehrani uniform of baggy black trousers and rumpled blue suit coat, invited us in. He gestured toward several knee-high stacks of carpets and indicated that we should sit. Everyone looked uncomfortable in variations of awkward semi-cross-legged positions. I smoothed my knit skirt over my knees and relaxed, giving due credit to daily yoga practice for my comfort.

A shop assistant served steaming tea in tiny tulip-shaped glasses. I shifted mine between my fingertips as quickly as I could without spilling. My first tentative sip scalded a raw spot on my tongue.

Abdul Abbas' opening remarks in rhythmically accented English drew my attention back to the carpets.

"I show to you that design in Persian carpets have many meanings. Each is named for the region where they are woven. Today I show beautiful examples of Bakhtiari, Kashan, Hamadan, and Karajeh." He pointed to a pile on his left. "Here you see tribal rugs, or Kilim, made by Kurdish peoples."

To me, one rug stood out from all the rest. The background comprised alternating stripes of chocolate and cinnamon wool. Each wide stripe bore embroidery in blue, gold, and white yarn in patterns that reminded me of Navajo designs.

"I wonder how much he wants for that one?" I whispered to Fred.

My limited experience so far led me to believe that success in Foreign Service life might depend on bargaining skills, but unfortunately I had none. Neither did Fred. We paid the full asking price of $300 for a four-foot by ten-foot Kurdish rug that we thought we couldn't afford and believed we had no place for. And we cherished it forever after as one of our best souvenirs, finding a place of honor for it in all our future homes.

It took both of us to carry the rug up those three flights of stairs. Back at the apartment, the loud click of the opening lock echoed in the hallway, then -- silence.

"Do you suppose…?" The absence of child noises carved a void in the pit of my stomach.

Najibey smiled at us from the bedroom doorway. She beckoned.

Two single beds, two occupants lying flat on their backs, eyes closed, covers pulled up to their chins and tucked in tight on both sides, eight inches of crisp white sheet folded back over the blanket. *My babies. Are they sleeping or unconscious?* No matter how fleeting, still a terrifying thought.

Fred patted my shoulder. "Didn't I tell you? You shouldn't worry so much…. Uh…do you think she drugged them?" He chuckled.

Not funny to me. How could I not worry about my children in these strange circumstances?

Amoebas

When we moved from temporary quarters to our permanent apartment, another third-world risk caught me by surprise. The move took us off the embassy compound and across town to a residential area directly behind the Tehran American School. Our two toddlers complicated things a bit, but the biggest difficulty on moving day was my need to visit the bathroom every few minutes. Urgently. Again and again. Eventually I realized that my problem was not going to go away on its own.

The doctor looked at the results of the tests. "I'm sorry, Mrs. LaTurner, but you have amoebic dysentery." He looked up from the sheaf of papers. "Perhaps you have eaten some contaminated salad? One must be cautious about raw foods, you know. But in any case, we must treat this illness aggressively to prevent peritonitis and liver infection. The prescribed medicine is Flagyl. Essentially I will be giving you a sub-lethal dose of poison in order to kill off the amoeba that are multiplying in your intestines."

In other words, I'm going to feel a lot worse before I get better? "Doctor, I'm nursing my youngest child. Will this medicine cross over?"

"Oh, most definitely. You must stop breast feeding immediately and start taking the Flagyl right away."

I cried. I worried. I fretted all the way home. As we nursed one last time I explained to Tina as gently as I could that Mama would have no more milk for Num-Num. She was only seventeen months old, but she seemed to understand. I cried myself to sleep that night, but she was fine.

Tina did not ask to nurse again. Once she climbed into my lap, patted my chest, and said, "No more milk." She gave me a hug, jumped down, and ran off to play.

I cried. My breasts grew into hard rock mountains, aching and hot. I was miserable. Tina was fine.

Unfortunately I could not keep the Flagyl down. If I swallowed my tablets at 5:00, I threw up at 5:15. I ran to the bathroom for two reasons now. The doctor prescribed another drug, one usually used in much smaller doses as a malaria suppressant. It stayed down, even though I started gagging on the anticipated bitter flavor ten minutes before the time for each dose. But the medicine worked and I got back to the business of unpacking boxes and re-creating our home in new surroundings with thoughts of danger pushed far to the back of my mind.

Terrorism and Traffic

Danger was real and present in Tehran in 1975, and we heard all about it from Fred's embassy colleagues. They described the revolutionaries' plot to depose the Shah of Iran, Mohammed Reza Pahlavi. Although the Shah was credited with the modernization of Iranian infrastructure, he was also guilty of using his ruthless intelligence agency SAVAK to crush all forms of political opposition. Religious leaders denounced his methods and criticized his doctrines as well as his alliance with the United States. Revolution was not a new idea -- the Shah's army had quelled an uprising in 1963 and forced the Ayatollah Khomeini into exile. Now, in 1975, dissidents again pursued the overthrow of the government by attacking high-level military and political figures, both Iranian and American. The revolutionaries included diplomats on their hit list, and during our two-year stay, they assassinated seven Americans in Tehran.

Fred and I asked each other why the career counselor had described Tehran in such glowing terms, making it seem like a grand resort serving caviar sandwiches, rather than a city fraught with unrest and violence. We concluded later, after years of experience in the Foreign Service, that most of the folks who chose to serve at Main State in Washington, DC, rarely left the United States. They might excel at their jobs; they might know all about foreign policy; but they had little or no idea of what was actually going on in everyday life in these far away corners of the world. Embassy security experts told us that women and children were not terrorist targets, so I felt safe, safer than in Washington, DC to be honest. But the risk for Fred worried me sick, even though the embassy provided armored cars with armed guards to transport staff members to work. Fred told me he felt uncomfortably like the bulls-eye in a large target while riding in the official car. He decided to drive by himself in our VW. He grew his hair long again and completed his disguise with a full beard. Even with blue eyes, he passed for an Iranian.

Of course driving alone also presented dangers. Drivers in Tehran defied every traffic rule known to mankind. Vehicles of all shapes and sizes darted from lane to lane, treating stop lights as nothing more than pretty decorations. If there were a gap on the opposite side of the street a vehicle soon filled it, dodging the oncoming traffic. Gridlock was common and led to shouting and fistfights. When we asked an embassy driver what all the yelling was about, we learned how colorful Iranian insults could be. "You son of a barren camel!" Or, "Try to paint my fart!" On several other occasions we had to maneuver around a car coming backwards on a one-way street. Did the drivers really believe that the arrow on the street sign referred to the direction of the car's position rather than the direction of its motion?

Because Fred took our car every day, when I wanted to go out I called a taxi. That is, until I discovered the buses. The city owned a fleet of faded green double-decker buses retired from service on the streets of London. Dakota, Tina, and I enjoyed the view from the upper deck where we could see over the high walls into all the gardens. No matter how crowded the bus was down below, we usually had the upper deck to ourselves. I commented on that fact to an Iranian friend and he laughed.

"Everyone knows it's not safe to ride up there," he said.

"Why is that?" I couldn't imagine what could be dangerous about the upper level that wouldn't also be true of the lower level of the bus.

My friend chuckled again. "Well, you see, it is very dangerous to ride on the upper deck because there is no driver up there, no driver, you see?"

3

Imps in the toy cupboard

June – September 1975

Home Turf

Our new apartment was bigger than the temporary quarters, about 3500 square feet, furnished in the same style of government issue, and decorated with typical Iranian flair. The floors provided the only neutral color, a grayish polished aggregate material, like Terrazzo but coarser than the fine Italian marble chip version. The walls virtually shouted their contrast in loud patterns and colors.

The gaudiest room was the nursery. Glaring orange wallpaper embellished with gold filigree designs clashed with floor to ceiling yellow draperies printed with a riot of disturbing doll faces. I don't think the kids noticed the garishness, but I felt a headache twinge every time I went in that room. Why didn't I make any changes? The thought simply didn't occur to me; I was that dedicated to adapting to everything, no matter what the significance. I focused on the coincidence that Dakota's crib was orange and Tina's was yellow – at least they blended with the nursery color scheme instead of causing another clash.

In the back yard our landlord had created a mini-paradise that we monopolized as the residents of the ground-floor apartment. A rich blend of spice, musk, and sweet from crimson, vermilion, and coral roses scented the air. Of all the trees and plants in the garden, the pear tree was our favorite. It was a dwarf variety, but that label only applied to its height; the fruit grew full-size, plump and juicy. I've never before, or since, tasted such robust and succulent pears. The kids preferred to eat their fruit whole, but there was no neat way to do it. The first bite unleashed a river of juice down chins, arms, and chubby tummies. I let the kids eat pears outdoors, naked, and play a squirting game with the hose afterward.

The centerpiece of the garden was an 8 by 16 foot rectangular pool made of cement and painted cobalt blue. I'm sure our landlord intended the pool to be ornamental. I wanted something more practical for my life with toddlers so I enlisted Fred's aid to make the pool functional. Rather than filling it to its full three-foot depth, we put in about a foot of water to make the most marvelous kiddy pool imaginable. All summer long we splashed and played in our own backyard spa. The pool had a slow leak, so the water self-cleaned before any sanitation issues arose. When the paint started to peel, we didn't bother the landlord; we bought pool paint in a turquoise shade that reminded me of New Mexico and did the job ourselves, with the surprisingly skillful assistance of our two artistic preschoolers.

All four of us enjoyed having a row of windows on the street side of the apartment where we could view the dusty road that passed in front of our building. We could hear the cling-clong-clang of camel bells before a caravan turned the corner, giving us enough time to pull chairs up to the windows for the kids to stand on. The camels came often in the spring, loaded with bags of their own dung offered for sale to eager gardeners along the way. Donkey carts clattered by every day, carrying anything and everything that might need to be transported from one place to another. Herders also drove flocks of fat-tailed sheep down the streets so that housewives could choose their meat on the hoof and verify that the slaughter met religious specifications. Although I understood the importance of this practice in Iranian culture, I was glad we didn't ever have to witness the sounds, sights, and smells of a butchering on our doorstep or see blood evidence anywhere in our neighborhood.

Most weekends (our embassy closed on Fridays and Saturdays to accommodate Muslim religious practice), we four went exploring in our neighborhood. We found a small vegetable stand that had the freshest produce available. After purchasing cucumbers, tomatoes, and onions, we followed the fragrance of fresh-baked bread a few doors down to the barbari store. If we were lucky, we'd be in time to see the baker lift a gigantic wooden spatula inside his beehive-shaped brick oven where the oval dough stuck to the ceiling as soon as it touched the hot surface. I admired the baker's nonchalance as he turned his back to the oven, whacked a hunk of raw dough from the mound on the table, and slapped another loaf into shape. How did he know the exact moment to pluck his spatula from the corner and hold it steady to catch the hot barbari bread as it fell from the oven ceiling, baked to toasty brown perfection? The music of "Swan Lake" would have completed the image of pas de deux, baker and bread. Barehanded, the baker then lifted the bread from his spatula and impaled the long flat loaf on one of the ten-penny nails on the wall behind the counter.

We lined up like the other customers to receive our loaf wrapped in newspaper, too hot for us to handle, best carried home in a shopping bag. Back in our kitchen, we wasted no time. Fred used a bread knife to open the loaf like a giant pita pocket while I sliced crisp cucumbers, juicy tomatoes, and a mild sweet onion. A smear of Miracle Whip (from the commissary), a dash of salt and pepper, grated cheddar cheese, and voila! The tastiest sandwich ever.

After lunch we often watched TV. The local Armed Forces Radio and Television Service (AFRTS) broadcast a few hours of television daily, re-runs of popular American shows like Gunsmoke, M*A*S*H, and our favorite, Sesame Street. We sat close to our 10-inch black and white TV to follow the antics of Bert, Ernie, Big Bird, and the rest of the crew. I think Sesame Street's episode on pets might have been the source of inspiration for Tina's request for a kitty.

Fred asked around at the embassy and in a matter of hours we acquired two kittens, one marshmallow white and the other milky white with smoky gray patches. Tina and Dakota named them Star Kitty and Moon Kitty. The kittens had to adapt to the love-style of toddlers, not always gentle, and the kids had to learn to avoid the sharp parts of the kitties. Thankfully, the good-natured cats reserved their claws for life-threatening situations and my supply of Band-Aids held up.

We gave the cats free access to our garden space so they could escape from kiddy adoration as needed. Soon after they reached maturity they both disappeared. I imagined they scaled the twelve-foot-high wall to search for mates and enjoyed their freedom too much to return. The kids' sadness lifted when I told them that their cats needed to find daddies and have babies of their own. They still missed Star Kitty and Moon Kitty, but they didn't have long to wait for a replacement.

That same week our friends from down the block began preparations to return to the States at the end of their contract with an oil company. They gave us their swing set and their cat, Tigger. We already knew Tigger, a full-grown male tabby, raised in the Johnson's family of three young children. Tigger enjoyed all forms of attention -- he even let the kids dress him in doll clothes, something the other kitties had never tolerated.

Farsi, Sakine, and Katrina

As the stay-at-home mother of two toddlers, my average day lacked adult interaction until Fred came home from work. I wanted to learn the local language so I could talk to neighbors and shopkeepers at least. The embassy offered free Farsi classes twice a week to employees and family members. To take advantage of the classes I had only to get a babysitter and call a taxi.

I had two options for a babysitter. First there was Sakine, our cleaning lady, who came three days a week. Dakota and Tina liked Sakine, but language was a barrier for them too. Even at their tender ages of two and not-quite-two, they were intensely verbal beings, and they caught on right away that Sakine didn't communicate in the same kind of words that they did. Dakota connected with Sakine more than Tina did. He had developed a taste for sugar and Sakine seemed always happy to oblige. The similarity between the sound of "sugar" and "shekar" (Farsi word for sugar) certainly aided his cause. I heeded the "white death" definition of refined sugar and did everything I could to discourage its consumption. But Sakine believed that sugar was healthy. No doubt she doled out sugar lumps as soon as the door closed behind me.

Sakine was our housekeeper for nearly two years. Our first domestic employee, she performed adequately and gave us no grief. We shared her time with another family, however, that was not as satisfied with her performance. They fired her on the spot when they caught her cleaning the rim of their jelly jar with her tongue. I wondered if I would have done the same or would I have used the opportunity to teach Sakine about germs and food handling in the American kitchen. A picture of Sakine's tongue running laps around the lip of the jelly jar stuck in my head for a long time, and I kept a closer eye on our kitchen from then on. I didn't see her do anything unsanitary or unsavory so Fred and I decided to continue employing her.

Our other babysitter was a thirteen-year-old American girl who lived on the second floor of our building. Katrina was available for my class periods only if she had a school holiday. She sat for us more often on winter weekends when Fred and I went skiing on day trips to nearby Shemshak or Dizin or rare evenings when Fred and I went out without the kids. It was a convenient arrangement since Katrina and her family lived on the second floor of our building. The kids loved her. Dakota especially. Maybe his love for Katrina explains his lifelong attraction to blondes! Katrina acted like a doting older sister. She even called Fred and me Dad and Mom. I always made time to listen to her problems when she had typical teenage difficulties with her parents.

Katrina's father worked for Bell Helicopter, and their benefits were different from ours. Instead of shipping a car for them, Bell gave them a transportation allowance. Katrina's mother hatched the idea that, because we had a car and they didn't, it was our obligation to drive them everywhere. That way they could add the transportation allowance to their savings and still get where they wanted to go. Her plan did not work for me, but it was torture for me to say no every time she asked for a ride. I started to avoid her just on the off chance that she might want to go somewhere. I wanted to be a good neighbor, but I dreaded feeling used and abused as Mrs. S's personal chauffeur.

One Saturday I almost didn't answer the knock, dreading that it was Katrina's mother. But I was hoping for a kerosene delivery for our space heater, so I opened the door. Katrina stood there, crying, shoulders slumped forward, a pitiful sight. I put my arm around her and guided her to the sofa. She wouldn't sit down.

"I don't know what to do. Can you help me?" She dabbed her eyes with a blob of sodden Kleenex.

"Tell me what's going on." I patted her arm and wondered what new criticism her parents had thought up.

"It's that time of the month and I used a tampon and I can't find the string to get it out." Her final word trailed off in a wail.

"Honey, your mother needs to help you with this kind of problem."

"No-o-o-o. She's the one who won't let me use tampons."

Oh, no is right. No-o-o-o, not me. I don't want to deal with this. Jeez.

"Sh-sh-sh, it's okay. Let's try this. Here, take this mirror, go into the bathroom and see if you can find the string that way."

"Are you sure? I've never looked down there before."

"Yes, I'm sure. It's okay to know what your own body looks like and it's good to understand how it works, now that you're doing grown-up things like using tampons."

I stood outside the door and fidgeted.

At last I heard Katrina shout, "Got it!" A rite of passage for both of us.

My Mommy Will Come Back

It wasn't long before I experienced another rite of passage into a new phase of motherhood. I remember Fred had trouble closing the door after arriving home that evening. Tina clung to one of his legs, Dakota to the other, and I vied for his attention above the clamor of the kids' welcome-home babble. I had to tell my big news or burst.

"There's a preschool for the kids. It's wonderful. Right in our own neighborhood. Run by an American lady with a degree in early childhood education. Betsy's her name. I'm going to check it out tomorrow."

"Great. How…?"

"Dakota can start right away. Tina will have to wait until she's two, that's the youngest Betsy accepts."

"Are you just a little excited?" Fred plopped down on the couch and pulled the kids up next to him.

"Just think, I'll have some time to myself. Two and a half hours, two days a week, for me and me alone."

Dakota loved Betsy's school from the very first minute. At the end of his third day, Tina and I came to pick him up and found him playing with a blonde boy.

"This is Dane." Betsy patted his head as she introduced us. "He's the same age as Dakota and he has a younger sister too."

The moment I met Dane's mother, Mary, we connected. In our first thirty minutes together I learned that her husband Jim taught at the American school, that they had adopted Dane in their hometown in Ohio, that they adopted Sarah in Tehran three months ago, and that they lived about two blocks from us. We agreed to get together the following morning for a play date.

Dane and Dakota played well together and Sarah and Tina seemed content with their typical toddler parallel play. Mary and I decided to take turns having the girls on the days the boys went to Betsy's School. I volunteered to have them first.

Mary dropped Sarah at our apartment and took Dakota and Dane to Betsy's. Sarah didn't even whimper when Mary left. She practically dove into the toy box and spent the rest of the morning enjoying the novelty of someone else's stuff. Tina kept her favorite doll, the one with long purple hair she called Bollack, tucked tightly under one arm. That was the only sign I caught that she might not be wholeheartedly in favor of this new arrangement.

Next time, it was Tina's turn to stay at Mary's house. She cried when I left with the boys. I had to believe she would settle down right away or this wouldn't work. Still, I couldn't concentrate on enjoying my freedom. A tear-streaked face with accusing eyes followed me from room to room as I searched for a task to validate my time alone. After the longest two and a half hour period of my life, I went to Betsy's School to get the boys and stopped off at Mary's house to exchange Dane for Tina. Tina ran to me and buried her face in my skirt.

"Don't worry, she stopped crying as soon as the door closed," Mary said.

"That's a relief. So she seemed happy to play with Sarah?"

"Yeah, for the most part. But just before you got back, I found her sitting over there looking out the window. She was whispering. I had to get real close to catch what she was saying. It was like a chant, the same thing over and over."

"My mommy will come back...my mommy will come back...my mommy will come back."

Six months later, Tina turned two and proudly packed her tiny duffle bag for that most important first day at Betsy's School. She never once cried for her mommy.

The Egg

Our weekdays settled into a comfortable routine of work for Fred, pre-school for the kids, Farsi lessons and household chores for me. I looked forward to the weekends when we could take short trips to explore Tehran and the surrounding countryside. One sunny autumn day we escaped from the hubbub of the frenetic city and made our way out of town with no planned destination.

After an hour or so on a narrow, winding road Fred spotted a convenient place to pull over and park on the bank of a brook. Dakota and Tina scrambled out of the car and ran to the water's edge. They threw rocks and sticks into the stream and chased alongside the sticks that floated with the current. The four of us climbed the smooth gray boulders and rock-hopped back and forth like mountain goats. Playing in the fresh air and sunshine soothed our country-bred souls.

"All this exercise makes me hungry." I've always been one of those people who want to eat every two or three hours.

"Me too," agreed Fred. "Let's drive back to that little café we saw on the way up."

"Yay!" Dakota and Tina cheered and clapped their sandy hands.

The small mud-brick building crouched in the middle of a packed-earth yard. Faded blue paint peeled here and there on the scarred and gouged walls. Three square wooden tables with rusty folding chairs sat vacant in the yard. A rickety bicycle leaned against the wall. Five red hens, exactly like our Rhode Island Reds back home, pecked in the dirt, giving wide berth to a scruffy brown dog napping in the sun.

Hand in hand, we walked toward the building. A short, thin man wearing an apron came out and swung one arm wide with a slight bow. We chose a table and sat down. The waiter greeted us and we returned his greeting.

"Salaam aleikum."

"Wa aleikum salaam."

"Chehar chello kebab." I practiced my primitive Farsi and ordered a national favorite dish made of chunks of savory charcoal-roasted mutton, steaming buttery white rice, and bold raw onion. I didn't ask Dakota and Tina what they wanted because I knew. Since the first time they tried it, they never wanted anything at a restaurant but chello kebab.

The waiter returned to the building, presumably to the kitchen. Wisps of smoke drifted from the chimney. The kids played with their forks and tablespoons as we waited for our food.

With no warning a strange choreography began. The waiter ambled toward us carrying four drinks. As we turned to watch the waiter approach, one of the red hens fluttered up, hunkered down right in the middle of our table, and startled us with a confident cackle. Four pairs of eyes opened wider and wider. In one fluid motion the waiter served our drinks, shooed the hen away, and plucked up her glistening wet brown egg, slipping it into his wide apron pocket.

Dakota started to cry. Tina wrapped her arms around my neck.

"What's wrong, Bubba? Did the chicken scare you?" I asked.

"No! That man took my egg! I want my egg!"

I held back a laugh. To Dakota, this was a serious offense. He stuck to his own logic. The egg appeared on his table. Therefore the egg was his. My explanation that the egg belonged to the restaurant because the chicken belonged to the restaurant did not appeal to him in the least.

Fred stood up to his full 5 feet 8 inches of Daddy-Hero height. He snapped to attention and executed a perfect military about-face and marched into the café. A few minutes later he returned with his hands behind his back.

"Which hand?" he asked Dakota.

Dakota knew how to retrieve a treat from Daddy. He tapped Fred's left elbow. Fred brought his left hand out and opened it.

"My egg!" A delighted boy forgot his tears.

"Which hand?" Fred asked Tina.

Tina tapped the other elbow.

"My egg!" She beamed at Fred and cradled her egg in both hands.

The Bastard

On the weekends that we didn't go exploring, we often visited the 22-acre American Embassy compound, which included the commissary, restaurant, swimming pool, volleyball courts, and two red clay tennis courts. On one memorable outing, the kids and I escorted Fred to a game of doubles with the Ambassador against his wife and one of the political officers.

On the way to the compound Fred said, "I'm afraid I'm out of my depth -- I've seen the Ambassador play – he's really good."

Fred's next comments about the Ambassador revealed that he was worried about more than his tennis partner's skills on the court. He told me that our ambassador's close personal friends included President Nixon, Secretary of State Kissinger, and the Shah of Iran.

"I heard that Ambassador Helms resigned his previous job as head of the CIA to take the ambassadorship as a favor to President Nixon."

Fred was most impressed that in his early days as a journalist Mr. Helms had interviewed Adolf Hitler at the Berlin Olympics in 1936. I agreed that the Ambassador was altogether an unlikely tennis partner for an ex-hippie from New Mexico.

As we walked from our car to the tennis courts Fred fretted about his backhand and repeated his hopes to play well, while I tried to keep our troops on track.

"Come on, let's hurry up. Daddy doesn't want to be late for his match."

"Daddy, I carry your racquet, okay?" Dakota always wanted to help.

Tina spoke up, "I carry balls," not to be outdone by her big brother.

"Look, Daddy, look, I seeum," Dakota shouted in his biggest big-boy voice.

Fred bent down to his level and whispered, "Hey, Buddy, use your quiet voice, please. Who do you see?"

Dakota couldn't contain his enthusiasm. "Daddy, Daddy, there he is! There's the Bastard!"

As usual on any weekend there were several other embassy employees sitting around the courts; not a single one missed Dakota's announcement. We realized this was probably not the best time to explain the correct pronunciation of Mr. Helms' title to our two-year-old. Fred hung onto his hopes that the Ambassador had a sense of humor or at least a forgiving heart and would not have him assassinated or sent to Siberia. He gamely nodded his red-faced head in the Ambassador's direction, waved and awaited his fate. Ambassador Helms merely smiled and raised his racquet in a jaunty salute. Fred somehow managed to play better than his best throughout the entire tennis match without ever learning how Ambassador Helms felt about Dakota's faux pas.

Hospitality

Later that evening, I had reason to worry about faux pas again. As dinner guests in our landlord's third floor apartment, we needed to be on our best behavior. I wished I could obey Mr. Madeni's command to relax while his wife laid out a splendid array of treats and tidbits, but I had to keep a sharp eye on my kids.

The feast included Iranian classics such as the golden rice crust called Tah-deeg and tender lamb stewed with tart quince and yellow split peas. We sampled garlic marinated in vinegar for "100" years, walnuts preserved in sugar syrup, dates, pomegranates, cheese, and halvah. We sipped hot tea from gold-rimmed glasses, imitating our landlord who sucked the brew through a sugar cube held in his front teeth. The sugar cubes fascinated Dakota and Tina, and our host indulged them with a stack of six cubes each. I prayed that the sugar would not send my kids into a hyper sugar rush and I invoked Lady Luck to prevent spills of any kind on the priceless Persian carpets layered fifteen-deep beneath us.

Our landlord explained what hospitality meant to Iranians, "The Koran teaches us to treat visitors and guests as precious gifts from Allah. We must offer our guests the best of whatever we have. I am sad to say that most people in the city no longer follow this tradition, but you will find it still practiced in the country."

Mr. Madeni dropped by a couple of times a month to see how we were getting along. He always asked if we needed anything. Fred recalled his career counselor's words about caviar being as common as peanut butter. He asked Mr. Madeni if he knew why we hadn't found caviar for sale anywhere. A blank look came over our landlord's face and his eyes shifted to the side. He mumbled something that I didn't quite catch. I thought I heard the words "black market." Fred hadn't heard him clearly either, but because Mr. Madeni seemed uncomfortable, he changed the subject.

A few days later, Mr. Madeni visited us again, bringing a small parcel. Inside we found a circular tin container about six inches in diameter and two inches deep.

"Caviar," he said. "I have a friend…."

We thanked him and Fred offered payment. The caviar cost the unbelievable equivalent of $5.00 U.S., which worked out to be just over thirty cents an ounce -- not quite comparable to peanut butter, but a great bargain for fine Iranian caviar even in 1975 dollars. Because of the mysterious dearth of caviar on the open market, we had only that one tin in our two years in Tehran. We savored it on crackers, on bread, and by the spoonful. Dakota and Tina both preferred the spoon method. Yes, we fed Iranian caviar to our two-year-olds and they loved it.

Mrs. Madeni, as hospitable as her husband, took me shopping for fabric and showed me how to sew a chador, the floor-length covering worn gracefully by most proper Muslim women. She helped me choose a summer-weight dark blue material with a subtle pattern of tiny flowers, and she stood beside me as I sat at my sewing machine and stitched the chador according to her instructions. I didn't express my opinion that the chador symbolized the repression of women, and I didn't laugh out loud when I discovered that young women wore hot pants and halter-tops under their modest covering.

To avoid calling unwanted attention to myself when I went out in public beyond our neighborhood unescorted, I wore the chador. Or tried to. I couldn't make the slippery thing stay on my head without using both hands to hold it there. Mrs. Madeni suggested bobby pins, but bobby pins wouldn't stay in my flyaway hair. As a last resort, she taught me how to hold the chador in my teeth, which resulted only in wet slobber marks on my falling garment. I did eventually develop some chador skills, but not to the extent that I felt confident, and certainly not graceful. I still have my chador, packed in a box labeled "Costumes," folded next to a miniature chador handed down to Tina from the Madeni's youngest daughter, Maheen.

Tina adored five-year-old Maheen and her hand-me-downs. One dress appealed to Tina more than any of the others. She wore it every day. She wanted to sleep in it. I thought I might have to bathe her in it, just to get it clean. The style was plain, a simple A-line shift. Perhaps she saw beauty in the shiny blue metallic threads running through the brown background. Or maybe she liked the way the skirt twirled. She didn't explain her devotion, but she wore that dress until she could no longer squeeze into it.

I wanted to absorb everything the Madenis had to share. Until we touched on personal hygiene, that is. Mrs. Madeni seemed keen to demonstrate how Iranian women removed unwanted leg hair. First, she used her own leg. The process involved a twisted string, hairs torn out by the roots. Then she wanted me to try her technique on myself. One hefty dose of pain was enough for me.

Although I couldn't follow all of Mrs. Madeni's advice, I did treasure her willingness to share with me. In these moments of openness, in Ms. Madeni's home with no males present, I learned that Iranian women were less shy with each other than typical American women. They spent most of their time at home cloistered together, shielded from the eyes of men, and developed an attitude of sisterhood that extended beyond family and embraced friends as well.

Although we thought Mr. and Mrs. Madeni's hospitality and generosity could not be equaled, we met many Iranians who welcomed us with the same enthusiasm. One man who hitched a short ride with Fred from the ski lift down to the village below invited Fred into his home for hours of eating, tea-drinking, and a dancing performance by his daughters.

"Visitors are to be treated as gifts from Allah." Mr. Madeni's words echoed as a reminder of our responsibilities as guests. Being gifts from Allah, we never dared to resist a host's kindness, even if we sometimes became hospitality's hostages, like the day we met the Armenian shopkeeper.

Within walking distance of our neighborhood we found a street lined with dozens of shops selling metal handicrafts made on the spot. While Fred and I shopped among the shiny brass and copper vessels on display, Tina and Dakota watched the craftsmen who pounded and polished their latest creations.

As we passed one building a tantalizing food aroma pulled us like a magnetic force. All four noses pointed like so many beagles at the narrow doorway.

"If that store doesn't sell salami, I'm having a hallucination." Fred had confessed earlier that he wanted some hard salami to add to our favorite barbari bread lunch. It was nearly noon and we looked forward to building those sandwiches as soon as we got home.

Inside the store more rich fragrances made my stomach rumble. My eyes devoured the bounty of cheeses and meats behind the glass-fronted display case. My mouth watered. We picked out a fat, dark red salami, 400 grams of sliced meat that resembled pastrami, and a small wheel of pale yellow cheese. The clerk behind the counter started to total our purchases, but a rotund swarthy man stepped in and took over.

"You are English?" he asked.

"Well, no, actually we're Americans," Fred replied.

"Ha. Your money no good here," the man exclaimed.

"I'm sorry…why?"

"Ha. You are Americans. You are Christians. I am Armenian. I am Christian. I not take your money. You will come to my house now and we will eat." His broad smile belied his gruff speech.

My danger antennae flickered a brief signal and I put a cautionary hand on Fred's arm. He winked, smiled and shrugged. If Fred wasn't worried there probably wasn't anything to worry about; I relaxed my guard. We all trooped along behind the Armenian through the back of the store and up a flight of stairs to his apartment. After introducing us, he rattled off instructions to his wife and ushered us into the living room. He brought out pictures of his children and grandchildren and told where they lived and their level of education. Then he patted our hands and said, "My friends, my friends, my good friends," grinning all the while.

His wife set the table (forks on the right, large tablespoons on the left) and served lunch: a savory vegetable soup, lavash bread, slices of the same pastrami-like meat we saw in the shop, chunks of cheese, and a platter heaped with fresh fruit. Our host talked more about the life of Armenians in Iran.

"We came for religious freedom, you know. The Shah guarantees religious freedom here. So we are free to be Christians. This is good. We have good business. We are treated not so very good but not so very bad. But we have only small community of Armenians. We are starving to know more Christians."

He rambled on throughout the afternoon. He seemed so desperate for company that I felt guilty about feeling equally desperate to leave. Dakota and Tina fell asleep on our laps. I laughed at my earlier sense of danger – the only danger here was injury from too much smiling and nodding.

Finally we managed to say our goodbyes. Before we left, our host presented us with our shop selections, wrapped neatly in newspaper. He refused to accept any payment, saying he wished only for us to return often.

An Important Ingredient

Another important ingredient in our daily lives had the initials MSG. No, not the flavor enhancer; this abbreviation stood for the Marine Security Guard detachment. Chosen from the top 10%, these elite Marines guarded our embassies all around the world, and they also became valued members of the extended embassy family. Young men, eighteen to twenty-two years old, they fulfilled the role of in-between cousins, younger than we parents and older than our children. They baby-sat for us occasionally, shared our Thanksgiving feasts, and hosted community events like spaghetti night, movie night, and holiday parties. Living overseas, we had to sacrifice everyday contact with family and friends back home, but "our" Marines helped fill in the empty spots.

One of the guys, James Vincent Viancourt from Cleveland, Ohio, was the last Marine to leave the embassy in Saigon during the evacuation of all personnel by helicopter just before the capitulation of South Vietnam. He took up his new assignment in Tehran soon after. James had the same birthday as Dakota. He turned twenty when Dakota turned two. The coincidence of a shared birthday contributed to our bonding, plus the fact that he loved our favorite musician Jackson Browne, especially the album "Late for the Sky." But there was more, that indefinable something that makes people click at soon as they meet. James fit our family like he had been part of us since birth.

Tragically, fate cut our relationship short. James escaped the violence of the war in Vietnam only to succumb to a freak swimming pool accident in Tehran, Iran on June 25, 1975. Fred and I suffered the sharp pain of the loss of a loved one for the first time in our lives. My heart still aches for James and for his parents and siblings.

4

Nancy and Fred visit a caravanserai

October 1975

Caravanserai

The October early morning chilly breeze penetrated my sweater and I bent down to secure the hood of Tina's cherry red windbreaker. Dakota, oblivious to the cold as usual, carried his jacket tucked in the crook of his left elbow. Our group of eight (my best friend Norma, her husband Tom, and their children Julie and Tommy plus Fred, Nancy, Dakota, and Tina) joined the other embassy folks lined up to board the small blue minibus and the full-sized red bus chartered to take us on an overnight adventure.

The driver of our bus and guide for the tour, a middle-aged balding man with an enormous bushy mustache, smiled and said his name, Rashidi, to each passenger as we boarded. He offered his hand to Dakota and as they shook hands, man-to-man, they became instant buddies.

Rashidi revved the engine and shifted into first gear with a grind and a jerk. We were on our way to a caravanserai in the desert – a historic Near East inn originally built to accommodate camel caravans on the famous trade route leading to Tehran.

Our first stop was the town of Rey (Shahr-e-Rey) where we watched the traditional carpet cleaning process. At the edge of the river, the rug cleaners spread fine Persian carpets flat on the smooth sandstone surface. Then they doused the carpets with buckets of water, followed by a sprinkling of ordinary powdered laundry detergent. The next step involved scraping the rugs with a long-handled tool that I could have sworn was a common garden hoe. The scraping action mixed water and detergent into foam and pushed the foam down into the fibers. After a few minutes of scraping, the workers tugged the carpets into the river to rinse them. This involved another vigorous scraping to force out the soapsuds. After dragging the carpets onto the riverbank once more, the workers attacked again, using their hoes to squeegee out the moisture. The last step left the rugs to air-dry on the sun-warmed sandstone.

Rashidi told us that some rug merchants were known to toss new carpets into the road and let passing traffic "age" them into "antiques." He said this with an enigmatic smile that made me wonder if he was kidding about this underhanded trick of the carpet trade.

Before lunchtime we made two other interesting stops, one at the Djomeh (Friday) Mosque of Varamin, which was in the process of being restored, and another at the imposing ruins of an ancient Zoroastrian fire temple perched atop a high hill. We followed a dirt track up the steep hillside to the fire temple, pausing a few times to rest. At the top I caught my breath as I enjoyed the panorama of patches of desert alternating with swatches of green all the way to the mountains on the horizon. The three older kids ran the dirt path down to the parking lot at top speed, little Tommy toddling behind. In spite of the headlong rush, no one fell.

Back on the bus, we listened to Rashidi's elegant English spoken with no accent other than the lyrical rhythm typical of Farsi speakers. "Here is the ancient Shah Abbas game preserve and the remaining walls of one old caravanserai. We'll stop here for our lunch hour. Look around, eat, rest, enjoy." He brought out a cooler of sodas and a container full of boxed lunches from the embassy restaurant, aptly named The Caravanserai. Our two busloads disembarked and dispersed, some to explore the ruins, some going straight for the food.

"Camel bells, Mommy." Dakota heard the harmonious tones first.

Moments later we saw the lead camel approaching. A dark brown dromedary, he carried two large bulging sacks cinched tightly with thick rope. The next animal, a shaggy sandy-colored fellow, carried two bales of straw hanging low on each side. Each of the fourteen animals, connected by rope from one camel's saddle to the next camel's halter, carried a similar burden and the last in line had her calf by her side. The wiry young man riding the lead animal noticed Tom's long telephoto lens and sprang into action. He stood up in the saddle, spread his arms wide, and showed his shiny white teeth in an impish smile. We watched the caravan glide by and disappear into the distance, followed by several sheep and goats that had been grazing among the ruins.

After lunch break we re-boarded the bus for two hours of bumpety-bump ride deeper into the heart of the desert. In spite of the rough road, the kids dozed off. Fred stared out at the ocean of sand, deep in his own thoughts. I imagined riding a camel across this desolate land, wrapped in a burnoose against dust storms, waiting with stoic patience for a sip of water at the end of the day.

When the buses stopped inside the caravanserai gate, we scrambled out to look around. The variety of materials struck me – stone, brick, adobe, all the same color as the surrounding expanse of endless sandy earth. Here and there a painted wooden door provided a splash of blue. The roofline humped with the symmetrical bulges of carefully crafted adobe domes, and all of the rooms had small porticos with distinctive peaked archways at the entrances.

Rashidi explained the general layout. "As you see, the caravanserai is built in a square shape. We have entered through the only door. Our buses passed easily because the gate was made wide enough for large or heavily burdened beasts to enter side by side. The central courtyard is open to the sky and the inside walls are lined with chambers that were used by merchants and their servants, animals, and merchandise. Oftentimes the merchants set up stalls in these chambers and sold goods to each other. I know you will laugh, but I swear this is true: outside the wall there is a separate building for concubines and the eunuchs who guarded them." Again, Rashidi flashed his brief quirky smile.

After the buzz of laughter died down, I asked, "What's the purpose of the pool in the middle of the courtyard?"

"In old times, this pool provided water for the travelers and their animals to drink, to wash, and also for ablutions before prayer. In present days, the pool is for decoration only. For health reasons, drinking water and washing water now come from separate sources."

After unloading our baggage and assigning our rooms, Rashidi called us back to the buses for a short trip to a fossil bed.

We found hundreds of shells; oysters, clams, all shapes and sizes of petrified seashells and imprints of underwater plants. The textures and patterns begged my fingers to touch, trace, and remember. If collecting had been allowed, I would have filled my backpack with souvenirs.

Darkness came all at once, soon after the buses brought us back to the caravanserai. Supper for the exhausted group of travelers was a filling but not otherwise memorable meal of meat/vegetable/rice stew with bread. The children drooped and offered no resistance to bedtime. Norma volunteered to stay with the kids while Tom, Fred, and I went out for Rashidi's stargazing walk.

In the sudden chill of evening I shivered. Fred wrapped his arm around my shoulder and pulled me close. "Kind of nippy out here now. Hard to believe it was so warm this afternoon. That's the desert though, huh? Like back home in New Mexico."

I cuddled up and tipped my head back. "Worth it, just to be able to see the stars like this with the sky so clear. Look, there's Orion."

We kissed, as we always did, when we saw our star – the middle star of Orion's belt. That star had become ours ten years earlier when the Army sent Fred to Sinop, Turkey, for eleven months and ten days. We pledged to send love to each other via that star until he returned and we could marry. Our Orion kisses had a way of lingering while we remembered the wrenching pain of separation and the luscious joy of reunion.

Rashidi's voice interrupted our love scene. "Now, everybody, get your flashlights out. We are going for a snake hunt."

"Doesn't that sound dangerous?" I whispered to Fred.

"Surely he doesn't mean poisonous snakes -- that would be crazy."

Tom made the first discovery and he laughed out loud. "Hey, you guys. There's no snakes. Just the cokes and beers Rashidi stashed over here in the bushes!"

Rashidi stroked his mustache and the glow from our flashlights reflected off his perfect teeth. "You like my joke?"

Breakfast the next morning brought out a few chuckles too. The meal tried to be typically American – fried eggs, toast with strawberry jam, and sausage. But the sausage looked and tasted exactly like sliced hot dogs.

The trip back to Tehran took a painfully long time. Our buses had a total of three flat tires, requiring a long stop for each. The road seemed to be much dustier and bumpier than it had on the way out. And we made a serious mistake in our choice of seating. We sat in the last row of the second bus. All of the windows were open because the bus lacked air-conditioning. Dust poured in and literally covered us. By the end of the trip Fred, Tina and I wore a visible coating even on our eyelashes.

Dakota fared a little better. He sat up front near Rashidi and benefited from the protection of the windshield. Rashidi kept up a steady patter that held Dakota in thrall. He also shared his bag of apples. Small, very green apples, which Dakota devoured, one after another.

It seemed later than 6:30 PM when we finally got home. I called for warm baths for everyone to scrub away the road dust. After his soak, Dakota, clean and shiny, cozy in his Mickey Mouse pajamas, took a flying leap and landed with a belly flop in the middle of our king-size bed.

He cried out from his prone position on our bed, "Mommy…. I puked."

"Oh, Ducky, you sure did. All apples! Here, let me wipe you up."

In the time it took me to wash his face and hands and change his pajamas, the vomit soaked through the bedspread, the blanket, the sheets, the mattress pad, and left a damp spot on the mattress. We didn't have a spare set of king sheets and had to improvise with a patchwork of other linens. At last we slept, like buns in a basket, all four tucked up as usual in the family bed.

5

Dakota, Nancy, and Tina at the Shah Monument

November 1975 – May 1976

My Yek Doh Punch

Like couples with young children anywhere in the world, Fred and I had to maneuver and finagle to find time for intimacy without interruptions. We also needed to develop other adult activities that we could enjoy as a couple, in addition to skiing, which we had learned to do in Japan. Fred suggested taking a class together. The Tehran American School offered a few classes in the evening for adults, and we finally agreed upon karate. Why karate, I'm not sure, but it must have seemed like a good idea at the time.

I don't remember how many classes I attended, but I know I stuck with it long enough to order and receive my uniform, complete with the white belt of no-status-whatsoever. It seemed I couldn't get with the program. What made me think that a martial art would not be violent? The screaming, punching, kicking, and thrusting put me into a constant state of flinch. So I dropped out.

Before the end of the semester, Fred had also lost interest and dropped the class, so neither of us attended the "graduation" demonstration. Dakota and Tina went, though, on a field trip from Betsy's School. Apparently it wasn't the highlight of Tina's day, but Dakota came home excited about karate and showed us how he had learned to "yek doh." After a minute of watching and listening I realized that yek doh was Dakota-speak for jumping jack: he simply used the Farsi words for one-two. As he executed a long series of lopsided jumping jacks, he chanted, "Yek-doh, yek-doh, yek-doh."

In the following months, I forgot my brief flirtation with karate -- until one day, about halfway home from Betsy's School, a man stopped me to ask the time. It was a reasonable request from a respectable-looking person so I let go of Tina's and Dakota's hands long enough to pull my sleeve back and look at my watch. The man stepped toward me, reached out with both hands and pinched my breasts. All sorts of horrible thoughts raced through my brain. Before I knew what I was doing, I planted two quick karate punches on my molester's breastbone, yek-doh, and watched him plunk down on his butt in the middle of the footpath, wearing an expression that could be used to define incredulity.

I grabbed my kids' hands and said, "Let's run fast."

When we were safely inside our apartment building, Dakota said, "Why did you hit that guy, Mommy?"

Not an easy question to answer in a way that's suitable for a preschooler, but a great opportunity to introduce the issue of strangers. Still pumped with adrenaline, I stammered through an explanation peppered with ums and ahs. I recall great relief when Dakota lost interest in my convoluted rambling.

Before long, Fred and I found a togetherness activity much better than karate. We joined a volleyball group made up of embassy couples, singles, and Marines. Our games had just the right balance of competition and camaraderie. My pleasure was doubled by the fact that I didn't have to arrange for a babysitter; those of us with children took turns watching the youngsters, who also played well together. Volleyball felt like a couples' event, but functioned as family fun too.

The Shah Monument

Family fun definitely came first in our lifestyle. We ventured into the country as often as we could, and we explored the city when we felt feisty enough to brave the legendary traffic. The Shah Monument was one spot that could motivate us to make the trek across town.

The official name was Shahyad Aryamehr, which translates to King Memorial Tower, but we called it The Shah Monument. The Shah of Iran commissioned it and dedicated it to himself and the Pahlavi Dynasty. A young architect, Hossein Amanat, won a nationwide competition for the design, and the structure was completed in 1971. Tall and marble white, a symphony of sweeping curves, the beautiful piece of architecture graced the mountain backdrop. It was so popular among the people that none of the revolutionaries dared to deface it when the Shah's regime fell. It still stands today, with a new name, Azadi Tower, also known as Freedom Monument, now a symbol of modern Iran and the nation's revival since the revolution.

We enjoyed numerous visits to the park that surrounded the monument. The open space provided a clean, safe place for our little ones to run and play. Even the jubes (deep open gutters that usually functioned as above-ground sewers, but were kept clean and dry here) became a playground. About armpit deep to Dakota, the jubes made a great racecourse for whatever vehicle he was pretending to drive. Tina's favorite part of an outing to the Shah Monument was the delicious soft ice cream she managed to smear all over her cheeks and chin.

Snow Removal

Winter's arrival precipitated more home-based indoor activities. Sometimes we stayed home because of bitter cold temperatures, and quite often a huge snowstorm kept us inside.

Early one December morning, shouts echoed down the alley, "Barfi! Barfiiiii! Barfiiiiii!"

I looked out the window and saw our landlord Mr. Madeni, standing knee-deep in snow, negotiating with two men in dark blue quilted jackets. They seemed to come to a mutually satisfactory agreement in less than a minute. All three men entered our building and clomped up the stairs to Mr. Madeni's apartment on the third floor.

"What's going on?" Fred brushed toast crumbs from his beard and joined me by the window.

"Not much. I think Mr. Madeni just hired a couple of workmen to fix something in his apartment. Must have been them doing the shouting – hawking their wares or whatever."

A few minutes later we heard loud thumps as clumps of heavy wet snow hit the ground outside. A louder bang with a metallic ring brought us running to the window again. A mound of white heaped on our little Volkswagen.

Mr. Madeni rushed downstairs to apologize. He explained that "barf" was Farsi for "snow." And a "barfi" was the itinerant worker who scraped snow from the roofs. Tehran's flat-roof construction and massive snowfall were a dangerous combination. If the snow weren't removed, the roof would collapse, as did the roof of the Tehran airport terminal in 1974, with twenty-five fatalities.

After the barfis left and it was safe to go outside, Fred went to inspect the damage. Under the snow pile he found a large crater in the VW roof. Luckily the dent popped up when pounded from the inside. Fred decided there was wisdom in parking in the underground garage, especially during the winter.

He's Only a Little Boy

Thanks to Fred's mom, Dakota and Tina had state-of-the-art snow-suits, perfect for Tehran's spectacular snow. When we wanted to play outdoors, I had to hurry to suit them up as quickly as I could. If I dawdled, the first one dressed got sweaty before the second zipper zipped. Bundled up in snowsuits, boots, mittens, hats, and hoods, they could barely walk and probably couldn't get up if they fell. I carried Tina and held Dakota's hand as we slip-slid down the steep half-flight of stairs leading from the balcony to our garden.

"Let's build a snow man." I packed a handful of snow into a ball and showed the kids how to roll it along to accumulate more snow.

"Wow. What a big ball you made. That can be the snowman's body."

We rolled a medium-sized ball for the torso and a smaller ball for the head. My chartreuse straw gardening hat sat on top. Dakota chose square blue Lego pieces for eyes and a green one for the nose. Tina picked out five small rectangular red pieces and I helped her form a smiling mouth.

I stepped back to admire our work. "Isn't that the best snowman in all the world? Hold on a second, I'm gonna run in the house and get the camera."

In less than two minutes I came back, ready to immortalize Mr. Snowman on film. But Mr. Snowman lay in a heap. Dakota held his red plastic baseball bat in a perfect home run follow-through, just the way I had taught him.

"I don't believe it! Young man, you better go to your room and think about what you have just done." Vapor puffed out of my mouth with every word. I imagined steam pouring out of my nose and ears.

Two-year-old Tina tugged at my pants leg. I looked down at her earnest little face.

"But, Mommy," she spoke softly in a soothing and reasonable voice, "he's only a little boy."

First Foreign Service Christmas

The high point of winter was Christmas of course. Our first Christmas in the Foreign Service pointed out how very far we were from our families and from normal American life. No crowded malls for shopping. No visits to grandparents to share the celebration with cousins, aunts and uncles. Just our little family of four and our small community of embassy folks.

The Marines hosted a Christmas party with a gift exchange, and

Santa Claus put in an appearance. Our two pre-schoolers knew Santa as a friendly storybook character. They weren't prepared to see him in the flesh, looming large in his overstuffed red costume. Tina pressed her face into my shoulder to make herself invisible. Dakota rode on Fred's shoulders, watching Santa's approach with suspicion, even from his safe perch. When Santa took Dakota in his arms to carry him the rest of the way to the throne, Dakota looked like he'd been struck by lightning. Then his face scrunched up and his arms stretched out for salvation. His eyes filled with tears and he let out a cry that sent Fred running to his rescue. Daddy-Hero completely foiled Santa's kidnapping attempt, but Dakota still kept his distance from the red-suited villain for the rest of the party.

Thanks to good advice from friends, we knew that Christmas overseas required advance catalog shopping. In those days, Sears, J.C. Penneys, and Montgomery Wards had full-color Christmas toy catalogs that came out in August. The kids and I spent hours poring over our wish books. Dakota was old enough to know what he wanted. Tina didn't have as much experience with Christmas, but she had been successfully following Dakota's lead all her life. So we ordered two big green dump trucks, two shiny red tricycles, and two brown plastic rifles. The tricycles needed some assembly and Fred spent the last hours of Christmas Eve struggling with incomprehensible instructions written by someone whose native tongue could not have been English. This did not improve Fred's vocabulary one iota.

In addition to the toys ordered from the catalogs, Fred bought a few presents at the commissary. He picked out a huge doll for Tina and kept it at the office until Christmas Eve. Sue, his supervisor, told him such a big doll would scare a little girl like Tina. Sue couldn't have been more wrong. It was love at first sight for Tina. Her rifle didn't get a second glance.

The dump trucks pulled extra duty in "the rock place," an unusual architectural feature of our apartment that we adapted to our own use. It was a 6 by 6 foot column of space that extended from the ground floor to the roof, intended as an airshaft perhaps. At our level, the space had glass walls on two sides – facing the kitchen on one side and the formal dining area on the other. The kitchen wall also had a glass door giving access to any plants that a tenant might want to grow in the large cement lotus-shaped planter in the center. Dakota and Tina called it "the rock place" because landscaping pebbles covered the floor in a thick layer. When I cooked or baked in the kitchen, they played with their dump trucks and matchbox cars among the stones.

Change of Season

Spring came early that year and we welcomed warm weather, blossoms on our pear tree, buds on the rosebushes, and freedom to resume our outdoor excursions. First on our list: the Tehran Zoo.

From any animal's viewpoint, the Tehran zoo in 1976 was a concentration camp. Most of the poor creatures barely survived in cages, not habitats, on questionable diets with no prohibition of inappropriate feeding by zoo-goers. To my everlasting horror, I saw spectators feeding lighted cigarettes to chimpanzees and then laughing like maniacs at the chimps' suffering. The only animals that looked groomed or even minimally cared for were the camels and horses and one small elephant that could be ridden for the price of a ticket. We rode the camels and horses tandem with the kids. Dakota rode solo on the little elephant, with some trepidation. He wanted the ride badly, in theory, but not so much in reality. He toughed it out, though, having matured in courage in the four months since his scary encounter with Santa.

Happy Birthdays

Springtime also heralded birthday season for the boys of our house. Perhaps remembering his recent ride at the zoo, Dakota chose an elephant shape for his cake. I made a paper pattern and cut a simple elephant outline from a chocolate 9X13 cake. The hardest part was getting the white frosting to cover the dark cake, and I fussed and cursed over it a long time. The adoring look on Dakota's face told me all I needed to know about my success.

Ignoring current wisdom to invite one guest per candle on the cake, we asked all the kids from Betsy's School to come and celebrate Dakota's third birthday at a party in our garden. Ten youngsters showed up and happy kiddie mayhem ensued. Most of the parents stayed for the party, which assured plenty of supervision. A generous supply of adult beverages kept the supervisors' spirits high. Busy with last minute preparations, I asked Fred to dress Tina in her party clothes, and it wasn't until the party was well underway that I noticed how cute she looked. She wore a yellow dress handmade by Aunt Pat and, oops, her lacy tights were on backwards with the seam running up the front.

On Fred's thirty-second birthday, May 12, 1976, we reminisced about the year gone by. The realization came as a shock: we had passed the halfway point in our Tehran tour. Despite my early fears and the real and present dangers, our life in Iran didn't seem perilous to us. As we coped and adapted, the extraordinary had become ordinary. We lived a normal family life, taking appropriate safety precautions but not dwelling on danger. We worked and we played, we studied the language and culture and explored the countryside. We established a rhythm and forged our niche as a Foreign Service family.

6

Dressed for London

June - August 1976

London

The time had come to plan our first R&R. The State Department designated Tehran as a two-year post with a hardship pay differential of 10% and a mid-tour R&R. The rules at that time established Athens as the R&R point. We could go anywhere we liked and the government would cover airfare up to the amount of economy fare to Athens. We chose to go to London (only $200 out of our pocket) to visit Fred's sister and family, the Coxes (Dick, Pat, Beth, Karen, and Kathy), who were living in Beaconsfield, just outside London, while Dick conducted business as regional manager for a Texas-based oilfield manufacturer and service company.

Judging by photos showing our travel clothes, we dressed for style rather than comfort. My getup was particularly fetching – a floral frock with eyelet edging at the neckline and sleeves, sheer stockings, and tidy black pumps. The pièce de résistance -- a dramatic curly wig with my usual shoulder length, straight hippy-do tucked underneath. Fred, also way out of character, wore plaid (yes, plaid) slacks, a brown sport coat, paisley tie, and, his flair for the day, polished cowboy boots. Dakota's outfit was spiffy too – yellow shorts to match the yellow Tweety-Bird on his brown t-shirt, coordinated with brown knee socks and shoes. And Tina looked precious in her green gingham pinafore, lace-trimmed anklets, and white Mary Janes. Was that really us?

Pat and Dick welcomed us with loving hospitality, and their girls (Beth 14, Karen 11, and Kathy 7) swept our kids away to the playroom. What followed was three weeks of fun, totally relaxing and mostly worry free.

Pat was active in the American Women's Club, and she signed us up for a bus trip to an old castle to see a Renaissance fair. A very realistic jousting tournament was the highlight of the day. Fred and I were less impressed by our introduction to typically British warm beer.

Another excursion took the whole bunch of us by train into London to visit the zoo, a much more animal-friendly place than Tehran's. Our kids couldn't wait to get to the petting zoo.

Tina sank to the ground next to a baby goat and gazed at it with unconditional love as she said, "This is the one, Mommy."

She explained that the petting zoo was the place you went to choose a pet and the baby goat was her choice. Dakota fell in love with a big rabbit. He would have spent the whole day stroking the velvety interior of the rabbit's long ear.

The London Zoo was also the setting for one of Dakota's famous observations. When he noticed a disabled man in a wheelchair, he announced, in his biggest, deepest, longest-carrying voice, "Lookit, Mommy, that guy got no legs!"

Back at the Cox home we enjoyed the pampering of their housekeeper, Maria. She became an instant substitute grandmother for our little ones, allowing Fred and me freedom that we had not dared to dream about. We went sightseeing and covered most of the popular London attractions – the Tower of London, Big Ben, the changing of the guard at Buckingham Palace, and Madame Tussauds Wax Museum. We went shopping at Harrod's and I found great outfits that I treasured for years. I still have the belt that came with some black slacks, saved because of the unique clasp that reminded me of a cameo.

Beth, Karen, and Kathy's summertime activities included riding lessons. They looked so very English in their proper riding breeches, boots, and hats. All three girls also played on softball teams graded by age. They played at the same time on different ball fields in a large sports complex. Luckily it didn't rain on their game day and we got to see them play. Dakota and Tina lost interest before the end of the first inning. Tina found a comfortable spot near me and recruited several sticks, stones, and leaves to act as extended family for the two little dolls she had with her. Dakota invented his own game of running through the tall grass on the outskirts of the outfield.

At the end of the day, Dakota complained that his eyes hurt. One look at his face and I knew he needed medical attention. Pat called the family doctor and he told us to meet him at his office (even though it was a Sunday evening).

Poor Dakota. "I can't see," he wailed, and, "It hurts!"

His whole face was swollen, his eyes reduced to slits. The slits looked like they were filled with egg whites, transforming him into a creature from another planet. I tried to keep from showing how worried I was as I applied cool cloths to reduce the swelling.

The doctor treated both of Dakota's eyes with adrenaline drops and diagnosed a probable allergy to blooming grass. He prescribed an antihistamine and sent home a boy who felt much better, accompanied by two very relieved parents who had no idea that allergies could cause a lifetime of problems.

The children cheered us up and kept us laughing with their costume inventions. The three older kids dressed the younger two in all manner of getups. Picture Tina in a gold sequined ballet dress two sizes too big, a long scarf tied around her waist, a plaid babushka on her head, and a pink umbrella in her hand. Or Dakota in a polka dot dress, wearing a snorkeling mask, breathing tube and long blue fins, saying (his nostrils pinched shut by the mask), "I'm a underwater surfer, Mommy."

When we saw the advertisements for the South African musical Ipi Tombi, somehow Fred and I knew Dakota and Tina would be able to behave at a big city theatrical event, something you can't expect of every two- or three-year-old. The South African performers twirled across the stage to the compelling beat of drums, telling the story of a young black man leaving his village and young wife to work in the mines of Johannesburg. The show used pastiches of a variety of South African indigenous musical styles that kept our toes tapping and our hands clapping. Not only did Dakota and Tina enjoy the entire performance, they also spent many hours listening to the recording after we returned home to Tehran.

Before we left London, Pat and Dick organized a gala barbeque to introduce us to their friends and neighbors. These people knew how to party. We sang, danced, played cards and games, and ended up executing (pun intended) a badminton tournament at dawn.

After we recovered from our hangovers, a night out on the town provided Fred and me a final special treat. We left the kids in Pat's capable hands and took the train to find the action. The action was "O Calcutta," live on stage. The nudity and adult humor both shocked and fascinated me. I felt like I might become a sophisticated grownup after all.

In spite of all the fun and love, I felt ready to go home when our vacation came to an end. When we landed in Tehran, though, a sinking sensation hit me all at once. I had forgotten how gray and dismal the city was. Everything looked grimy and worn down. Compared to the Coxes' lovely home in Beaconsfield, our apartment was a third-world tenement, rimed with kerosene soot. My honeymoon with Tehran ended and I had to notch up my resolve to face the final months of our assignment.

Costumes

Dakota and Tina, on the other hand, had no trouble slipping back into life as usual. They brought home inspiration from their cousins and created more and crazier costumes than ever before. If they couldn't go naked, which they much preferred, they settled for dressing up. Our landlord didn't comment on the costumes, but he did express disapproval of their nakedness. He told me I should dress them warmly all the time so they didn't catch their deaths from cold. I've always had a talent for ignoring unsolicited advice, however.

One day, the kids outdid themselves. They dressed up in everything they could get their hands on, including ski gloves, backpacks, pantyhose, silk scarves, high heels, headbands, bedroom slippers (Big Bird, worn on the hands), a bathing cap that mimicked a blonde shag, and (no surprise) Mom's curly wig.

Another day, Dakota put on his red embroidered sombrero and matching vest, strapped on his six-shooter, donned an eye mask left over from Halloween, and called himself "Dangerous Cowboy the Elephant Rider." In the meantime, Tina stripped off every stitch and danced around naked holding a couple of balloons. I had never seen a more adorable "Bubble Dancer."

Tabriz

In an effort to pry me out of my end-of-Tehran-honeymoon funk, Fred suggested that we volunteer to make the non-pro courier run to Tabriz. The city of Tabriz, the fourth largest city in Iran and a commercial, industrial, and transportation center, had an American consular office that was a one-person outpost. For such a small operation, the embassy recruited volunteers to carry the diplomatic pouch, and designated them "non-pro couriers." Fred hadn't taken a turn because he didn't want to leave the rest of us home alone. After we made friends with the Goffs, though, a couple of months before the Caravanserai trip, we hatched a plan to trade off caring for each other's children occasionally. That gave us the option of evenings out, and, if all went well, an overnight trip. I called Norma for her approval and Fred requested the courier run to Tabriz.

The trip involved flying to Tabriz, delivering the pouch, spending the night at a hotel, and returning to Tehran the next afternoon. I had a few moments of terror when I thought about the distance between my babies and me, but Norma Goff's unfaltering calm quieted my fears. Fred and I took off as excited as a bride and groom embarking on a real honeymoon.

Couriers, even the non-pro, flew first class so they could get off the plane quickly and secure the pouches. First class status also enhanced our honeymoon atmosphere. Once we arrived in Tabriz, an official car met us at the air terminal and took us to the consular office where we delivered the pouch. Mr. Ex, the consular officer, suggested sightseeing possibilities and several restaurants that we might enjoy for our evening meal. He invited us to lunch at his home the following day.

After checking into our hotel, we set out to see the city. We intended to take in all the sights recommended by Mr. Ex, but we spent most of the day wandering in the extensive covered bazaar, admiring the amazing variety of beautiful and precious things for sale. When we stopped at a tea stall for refreshments, a group of older men invited Fred to share their hookah (galyan in Farsi). As the smoke from flavored tobacco leaves burbled through the water pipe, I watched my husband blend into the exotic surroundings and become a romantic figure of mystery and intrigue. It's possible I enjoyed the experience more than he did, struggling as he was to stifle a coughing fit from the harshness of the tobacco.

I don't remember what we ate that night, but I do remember our conversation at dinner. Try as we might to find another subject, we kept coming back to what was foremost on both our minds – yep, our kiddos. We spent the whole evening talking about them, how wonderful and clever they were, and how much we missed them.

The next day we arrived at Ex's home unfashionably early, revealing our eagerness to get home. Ex waxed eloquent through the appetizer, soup, main course, salad, dessert and coffee. He showed off his broad knowledge of all things Iranian and demonstrated his fluency in Farsi. I sneaked peeks at my watch as time plodded on. Shortly after the last bite of dessert, time sped up as I realized we needed to leave for the airport soon. I mentioned the time to Ex, and he said, "Don't worry, my driver is ready and waiting, you won't miss your flight, if that's what you're thinking." He changed the subject to his favorite, carpets, and off he went on a never-ending monologue.

As Ex droned on, I stopped sneaking peeks and began to make exaggerated time-checks. Finally, I stood up and made a direct request to leave for the airport. Fred looked surprised but didn't object. Ex's face showed his exasperation, but he did let us go. When we arrived at the airport, boarding had already completed and we had to scurry across the tarmac in order to make our flight with zero time to spare.

Thirty-some years later, I'm still annoyed with Mr. Ex. When I heard that he had been taken hostage at the embassy during the long siege, I pondered the mysterious workings of karma. One of the popular inside stories of that time described Ex as a constant irritant to his captors. He allegedly harassed them with scathing insults and angered them with frequent escape attempts. We heard that the hostage takers hated him so much they stopped the prisoners' bus on the way to the release point, simply to give Ex one last beating.

Back home in Tehran we reunited with our kids and learned that they had had their own excitement during our absence. After dinner the night before our return, Dakota went to the bathroom by himself. When Norma checked on him a few minutes later, she discovered he had locked the door and couldn't get out. He started to cry. Norma used her best powers of persuasion to get him to calm down. The old-fashioned locks used a large key, the type we used to call a skeleton key, and Norma convinced him to pull the key out of the lock and slide it under the door toward her. She could then unlock the door from her side and free the prisoner. The experience taught Dakota something about locks and keys and foreshadowed an adventure to come years later in another country.

7

Fred, Tina, and Dakota with our Cypriot family

1976 – 1977

Nicosia

When Fred's turn came for his first TDY (temporary duty assignment) he danced a victory two-step at the thought of a month in Beijing, an opportunity of a lifetime for a guy enchanted by exotic places. The reason for the TDY - President Nixon's historic visit - added spice to his anticipation. But the official announcement overturned Fred's hopes; someone else had been named for the Beijing trip. One of his colleagues had intercepted the official telegram and submitted his own name for the TDY assignment without authorization. Fred objected, but the boss only shrugged and promised him the next trip. It will always rankle Fred that he didn't go to Beijing; I have to admit my guilty relief that he didn't leave me on my own for a whole month in Tehran.

Fred almost turned down the next TDY because of hearsay. The war between the Greeks and Turks had only recently ended, and some people still talked of unrest, danger in the streets, and razor wire around the embassy compound in Nicosia, Cyprus. After a phone conversation with the guy he would be replacing, Fred concluded that most of what we heard about Nicosia was unfounded rumor. He accepted the assignment, and, after some discussion, we decided the whole family would go.

A furnished apartment was available within walking distance of the embassy, and we looked forward to playing house there for three weeks. My thirty-sixth birthday fell within that time period, so I considered the adventure part of my celebration.

Our itinerary required a change of planes in Tel Aviv, and we had instructions to request that the Israelis not stamp our official passports in order to avoid complications upon our return to Iran. Easier said than done, given the extremely strict security procedures at the Tel Aviv airport. At that time most airport security around the world was casual; security in Israel, in contrast, appeared to be designed for a police state. What I saw made me nervous and paranoid. The burly, scowling female soldiers on duty carried Uzis and looked trigger-happy to me. I saw a British journalist, a woman who published anti-Israeli articles in Arab newspapers, subjected to a ruthless search. Glowering officials tore her carry-on luggage apart and one inspector scooped her cold cream out of the jar while another ripped the heels off her shoes. I couldn't tell if they were searching for something specific or simply harassing her.

Uniformed security guards divided our little family by gender for a frisk-type search of our bodies and clothing. All of the authorities wore mean expressions, used rough gestures, and barked harsh commands. I wouldn't have been surprised to find a prison cell at the end of the queue, but an ordinary waiting room followed the security gauntlet.

The baggage inspections and personal searches had taken two hours. We expected our flight to begin boarding immediately. I checked my watch every few minutes while the next hour ticked by. Then an announcement stated the obvious fact that our fight had been delayed. No one in the waiting room had any idea what caused the delay or when our flight would continue. Another hour passed.

A crackly voice rattled the speakers of the public address system. "A British Airways representative will be arriving momentarily to clarify the schedule of Flight BA444."

The airline rep explained that a hijacked Egyptian Airways plane had landed at Larnaca Airport, our intended destination, and the government had closed that facility until the situation could be resolved. In the meantime, we passengers would be the guests of British Airways at a nearby Tel Aviv resort hotel. A bus waited to take us there once we had reclaimed our checked baggage.

We spent three days in Tel Aviv as guests of British Airways at that very lovely hotel, swimming in each of the three crystal blue pools, quaffing icy beers (apple juice for the juniors, of course) in the resort's pub, and stuffing our tummies at the sumptuous buffet.

However, our mini-holiday had a hideous downside -- daily bus trips to the airport. On every trip the bus stopped at the airport checkpoint to pick up two inspectors who scrutinized each passenger's documents. On the first day, the officials found something suspicious enough to warrant escorting one of the passengers off the bus and into their military van. That man, completely ordinary looking to me, did not rejoin our group, ever. The bus transported the rest of us to the airport proper where we had to go through the whole security procedure again only to turn around and board the bus back to the resort because our flight was not yet available. My emotions caromed between anxiety and anger as I dreaded each of these encounters. The pervasive hostility in the air chilled my marrow.

At long last the hijacking ended and Larnaca Airport reopened. I didn't take a full breath until our plane was airborne. When the wheels touched down in Cyprus, I let out an audible sigh.

We rented a Morris Minor, unfurled the road map, and headed for Nicosia, driving on the left, as is the custom. We were equal to the challenge, having learned to drive on the left during the two years of Fred's Army service in Japan.

A moment of déjà vu overtook me. The landscape didn't remind me of any place I could name, but it felt eerily familiar. The rolling hills covered in olive groves, scattered cactus, and the hint of salt on the breeze made me think of a desert island, a marvelous place to seek tranquility.

Our temporary sanctuary perched on concrete pillars. The three-story apartment building had parking space underneath and an apartment for us on the top floor. The furniture seemed familiar – in fact, it duplicated what we had in temporary quarters in Tehran (and probably at every other post in the world) – it felt like home to us. We unpacked immediately and set out to explore the neighborhood.

Dakota streaked out the door ahead of the rest of us. "Stop when you get to the bottom of the stairs," I yelled at his disappearing back. I could hear music wafting up the stairwell along with the unintelligible babble of voices and a whiff of appetizing aromas. The door to the second floor apartment stood wide open, and that's where we found Dakota, already absorbed into the festivities. The host of the party, Loullis Kozakis, introduced himself in perfect English and explained how the party, in honor of his daughter's fifth birthday, had enticed our son inside. Fred and Loullis became instant brothers and we joined the party.

We met Loullis' wife, daughter, and brother as well as the neighbors from downstairs, the Pabalambrianou family, who owned the building, and Loullis' best friend, Stavros. They treated us like long-lost American cousins. The warmth of their welcome wrapped around us like a homecoming hug.

Over the next three weeks I had to strain to remember the purpose of our visit. We came to Cyprus for Fred's work and he did go to work, of course, but the schedule turned out to be short days, no after-hour call-ins, a five-minute commute, and weekends free. He went to the embassy communications center at nine in the morning, performed the usual duties of the absent information management employee, and came home at five in the afternoon with no worries.

While Fred worked, the kids and I played. They liked the shady parking area under the building where they could dig in the dirt or play hide and seek among the concrete pillars. I enjoyed our walks downtown. We passed goats grazing in empty lots and homes sheltered by grape arbors and shaded by date palms. The balmy September air carried the scents of flowers and warm earth. Every time we went to the shops, I bought a new food to try. We sampled superb smoked trout and the best red flame grapes in the universe. Plump dates fresh from local trees begged to be eaten straight from the shopping bag. The abundance of a wide variety of fresh fruits and vegetables injected new life into our diet. Our palates perked up and everything tasted better in new flavor combinations.

Our new friends introduced us to their favorite restaurant, a simple family-owned café with oilcloth table coverings, rustic wooden tables, and homey atmosphere. "Just a sandwich shop," Loullis said. I salivate when I recall that meal. Fresh, lively flavors. Aromas succulent enough to send a lady into a fainting spell. As soon as we sat down, a waiter appeared and whisked the children to the kitchen where the staff fed them tidbits and entertained them with stories and games. I wanted to stay forever in the company of friends and eat only Greek Cypriot warm pita pockets filled with thin roast pork and yogurt-dill-cucumber sauce.

The next evening, Petros and Andrula invited us for dinner at their place downstairs. I'm sure Andrula got up early that morning to start cooking. She served us delicacy after delicacy, even tiny sparrow-size birds that Petros had hunted that very day out on their farm property in the country outside Nicosia. I experienced a brief case of the willies when I realized that these birds were far too small to eviscerate, but oh well…. This meal also introduced me to fried Halloumi cheese, a taste-treat that I long for, even now, so many years later. The cheese is made from a mixture of goat and sheep milk and the flavor is a cross between mozzarella and feta. The texture is crusty on the outside and the inside is silken but not quite melted. Unforgettable.

The following night, Loullis stopped by to invite us out to his mother's home for the coming weekend. His mother lived right on the Green Line (United Nations Buffer Zone), the very edge of no man's land between the Greek and the Turkish sides, impassable since the most recent

Turkish invasion two years before in 1974. Loullis said he wanted to show us where the battles raged (his mother's wall had bullet holes in it) and tell us stories of the war.

Loullis' mother must have spent days in the kitchen preparing the feast she spread before us. The rabbit stew (kouneli stifado) had more than one magic ingredient, melding into an unidentifiably delightful complex flavor. She lavished us with enough food for twenty people and Loullis made sure the beer glasses were always full. Delicious Cypriot wine and brandy flowed throughout the afternoon as the history lessons kept us spellbound and secured our allegiance to the Greek cause. These were not rich people and yet they shared all of their best food and drink with us, at what cost to the rest of their diet, we'll never know.

During the feast we learned more than history. We heard for the first time about American jokes. These witticisms sounded the same as Polish jokes Fred and I heard when we were growing up. For example, "Question: How many Americans does it take to screw in a light bulb? Answer: Three – one to hold the light bulb and two to turn the ladder." We laughed along with our host before turning the tables with a couple of Cypriot jokes in the same style.

On the advice of our new friends, we took a road trip to Limassol on the following weekend. We had heard that the best Cypriot resorts were on the Turkish-held territory, but I can't imagine how those beaches on the other side of the island could be more beautiful than Limassol's. The warm, clear, Mediterranean blue water gently lapping on the sun-drenched sandy shore – dreams are made of this.

After we returned from Limassol, Loullis and company escorted us out again, this time to a large restaurant with a dance floor and live music. Our dinner of dolmas, moussaka, souvlaki, and a sumptuous array of vegetables and breads exceeded our expectations and we had to loosen our belts another notch. Loullis soon urged us out of our after-dinner lethargy and set about teaching us to dance Greek-style. "Opa!" Our shouts rang out with the other dancers as we spun around the circle, doing our best to follow the pattern of steps, becoming breathless in the process. When the long music set ended and we returned, laughing and panting, to our table, we found a huge platter mounded high with fruit and cheese. I don't know how the Cypriots maintained their slim figures; perhaps it was the dancing.

On one of our evening explorations, we stumbled upon another uniquely Cypriot entertainment - Papa Philippe's amusement park. For the equivalent of pennies, Dakota and Tina rode a fairyland's worth of rides, all designed to suit the size and interest of toddlers. I haven't seen an amusement park quite like this one anywhere else in the world.

When our departure date approached, Loullis stopped by to announce he had special plans for Fred before we left the country. Loullis' brother played on the Cypriot national basketball team, and Loullis wanted Fred to go with him and his friend Stavros to the next game. Sounded innocent enough to me.

So Loullis and Stavros spirited my husband away, and he had the time of his life, which he reported (in full?) the following morning:

The basketball game took place on an outdoor court, and the Cypriots won. Of course the victory required a celebration and a large group of fans, including Loullis' bunch, migrated to the most popular nightclub in the area. Stavros' uncle, Cyprus' most famous bouzouki (Greek stringed instrument similar to a mandolin) player, was performing onstage when Fred and pals arrived.

When the uncle saw Stavros, he stopped playing and beckoned Stavros to the stage. The crowd erupted into a shouted chant, "Stavros, Stavros, Stavros!" Apparently Stavros, a movie and television actor, enjoyed rock-star popularity in this neighborhood. The uncle started playing again and the crowd swept Stavros onto the dance floor. Stavros obliged by breaking into a dance that whirled into a wild frenzy. At the finale, Stavros executed a backflip but landed wrong and sprained his wrist. With a nonchalant Walter Mitty air, he wrapped a napkin around his injury and ordered drinks all around.

The crowd started throwing plates (a Greek custom, we were told) and the management team scurried around, unsuccessfully trying to subdue the high jinks. Someone gathered an armload of broken crockery, dumped it on a table, gathered the tablecloth and dishes into a bundle, drenched the pile with Johnny Walker Red, and lit a match. When the flames flared high, Loullis' better judgment prompted him to shoo Fred out the door before unrivaled revelry turned to prosecutable hullabaloo.

Were we in Cyprus only three weeks? We certainly packed in the fun. We couldn't imagine never seeing our new friends again, and we exchanged Christmas cards for many years afterward, always hoping that we would reunite someday.

Choices

Back to reality, harsh reality. My friend Norma told me when she returned to Tehran after R&R she spent the first five days in the house with the drapes pulled shut, pretending she was not there. I thought she might be a little crazy until I had the same experience returning from Cyprus. Urban terrorism seemed to have escalated to a level beyond frightening. A U.S. Army colonel had been assassinated mere blocks from our home, revolutionaries and supporters of the Shah battled on the streets, and an embassy vehicle had been carjacked and one passenger killed. I felt mentally and emotionally unequipped to deal with the increased violence, but we had six months left in Tehran. I needed a better coping mechanism than closed drapes.

Fortunately, the arrival of the open assignments list came as a welcome distraction soon after we returned from Cyprus. Fred and I set upon the task of formulating a bid list. With several pages of openings in front of us, we looked at each other and shrugged. Where to begin? Eventually we developed a technique and continued to refine it over the years. We identified posts that had a school with an American curriculum and instruction in English. We placed a high priority on furnished quarters, since we had no furniture other than odds and ends in storage. The less-traveled places attracted both of us, so smaller posts got our attention. We liked the idea of hardship posts (offering a 10-15% pay benefit), as long as the hardship didn't include war.

I made a chart and we rated our choices. Fred submitted a bid list of ten to fifteen posts and then we faced a long, hard wait until the assignment telegram arrived several months later. Our first list included London, Vienna, Santo Domingo, Nairobi, Yaounde, Dakar, Manila, Brussels, Warsaw, and Accra. No one could tell us whether we could expect to be assigned to our first choice or any of the choices on our list. Assignments were made "for the good of the service." We didn't know what that meant either.

Jones

While we awaited our fate, a new guy was assigned to Fred's office and the Personnel Office designated us as sponsors. Fred read the name on the telegram, "Glenn Jones – you know what -- I hope he's black. Our shop could stand some diversity."

We looked forward to welcoming Glenn and his wife Christa to the embassy community and added them to our guest list for Tina's third birthday party.

Fred met Glenn and Christa at the airport and delivered them to their home on the embassy compound. When he got home, he told me how Glenn's appearance dashed his hopes of gaining an ally in his struggle against conformity. First, Glenn was not black, and second, he was wearing a suit and tie, "Just like all the rest of the polyester club." This first impression did not prove true. Glenn demonstrated later he was anything but another member of the polyester club. Glenn and Christa both played important roles in our lives from then on.

Packing Out and Moving On

After the Joneses' arrival, Fred received the cable announcing his assignment to Yaounde (pronounced yah OON day), Cameroon -- number five on our bid list. Eagerly we started the packing out process, sorting our belongings into piles for sea freight, airfreight, accompanied baggage, and give-aways. Since sea freight could take six months to arrive, it made sense for us to send it on its way and move back into temporary quarters on the embassy compound during our final three months at post.

As I deliberated over our possessions, I had to visualize what we would need to carry in our suitcases for six weeks of home leave. Our airfreight allowance could be divided in two shipments – one to our home leave address and one to our new post. Experienced friends advised me to pack plenty of toys, games, and books in airfreight along with clothing and toiletry refills. They also recommended including my favorite kitchen utensils to supplement the standard welcome kit supplied at our new post. I stacked airfreight bound for the U.S. in a corner of the kids' room. Airfreight destined for Cameroon piled up on the kitchen table and give-away items accumulated on the dining room table. I practiced packing our suitcases and tried to confine that stuff in our bedroom. What remained was sea freight and embassy property. A few things migrated from pile to pile until the final reckoning – pack out day.

As soon as the packers finished loading our containers, we stowed our personal baggage in the car and called for Tigger the cat. We searched everywhere. No Tigger. I hoped we might find him waiting for us when we returned to the apartment a few days later to run through the embassy check out list, but he wasn't there. As we drove off for the last time, I swear I glimpsed a familiar gray form sneaking into the garage of the Johnson's (Tigger's original family) former home where a new family had recently moved in. Perhaps he chose a new family in his own country rather than go to Africa and who-knew-where-else with us. I felt so sorry for the kids' sadness, I promised to get them a new kitty in Cameroon.

Unexpected Twist

A few days before our final departure, while I stood at the stove cooking oatmeal, a severe pain in my side made me double over and almost faint. When the pain subsided a bit I made some calls to arrange a visit to the Army clinic.

Tests for appendicitis came back negative, so the Army doctor referred me to a local gynecologist. The consultation provided an external exam only. Do I remember correctly that a male Iranian doctor could not perform a gynecological examination unless the woman's husband was present? I left the doctor's office without a diagnosis, reconciled to tolerating the pain until I could get proper medical attention. Since our plans included a week's stopover in London with the Coxes, that seemed like my best bet. Fred called Pat and asked her to arrange an appointment with their family doctor.

As our flight took off from Tehran, I reflected on the good times we had there. Abruptly the load of worry about the increasing level of terrorist activity lifted only to be replaced by concerns about my health. The pain in my side waxed and waned throughout the trip, never disappearing completely.

In London, physician Sir Peter Lord finished his examination and stood by the side of the examining table where I lay on my side, the position preferred by Brits in those days for the pelvic exam. "Now, if you were a home-town girl, I would do an exploratory operation, but as you're not, I want to admit you to the hospital for a few days' observation. We'll starve you and see what shows up. If surgery is recommended you can arrange to have that taken care of when you get back to The States."

That's how I got to spend the greater part of our London visit starving in the hospital. No, Sir Peter Lord was not kidding. Once checked into the hospital, I got nothing to eat. The British addiction to tea kept me alive. Served with milk and sugar five or six times a day, tea can keep a person going for at least three days, I am proof of that.

Fred and the kids had a great time with Pat, Dick, Beth, Karen and Kathy. Although they all swore they missed me, I think they were having way too much fun to feel sorry for me. I, on the other hand, felt plenty sorry for myself. After all, I had only teatime to enjoy.

Nothing showed up during my three days of starvation and the doctor released me without a diagnosis. We kept to our travel itinerary and I went on feeling miserable. My memory of that period is blurred, but I know we stopped in Pompano Beach, Florida, for a few days to visit my aunts before continuing on to Roswell, New Mexico, where I had an appointment with Dr. Ray, the OB/GYN who had delivered several babies of the LaTurner clan.

Dr. Ray found what the other three doctors had missed, an ovarian mass that had grown by then to the size of a grapefruit. It would have to be removed and biopsied to rule out cancer. And that's how I got to spend most of our first home leave recuperating from abdominal surgery.

I went into surgery with paralyzing fear that I would not wake up, never see Fred again, not be able to raise my wonderful children or see them graduate, get married and have children of their own. As the hours crept along, Fred wore a path between the visitors' lounge and the coffee machine. The surgery took much longer than anticipated because Dr. Ray had to remove an extensive entanglement of endometriosis that no one knew was there. The ovarian cyst was benign, but because of the endometriosis, I ended up without uterus and ovaries: even my appendix had to go.

After I returned to my hospital room, Fred brought Dakota and Tina to the hospital grounds outside my window so I could see them. They stood in the green grass on tiptoe to peer over the hedge and wave to me. I yearned to wrap my arms around them, but the hospital allowed no visitors under the age of twelve. I had to wait a whole week until I could kiss my babies.

During my recovery, we stayed with Fred's parents who lived in a spacious stone house a block from the hospital. I couldn't get around much and the doctor absolutely forbade lifting, so Fred and Granny cared for the kids while I played referee from Grandpa's big recliner. When I had to move -- to visit the bathroom, for example – I summoned all my strength and gumption to inch my way out of the chair. A physical sensation of emptiness in my belly made me grit my teeth. That hollow feeling persisted for weeks, until the rest of my organs shifted to new positions and filled the gap. Thanks to hefty injections of hormones, I didn't have to feel any emotional sense of loss at least.

The doctor said I could do anything I wanted after six weeks. To tell the truth, after six weeks I still didn't want to do much of anything. Fred requested an extension of our home leave to give me some precious extra time to gain strength.

We shopped for a replacement for our VW that we had sold before leaving Iran and found an excellent deal on a VW bus. Our blue and white chariot made us puff out our chests with pride, all four of us. In the chaos surrounding my illness and surgery, my driver's license had expired and I took the road test in our new bus, hoping the examiner would cut me some slack because I could hardly manage the step up into the bus. He didn't lower his standards, but I passed the test anyway.

While visiting my folks in Los Lunas, New Mexico, we turned our beautiful bus over to the shipping company for transport to Cameroon. We expected to pick up our U.S. airfreight at this time, but it had not arrived. After several phone calls and some clever detective work done by State Department transportation clerks, we learned that our shipment had been sent to Mexico. Unfortunately the shipping agent in Tehran thought that Mexico City was the airport closest to Los Lunas, rather than Albuquerque, which is about ten miles north on Interstate 25. Mexican Customs impounded our shipment for lack of proper documentation and began charging an impound fee.

When home leave ended and we left the States to begin our journey to Yaounde, Cameroon, we didn't know that it would take a year of negotiation and a pound of paperwork to get our airfreight released from Mexican Customs and delivered to my parents in Los Lunas. We had more important things to think about: we were on our way to Africa.

PART THREE
CAMEROON TALES

Architecture in the country

8

Fred's t-shirt says, "I'm Not a Tourist – I Live Here."

June - August 1977

Paris Quicky

Our itinerary to our assignment to Yaounde included an overnight stop in
Paris. Brother-in-law Dick, who traveled to Paris often, recommended the

Hotel Mac Mahon. The cabby on our taxi ride from airport to hotel drove like he was auditioning for a high-speed car chase in a B movie. As he swerved, passed, and gunned his way through heavy Paris traffic, he called out the names of famous buildings. One of his near sideswipes made me miss seeing the Sacred Heart Basilica, but it was worth the sacrifice if my concentrated will actually saved the day by pulling our fender in at the last instant before impact.

The Mac Mahon was a charming hotel in a historic dressed-stone building a few steps away from the Arc de Triomphe and Champs-Elysees. We four travelers walked the whole star-shaped perimeter of the hill of Chaillot where the Arc stands triumphant. When we got back to the hotel, we snuggled into bed and slept until jet lag interrupted our slumber at 2:00 AM. We woke hungry, ravenously hungry. Fred braved the streets of Paris in the wee hours to hunt provisions. Fortunately he found a bar that was both open and served sandwiches. Expecting the stereotypical French disdain for everything and everybody non-French, Fred was delighted to meet a friendly and helpful bartender who offered a selection of meat and cheese sandwiches on crispy-crusted baguettes.

We tore into those sandwiches like savages. It's hard to imagine a more satisfying meal. When we were finished, the carpet looked like we had dismembered an entire French bakery. On hands and knees I picked up crusty flakes for half an hour, but incriminating evidence of sandwich mutilation still sullied the deep blue carpet.

Barely minutes, or so it seemed, after we finished our middle of the night snack and finally fell asleep, banging drums and loud brass music woke us again. Fred opened the curtains and we watched a long parade of war veterans pass below, on their way to the Arc de Triomphe, solemn and stark in the cool light of dawn, like a scene from a 1940s black and white war movie.

Jungle Drums

The following day, in living color and 3D, we had a striking introduction to 1977 Africa when our flight to Yaounde required a plane change at the international airport in Douala, Cameroon's largest city. The humid heat struck with full force.

"There's something wrong with this air," Dakota said, "I can't breathe it."

A monkey on the shoulder of a passer-by drew our attention to the riot of colors, odors, noises, and activity in the air terminal. Women wearing jewel-toned cotton print ankle-length gowns with matching head wraps swirled through the crowd of travelers dressed in drab neutral colors. Vendors sang their spiels like Sirens of the sea with rooster crows and monkey screeches in counterpoint. We four held hands and formed a tiny minority island in an ocean of inquisitive faces, all smiling with dazzling white teeth against purple-black skin. A few passersby tried to make conversation, but when we responded to their patois with puzzled expressions, they gave Dakota a pat on the head or ruffled Tina's hair and walked away. I knew I needed to dive into French lessons as soon as we checked in at Amembassy Yaounde.

My white knuckles showed what I thought of our chances of survival as our small plane bounced and skidded to a stop only a few feet from a steep drop into the jungle surrounding Yaounde's airport. An embassy official facilitated our passage through the formalities and a small group of embassy folks met us at the gate. Our entourage buffered us from the chaotic swarm of arrivals, departures, hucksters, and taxi hawkers. Our welcoming committee ushered us through pandemonium into the sanctuary of an embassy vehicle and swept us to our temporary quarters.

The cement block building squatted at the edge of a road that cut a narrow slice through the dense tangle of trees, undergrowth, and vines. Our apartment had that nobody-really-lives-here look. The smell made an indelible impression -- the tangy nose-crinkling mixture of propane, cleaning products, insect spray and overripe fruit. I followed the odor to the kitchen and pantry area where it intensified. I made a quick survey of the groceries provided by our sponsors. Good enough -- Cheerios with milk, a whole pineapple, and Kraft Macaroni and Cheese would keep us going until I could go shopping.

The welcoming committee flocked around Fred, babbling, while Dakota, Tina, and I inspected the rest of the apartment. Fred reported later that this group of "young turks" tried to enlist him in their war against the establishment. Fred decided to stall them until he had a chance to talk to the "old guard" and figure out how he could best stay out of the political struggles entirely.

Twilight descended as the young turks left. I served bowls of mac and cheese on the veranda. Trees, green fading to black, filled the view. Vines intertwined everywhere. Jungle reached to the horizon. A few pieces of macaroni fell from Tina's fork and we watched the ants discover the spill. Within minutes no evidence remained, not even a grease spot on the cement floor. No doubt Cameroon had a lot to teach us about the job of insects in the tropics.

A few twinkling lights appeared among the trees that showed only their outline against the darkening sky. And the drums began. The hairs on my arms stood up. I thrilled inside with a shivery feeling of anticipation. Real African jungle drums! I felt as excited as a six-year-old watching "King Solomon's Mines" for the first time. The drumming grew more intense and I half rose from my chair before I realized that the louder sounds came from rain pounding on tin roofs as a tropical storm approached. When the storm reached its peak and the rain crashed on our own tin roof, it roared as if a locomotive were thundering overhead.

After the brief squall passed, we listened to the magic of the jungle drums until we could no longer keep our eyes open. Four sleepyheads stumbled to bed and all four hit the pillow snoring.

"Patron, Patron!" Screams in French jerked me from a sound, dreamless sleep.

Loud pounding on the door woke Fred at the same time and he jumped out of bed. He opened the door to find two Cameroonians, our night guards, one bleeding from a cut on his foot, the other holding the injured man upright. Through pantomime accompanied by hysterical jabbering in French patois, they managed to convey that a snake had bitten the injured man. They asked Fred to bandage the wound, provide a container for the dead snake (for identification whether venomous or non-venomous), and drive them to the hospital. I found a clean dishtowel for a bandage and emptied a pickle jar to carry the snake carcass. Since we had no car, Fred radioed the embassy for an official vehicle. In the silence that followed their departure, Fred and I gave each other the look that says, "Here we go again!"

We learned later that the snake wasn't venomous, but the guard nearly died from infection. The cut on his foot came from an old razor blade he pulled from his wallet to slash the site of the bite so his partner could suck out the venom. This was a common practice, although not considered safe or useful by medical experts. Everyone we met after that had at least one story about black mambas or green mambas or close encounters with other venomous snakes. I vowed to walk only on cleared paths with good visibility and to keep an eagle eye on my children at all times.

School and Trauma

Our sponsors, the Grimstes, Bob, Antje, Bobby and Andy (short for Andrea), took good care of us. Antje made sure I connected with the gracious proprietor of Mrs. Addoh's Preschool. Mrs. Addoh had converted a residence, within walking distance of our temporary digs, into an international day school for three to five year olds. I enrolled Dakota and Tina for a class that met for two hours every morning, confident that they would enjoy the opportunity to make new friends and play with other children.

While the kids were at school, I puttered around the house, taking care of the usual housekeeping chores and studying French with the Foreign Service Institute language tapes, until time to walk back up the hill and bring my scholars home again. One day, in the middle of the morning, I heard a knock at the door. I wasn't expecting any visitors. Curiosity mixed with apprehension as I opened the door a crack. Mrs. Addoh's assistant, Sandra, stood there with an arm around Dakota's shoulder. Dakota lifted his tear-streaked face and burst into a new flood of tears as he lurched into my arms. Sandra picked up Dakota's left hand and showed me his ring finger swathed in a cocoon of cotton wool. She explained that he had shinned up the swing set pole during recess and the hinge of the two-person swing had smashed his finger.

"I'm afraid he might lose his finger-tip. You should get him to a doctor right away."

I radioed for a car to take us to the Embassy Medical Unit. Sandra assured me that she and Mrs. Addoh would take care of Tina for the rest of the day.

Fred met us at the Medical Unit and held Dakota on his lap while our embassy nurse, Donna Schloss, used a whole bottle of peroxide to remove the cotton fibers stuck to Dakota's mangled finger. When she saw the severity of the injury, she phoned ahead and sent us to Central Hospital Yaounde.

We moved down the long hospital corridor as fast as we could. If the Devil had shown up, I would have latched onto any deal he offered to get us out of there. Moaning patients lay on makeshift pallets in the hallway. Blood spatter stained the pockmarked walls and scuffed floors. We had walked into a giant petri dish, a breeding ground for new strains of virulent bacteria and we were carrying our sweet boy straight into the center of it.

Thank goodness, Dr. Budzynski's tiny cramped office was an oasis of cleanliness, and the doctor's manner radiated competence and confidence. He told us about his career as a surgeon in his home country, Poland, and his current status as volunteer physician, inexplicably assigned to deliver babies rather than perform surgery. He pondered the x-rays of Dakota's hand and announced that he could reattach the fingertip and probably salvage the nail bed as well. Then he explained that the fingertip was too small to allow numbing the area.

I turned to Dakota and said, "You are a brave boy, but it's okay to cry. If you feel like screaming, Mommy and Daddy will scream with you."

Dr. Budzynski stitched, his face a mask of concentration. Dakota stayed brave throughout the surgery and all the painful dressing changes thereafter. He cried, yes, but he held still, firm as a rock. And his wound healed beautifully without any of the hideous infections of my nightmares.

Getting Acquainted

Once we recovered from the injured finger trauma, we focused on getting acquainted with the city of Yaounde. The American Club functioned as the hub of social activity for the international community. There was always something going on at the tennis courts, swimming pool, bridge tables, snack bar, and elementary school. We gravitated toward families with similar interests and children about the same age as ours: the Grimstes (our sponsors from Fred's office), the Ekstroms (Peace Corp Director Jim and his wife Leslie and their children Matt and Becca) and the Rowans (Embassy Security Officer Richie and his wife Kathy and their two boys Richard and Justin) became our boon companions.

We learned that grocery shopping could be done at the outdoor market for most of our needs; at SCORE, a French style supermarket, for special occasions; and at the spartan embassy commissary for American cereals and canned goods. The open market offered all varieties of fresh fruits and vegetables, meats, grains, and spices in a hustle-bustle atmosphere that appealed to Fred's sense of adventure. When I first saw the skinned monkeys, hanging from the rafters of the meat shack and crawling with flies, I passed the marketing baton with no regrets. On my few unavoidable trips to the market, I skirted the meat section and I always followed our friend's advice to wear rubber boots.

Fred continued to enjoy it all and didn't mind the squish of fetid muck between his sandaled toes. He told me, "A trip to the market is the highlight of my week. I love it all – the vendors' bright dresses among the tomatoes, mangoes, papayas, onions, okra, beans, seeds and the screeching animals, laughing people, lively music pounding on the radio and the horrible smells, mud, blood, ooze – I love it all!"

SCORE grocery store, a small oasis of French culinary culture, tempted us with an abundance of cheeses and rare treats like caviar, fresh strawberries, and fine wine, all at a premium price, which was a good reason to make shopping there a special occasion. I had a secret reason for avoiding SCORE. I dreaded seeing the lepers who begged outside the entrance. My spare change charity didn't blunt the claws of guilt that tore at my heart. What could one person do to help so many?

While we got acquainted with Yaounde, we waited for our airfreight, our car, our household effects, and our permanent housing assignment. With no houses available in the neighborhood where most of the embassy families lived, the Housing Unit leased a brand new house for us in a small development on Airport Road, just beyond the "33" brewery.

"Oh you lucked out," Bob Grimste said. "The area around the brewery always has electricity."

The area around the brewery also had a distinctive odor, sweetly pungent and yeasty. I expected the air to reek like spilled beer the morning after a kegger, but the smell was as pleasant as toasted bread.

Our new home, even without a twig or blade of landscaping, appealed to my eye. The house balanced gracefully on a steep slope. A tiled veranda ran the full length of the building on the side facing the street. The driveway descended sharply and turned abruptly to enter a carport. In addition to the carport the lower level included servant's quarters, a powder room, laundry room, storage closet, and a stairway to the upper level. The backyard continued sloping down to a retaining wall at the foot of the property. Upstairs, floor to ceiling windows faced jungle that stretched all the way to the "33" beer factory.

Inside the house, the brisk odor of fresh paint on new plaster blended with the clean fragrance of pine disinfectant. A complete set of furniture and appliances in their factory wrappings awaited their unveiling and our approval. New furniture might have pleased me more if the upholstery hadn't been pure white velour. I envisioned my two small children playing in our huge expanse of naked coppery red earth. I imagined them running indoors and belly flopping on the white sofa. My mind's eye foretold the future of pristine white turned to grubby pinkish brown, in spite of precautions like protective covers or attempts at stain removal.

I loved the floor in this house, glossy ceramic tile the color of devil's food cake. Dangerous when wet, but beautiful. There was nothing unusual about the floor plan – kitchen next to the dining room, living room at the front of the house, and three bedrooms along a hall on the side opposite the dining room. I laughed about the number of toilets in this modest home – six in all – and declared this a good time and place to have a servant.

Sampson and Joseph

Servants. Not in my wildest fantasy would I have become the mistress of servants. Even my childhood daydream of having been born to royalty and kidnapped by my evil faux-parents didn't include servants. Of course Fred and I called them employees, not servants. But they called us Master and Madame, a habit so ingrained that our efforts to change it had little impact.

First we hired Sampson Atanga. Tall, slim, dignified Sampson came to us from years with a British family. He carried a glowing reference letter that praised his abilities, his honesty, and his fine character. The letter also mentioned that Sampson held the title of Chief in his village. He cooked, cleaned, grocery-shopped (on his own motorbike), laundered, ironed, and occasionally babysat. He said he preferred to live in his village and commute, doing our daily shopping en route.

The Brits had trained Sampson in the fine art of table service. When he served dinner, he wore a starched white uniform with shiny brass buttons. His elegant attire and formal demeanor were slightly intimidating until I noticed that his feet were bare. His fashion statement told me that he might pay lip service to colonial code, but he had limits. He took a stand for freedom from shoe leather for his gnarled and calloused toes.

Sampson gave us lessons in British table service. As he served the first course he instructed Master to ring the silver bell sitting next to his wine glass to signal the next course. For our first meal, Sampson presented chilled cream of asparagus soup, followed by the best fish and chips in the world (made from barracuda fresh from that morning's market), then crisp green salad lush with ripe avocado, and the final ecstasy, coconut pineapple cream pie worthy of a French pastry chef magically transported to tropical fruit heaven. We couldn't keep up the pace. Although I worried about offending Sampson, I had to tell him to cease and desist before we four turned into the Goodyear Blimp family. We compromised on a protein-plus-two-veggies meal plan and reserved dessert for special occasions. Also, Fred asked to be excused from bell-ringing duty.

Another quirk of Sampson's training involved ironing. Sampson had been taught to iron everything, including jockey shorts, to kill the eggs of the tumbu or mango fly, a species of blowfly. Never mind the fact that our laundry went from the washer directly into the hot dryer, not hung out to dry where mango flies could lay their eggs on our damp clothing. The reason for mango fly paranoia came from the larvae's habit of moving out of the clothing and burrowing into a host's skin where painful lesions developed around the growing worms. Tumbu fly boils typically developed an opening on top that drained small amounts of the host's blood mixed with waste products from the maggot. I did not discourage Sampson from taking the extra precautions.

A common scene in our laundry room found Sampson ironing underwear, jeans and t-shirts, a cold bottle of "33" at the ready, Dakota and Tina sitting on top of the washer and dryer, listening to Sampson's stories delivered around a smoldering cigarette clamped in the corner of his mouth. I got used to having everything wrinkle-free and Fred told me the neat creases pressed into his t-shirts and jeans made him feel well dressed.

Besides Sampson, our staff included security guards. The Embassy contracted a security company to provide night guards for embassy-leased residences. Our guard might be any one of dozens employed by the agency, and a different guy showed up before dusk and left after dawn every day. We provided a wool blanket to ward off the night chill. More sleeping than guarding went on, but I gathered that the employment of hundreds of men provided a politic of mutual security -- jobs for them and safety for us. Thieves seemed to understand that tampering with a home under the protection of the large security company would bring quick and certain repercussion.

Every household also required a gardener. We hired Joseph Tazenou, a beautiful naïve boy from a village far to the north. Joseph told us he had come to the capital city to make his fortune. With his mother's permission, he added. Joseph started our garden from absolute scratch and created a botanical marvel, mostly from free cuttings he brought from other embassy-leased properties. He cultivated bougainvillea in shades of fuchsia, amethyst, and gold. He planted snake-repellent grasses along the walkways and bamboo along the property line. Many perennials that I thought of as houseplants grew to gigantic trees under his care. He said he loved Nature and he proved it every day. In a matter of months we had a small banana plantation, several papaya trees bearing fruit, and a kitchen garden that provided Swiss chard, peanuts, pineapples, and potatoes.

Like Sampson, Joseph also commuted to work, so I laid claim on the servant's quarters as my sewing room. That lasted until our first visit to Joseph's home.

Joseph had acquired a table and he asked us to help him get it to his place. He lived in a typical housing area where individual rooms could be rented. Joseph pointed out the central well where the neighborhood residents drew drinking and cooking water. I could see that everyone bathed there as well, rinsing their clothes right on their bodies, without soap in most cases, perhaps because of the cost of that luxury.

We watched as Joseph unlatched the door to his windowless room. Sunlight cut a wide path into the darkness. A creepy flurry of scuttling startled me and I saw that the walls, floor, and ceiling were in motion. I turned away, dizzy and sick with the realization that Joseph shared his room with a million cockroaches.

We didn't even take Joseph's table out of our bus. Fred helped him gather the rest of his few belongings, leaving his mangy cot for the cockroaches, and we drove directly home to install Joseph in the ex-sewing room. The embassy warehouse delivered a single bed and chest of drawers. And Joseph started calling Fred "Father."

I asked Joseph if he would be able to baby-sit occasionally. "Yes, Madame, I consider it an honor." So Fred and I finally accepted an invitation to a party. To simplify matters, I made sure the kids went to sleep before we left. Both of them usually slept soundly through the night, and I had no reason to think Joseph would encounter any problems. Apparently he didn't share my confidence. We returned before midnight to find every light on, Joseph sitting at the dining room table with Fred's NMMI (New Mexico Military Institute) Lieutenant's sword unsheathed and at the ready. The children slept blissfully in their beds, unaware that Joseph stood guard, armed to do battle with "the bad boys" of his own imagination. Fred and I went back to our routine of accepting only the invitations that included our whole family.

Daily Life

Our daily life settled into a predictable pattern. In order for me to have our bus during the day, Fred would walk to the corner on weekday mornings and catch a share-taxi to work. He claimed to enjoy the experience, the body odors, the sloshing bucket of animal entrails between the feet of his fellow passenger, and the vibrant colors of the passing scenes of Cameroonian early morning activity.

"Africans just smell so good," he exclaimed.

Not that good, I thought, compared to the fragrances of soap, deodorant, clean clothes, and perfume that I was used to.

Most mornings I drove Dakota and Tina to Mrs. Addoh's School and then went on to run errands, attend French class, or have a tennis lesson. After lunch, the kids and I usually went to the American Club for a swim and often we would hang out there with friends until it was time to pick Fred up.

The American Club had the best pommes frites (we couldn't call them French Fries in a French-speaking country). Kitchen staff sat on folding chairs outside the kitchen door, peeling potatoes all day long. One guy could peel a whole potato in one long spiral, a source of wonderment to the crowd of children who gathered to watch.

Often on the weekends, our whole family trooped over to our friend Earl's place. Earl worked for USIS (United States Information Service), the agency affectionately known as "culture vultures" because of their emphasis on the importance of cultural exchange with other nations. A single man, Earl had a remarkable tolerance for children and always made the LaTurner tribe feel welcome. Fred and Earl played chess while I relaxed in Earl's leather recliner listening through earphones to Jean-Luc Ponty's enthralling electric violin. Dakota and Tina played with the toys they brought with them or browsed through Earl's collection of souvenirs from previous posts. Those lazy afternoons and evenings mellowed further with the addition of "33" or Gold Harp beer and occasionally the special treat of sweet, intoxicating Black Russians.

Earl's apartment covered half of the twelfth floor of a building across the street from SCORE. The elevator reminded me of an upright coffin. I didn't trust it. Earl told us that the elevator broke down at least three times a week, sometimes stuck between floors for hours. I hated all elevators, but this one struck me as particularly odious. I insisted that we use the stairs, and my family humored me throughout the twelve flights up and the twelve flights down.

When we weren't visiting Earl, Earl visited us. As the grown-ups exchanged stories on the veranda, the kids played. Hydroplaning was one of their favorite activities. Hose a little water on the veranda's tile floor, get a running start and slide, slide, slide the length of the house. As nighttime and bedtime approached, Fred put Jackson Browne on the stereo, and the kids lay down on floor cushions to fall sleep listening to the murmur of adult voices.

9

Our kids frolic on the beach at Kribi

September 1977 – February 1978

The Great Washout

Once again, Fred's turn for temporary duty (TDY) came around. Three weeks in Nairobi, Kenya, sounded like fun, but it wouldn't be a family trip this time because of finances. Our extended home leave cost more than we expected, and we didn't have enough savings to cover airfare and hotel costs for three tag-alongs. Fred's boss made it easier for me to stay behind. He requested a temporary SECRET clearance for me and hired me to do clerical tasks during Fred's three-week TDY. A supplement to our income at that point meant merrier Christmas shopping from the new toy catalogs.

The kids and I took Daddy to the airport and shared his excitement right up until the plane started to move down the runway. My heart ached with a pang of regret and I felt the kids move closer and cling to my legs. I looked down at them. They looked up at me, and we all three burst into tears.

Fred kept a diary during the Nairobi TDY. The first entry showed how he felt about our separation:

"8:40 PM Sept 3, 1977. Left Yaounde. Saw Nancy, T & D from plane window. Tina waved like crazy. Beginning to feel like going was big mistake. Miss you guys already."

His troubles began to multiply when he landed in Douala forty minutes later and had to go through customs and security before boarding his flight to Nairobi. The customs official glared at him like he was an insect when he confessed that he had forgotten his shot record. The sour faced officer stamped his official passport, and Fred proceeded to the security booth for a frisk search. The guard's hand strayed into Fred's pocket and found his cash. Heart pounding, Fred grabbed the guard's hand and gave him the most menacing grimace he could summon. The stare-down lasted until the guard shifted his eyes and turned the money loose.

Fred's shaky legs carried him to a seat in the waiting room where he eased into a hard plastic chair and pulled out his diary. "Very lonesome sitting in airport until plane leaves at 1:15 AM"

Nairobi Customs almost didn't clear him because he had no shot record. The official said, "We don't let people like you in our country." But he stamped the visa anyway when he learned that Fred was traveling as an official of the United States Government.

For the next few weeks, work occupied Fred's days. He tried to stave off his nighttime loneliness by going to restaurants and watching movies.

Guys from the office, Rudy Kiel and Bob Burkhardt, took him out a few times, once to The New Stanley Hotel where Ernest Hemingway used to hang out, and once to Bob's home for dinner. The route to Bob's home followed Uhuru highway through scenery that reminded Fred of England in the summer, with the additional beauty of palm and banana trees. Bob's house was as cozy as an English cottage with moss-covered red tile roof and fireplace chimney wafting curls of wood smoke. That evening Fred returned to his room in the cylindrical tower of the Nairobi Hilton and continued his battle with loneliness and boredom.

As his struggle wore on, Fred went out to a dozen restaurants – Italian, Chinese, Indian, and many variations on those themes. He saw many movies, some so bad they weren't worth sitting through. He spent hours by the hotel pool. He read novels, a total of eight in eighteen days. Time dragged. He wrote in his diary, "Wish you guys were here."

The weekend loomed as a dark blob of wretchedness. Fred decided to book a tour to Nairobi National Park and Lake Nakuru, and his outlook brightened as he anticipated stepping into the Africa of Hollywood movies and National Geographic centerfolds.

The tour fulfilled his savanna fantasies. He saw lions, giraffe, antelope, buffalo, and ostriches roaming free. He watched a lion chase a giraffe through tawny grasses waving tall against blue gray folds of mountains in the distance. And he marveled at the rosy aura of Lake Nakuru, filled with thousands of wading flamingoes.

At the end of this marvelous interlude, Fred returned to hotel, room service vodka tonics, melancholy, and sleep.

Monday's diary entry read, "I sure miss you guys. I'll never take another TDY unless you all can come with me. This is definitely a drag. I just don't operate well on my own...I love you Nancy."

Even though he thought it might never happen, Fred's exile did end. As he sat in the departure lounge at Nairobi Airport he wrote his final diary entry for the trip: "Have an hour and a half to kill before plane leaves. Just realize I locked the key to suitcase inside suitcase. Oh well!"

While Fred was gone, Dakota, Tina and I suffered from the blues too.

Every single day began with, "Is this the day Daddy comes home?" In the evening, we snuggled together on the couch and played Fred's favorite Jackson Browne records until bedtime.

The weekend after Fred's departure, I heard that the Marines planned to show a kids' matinee movie at the American Club. The Marines often shared their movies with us, but only rarely did they have features for kids. I liked the idea of a matinee for two reasons: no need to drive home in the dark, and less likelihood of seeing the disgusting nocturnal parade of huge rats across the top of the movie screen.

We arrived early, ordered our hamburgers with pommes frites, and found seats with our friends, the Grimstes, and the Ekstroms. About half way through the movie, a deafening noise drowned out the sound track, followed shortly by a blackout. The audience groaned. A typical afternoon tropical storm dumped pounding rain for about an hour. The tin roof of the American Club amplified the sound to a painful level. We tried shouting at each other, but no one could hear anything besides the rain's roar. I knew from experience that the power outage could last until the next morning. That left nothing to do but wait for the end of the storm and go home.

The air had that unique fresh quality that follows a tropical storm. The sun came out, and a broad rainbow arched over the steaming jungle. All the green leaves glistened as if bedazzled with rhinestones. The world gleamed, renewed and washed clean of the ubiquitous red dust. My skin felt both feverish and chilled and my lungs labored to find oxygen shrouded in humidity.

We sang nursery rhyme songs all the way home. When we reached the bottom of the driveway, I was struck dumb. With the kids' piping voices in the background, I surveyed the damage in our yard. The storm had washed our whole backyard, including the stout block wall, into the jungle below, as if a hurricane had passed straight down the slope. Not only a huge mess, the loss of our wall also presented a security issue. If Fred were here, he would handle it, but he wouldn't be home for another two weeks.

GSO (General Services Office) and Embassy Security responded to my radio call and sent a crew out the next day. It took a week to put up a chain link fence and clean up the debris. Our faithful gardener Joseph had to start over with the garden, and he gallantly rose to the challenge.

Commissary

I didn't know it at the time, but I was about to face a challenge of my own. I had always believed in the importance of having one parent devoted to full time child rearing during those early formative years. Fred agreed. In fact, he volunteered for the position of stay-at-home dad right from the start. Lucky for me, I had an equipment advantage. The fact that I could breastfeed tipped the scales in my favor and Fred accepted his assignment as breadwinner. I fully intended to stay at home to care for our children until they reached at least school age.

No employment opportunities had tempted me in Tehran, but Yaounde was different. Fred and the Administrative Officer, Warren Littrell, became tennis buddies, and Warren apparently viewed me as an untapped fountain going to waste in a personnel drought. He dropped broad hints about this position and that job yet to be filled by someone with my "many talents." I sidestepped, gracefully (I hope) refusing to succumb.

Finally, Warren found a way to make me an offer I could not turn down. The embassy commissary needed a manager and Warren wooed me with a liberal schedule, great pay, and permission to bring my kids to work. I sensed that Warren was impressed by the fact that Fred and I had owned and operated a natural foods store in Albuquerque back in the early 70s. He said he would be counting on me to work with minimum supervision. My excitement increased as I signed the personal services contract and started imagining the improvements I could make with my "many talents."

Our commissary depended upon the monthly West Africa Support Flight and occasional bulk orders from a Danish supplier that delivered by ship. GSO equipped a bare-bones dirt-floor shack with minimal air-conditioning, shelving, several refrigerators, and a couple of freezers. A

CAMEROON TALES ✍ 99

table, chair, and an adding machine with paper tape printout completed the enterprise. The kids and I set up shop for four hours on Tuesdays, Thursdays, and Saturdays.

In addition to store hours, I had to do a little bookkeeping, manage the inventory, keep track of bulk orders, and recruit volunteers to meet and unload the monthly support flights and truck the goods to the commissary. Power failures, mice, and cockroaches wreaked havoc, but the commissary stayed in the black under my management. Most of the customers adapted to the less-than-perfect conditions. However, I usually had at least one "You won't believe what So-and-So did" story to tell Fred at the end of the day.

The Magic Bus

On weekends, holidays, and vacations we made road trips. Our beautiful blue Volkswagen bus carried us on paved or gravel roads, and we borrowed a Peugeot 504 from the embassy motor pool for the unimproved byways. Some trips we caravanned with the Ekstroms and Grimtes, and other trips we made with our close friend Earl. We could travel by road only during the dry season because paved roads ended at the city limits. Any dirt extension of a paved highway turned to a massive impassable quagmire in the rainy season; only planes or trains carried passengers out of Yaounde from June to October.

One of our first adventures took us to the city of Victoria's Atlantic Beach Hotel on the coast of the Atlantic Ocean west of Douala. This was a Grimste, Ekstrom, LaTurner excursion, with all six children riding in the bus with Fred and me, the other adults in the Ekstrom's vehicle borrowed from the Peace Corp (Jim Ekstrom was Director of PC then).

Cameroon inherited both the benefits and the flaws of the arbitrary borders imposed by colonialism's collapse. The country's borders enclosed some territory formerly dominated by English speakers, some Francophone, and a small portion German. Yaounde was primarily French speaking, and our destination on the trip to the Atlantic Beach Hotel fell within the English-speaking area.

Our hotel harked back to the days of British rule and interpreted English style with African flare. Our group monopolized the stone wall that separated the ocean from the saltwater swimming pool. As the gentle breakers washed over our knees we oohed and aahed at the vermilion sunset that radiated a constantly changing light show.

Many of our most treasured souvenirs came from the Peace Corp sponsored handicraft market that we visited on this road trip. We bought baskets, beadwork, brass figurines made by the ancient lost wax process, and woodcarvings. The Peace Corp could be proud of the success of this project that encouraged craft as well as entrepreneurship.

The next long weekend, Thanksgiving, lured us out on the highway once again. This time we (the same old bunch) reserved rooms at a safari lodge in the midst of the western savanna. We arranged to have dinner the next day at a place recommended by the hotel manager. He told us that the Swiss proprietor had trained as a chef in France and featured fresh-caught game on his unusual menu. Reservations had to be made a day in advance to allow time for his hunters to do their job.

At 8:00 PM precisely, timed by a Swiss watch I suppose, the dining room doors opened and we filed in and took our places at the long table. The flickering light of dozens of candles created a ballet of shadows on the gray stone walls. Our host sat down with us. He spoke very little English and French was not his native tongue either. Fortunately, Antje Grimste, being originally from Germany, could carry on in two languages at once. Through her translating skills we learned that our host had built the restaurant himself, stone by stone, from local materials. He explained that the candlelight was not mere ambiance; electricity was not available in this remote location.

Most of the conversation focused on what we were eating, everything caught and prepared that same day: snake, an enormous whole freshwater fish, wild birds, and the main course – "cutting grass" – a rodent about the size of a beaver (also known as cane rat). Our unique Thanksgiving dinner was delicious, but in my opinion the fine flavors came from the chef's sauces rather than from the strange meat they smothered.

Kribi

Many of our most memorable trips had a beach destination, the beach near Kribi, far to the southeast, about 100 miles from the border with Equatorial Guinea. The kids and I made the trip three times, Fred twice.

The first time, all four of us plus Earl drove down on the lumber road, known as Le Route Forestiere, using a friend's hand-drawn map to guide us. We borrowed one of those terrific Peugeot 504 all-wheel drive station wagons from the embassy motor pool, filed our travel plans with the embassy security office, loaded our camping gear, and headed out.

The hardwood forest resembled the rest of the jungle, only taller. Heavy lumber truck traffic had worn deep ruts in the dirt road. Fred and Earl took turns driving, and the kids and I bounced around in back. I had prepared a picnic lunch, and Earl chose a convenient spot to pull over and park. We opened the car doors into a world of sound effects right out of a Tarzan movie – birds, monkeys, and insects screeched, howled, and buzzed. Earl pulled out a Frisbee to play with while I dug around in the coolers for our sandwiches. Earl's first toss went wide and the Frisbee disappeared, swallowed whole by the vegetation. Nobody wanted to venture into the tangle of vines, so Earl hacked away at the bushes with the Army entrenching tool from our camping gear. He located the hidden toy, but the Frisbee fell by the wayside as Dakota started yowling and jumping like an agitated baboon.

Fred discovered that ants had crawled up inside Dakota's pants where they munched furiously on his privates. By the time the boys had quelled the ant invasion and applied ointment to the bites, an estimated gazillion flying insects had formed a cloud around us with obvious intent to enter our bodies through eye, nose, and ear openings. We dashed to the car, rolled up the windows as fast as the cranks could go, and reassembled our picnic inside.

Down the road, a troop of colobus monkeys swung across our path, flaunting their gorgeous black and white coats against the jungle green. Later I caught a fleeting glimpse of what I thought might be an okapi, elusive relative of the giraffe.

About five miles south of the town of Kribi we looked for the ferry that would carry us, and our car, across the river. I saw a couple of dug-out canoes and another contraption that might be a floating dock. The floating dock look-alike proved to be the one-car ferry, pulled across the river by a rickety rope and pulley arrangement. I held my breath to get us across. It worked.

Our map told us we would find Paradise Beach about fifteen miles south of the ferry and then go a quarter mile further to another place called Lolabe Beach, where a fresh water stream flowed into the ocean. Thanks to that accurate map, we found our beach and hurried to set up camp before dark.

In a few minutes, we had visitors. One gentleman stepped forward from the group of five men and introduced himself as the chief of the nearest village. There was nothing in his appearance to set him apart from the rest of the group; all six men wore shapeless shorts in various stages of tatter, and all six were bare-chested.

The chief welcomed us, presented a bag of local tangerines and a container of live miniature shrimp. The men placed a wide log across two shorter pieces of wood and invited us to sit. Then they took their leave, the chief bidding us enjoy the beach "in tranquility." Earl asked if there was anything we could do to repay their hospitality and the chief asked only that we leave our empty bottles for the villagers.

In celebration, Earl broke out his surprise treat: chilled vodka for the grownups, iced Fanta Orange for the kids, boiled eggs and caviar with lemon for everyone. In a sudden rush of compassion, Fred decided to let the headman's shrimp go free. Oops, they weren't shrimp after all, but fresh water crawdads, which perished instantly in the saltwater of the Atlantic Ocean.

Tranquility did indeed reign during our entire stay at the beach. The freshwater stream saved the day, washing our bodies clean of sand and salt every night before bedtime. We slept like babes, snug in our tents, soothed by the lullaby of surf caressing sand. Our children ran naked and we wore the minimum.

One day, a single fisherman passed by, and Dakota followed him down the beach a long way. I could see the fisherman gesturing back in our direction and I imagined him saying, "Boy, go back, I hear your mother calling."

I whistled our signal and Dakota came running.

Earl's tranquility persisted too, despite close contact with a three-year-old and a very inquisitive four-year-old. He told us later about the morning when Dakota followed him into the trees and asked, "Whatcha doin'?" Earl said he couldn't think of anything funny, so he answered, "Just taking a dump." Curiosity satisfied, Dakota left Earl alone for the rest of his morning ritual.

We departed from our mini-paradise reluctantly, facing a long trip back across the ferry and through the jungle. The further we went, the worse the road. Recent rain had added considerable moisture to the dirt and the result was gooey and slimy and slippery and, as the kids said, sucky. In spite of Earl's extremely skillful maneuvering, our car came to a complete, squishy halt. Mired in the goosh in the middle of the rainforest in unpopulated West Africa, there we sat. As carefully as we had over-prepared for camping, we probably had enough food and water to keep us alive until Embassy Security sent a search and rescue team, but I hoped for better options.

We got out of the car to assess the situation. Earl thought he might be able to steer to dryer ground if Fred could push. The spinning rear tires plastered Fred with a mud coating, but the car stayed put. They tried again and yet again. I started to worry about the car running out of gas if they made many more tries.

Dakota tugged my skirt and pointed toward the forest's edge. We had company. This part of unpopulated West Africa had a population after all. The headline, "Cannibals Have Stranded Family for Dinner," flashed through my mind. Six of the heftiest men in the group of ten stepped forward. These guys had muscle definition that would put Arnold Schwarzenegger to shame. Like our visitors at Kribi beach, they wore nothing but ragged shorts that left little to the imagination. With muscles rippling and bulging, they simply hoisted the car out of the mud, using sheer muscle strength more than leverage.

Then they invited us to their village to clean up. They offered us a meal as well. Using his most polite FSI (Foreign Service Institute) French, Earl gave our thanks, offered payment (they refused), and made our excuses to get us back on our way. We had but a few hours of daylight to complete our journey.

Three months later we had our second Kribi trip all set. This time we wanted to fly down and, rather than camp, we reserved a beach house in the town of Kribi. Earl planned to come too, as well as his brother Doug (visiting from North Carolina) and our friends the Rowans (Ritchie, Kathy, five-year-old Richard, and two-year-old Justin). At the last minute, Fred had to cancel because of work.

The work situation was dire. Because of a coup in neighboring Chad, the emergency radio in the Ambassador's Residence in Chad's capital was the only contact between Embassy N'djamena and the outside world. Back at our embassy, Fred manned his radio 24 hours a day until the American families were evacuated from Chad a week later.

Meanwhile, our intrepid band boarded a tiny puddle-jumper aircraft and flew off to Kribi. When the hour of our arrival approached I peered out the window for signs of the airport. I saw treetops. The plane started to descend and still I saw treetops. We touched down before I could spot the runway. A wall of trees blurred by on both sides and I wondered how the pilot could avoid crashing into the jungle. Was smoke pouring from the brakes? The plane stopped with few feet to spare. I stood on rubbery legs and helped the kids deplane.

We entered the terminal shack and waited next to the baggage claim sign. The sign was tacked above a rectangular opening in the exterior wall of the shack. Five minutes later I saw our suitcase sail through the opening and crash to the floor. Outside stood the baggage handler grabbing bags from a wooden cart and tossing them into the terminal through the baggage "window."

Our rented beach house had the beach for a front yard. The three bedrooms held six mosquito-netted bunks each. We made our bed choices, unpacked our bags and stripped for beach action. A fisherman approached and Earl negotiated a good price for his catch of the day. I didn't know if all my companions spoke the truth, but every one of them professed ignorance of the time-honored art of fish cleaning. So the task fell to bigmouth me. Dakota helped, as much as a four year old can.

Next day, Kathy said she didn't mind watching the four kids so I could play tennis with the guys -- Ritchie and I against the Simmerson brothers (or The Blues Brothers, as I called them). Doug and Earl beat us beginners with their repertoire of drop shots, lobs, and backspin trickiness. We laughed as we replayed the match during our mile-long walk back to the beach house. We joked about whether the winners or the losers should pop the first ice-cold beers.

Kathy put her book down and slid her reading glasses to the top of her head. "Hi, how was tennis?"

"Terrific," I said. "How did the kids do?"

"No trouble at all. They paired off as usual. Dakota and Richard have been working on their sand fort the whole time." Kathy pointed at our two boys digging and tamping in the shade of a nearby coconut palm. "Justin and Tina are playing dress-up in the house."

I dropped my racquet and backpack on the porch and went inside to find the little ones. My voice echoed in the empty house. "Tina? Justin? Are you hiding? Come out, come out, wherever you are."

I expected to hear telltale giggles from under a bed or behind a closet door. Cold silence drove me outside to call for help. As the other adults did a thorough search of the house and yard, I questioned Dakota and Richard. They swore they hadn't seen the younger pair since breakfast.

Doug volunteered to stay with the boys while the rest of us split into two teams. Ritchie and Kathy went south on the main road, and Earl and I headed north. Earl spotted a woman at the front door of a house, sweeping the steps. He asked if she had seen two small white children.

"Oh, yes," she said, in French. "Two little white girls passed this way half an hour ago."

My heart flip-flopped with hope. Justin seemed all boy to me, but perhaps his golden curls made him more feminine in the eyes of a stranger. Or perhaps all whites looked the same to Africans. Earl and I forged on.

Around the next corner we saw a vendor selling fruits and vegetables from a wooden wheelbarrow. "Yes, I saw the English girls. The older one told me that they were going to meet their parents at the tennis courts. Are you the parents? Don't worry, all the neighborhood is watching out for them."

I realized we must have just missed them when we took a shortcut on the way back from the courts.

I ran the last quarter mile. Earl couldn't keep up. Granted, he had a bad knee, but still....

I found the "English girls" sitting in the shade beside the road, oblivious to the rest of the world, deep in their imagination game. Tina wore her favorite ankle-length muumuu, and curly-haired Justin portrayed delicate femininity in Tina's paisley sundress. Tina admitted that she instigated the whole plot, intending to surprise us. I forced myself to concentrate on the happy ending and avoided pondering on the grisly alternatives.

Before our flight home, we saw the other side of the baggage handling system; our suitcases got tossed outside through the window and landed in a heap on the ground, awaiting transfer to the wooden cart that was pulled by hand to the aircraft. The last item added to the top of the pile was a huge fish, probably weighing fifty pounds or more. Earl used his French skills again to ask what kind of fish.

"Why, an ocean fish, Monsieur," the baggage handler said.

The fish, long, long dead, shared its odor with all of the contents of the baggage compartment. When we got home, I unpacked in the garage and held my breath while I stuffed the ruined suitcase into the bottom of our galvanized garbage can and lit the mess on fire.

We reunited with a very weary Fred who had just finished his grueling radio stint. The French Foreign Legion had come to the rescue in Chad and a unit of Legionnaires ferried our stranded people across the Chari River to relative safety in Cameroon. Once the evacuees were transported to Yaounde, our embassy families clothed, housed, and fed them until their repatriation orders came through.

We opened our home to an energetic group of Peace Corps volunteers who had been evacuated with the embassy staff. They fascinated us with stories about living and working in remote areas of Chad. Their experiences during the coup and the Foreign Legion rescue were hair-raising. One young woman spent three days under her bed while mortar fire boomed all around. She was evacuated in her pajamas and that's all she had left of her possessions. Almost all of the evacuees escaped with only the clothes they were wearing. They considered themselves lucky if they had a chance to grab wallet, purse, or passport.

I joined the efforts to collect and distribute clothing and toiletries to our stranded compatriots. It felt good to be able to help, and the recipients' gratitude was very rewarding. I knocked on wood to seal my willingness to assist evacuees any number of times in exchange for never having to be one.

A few months later, we went to Kribi again, by car (without getting stuck), with Earl (he still enjoyed our company). We rented the same beach house as before and had a quiet, relaxing, and uneventful (for once) beach vacation. Amen.

10

Joseph, Dakota, Tina, and the wheelbarrow

March – July 1978

Tina and the Wheelbarrow

When we hung around at home, Dakota and Tina tagged after Joseph, worked bare-chested like Joseph, dug and raked the red dirt just like Joseph. Sweet, kind Joseph treated them like prince and princess, letting them "help" as much as they liked. He gave them rides in the wheelbarrow up and down the steep drive from backyard to front yard and back again.

I was busy with commissary bookkeeping at the dining room table when Dakota's screams brought me to my feet. I ran to the front door. Joseph stood there with Tina in his arms, Dakota by his side, wailing. Tina wasn't crying, but her face was unnaturally pale and wide-eyed. Blood dripped from her leg.

"Oh my God what happened?" I reached out to take Tina from Joseph. I held her tight to my chest as I knelt down to comfort Dakota. "Shsh, Honey, it's okay. Shsh, everything will be all right. Shsh."

Dakota trotted along behind me as I swooped Tina to the bathtub. I ran a gentle stream of water on her leg. Cleared of blood, a four-inch gash gaped like an obscene grin on the outside of her right knee.

I'm not good at this. I think I'm going to throw up. Oh God what should I do. Calm down. Sure, sure, but what can I DO?

I grabbed a clean bath towel and wrapped it round and round Tina's leg. I carried her to the emergency radio, our only source of communication, and called the Marine Security desk. I had to call for transportation because Fred had taken our car to go to Earl's to play chess and I didn't know when to expect him back.

While we waited for an embassy car to come for us, I reassured Tina, comforted Dakota, and interrogated Joseph. I blamed him for letting Tina get hurt. I regretted it later, of course, because the injury was accidental. Tina was walking beside the wheelbarrow while Dakota took his turn riding. Dakota must have shifted his weight at the same time the tire hit a stone, and the edge of the tipping metal barrow hit the side of Tina's knee and split skin and flesh.

I felt a cheer rise in my chest when Fred drove up before the embassy car arrived. Fred, who had always wanted to be a veterinarian, could handle injuries like this. He unwrapped the towel, surveyed the damage, pinched the wound together and announced, "She'll need a few stitches, that's all."

Our embassy nurse called in the Peace Corp doctor who tried to jolly Tina along by asking how many stitches she wanted.

"Four, because I'm four years old."

"Four it is then, Sweetheart."

The wound healed as expected and the nurse removed Tina's stitches on a Friday afternoon, rather than wait until Monday morning. It looked like the scar would be pencil-line thin and hardly noticeable. However, the next day, at an embassy picnic, Tina ran and played so hard that the wound reopened. A doctor at the picnic closed it with a butterfly bandage, but that closure left her with a wide, laddered scar – a lasting memento of Africa days.

Only in the Bush

When the time came to plan our R&R, Fred worked with the travel unit to create an itinerary that would take us to Albuquerque instead of Marseilles, which was the designated R&R point. In May we boarded a Cameroonian Airlines flight bound for Dakar, Senegal, connecting with Air France to New York and American Airlines to Albuquerque.

The Cam Air flight, depending on the day of the week, made stops in Lagos, Nigeria; Cotonou, Benin; Accra, Ghana; Abidjan, Ivory Coast; Monrovia, Liberia; Freetown, Sierra Leone; and/or Conakry, Guinea – the major cities along the bulge of West Africa. Our flight on that particular day touched down in Cotonou, Abidjan, and Freetown. We didn't leave the plane at any of these stops. The wait in Cotonou seemed interminable. Maybe that delay caused our late arrival in Dakar, too late to make our Air France flight to New York.

The airline accepted responsibility and arranged for hotel and meals until the next available flight, scheduled late the following evening. They gave us two rooms in a luxury beach hotel, even though we needed only one. We lived it up like royalty with room service and all the trimmings.

Next morning we walked on the waterfront where a crowd had gathered to watch fishermen casting seine nets. Dakota melted into a group of Senegalese children and got a close-up view of seine fishing for sardines. A little girl offered Tina one of the flopping fish, but Tina turned suddenly shy and buried her face in the folds of my skirt. Fred snapped a wealth of pictures to immortalize that sunny memory, another unexpected gift of world travel.

Underway again, we assumed that our plane would land in New York, where our flight to Albuquerque originated. Rarely is it wise to assume anything. Our plane landed in Newark, New Jersey. We had to take a helicopter to LaGuardia and then run for our departure gate. We missed our flight.

It wasn't so bad being stranded in New York City. After the enticing helicopter overview of the wonderland of Manhattan's twinkling lights, Fred made a couple phone calls to locate a decent hotel. We had an exciting, hair-raising taxi ride, and capped the evening with a marvelous steak dinner in the hotel dining room. We seemed to be gathering accidental adventures at an accelerated rate.

After such a long journey, New Mexico looked mighty fine to me. We divided our time equally between my parents in Los Lunas and Fred's folks in Roswell where the LaTurner clan gathered for a family reunion.

"We won't be needing this," Grandpa said. He huffed his words through his own cigar smoke as he tossed the cap of the half-gallon bourbon bottle over his shoulder and dealt the cards for stud poker.

Granny suggested a day trip to Peppermint Park Zoo. She asked Dakota if he had ever seen a lion.

"Only in the bush," he said.

She told that story over and over, making all the cousins squirm with jealousy. Up to that point, Granny had convinced each and every grandchild that he or she was the favorite. Now, however, some doubt had been cast.

At the very end of R&R, as we hopped, skipped, jumped our way back down the bulge of Africa to Yaounde, we stopped off in Liberia to visit our friends the Goffs at their new post. The Goff family made us welcome at their palatial home in Monrovia. Julie, Tommy, Dakota and Tina played as if they were still together in Tehran, while Norma and I brought each other up to date on family happenings over the past year. Tom persuaded Fred to go fishing.

Tom kept his boat at a dock on the St. Paul River, a short distance from their neighborhood. The river spilled into the Atlantic two or three miles downstream, but a boat like Tom's wouldn't survive the roiling waters where river met ocean, so Tom and his buddies fished only in the river.

Our guys packed up fishing gear, bait, a cooler full of beverages and a bag of sandwiches and snacks. They promised to return before four o'clock -- with plenty of fish for dinner, of course.

I lost track of time as Norma and I chattered away. I noticed the length of the afternoon shadows when I caught her checking her watch.

"They should be back by now, shouldn't they?" I could sense her anxiety and feel my own worry rising.

"I'm trying not to fret…it's just that Tom is always so reliable. When he says four o'clock, he shows up at three forty-five, you know?"

"I know…what time is it now?"

"Four fifteen."

Norma and I herded the kids toward the dock where they could play in the sand while we stared at the water, conjuring the safe return of our fisherman.

At five thirty, with equatorial twilight fast approaching, Norma made a command decision. "If they're not back by six, I'm going to call Tom's friends for help."

At five fifty-nine exactly two boats came putt-putting up the river. Could that be Fred's red baseball cap on the front figure in the second boat?

The whole story came out in bits from Tom and pieces from Fred. After leaving the dock they had made a beeline to Tom's favorite fishing spot. The fish weren't biting there, so they pulled anchor and scouted for another place. It just didn't seem to be a good fishing day. By lunchtime they were bored and ready to quit.

Tom pulled the starter cord on the outboard motor. He pulled again. And again. Again. Tom lifted both hands heavenward and brought them down in a hard slap against the sides of the boat. Fred tried several pulls on the starter. The stubborn motor stayed silent.

Fred knew it before Tom noticed; the boat was moving downstream. The anchor must have come untied. The boat bobbed in the current, inexorably bound for disaster where the ocean's thundering tide battled the river's roiling force. The oars, shapeless two by four imitations of the real thing, were useless against the ever-faster moving water.

A giant boulder loomed in their path. The heavy metal boat crashed against granite rock and the bow slid into a crevice between the big boulder and a somewhat smaller one. Safe for the moment, Tom and Fred went over their options. Wait for rescue? Abandon the boat and swim to shore? With no way to call for help, they couldn't expect to be rescued. They couldn't guess how secure the boat's temporary mooring was. Tom said he wanted to stay with the boat; he admitted that he couldn't swim very well. Brave or foolish, he couldn't say which, Fred volunteered to swim to shore and go for help, heedless of the danger of crocodiles.

Fred gave credit to adrenaline for the extra boost that powered him across the river and carried him through the long walk to Tom's friend Bill's dock. Luckily, Bill was right there, getting ready to go out fishing. He grabbed a long rope and set off with Fred to rescue Tom. Bill's bigger boat with its heavy-duty motor towed Tom's wreck easily.

After all that, nobody seemed interested in having fish for dinner, so Tom whipped up a hamburger/hot dog cookout to celebrate the happy ending of that tale.

Next morning the Goffs treated us to a tour of Monrovia, the capital of the Republic of Liberia, a country with a unique beginning. Liberia was founded and colonized by freed American slaves with the help of a private organization called the American Colonization Society. In 1847 the Republic of Liberia established a government based on that of the United States. The capital is named after President James Monroe who was a prominent supporter of the colonization.

Conflict dominated Liberian history from the start. Relations between the colonists and the native people were contentious at best and uprisings became a common occurrence. All over the city we could see the toll taken by generations of political unrest and civil war.

One endearing scene had the strength to brighten the gloomy portrait of Liberia --a tableau of adolescent girls giggling together at the side of the road. They seemed as skittish as teens anywhere, except that they had additional reason to be self-conscious: they were stark naked and painted white all over. Norma explained that the girls were undergoing a tribal rite of passage into womanhood. Cynical city folk called them Bush Babies but to me their public innocence symbolized hope for their battered nation's future.

Voodoo

Once back at home in Yaounde, our daily routine reclaimed us as if we hadn't been gone at all. Fred decided he would like to have a quicker way to get to work than the share-taxi, so I added another leg to my route as chauffeur. My day included taking Fred to work, return home, take the kids to preschool, return home, pick the kids up from school, return home, take the kids to the American Club, pick Fred up after work, return home. And I squeezed in my commissary work on Tuesdays and Thursdays. After a few weeks of this new schedule, I had to make some changes or go mad.

Life seemed simpler when I saved two trips across town by taking Dakota and Tina out of Mrs. Addoh's school. I created a preschool program at home. My favorite project was alphabet books made from construction paper and catalog or magazine cutouts. We paged through the toy catalogs and various magazines while I encouraged the kids to cut out pictures that appealed to them. I helped them identify the initial letter of each picture's subject, and they pasted the picture on the appropriate page of their booklets. I loved playing school with my children. I still keep those dear little alphabet creations in a box of treasured memorabilia.

Occasionally my chauffeur route included a stop at SCORE for special treats. The kids came too. They liked to give coins to the lepers as we left the store. I hoped we were accumulating good karma with our small acts of charity.

Perhaps I should have been making donations in higher denominations. One afternoon, after handing out alms, I shlepped my shopping bags and children to the car, opened the windows to catch a breeze, and dropped my wallet into the well between the two front seats. Dakota claimed his turn at riding shotgun and Tina sat in the back. Before I could turn the ignition key, a hand shot through the window, passed over

Dakota, and snatched my wallet. I jumped out of the car, but I was afraid to leave the kids alone to chase after the running man.

"Stop! Thief!" The volume of my shout surprised me and startled the children.

The running man disappeared around the corner of a building. *Damn. Driver's license, identity card, photos...not much cash thank goodness.* Replacing the documents would be a never-ending bureaucratic pain in the butt. And I felt violated, a victim.

A different man came running around the corner where my thief had disappeared. He handed over my wallet. The money was gone but license and identity cards nestled in their proper places. With all my money gone, how could I reward this Good Samaritan? I picked out a loaf of bread and a bottle of beer from my shopping bag, but he waved my offering away, flashed a brilliant smile and said goodbye.

During the short drive to Fred's office, I ruminated about the theft and marveled at the gallantry of the Samaritan. I came to a stop at one of Yaounde's few traffic lights and stayed in my daydream, unaffected by kiddy chatter in the background, until a hand thrust through the open window and jolted me back into the moment. It was a begging hand, no mistake about that, and me without money.

The beggar mumbled in French and I yelled at him in English, "I don't understand you. I don't know what you want. Leave me alone."

The begging hand turned into a grasping claw that tore strands of hair from my head. The light turned green and I pulled away, watching the beggar in the rearview mirror as he wandered down the middle of the street, holding my hair close in front of his face. I was sure I could see his lips moving in a dark voodoo chant. I jerked the car to a stop at the curb and burrowed hand over hand through the contents of the glove box. Yes, a coin lay at the bottom of the compartment. I speed-shifted around the block, found the beggar and tossed him the coin.

"Is this what you're after?" I shouted.

He made a grand gesture of throwing my hair to the wind, and I let out a crazy laugh, knowing how narrowly I escaped a terrible curse.

I felt glad to put voodoo behind me. However, poor Joseph wasn't as lucky with curses as I was.

I thought he might have malaria. His glowing black skin had lost its luster and his face was drawn and gray. His robust and muscular body sagged now, weak and frail. Fred advised him to go to a doctor.

"Father, a medical doctor cannot help me, for I have a demon in my back. You don't believe me, but this is the truth. I know about modern psychology, but that is no help either. The boys I work with in the Ambassador's garden hate me because I come from Dschang and belong to a different tribe. To get rid of me they sprinkled a curse on the grass and it entered my body through the bottoms of my feet and lodged in my back. I cannot stand the pain. It will kill me if I don't go to my home village and have it removed by the medicine man."

Fred pulled out his wallet and gave Joseph bus fare to Dschang.

Three weeks later, Joseph returned, hale and hearty, his exorcism an apparent success. Fred interceded on his behalf and Joseph transferred to other duties for his part-time work at the ambassador's residence, guaranteed to be at a safe distance from the rival tribesmen and their toxic magic.

Fred and I discussed other ways to help Joseph improve his lot in life. We asked him if he would consider doing any kind of work other than gardening. He expressed an interest in office work, so we bought him a portable typewriter and paid for his enrollment in a typing class. Too bad the breadth of his fingers made typing impossible. He hit two keys with every stroke.

Joseph suggested that he might like to be an embassy driver, if only he had the chance to learn to drive. We sent him to a local driving school.

License in hand, he invited Fred to go for a drive with him to demonstrate his skills. Fred borrowed a car from the motor pool and off they went. I thought it odd when they returned so soon, with Fred behind the wheel, his lips taut and grim. Joseph retreated to his room and Fred launched into the story of his near-death experience. Joseph drove as if he had never before been behind a steering wheel. His attention flitted everywhere but the road ahead. The car weaved and wandered, slowed and speeded in random surges. Fred made him stop and change places. We shared a rueful laugh about the quality of training at the local driving school and the futility of our attempts to help Joseph find a new career.

11

The Ekstrom, Grimste, LaTurner crew

August 1978 – April 1979

Milestones

Time marched on and the kids grew and thrived. In August 1978, Tina measured 41 inches tall and weighed 36 pounds; Dakota was 5 inches taller and 12 pounds heavier. Dakota earned a soccer ball by staying dry seven consecutive nights, and I gave Tina a prize too, a doll, to acknowledge that she hadn't wet the bed since she was two. In my opinion, they were both ready for kindergarten, although Tina's birthday was nine days past the limit and her enrollment required school board approval.

I went to the school, located on the grounds of the American Club, to talk to the principal about kindergarten for Tina. I told Dakota and Tina to wait in the car while the principal and I stood nearby.

"Mommy. Mommy?" As soon as I shut the car door, Tina started calling to me.

"In a minute, Honey, I need to talk to Mr. B real quick."

"Mommy, Mommy!" What had gotten into her? Was the most compliant child on the planet trying to ruin her chances of going to school?

As I turned to Mr. B to finish my interrupted sentence, Dakota reached out of the window and grabbed my sleeve. "Mom! You shut the car door on Tina's hand and she can't pull it out."

Tina's little hand suffered no permanent damage thanks to the cushioning provided by the door's thick rubber gasket. But my self-respect took a devastating hit. What kind of mother slams her child's hand in the door and walks away oblivious?

The school board did approve Tina's enrollment in kindergarten. Perhaps Mr. B. agreed that she was ready or maybe he advised the board that this child would be safer in school than stuck at home alone with her careless mother.

Before school started, Dakota surprised us by riding a neighbor boy's bicycle on the first try, without the aid of training wheels. He had a knack for learning a skill by watching someone else do it. I don't understand how his brain translated a visual experience into muscle memory, but it happened again and again as he learned to swim, play tennis, ski and snowboard without the usual trial and error period.

My learning style was more traditional. I enrolled in formal tennis lessons and I practiced, practiced, practiced. I played singles with my coach's girlfriend and doubles with Fred as my partner. I entered a club tournament and made it to the finals. Who knows, I might have won if the rains hadn't interfered.

I had the most fun playing doubles with Fred and the Blues Brothers. We met our buddy Earl and his brother Doug on Sunday mornings with a jug of Bloody Marys and a basket of hot croissants. Fred and I couldn't beat Earl and Doug, but we had a fine time trying. We almost closed the gap after we both quit smoking and improved our fitness considerably.

Our achievements expanded. Fred learned to crochet and he worked on a lovely zigzag patterned afghan in earthy tones of brown and tan. Tina figured out how to whistle and also perfected the art of shoe tying. Midway through the third term, the kindergarten teacher recommended skipping Dakota to the first grade and he soon caught up with the class and learned to read. And I learned new sewing skills while preparing for Halloween.

The school Halloween party included a Marine-sponsored spook house, a carnival of games played for prizes, and a costume parade. Costumes had to be homemade by the kids, their parents, or both. Tina wanted to be a rose. She wore her green pajamas and I made a tie-dyed green collar and a red pleated hood to frame her face. Dakota became a pirate with eye-patch, bandana, gold hoop earring, eyebrow-pencil beard, and a gleaming sword made by Fred out of cardboard and tin foil.

Bob's Prophecy

From time to time during the rainy season, we had reason to remember Bob Grimste's prediction about electric power for those lucky enough to live in the "33" brewery neighborhood. On those rare occasions when an outage happened and even the brewery lost power, a string of events occurred that always made us smile, despite the knowledge that we might be without electricity for several hours. First came the loud sound of clinking glass as the beer bottles on the conveyor belt bumped together after jolting to a stop. Then came the loud groans of frustration from the hundreds of brewery employees, followed almost immediately by peals of laughter and good-natured shouting by the same folks – a perfect example of the basic optimistic attitude of the Cameroonian national character: darn, the power's off – oh, yay, we get recess!

Quinsy

After the wet season, we could enjoy afternoon barbeques again. At a cookout at the Grimstes' Tina left her group of playmates and slumped down beside me.

"Mommy, my head hurts."

My hand on Tina's forehead registered fever. I called to Fred and Dakota and we said our goodbyes to the other guests. Once home, I gave Tina a dose of Tylenol and tucked her in bed where she went straight to sleep.

In the morning I knew she had a serious illness. Not only did she have an unusually high fever and complained of headache and sore throat, she had also wet the bed. This is the girl who had slept dry since age two. I took her to the embassy medical unit.

The nurse, Barbara Koch, referred us to a British doctor downtown. Dr. F. palpated the swelling on Tina's neck and stated that the obscuring of her jaw line suggested mumps. She advised us to push fluids, encourage Tina to rest, give her Tylenol for pain, and wait for the disease to run its course.

Instead of getting better, Tina got worse. The fever rose. Tina stopped eating. She sipped water only if I begged her. I radioed Nurse Barbara, who called the Regional Medical Officer stationed in Lagos, Nigeria. He immediately booked a flight to Yaounde and examined Tina the next day. In Dr. R's opinion, Tina's illness was not the mumps. He diagnosed a peritonsillar abscess, an illness also known as quinsy. The doctor said that under normal circumstances he would recommend admitting Tina to the hospital, lancing the abscess, and initiating treatment with penicillin. Given the deplorable conditions of the local hospital, Dr R. suggested either a medevac (medical evacuation) to Army medical facilities in Frankfurt or forgo the lancing in favor of home treatment with antibiotics.

Fred and I couldn't approve of taking our sick child on a long plane trip from the tropics directly into winter in Germany, so we chose the home treatment. Tina's allergy to penicillin required an alternative antibiotic. Barbara volunteered to stay by Tina's bedside throughout the first night of treatment with a tracheotomy kit ready in case of allergic reaction to the penicillin substitute.

I lay awake that night, listening to Tina's every breath. In the morning, Barbara closed her trache kit and went to work as usual. Fred took Dakota to school and went on to his office. I continued my vigil with

Tina. Dr. R. had instructed me to record her temperature every hour and get her to drink fluids as often as possible. He told me to take her to the Peace Corp lab every day for a blood test to monitor her white cell count.

Tina did not complain, but she didn't eat either. She survived for three weeks on sips of water and four or five tiny bites of yogurt a day. She lay on the couch and listened to the recorded book "Tina the Ballerina" over and over.

The antibiotic did work and her white count came back down to normal. The abscess disappeared and Tina's appetite returned. Months passed before she regained her health and her weight. Her knees stuck out like knobs on her matchstick legs, and her complexion held the pallor of sickness for weeks.

Before her recovery was quite complete, I wrapped our little ballerina in a blanket and carried her to the embassy Christmas party. She laughed for the first time in a month when she saw her slim Daddy dressed in a pillow-padded Santa suit, distributing gifts to all the embassy kids. She laughed again when I asked Joseph to pot a banana tree and bring it in the house. And she giggled while I sewed Christmas ornaments on the broad leaves of our unorthodox Christmas tree. I laughed with her, so happy to see her getting well.

We went all out for Tina's fifth birthday in January 1979. We invited the whole kindergarten class as well as our group of friends and their children. Tina chose a Winnie-the-Pooh theme and I drew a big picture of Eeyore for pin the tail on the donkey. While everyone else sang happy birthday, I silently sang a prayer of thanksgiving that our daughter had survived quinsy.

Bye Bye Bus

After Tina recovered, we resumed road trips with our group of friends. Luna Park, about ten miles out of town, was a popular destination. The kids enjoyed the playground and shallow splashing pool and we adults hungered for the restaurant's special couscous and chicken spiced with the devilish heat of piri piri pepper sauce.

On our way home from Luna Park one Sunday afternoon, I think we might have blown a gasket. The cause didn't matter as much as the outcome. The engine, the heart of our fantastic chariot, seized up. Fred had the carcass towed to a bush mechanic and we waited for the prognosis. According to our local consultant, the bus needed a new engine block. Fred mailed the specifications to my dad in New Mexico and asked him to send a replacement.

Our correspondence traveled by government pouch, not quite as fast as the pony express, so Fred started searching for some sort of transportation to tide us over. Our friend Jim Ekstrom solved the problem by offering a great deal on the valiant little yellow Fiat that carried his family to Yaounde from their previous post, Niamey, Niger. This tiny, battered, four-cylinder wonder chugged along like "The Little Engine That Could," heedless of the holes in the floorboards or the window that didn't quite close all the way.

My dad sent the engine block for our ailing bus and Fred delivered it to the bush mechanic. When Fred heard from the mechanic in less than two weeks, it seemed like a miracle. But the news was not good. The new engine block had disappeared. The mechanic's Nigerian night guard had been arrested for the theft, and Fred was summoned to the police station.

The police captain escorted Fred inside to see the prisoner. Fred told me that the man's face was bloody and bruised, but there was no way of knowing whether his beating had been dealt by the mechanic or by the police. The prisoner held a large gunnysack at his side. When the captain spoke a harsh command, the cowering fellow dumped out the bag's contents -- a large aluminum cooking pot.

"There, Monsieur, is your missing engine block," the policeman said.

The captain went on to say that the Nigerian's family had raised a considerable amount of money that they wished to offer as restitution, if Fred agreed not to press charges. Fred left the police station with cash in hand.

We sent another letter to my dad, and he sent another engine block. When Fred delivered it to the shop, the mechanic told him that he knew of a buyer if Fred were willing to sell the bus. Several months had passed since the engine meltdown and by that time we were close to the end of our tour in Cameroon, so Fred set a price and finalized the deal before the bus was ready to leave the shop.

A few days before our final departure from Yaounde, the new owner of the bus, chief of a nearby village, resplendent in his white Muslim robe and mitre-like headwrap, came to our house expecting to get the bus's middle seat. Our night guard had been using it to sleep on until recently when Fred gave it to Joseph, who hauled it away to parts unknown. Fred told the chief that the seat had "disappeared," and the chief laughed and left without further comment.

I regretted that we couldn't keep the engine block pot as a memento of our tour in Cameroon and a symbol of the many unexpected elements of life in the Foreign Service.

Yet another of those unexpected details aroused a more poignant emotion than regret. I almost cried when I heard Joseph make his proud announcement, "Father, my mother has given her permission for me to go with you to America."

Fred explained gently that we were not going to America but rather to another country where we could not take him. He accepted Fred's explanation with resignation, even though his hopes of a fairy tale future were struck down.

I hoped our contact with Joseph enriched his life as much as it did ours. Maybe he tells his children the same stories that we tell ours about the experiences we shared.

Tourists in Our Own Land

I attacked the pack out process with confidence this time. No need for an old hand like me to dither about sea freight/airfreight decisions. A tingly thrill brought a smile to my lips every time my glance landed on the bold red circle drawn around the first choice on our bid list: Wellington, New Zealand. The list included Kuala Lumpur, Seoul, Manila, Vienna, Ottawa, and Kathmandu, but Wellington stood out as number one. We gave credit to our good friend and admin officer Warren Littrell for recommending Fred to his contacts in Washington and clinching this plum assignment. Not that I wouldn't have been pleased to go to any of the other places, but I was glad to be moving on to a developed, English-speaking country for a change.

Apparently excitement over our good fortune carried us away – we heard later from a friend in GSO that we left for the airport without closing our back door, much less locking up properly.

We left Cameroon on Dakota's sixth birthday, May 2, 1979. We planned to have a proper birthday party later at my folks' place, but I couldn't let the actual day pass without marking it somehow. During our hour layover in Douala, I bought Dakota a brioche and stuck six candles in it. We sang "Happy Birthday" in the airport departure lounge. Dakota beamed.

Our first stop was Washington, DC, where we rented a VW Rabbit from an agency that catered to diplomats. On Mother's Day we were standing in the Pirates of the Caribbean line at Disney World in Orlando, Florida, when Dakota lost his first baby tooth.

With our maiden Disney World and Sea World experiences behind us, we headed south to Pompano Beach to see my aunts and uncles. Tina held her head high to show off her Mickey Mouse ears. My relatives wined and dined us, showed us the African Queen, treated us to a day of deep-sea fishing, and introduced our kids to the wonderful fun of giant water slides.

Next, we hit the Texas Triangle, the LaTurner term for Conroe/LaPorte/Austin where Fred's three sisters lived. I remember best our stay in Austin with Beth at the University of Texas married student housing. Beth had created a cozy home for her children Pam (13) and Ronnie (9) and they shared it, and their beds, with us. We went to Barton Springs and Deep Eddy to swim. Dakota rode Ronnie's big bike all around the neighborhood, and Tina played with a group of adorable girls, children of other graduate students from Africa, Asia, and the Middle East. Dakota and I attended a raptor show at the Austin Nature and Science Center, and he impressed me yet again with his maturity and cooperative behavior.

After visiting our parents in Roswell, where the kids raided Granny's closet to play dress-up in her clothes, and Los Lunas, where Dakota had his official birthday party, we zoomed back to Washington, DC for Fred's training course.

While in Washington we visited with various friends who happened to be in the area. The Goffs (from Tehran days) showed us their new home and stomping grounds in Manassas, VA. The Ekstroms, who had left Yaounde several months ahead of us, had settled in Reston, VA. And the Rowans (also from Yaounde) were in transit the same as we were. We partied, camped out, and went to King's Dominion amusement park where Tina lost her first baby tooth. Dakota suffered a bit of trauma at the Smithsonian when he saw a painting that depicted brain surgery as performed by the Incas. He talked about that bloody scene for years afterward. We joked that it might have been that experience that kept him from becoming a brain surgeon.

PART FOUR
NEW ZEALAND YARNS

Beautiful Wellington Harbour

12

Nancy hiking in New Zealand

1979

Aotearoa
The Land of the Long White Cloud

Our flight from Los Angeles to Auckland was packed. We squeezed into four seats in the center section behind the bulkhead. The flight lasted forever, or sixteen hours, whichever is longer in that kind of confinement. The kids were fine. They colored, read books, listened to music on the airline headsets, and fell asleep curled up on the floor at our feet. Fred read and slept. I struggled to keep my head from falling into my lap and snapping my neck off.

After a lifetime in the air, and one quick stop for fuel in Tahiti, we landed in Auckland. As soon as the plane reached the gate, a crew of men in coveralls came aboard and passed down the aisle spraying a mist into the air and over us passengers from large canisters strapped on their backs. The idea of being fumigated with no warning or explanation riled me. I didn't say or do anything; I just rankled for a while. We deplaned to stretch our legs a bit, and re-boarded for the final short hop to Wellington. My left foot hurt, from lack of circulation, I thought.

Fred exclaimed about the beauty of the view of Wellington harbor as we landed, but I was preoccupied with my sore foot. When I stood up to get off the plane I couldn't bear the pain. It felt like a hot needle stabbed into my heel with every step. I hobbled along, hanging on to Fred for support. Our sponsor, Dave Smith, Fred's boss, delivered us to our tempo- rary quarters, the Capital Hill Apartments next door to the New Zealand House of Parliament, to freshen up before dinner. I removed my shoe and didn't like what I saw. My red, hot, swollen paw wouldn't fit back into the shoe. I covered it with one of Fred's big athletic socks and hopped to the car that waited to take us to the Smith's home for dinner.

Next morning the doctor recommended by our sponsors pulled a splinter of coral out of my heel and gave me a prescription for an anti- biotic. My splinter was a souvenir of a day at the beach during our brief visit with Fred's brother Mike in Los Angeles. I didn't want a souvenir of that day; the beach swarmed with near naked sun worshipers who littered with thoughtless abandon, leaving no space for our kids to play safely. My sore foot brought back the grumpy mood I fell into that day at the beach and doubled it.

Good news changed my outlook. The embassy housing office left a message that a house had already been leased for us out in a suburb called Tawa where there was a good elementary school. The embassy had run out of furniture but had contracted with a local furniture store where newcomers could select their allotments. I recognized this as an un- usual opportunity to dabble in interior decorating. The usual repertoire of embassy furnishings included Ethan Allen suites or the style I called Government Issue Teak or a mix of wicker and rattan. This time we would have unique décor chosen by none other than moi, as Miss Piggy would say. I rubbed my hands together in greedy egotistical glee.

Our street, Oriel Avenue, curved along the hilly terrain of Tawa, a suburb about ten miles northeast of Wellington's center. Another American Embassy family lived down the block, and their teenage daughter Mackenzie was a potential babysitter for the rare occasions that Fred and I went anywhere without our kids.

The house exceeded our expectations and topped our standard of luxury and size, two-car garage and all. The lot was so steep that the garage sat at street level in front while the kitchen one floor above was at ground level at the back of the house. The backyard rose like a cliff fit for mountain goats. The landscaping consisted of rocks, moss roses, periwinkles, and a perennial crop of prolific weeds. Thick, lush grass covered the front yard. The landlord provided a gas-powered lawnmower.

It had been several years since Fred had last taken care of a lawn. He had never taken care of such a steep lawn. It would have been easier without the narrow strip of grass on the upper level. To get to the upper level, Fred had to drag the mower up the slope, open the gate that was mounted on heavy springs, and prop it open while maneuvering the mower through the narrow opening. He learned to keep one hand on the mower at all times. How did he learn this important lesson? By leaving the mower unattended once. He turned away for less than a minute, long enough to open the gate and fix a prop to keep it open. When he turned back, the mower was out of reach. He watched it chug down the sloped lawn, over the curb, down the street, up a driveway, and into a neighbor's flowerbed, chopping that to bits before it ground to a stop against a retaining wall. Our neighbors kept this story alive for a long time -- much, much longer than Fred wished.

Next door to us lived a family with children the same age as ours. In typical kiwi fashion they welcomed us into their home like favorite relatives. Up the hill behind us lived the Tock family, whose son Chris befriended Dakota the very first day. Chris's older sister Tracy offered to baby sit for us any day of the week.

Tina also found a new best friend in Sarah, whose house was across the street from ours. Sarah showed Tina and Dakota her shortcut to school. Sarah's mother showed me how to make a regulation book bag for Tina.

In New Zealand, every child started school on his fifth birthday (or the next school day). The class for new entrants was called New Entrants (consistent with one of the most popular naming conventions in New Zealand – for example, North Island, South Island, West Shore, Beach View). All books and school supplies were standardized and all new entrants were required to have the same type of book bag to hang on the back of their chairs in school. The new entrants class curriculum focused on reading and taught students to read before their advancement to Standard One at the end of the school year. I couldn't imagine how the school managed to integrate new children in a steady stream all year long and still teach all of them to read by the end of the year, but the system did work. Tina joined the new entrants late -- six months past her fifth birthday and mid way through the school year. She learned to read in a couple of months, well before the end of the year.

Dakota and Tina were the first American children to attend Redwood School and the headmaster gave them a personal welcome. He drew me aside to chat about his love of American history and his admiration of American character. He encouraged our family to tour and learn about New Zealand. He said to feel free to take the kids out of school as often as we wished for educational travel; he promised to instruct the teachers to provide homework so they wouldn't fall behind in their studies. I wished I could hug him for giving us exactly what we wished for – freedom to explore – but I settled for a most heartfelt thank you.

Climate and Culture

We arrived in New Zealand in the midst of a worldwide energy crisis, brought on by the Iranian Revolution, so the pundits said. The New Zealand government proclaimed an energy-saving scheme they called "Car-less Days." Every car owner chose one day of the week that his car would not be driven. The government issued windshield stickers to indicate the selected car-less day. A fine would be levied on violators, like a traffic ticket only heftier. Although we had diplomatic exemption, we decided to participate too, in our own fashion. I walked to do my shopping and Fred ran home from work as often as once a week.

A commuter train was available too, and many of our neighbors took advantage of that. The men on their march to the station made quite a picture, dressed in their business suits, carrying umbrellas and briefcases, like clones of one another. Oddly enough, on the first day of spring, all of these same gents started wearing short pants and knee socks with their coats and ties. The summer uniform code prevailed until the first day of fall when everyone reverted back to long pants.

I would like to have good things to say about the climate in New Zealand, but I didn't enjoy it. It rained too much to suit me. We arrived in winter, but even summer didn't get warm enough – during an unprecedented heat wave, the temperature rose no higher than a mild 78 degrees Fahrenheit.

And the wind blew. All of the time the wind blew, several days from the north, and then several days from the south. The southerly carried frigid air from Antarctica; add rain and you had instant bone-chilling misery. Our house did not have central heating or adequate insulation. Brrrrr. Fred and I complained about the weather too much, according to Dakota and Tina who denied any discomfort from their chapped hands and wind-burnt cheeks.

In some ways, though, New Zealand could qualify as my favorite post so far. I liked living in a country where Americans had hero status. Kiwis still remembered us Yanks saving them from Japanese invasion/occupation in WWII. I enjoyed being a respected member of a community and having a head start on the language. New Zealand English isn't the same as United States English, but close enough to make communication easy. I appreciated the pace and quality of life, much like my own childhood era in Minnesota in the 1950s. The nation could boast of political stability and a low crime rate. There were no strange diseases running rampant and there were no venomous creatures lurking in the shadows. In light of all that, it did seem petty to complain about the weather.

New Zealand had something else we weren't used to – regular television programming. In Tehran we watched AFRTS (Armed Forced Radio Television Service) – old movies, ancient sitcom reruns, and Sesame Street – on a 13-inch black and white set. In Yaounde we had no television programs period. In Wellington, TV came on in the afternoon and shut down at 10 PM, unless there was a special cricket, soccer or rugby broadcast (those could happen in the middle of the night, depending upon where in the world the match took place). And in Wellington, TV could be viewed in color. I questioned whether television was damaging, worthless, or beneficial to children. Fred favored getting a color TV if we were going to watch at all. I leaned toward banishing the idiot box altogether. Dakota and Tina didn't care. They went next door and joined the neighbors in front of their large color screen. That was the temporary solution. The permanent solution came later, entirely by accident.

Day to Day

During the week, Fred went to work in Wellington, the kids walked to school, and I walked down the hill to the shopping street of Tawa, carrying a daypack for my purchases.

The supermarket, not super by US standards but more like the neighborhood grocery stores of 1950s America, had a narrow selection of brands I had to get to know. The meat market displayed the usual cuts plus some I did not want to know (blood sausage, for example). The greengrocer's shop became my regular hangout.

Tony Ng, the proprietor, and his wife, Christine, became my mentors. New Zealand born, both Tony and Christine came from Chinese heritage. Hearing the distinctive kiwi accent from their distinctly Asian faces surprised and fascinated me. Christine showed me the Chinese technique for roasting a whole chicken (plunge it into boiling water first for a few seconds to tighten the skin) and she taught me how to prepare dim sum.

Tony and Christine's shop, smaller than most produce sections in American supermarkets, displayed a bounty of fruits and vegetables. I learned that they stored more in the back room. Tony liked to keep a stash of favorites for each of his best customers. He had an uncanny ability to remember what his patrons liked and to predict their shopping patterns. He told me to ring (telephone) him if I had any special requests and he would try to find what I wanted at the wholesale market.

"How does that work, Tony? The wholesale market, I mean…"

"Have you seen my lorry – I go to the Wellington market once a week and fill it with fresh vegs. Speak up if you'd like to go with me."

Tony's wink showed me he was joking, but I was serious. I had a couple of fleeting second thoughts when Tony told me to meet him at the shop at four o'clock in the morning on Thursday, but the early hour didn't make me change my mind.

In the pre-dawn darkness, Tony handed me a thermos of tea Christine had brewed for us. "Pour us a cuppa, there's a good girl."

As we roared along in the old truck, sipping strong, sweet, milky tea, I tuned in to Tony's love for his work. His enthusiasm opened my eyes to the magic of a city caught in the lull between nightlife and workaday, a mysterious combination of suspended animation and pent up energy pressing for release.

Tony parked his truck with several others in a shadowy car park at the rear of an enormous building. He held the warehouse door for me and I passed through into sensory overload. My poor eyes squinted shut against the brilliant overhead lights. My hands covered my ears against the shrill whistles, shouts and bangs. My nostrils tingled from the riot of pungent odors of fish, seafood, tealeaves, and spices. The vendors whistled and banged to attract attention to their wares, and the buyers shouted their bids above the racket. Tony pantomimed that I should roam around while he made his purchases. He hurried off to bid on the best and freshest of the day.

Even though I paid close attention, the bidding process remained a mystery. Like a foreign language, a flurry of gestures and jargon communicated clearly between vendor and buyer and left me bewildered. I wound my way among the stalls and absorbed the symphony of sounds and smells without trying to analyze what was going on.

I regained normal consciousness when Tony tapped my shoulder. "Sorry to tear you away from all this, but the party's over, by Jingoes."

In little more than an hour, Tony had completed his bargaining, made his purchases, and loaded the truck. As we stepped out of the glare into the twilight of early morning, I wondered why the crazy market appealed to me so much. I couldn't put it into words. As the kiwis might say, it was "simply brilliant" to peek inside a hidden part of city life and find its colorful and vibrant secret heart.

That outing with Tony encouraged me to look for other activities to fill my days. With the kids in school and Fred at work all day, I had time on my hands. Housework didn't take much effort, even if I did have to do it by myself. New Zealand air wasn't dusty like Cameroon's or sooty like Iran's. And we had a dishwasher, the first of my life, and a new vacuum cleaner. I turned my back on the aggravation of weeds in the rock garden, and went out in search of a tennis court.

I found the local tennis club. The rules were confusing, but I joined and signed up for Midweek Ladies. My name appeared on the bottom of the list, or ladder, as it is called. A committee assigned matches; winning or losing a match moved a player up or down the ladder.

I don't know where my tennis skills went, but I played my first match like a clown, a caricature of bumbling ineptitude. I read the judgment in the eyes of the other ladies: Loser. I tried to overcome my nervousness and loss of confidence, but my game didn't improve. The cold and windy weather didn't help either. Then Eunice came to my rescue. Eunice Weemys, from England, also branded an outsider, commiserated with me about the climate (both the weather's chill and the social frost at the tennis club) and suggested we give squash a try. Her husband Michael played squash at the Tawa club and praised the indoor courts and the amicable participants.

Much better, although I couldn't adjust to the ten o'clock bell when all play suspended forthwith for tea and biscuits (cookies). I did enjoy the game and the fact that joining the competition ladder was optional and members were allowed to make their own matches. The greatest benefit came from my growing friendship with Eunice and the happy blend of our families.

Fred and Michael shared an interest in music. They introduced each other to their favorite bands and kept up a steady exchange of records and tapes. Michael turned Fred on to Pink Floyd and The Who, and Fred gave Michael his first taste of The Eagles. Dakota knew the Weemys' son Simon from school – they were in the same class. Tina and Catherine, a year younger, clicked on the spot.

I still managed to have time on my hands. I investigated the adult education program at Tawa College (college in New Zealand is the same as high school in the US; university is the term used for education beyond the first twelve grades). "Pottery" leaped out of the list of courses. When I read the word, I had a strong sensory memory of the fragrance of clay in the zinc-lined damp box in my junior high school art room. Then I flashed back to the ceramic sculpture class I had taken at a community center in Minnesota in 1964.

Pottery hooked me. I started with the Tawa College evening classes and soon created my own work space at home in the unused half of our two-car garage. I equipped my studio with potter's wheel, kiln, and shelving installed by my faithful handyman Fred. Good thing embassy dependents were not allowed to work on the local economy; now I had no time for a job.

Having Fun

Wellington offered a variety of entertainment possibilities. Movies at a movie theater for instance, matinees for children in particular. Parents dropped their children off and didn't worry. We stayed with our kids because we thought they were too young to be left alone in a public place. The Tawa school system hosted movie afternoons from time to time, and we let Dakota and Tina go there by themselves as those events were well supervised. But the downtown movie theaters had no supervision at all.

At some point in every movie we went to, some kid would throw a piece of candy (sugar coated almonds were very popular for this) and ignite a fusillade of hard, sweet missiles. I learned to turn up my collar and duck during the flurry. At the end of the war, walking up the aisle was like walking on marbles.

We saw Star Wars at the movie theater and Quest For Fire, although I couldn't understand how the latter earned classification as a children's feature. "Quest-For-Fire" became our family's euphemism for intercourse, thanks to the scene by the river where the cave man and the cave woman…well, you get the idea.

Dakota, a music lover since infancy, having cut his teeth on the artistry of Jackson Browne, The Rolling Stones, and Rod Stewart (and on their cardboard album covers as well), began to establish his own taste in music at about age six. He joined the KISS Army, played air guitar, and asked Santa for a real KISS guitar for Christmas. When KISS came to Wellington we had to go to the concert, no question about it. We didn't have very good seats, so Fred put Dakota on his shoulders and carried him down to the front of the crowd. We adopted "I Wanna Rock and Roll All Nite and Party Every Day!" as our family anthem.

Having broken ourselves in right, we went on to attend concerts by Elton John and Men at Work. The best entertainment in the world, though, came from the Maori tribes people who demonstrated the haka war dance and other dances on stage with contagious enthusiasm. It's hard to watch a haka without wanting to join the loud chanting, foot stomping, arm flailing, fierce face making and the final tongue-thrusting grimace.

When Fred accumulated vacation days, we remembered what the headmaster said about taking our kids out of school for educational travel, and we explored the country as often as we could. Sometimes we camped, but more often we opted for the luxury of New Zealand's comfortable motels. Not that we stayed in fancy places. No, the motels we chose were more like the mama/papa small town places in 1950s America, with one big difference – each room had a kitchenette furnished with every utensil imaginable, including tea cozy, sugar tongs (one lump or two?), and crumpet toaster. Tina and I developed a ritual – kitchen inventory – to delight each other with our discoveries in drawers and cupboards. We played house while the guys unpacked the car and looked around the motel grounds.

We went to Lake Taupo for my thirty-ninth, fortieth, and forty-first birthdays. Lake Taupo's setting had the magic allure of hot springs. The lake was cold enough to support splendid trout, yet it had an area where the water was heated by hot springs welling from the lakebed. The lakeside motel we returned to year after year had hot springs within it, as did many inns in town. One of our favorite restaurants had a large pool in a man-made cave with a faux-grotto theme. The lakeshore was dotted with rocks, most of them pumice, porous and light as balsa wood. I called Taupo a kids' paradise, for this kid's birthday trip especially.

Not long after our first trip to Taupo, Fred caught the marathon bug. He met some local runners while pounding the pavement to improve his cardiovascular fitness, and they encouraged him to try longer distances. Then they invited him to come to the Wellington Marathon Clinic, a running club that met on Sunday mornings for an inspirational or informative talk before setting out on group runs of varying distances and paces. The club was the creation of two Scottish physicians who believed that anyone, literally any one, could complete a marathon and benefit from the resulting improvement in cardiovascular health. Fred told me all of this with enthusiasm.

Not me, I thought, remembering how my sadistic PE teacher punished us with laps of the football field. *Fine for Fred, but definitely not for me.*

Fred can be very persuasive when he wants to be. He convinced me to give running a try. He suggested a mile for my trial run and measured the distance for me with our car. Hoo! I thought I was having a heart attack. But as bad as I felt, I recognized the pleasure and pride of accomplishment. I ran a mile! Fred wanted to sign me up at the Marathon Clinic that very day.

Whoa, slow down, I thought. That was October 1979 when I said,

"How about I use the next eleven months to work my way up to five miles before my fortieth birthday, and then think about joining the Marathon Clinic? Just to participate in the pack runs and the fellowship, though, no marathon for me, all right?"

When Thanksgiving time rolled around, I pushed thoughts of running aside and invited our best Marine pal, Scott Geater, to join us for dinner. He offered to provide the turkey. He showed up with not only a wild turkey but also several plump trout that he had caught. I pulled the newspaper wrapping off the turkey to get it ready for the oven.

"Psssst, Fred, come here." I beckoned Fred to the kitchen and pointed to the turkey. "Does this look strange to you?"

Fred poked at the bird. "One breast is missing. Hey, Scott!" He directed his shout through the archway to the living room, and Scott joined us at the cutting board.

"Yeah, sorry about that. I shot it with a 30-30 deer rifle. Guess it was too much weapon for the job."

Kiwi Christmas

Dakota woke us at dawn's early light on Christmas day, eager to see if Santa remembered his KISS guitar. Good old Santa also brought a stereo system to play Dakota's favorite music and Tina's storybook records.

Mid-morning on Christmas day we did the traditional New Zealand thing – we visited various folks who had invited us for a drink.

First we went to the embassy receptionist's home. Her husband was an officer in the New Zealand military and they lived up to their elevated status by serving champagne punch with floating strawberries.

Next we dropped in on the family who formed the team that did janitorial work at the embassy. These were real down-to-earth family folk who served beer in a giant 2-quart goblet passed 'round the room. We heard there was also a joint to share, but the papa of the clan, who was about Fred's age, didn't approve. The young adults found reasons to go for a car ride to sneak a toke.

We made a third stop at the home of Dakota's best friend. There we had a cup of tea and a tour of their new home. The house seemed enormous and it featured the classic symbol of New Zealand middle class success: an extravagant master bath. This one boasted gold faucets and lurid flocked wallpaper imitating cut-velvet wall hangings of the 17th century – stark black and white in color and stark naked Polynesian female in pattern.

Our last social call introduced us to a Chinese-New Zealand Christmas. The gathering included the elder couple and all their children and grandchildren plus a couple of neighbors and us. This party centered on a buffet table covered with platters of dim sum and jugs of soft drinks. The eldest son, our friend and greengrocer Tony, played Father Christmas and handed out small gifts to all the guests, assisted by his brother-in-law Rob.

To tell the truth, Rob completely upstaged Tony. In his role as Christmas Fairy, he wore a yellow hairnet, a mini skirt, and a D-cup bra rounded out with grapefruits. He flounced around the room waving a sparkling magic wand and flashing his apron. The apron had pocket flaps labeled "His" and "Hers." Under the "His" flap lay a small, stuffed cloth item that resembled a tiny white, red-tipped penis; under "Hers" was a triangular patch of black fur; and from a slit in the front of the apron, the fairy could pull a fourteen-inch well-stuffed phallus labeled "Mine." When he wasn't distributing gifts, the fairy tormented the guests, both male (rear assault) and female (frontal attack), using "Mine" as his primary weapon. I laughed 'til my sides ached.

I had never known a more thoughtful, considerate, and kind group of people, so I chalked up the weird fairy shenanigans to Chinese humor. Tony told us that an 80-year old lady made the apron – all in good fun, right, Mate?

South Island

The long summer break from school (which started in December, due to the reversal of seasons in the southern hemisphere) seemed like the best time to explore the South Island. Our Marine buddy Scott suggested a camping trip. No argument from any of us eager campers.

To get to the South Island, we loaded our Toyota station wagon on the Cook Strait Ferry that crossed the strait and continued down Queen Charlotte Sound to Picton where we left the ferry and caught the main road south.

The three-hour ferry crossing was Tina's favorite part of the trip. She hung on the rail, hair whipping in the salty wind, the words of her song whisked away before any ears could hear. I wished I could peek inside her fantasy for a second to experience what entranced her so.

The ferry moved along at a steady clip so seasickness was not an issue. The weather treated us with kindness. We enjoyed clear sailing followed by rainless driving, perfect conditions to enjoy the extraordinary scenery along the way. We took long lunch breaks, so the kids could work off some of their stored energy. They traveled well as always, amusing themselves and each other. Tina played imagination games with her dolls. If she didn't have dolls handy, she could create a community of families out of matchsticks or pebbles or her own drawings. Dakota liked reading and activity books. His favorite author was Roald Dahl and he chose math workbooks for fun.

Near the end of each day, we searched for a good campsite. Somewhere in the vicinity of the Fox Glacier, which we planned to explore the following day, we found the perfect spot. Scott pointed out the ring of rocks that had contained the previous camper's fire, and we flipped a coin for the two nearly level tent sites. I helped Fred erect our tent while Dakota and Tina hunted for kindling for the fire. Scott put up his smaller tent in minutes and gathered a large pile of bigger pieces of wood.

Rain forced us inside early in the evening. We didn't get to have a campfire or our s'mores.

In the middle of the night I woke with a cramp in my calf and realized that I had pulled my legs up into an awkward quasi-fetal position. I reached over my head and patted around to find the kids, sound asleep in their sleeping bags, which lay at a 90-degree angle to ours. I checked Fred too and felt his legs drawn up as high as mine. I straightened my legs and felt cold wetness on my feet.

I patted Fred's shoulder and whispered in his ear. "Where's the torch (flashlight in New Zealand parlance)? I think the tent is leaking."

Fred groped for the flashlight, flicked the switch, and illuminated the ceiling of the tent. No sign of a leak. He directed the beam down to the floor. Reflection bounced back from the foot-wide stream running past our feet.

Scott poked his head in. "Looks like we pitched our tents in a dry stream bed… I mean, a formerly dry stream bed."

I underestimated the wicking power of sleeping bags. By the time we finished discussing our options, our bags were soaked. Since it had stopped raining, Scott offered to start a fire to dry our stuff.

With wet wood? Fat chance.

I didn't voice my thoughts. Instead, I turned my attention to settling the kids in the backseat of the station wagon and then attempting to wring out our bedding. Fred dismantled our tent and stuffed it into the cargo area of the car. He sloshed over to Scott who bent over the fire ring, blowing gentle puffs to try to encourage a flame.

"Hey, never mind the fire, we need to get out of here and find a motel."

"No – look – I've almost got a fire going – a few more minutes, okay?"

Poor Scott. He was determined to make fire and save the day. Fred gave him a hard time about such a big, tough Marine letting a little rain defeat him. Scott pulled out his container of lantern fuel and emptied it over the wet firewood. His huge blaze lasted all of twenty seconds, long enough, according to Scott, to save face for the Marine Corps.

The next day dawned bright with sunshine. We draped our sleeping bags over the patio rail of our comfy motel in Queenstown. This jewel of a city overlooks the shore of Lake Wakatipu, which means "space of the giant" in Maori. In mythology this area belonged to a tipua (demon) who captured a beautiful girl and took her back to his mountain home. Her lover rescued her by setting fire to the demon while he slept on a bed of fern. The flames licked his body, causing him to draw his knees up in pain, but before he could regain consciousness the smoke suffocated him. The flames were fed by fat from his enormous body, and as the fire burned he sank deeper and deeper into the earth and formed a vast chasm. The fire's heat melted all the snow on the mountains and the chasm filled with water, forming a lake that mirrors the outline of the giant with his knees drawn up in agony.

Scott wanted to try his hand at parasailing on the lake, and the rest of us tagged along to watch. He put on water-skis, snapped the belt of the parasailing harness, and gave the boat operator the high sign. The boat surged ahead, pulling Scott faster and faster until the parasail filled with air and lifted him high into the sky. Scott's adrenaline rush lasted for days. He wanted to tell the story of his flight again and again. I wore out first. I remember Dakota was the last to tune him out.

Our motel stop in Queenstown dried our gear and we went back to camping for the rest of the vacation. Queenstown also marked the southernmost point of our trip. I wished we had more time to see the famed alps and fjords, to go all the way south to Invercargill or west to Fiordland.

One of the last nights, I woke again in the wee hours. This time a noise roused me -- the flap, flap, flap of nylon in the wind. I nudged Fred. He crawled outside to see what had come loose. A fierce windstorm threatened to blow our tent away. All the pegs had come loose and Fred had to bring the cooler and several large rocks inside the tent to hold the floor down. By placing the cooler on the windward side, he kept the tent from collapsing on top of us.

"What's going on?" Dakota sat up and clutched my hand.

"The tent started to blow down, but Dad's fixing it."

"Oh, okay." He lay back down to instant sleep.

13

Tina and her beloved swans

1980

Tina's Swan Song

We returned home to North Island after that South Island trip and continued with our weekend and vacation explorations, staying in motels more often than camping. One place we found on our travels offered cabins for rent on the shore of a small lake. Our cabin had its own dock where Tina liked to throw breadcrumbs to the swans and ducks. The cabin porch had two rocking chairs. While Dakota went off to play with a newfound friend, Fred and I rocked and talked. I kept one eye on Tina playing her imagination game at the end of the dock.

Perhaps I should have kept two eyes on her – I blinked and she was gone. I jumped up to sprint to the dock, but she had already bobbed up, spluttering, hair and weeds covering her face. She reverted to a desperate dog paddle and reached shore before Fred and I got to her. Funny thing is that the water at the deepest point surrounding the dock came up to her armpits at most. If she hadn't been terrified, she could have stood and walked all the way. We teased her about it, and she claimed that she knew the water wasn't deep; she just couldn't bear to step down on the mucky, weedy bottom. She confessed that her downfall that day was her closed-eye pirouette as she sang a happy song for the swans.

Feast

Although we did travel quite a lot, we stayed in Wellington some weekends for a special event or simply to catch up with home chores. Fred came home from work one day with an invitation for a very special weekend event. His friend John, a Maori who worked at the embassy, invited our family to his home to share a feast, called a hangi, with his extended family. He asked us to come over early in the morning to help set it up, and he advised us to bring a change of clothes in case we got dirty and sweaty during the preparations.

First task: dig a trench three feet deep, three feet wide, and six feet long. Fred and Dakota grabbed spades and pitched right in. When John declared the pit perfect, he and his brothers layered the bottom with large rocks. They piled wood on top and lit the bonfire to heat the rocks.

Tina and I helped the women of the family carry bowls and platters of food from the kitchen. We watched the ladies arrange the pieces of food in big metal baskets lined with dampened white cotton sheets. I recognized carrots, potatoes, onions, squash, sweet potatoes, pumpkins, cabbage, a lot of cabbage, whole chickens, haunches of pork and lamb, strips of smoked eel (John pointed it out to me), and more cabbage.

When the wood had burned down to hot coals among the stones, John's crew put down a layer of wet burlap sacks, followed by the food baskets, followed by another layer of wet burlap. They shoveled dirt on top as fast as they could and tamped it down to seal in the heat and steam.

After breathing the dominant smell, burnt cabbage, for four hours, I wondered if I could choke down a single bite. But the meal was marvelous once the overpowering cabbage stink blew away and the enticing fragrances of succulent meats and roasted sweet potatoes came through. Good food, jovial companions, Stevie Nicks on the stereo speakers, and uncounted liter bottles of Lion Brown combined to make a memorable party.

The hangi didn't rate in the top four of New Zealand eating experiences, however. Of all the many foods available in New Zealand, we each had our favorite. For Tina it was lamb chops, always, every meal if she could have them. Nothing tempted Dakota more than meat pies from the Dairy (kiwi lingo for corner convenience store). Fred loved bouillabaisse from a recipe that evolved to take advantage of the vast variety of fresh seafood at the fishmongers shop. For me, the best taste-treat was gold fruit, a cross between grapefruit and orange, better than either one; I bought them in ten-kilo (twenty-two pound) mesh bags from Tony's greengrocer shop.

Good and Bad

In the new school year, Dakota and Tina excelled in their studies and made many new friends. Dakota started playing soccer on a community team and earned a nickname. His teammates called him "The Boot" because of his strong and accurate kick. Tina won all her running races, looking back and slowing down because she ran so far ahead of the rest.

Redwood School had an aboveground pool and provided swimming instruction. Both of our kids knew how to swim from many hours in the American Club pool in Yaounde. They had perfected their own cannon ball dives and dog-paddle style, but the lessons at school taught them proper strokes, even the butterfly. Dakota was invited to participate in a swim meet to benefit the local police and the newspaper report praised his outstanding performance.

All was not sweetness and light, however. The ugly monster Prejudice made a surprise appearance. Some boys at school called Dakota "Black Ass" and refused to play with him. I awoke to the fact that New Zealand society had significant race issues. They took care of "their" Maoris in a paternalistic sort of way, but some folks couldn't bear to see complete integration with other races -- similar to New Mexico and the rest of the States in those days.

In Iran and Cameroon, Dakota's complexion had blended better with the local population while Fred and Tina and I stuck out in a crowd as foreigners. New Zealand was not the only nor the last time Dakota faced discrimination on the basis of skin color. Fred and I always rose to his defense and Dakota handled himself with dignity and poise.

Most of the time, however, we had no reason to be concerned about prejudice and discrimination. We traveled widely and found virtually universal acceptance of our mixed-racial family.

Flora and Fauna

Often our travels took us to a place that required hiking. Dakota and Tina didn't love hiking, but they tolerated it for the most part. We hiked Mt. Victoria and Tinakori Hill to get the splendid views of Wellington. We strolled through the Otari Museum of Native Plants to learn about New Zealand flora. We combed the beaches of Paekakariki and Waikanae and scoured the sand dunes of Paraparaumu.

One Sunday in July we bundled up against the chill wind and drove out to Turakirae Head. At road's end a two-mile trail began on the rocky beach. We picked up some fine Paua shells (mother of pearl) and watched enormous waves crash on the rocks. Out in deep water a handful of surfers sat on their boards, bobbing about but not catching any rides. Fur seals enjoyed protected status here and viewing them was a popular family outing for the locals. The kiwis brought their thermos of tea, of course. The seals accepted their celebrity with indifference; having visitors didn't disturb their sleep or their courtship. We didn't stay long. The freezing wind and bitter stench of concentrated seal droppings drove us back to the car to go home for a comforting bowl of hot bouillabaisse.

A spell of fine weather inspired us to take a camping trip, this time on the North Island, to see the gannet breeding grounds, and the sea world show in Napier.

The Cape Kidnappers' Gannet Sanctuary brochure promised a pleasant two-hour walk along five miles of sandy beach. Dakota wouldn't agree with the pleasant part. He covered the first four miles in good spirits, but faded in the last mile.

"Just leave me here and go on. My stomach is sick and I want to lay down."

I checked his forehead - nice and warm but no fever. I wadded up my sweatshirt and stuffed it between his back and the rock he leaned against. "Promise me you will wait right here. We'll take a quick look at the birds and come right back."

Dakota wasn't above feigning illness to get out of something he didn't want to do. I suspected that the gannets didn't interest him as much as the Incredible Hulk comic book in his pocket.

Fred and Tina and I walked on. I looked back several times. Dakota was wearing his bright red hoodie that could be seen from a long distance. The red spot shrank each time I looked back and it dipped out of sight when we descended the slope to the birds' breeding ground.

Gannets are large seabirds with long, pointed wings and tails, and strong beaks. They perform elaborate and involved mating dances. Chicks are born naked and later grow a white down that turns to grey plumage in about four months. We arrived at the chicks' most adorable white fluffy stage. Tina could have stayed forever watching the cute chicks, but I insisted that we get back to our stranded child.

A middle-aged couple crouched next to Dakota. They stood up as we approached.

"Quite an independent lad this," said the man.

"You can be proud of him," added the woman.

Nice of them to keep him company, I thought. We said our thanks and goodbyes and hurried to catch the tractor-pulled trailer that offered lifts to tired hikers.

Back at camp, Dakota continued to complain about his tummy ache. I gave him a dose of Pepto Bismol and tucked him into his sleeping bag. I stepped out through the tent flap and heard him call out, "Mom?"

Right then he threw up. Not a little, a lot. Vomit soaked his sleeping bag and splattered all over the tent walls.

Our decision didn't require much discussion. We abandoned our smelly camping gear and took the shortest route to a motel, leaving the cleanup of our campsite until the next day. After throwing up, Dakota felt great and enjoyed the rest of the trip in fine fettle.

The sea world show in Napier might not measure up to San Diego's or Orlando's in size, but it did in every other way. Fred and I thought of it as entertainment for the kids, but we enjoyed it at least as much as they did.

On another trip we went to Waitomo Caves to see the famous glowworms. The action of water on limestone formed these caves and, just like our own Carlsbad Caverns in New Mexico, they have stalactites and stalagmites hanging from the ceiling and growing from the floor. The glowworms are the larval stage of a species of gnat. The gnats lay their eggs on the cave ceiling and the eggs hatch into larvae that grow to about two inches in length. The larvae develop long, sticky threads that drape down to catch insects to feed their hearty appetites. The glow of the glowworm attracts prey to its sticky lure. Scientists suggest that the glowworm can turn its light on and off at will. The larval stage lasts for nine months of the insect's twelve-month life span.

All those dry facts belie the beauty of the Glowworm Grotto. We purchased our tickets at the kiosk and joined the queue at the entrance to the grotto. We stepped into one of a single-file row of flat-bottomed wooden boats, old and worn, bearing flakes of blue paint from long ago. As soon as all the passengers had taken a seat, the boats moved forward, the drifting pace determined by the river's current. Fred whispered that the Beatles visited here and sang one of their songs in the cave to enjoy the unique acoustics.

In silence, we floated into the dark mouth of the cave. The total darkness felt heavy and thick as if it had substance. As long as no one spoke, we could hear small watery sounds, the occasional dull thud as the boats bumped gently, and a suppressed nervous giggle from time to time. The air had a clean mineral smell, with a faint undertone of sulfur. Floating in black, who knew how much time passed? Too much, I thought. Have we hit the glowworms on a bad day? Are they on a hunger strike?

When our boats entered the grotto, my silly thoughts evaporated. Our heads tipped back, our mouths flew open in a unanimous, "Oooooo." The cave ceiling luminesced with a golden, pulsating radiance. A lacy drapery of light festooned in luxurious swags, forming a canopy that fluttered like feather boas in the breeze – Nature's astounding magic.

Tracy Ann Jones

Mother Nature brought more of her magic to our family through the miracle of birth. We had kept in touch with Glenn and Christa Jones ever since leaving Iran. They had been evacuated to Athens shortly before Embassy Tehran fell and they served in Bonn while we were in Yaounde. We welcomed the news that their next assignment would bring them to our side of the world, to Suva, Fiji. When they announced Christa's pregnancy and described the facilities in Suva, explaining their decision to deliver the baby in New Zealand, Fred and I invited Christa to stay with us; she arrived in Wellington six weeks before her due date. Tina moved to the extra bed in Dakota's room and Christa settled into Tina's room. Glenn didn't want to base his plans on the old wives' tale that first babies always came late, so he arranged to arrive two weeks before the baby's predicted birth.

At 2:00 AM on October 4, 1980, a soft knock on our bedroom door roused us.

"My water broke two hours ago – I'm so sorry for the mess – and the pains are coming on top of each other. I'm so sorry to wake you in the middle of the night – I think I should perhaps go to the hospital now."

Oh, Christa. She would do anything for her family and friends, but she had a terrible time letting anyone do anything for her. Fred swept her down the stairs and into the car while I fetched her pre-packed birthing suitcase. Fred broke the speed limit on the deserted road to Wellington.

After a quick exam, the doctor parted the curtains and announced;

"She'll be on her way to labor and delivery now." He patted Fred on the shoulder. "The father can follow along, but, you, ma'am, will have to wait in the lounge."

Fred blushed and denied paternity, and we waved goodbye to Christa as her gurney rolled through the double doors at the end of the hall. We decided to go home, call Glenn, and be ready to welcome our kids back from their sleepover at our neighbor's house. It took an hour to make the phone connection with Fiji. Fred said he expected Glenn to explode with surprise that his baby had arrived twenty-five days early, but no, Glenn announced with exaggerated nonchalance that Christa had already called from her hospital bed to tell him about the birth of their daughter.

Glenn told us about the new tradition he started that day. Instead of cigars, he bought one hundred bananas to pass out among friends and colleagues to announce his baby's birth.

14

Dakota the snake charmer

1981

Fiji

For about a minute we considered taking a trip to Australia as a change of scene from New Zealand, but Australia couldn't compete with Fiji as a vacation destination. Glenn and Christa extended an open invitation when they returned home to Suva following Tracy's birth. And we embarked on a dream trip to a tropical paradise.

The gleaming hardwood and polished brass of the Joneses' home brought "Gone With the Wind" to mind. I could almost hear the rustle of silk hoopskirts. The kitchen, however, counterbalanced the antebellum ambiance. The electric appliances and chrome utensils gleamed in a perfect display of modern efficiency. Christa and Glenn were experimenting with a macrobiotic diet and they equipped their kitchen with dozens of cutting boards, arranged in groups dedicated to different uses (one set for garlic, one for yin vegetables, another for yang, one for fruit, and so forth.) Their pantry overflowed with bags of organically grown grains, seeds, and nuts mail ordered from Walnut Acres in Pennsylvania.

In honor of Tina's seventh birthday, though, Christa ignored diet restrictions and bought a bakery cake that formed the hoop skirt of a Barbie doll. Then back to brown rice and vegetables, familiar fare to us ever since our days as health food storeowners.

Glenn and Christa squired us around like visiting dignitaries. We sampled the memorable flavors of Indian food cooked with Fijian flair at the Jones' favorite restaurants. They took us out of town to Tholo-i-Suva Park where Glenn taught Fred and Dakota to snorkel in a gin-clear waterhole. The main attraction at this natural swimming pool was a rope swing suspended over the deepest part. I watched and cheered as my husband, children, and friends lined up to swing out over the water and plummet down into the depths. They were having fun, but I couldn't get up the courage to try it, thanks to my lifelong phobia about heights and my fear of deep water.

Not long after our excursion to Tholo-i-Suva, news of a hurricane came over the radio. Instead of staying at home in safety, we let Glenn persuade us to go to the Grand Pacific hotel before the storm hit. When I saw the hotel I realized why Glenn was so eager to show it to us. The architect modeled the hotel after a luxury cruise ship. The décor looked authentic enough to convince visitors from a real cruise ship that they had never left their original vessel.

We heard rain falling while we sipped our drinks in the elegant hotel lounge, but it was only typical tropical rainfall, not a torrent driven by high velocity wind. Glenn announced that he had a great idea. We followed our pied piper to the car and he drove us to Albert Park. I chose to stay in the car with Christa and three-month-old Tracy, who slept like an angel in her mother's arms. The rest of the mob ran out into the rain-drenched field where Glenn gave them their first lesson in butt-sliding, the fine art of running full speed on wet grass and dropping to one's bottom to skid as far as possible. They had too much fun to notice the wind whipping up and the rain falling like Victoria Falls. Christa and I yelled at them to get the hell back to the car.

Back on the road, Glenn navigated around fallen trees and branches littering the main thoroughfare. Lack of streetlights reduced visibility to near zero, and the wipers failed to keep up with the downpour. Bad as that seemed, the storm didn't reach full hurricane force until later that night, long after our crew settled down and went to bed.

The hurricane caused minimal damage in the city of Suva, but hit harder in the northern part of the islands. Glenn checked to be sure that all the main roads were open before sending us off, in the Jones' family car, on the circle tour he had planned for us. Our itinerary included a two-day road trip north to the town of Rakiraki where we would park the car and board a launch to Nananu-i-Ra, one of the smaller Fiji islands, where we would spend the next three days in a rented cottage. At the end of our stay on Nananu-i-Ra, the launch would return us to the car for our two-day drive back to Suva.

First stop – the Man Friday Resort. How I loved that place! The rooms were built like tree houses, elevated on stilts, half-hidden among the leaves. The swimming pool was shaped like a giant footprint, a bare foot, of course. Hammocks hung between trees and promised breeze-caressed naps and magical dreams. And the hotel offered babysitting service. We hopped on that right away so Fred could teach me how to snorkel.

I had trouble breathing, but not because of the snorkeling gear – the glory of the underwater world made me forget to exhale. One starfish glowed like something from another world. It must have measured two feet across and the colors, wow – neon red, blue, green, and yellow gleamed against the white sandy bottom of the lagoon. Fish surrounded us -- angelfish, dragon fish, wrasse, puffer fish, and many whose names we didn't know flashed their brilliant blues, greens, and yellows. Orange and white clownfish darted in and out of pale pink and lavender anemones.

Oh, and the coral! Giant clumps of brain coral, bright blue fan coral, fuchsia feathery formations, stag horn, fire coral. I couldn't have picked a better place for my first snorkeling experience, and I never saw the equal of this spot again. I shed a small tear when we left Man Friday.

On the way to Rakiraki we stopped at the Pacific Harbour Resort, one of the most popular tourist attractions in Fiji. We toured the mock native village and watched demonstrations of typical tribal dances. We walked through the animal collection and discovered a show in progress.

Two animal handlers fed mangoes and other fruits to several giant fruit bats. These bats were as big as Chihuahua dogs, their sharp teeth quite intimidating up close. A reticulated python starred in the animal show. The animal handler selected Dakota from the potential volunteers and brought him center front, then draped the python around Dakota's shoulders like a stole. The handler turned to the audience and went on talking about pythons, their habitat, diet, and hunting style. Dakota stood still as a statue while the snake's head rose slowly, tongue flickering, moving across Dakota's chest toward the opposite shoulder. The handler answered questions from the audience and didn't notice the snake's progress.

When the snake's eyes were even with his collarbone, Dakota called out in a desperate whisper, "Hey, Mom, can you tell them to take it off me now?"

Leaving the Pacific Harbour Resort behind, we drove on to Rakiraki where we shopped for groceries before catching the launch for Nananu-i-Ra. We knew that our cottage had a refrigerator, so we bought the usual breakfast cereal and milk, bread, a selection of canned goods, some fresh tomatoes, a plentiful supply of beer, and four pineapples. I can't say why we bought so many pineapples for a three-day weekend, maybe they were cheap, but I do know that we ate them all and relished every juicy bite.

The launch, barely big enough to carry us and our baggage and groceries, dropped us off at our landlord's dock after a 30-minute trip across calm water. The landlord showed us around the simple cement block cottage and explained that the fridge operated on kerosene and a generator would provide electricity for lamps in the evening from six to nine o'clock.

While I put the groceries away, Fred and the kids went out to check the seashore. Dakota scavenged a length of fishing line and a hook from the rocks near the dock. He cracked open a few small clams for bait, put on his mask and fins, and snorkeled around in the shallows. By dangling his baited hook in front of tasty-looking fish, he managed to catch enough for our supper. I hope I praised him for his remarkable ingenuity. I kept returning to the same thought, this boy of ours is not quite eight years old and he can put food on the table.

In the morning Fred and I talked the kids into going on a hike. We figured we could beach comb all the way around our little island, investigate tide pools, see some wildlife, and collect an assortment of pretty shells. I packed a few snacks and we marched down the waterline.

I picked up the first rubber flip-flop flotsam and challenged the kids to find another to make a pair. Fred found one and said he wanted a pair too. The race was on. We found washed up flip-flops in all sizes and colors, and we rejected any that had torn straps. Before long we each had an intact, although not color-matched, pair. And it was time to invent another game.

Fred found a long, sturdy stick and dragged it behind him to create a snaky trail in the sand. "Walk this way," he said, and we three slithered along in his tracks. Everybody had a turn at being the leader.

The sun had reached its high point before I realized how much time had passed. I passed out the snacks and wished I had brought a real picnic and cold drinks. Surely we must be well beyond the halfway mark by now. Fred guessed we might have one more hour at the most until we reached the short row of houses and cabins that housed Nananu-i-Ra's population and included our cottage.

Further down the beach, I slipped off my flip-flops and walked in the water to cool my feet. As I passed some rocks, the water came alive, boiled up and splashed around my knees. I yelped and leaped shoreward, heart pounding, arms flailing.

The kids screamed and Fred ran toward me. It was only an eel protecting its lair, but its expression was evil. When Fred came closer to get a better look, the eel thrashed the water again, thrusting forward as if to bite a chunk out of anything in its way, namely, Fred's ankles.

Now I took much more care to look where I was stepping. I'm sure that's why I found my treasure, a small nautilus shell, empty and almost perfect. This was a lucky find because nautiluses live in the depths of the ocean and their fragile shells don't often survive the long, tumbling journey to shore.

Ahead of us lay a spit of land that jutted into the sea. As we approached the small peninsula, the sand turned thick and viscous. Strange trees standing on a forest of arched roots covered the ground. I wondered if it would be better to try to cut inland instead of slogging through the mire, but Fred pointed out that we would need a machete to hack through the vines of the interior. We trudged on and entered our first mangrove swamp.

Tiny black fiddler crabs swarmed and scurried out of our path, brandishing their over-sized orange "fiddle" claws like medieval weapons. Tina tried to catch one. Maybe she was thinking of catching several and making a family out of them. Ploop, ploop, one after another the feisty crabs evaded Tina's grasp and darted down a handy escape hole.

I started wishing for some sign of civilization. Maybe when we rounded the point…but no, beyond the mangrove swamp the muck changed back to sandy beach that went on forever, and taller trees filled the inland view. No one had complained yet, but I knew the kids would soon be hungry and thirsty. Our shadows stretched further and further ahead of us as we plodded along.

"Let's go up closer to the trees for a minute," Fred said, "and see if there's a path or an opening through the woods."

We turned to look where he pointed and all four of us saw the same thing at the same time. A gigantic black cloud swept back and forth across the treetops. Not a sky cloud, of course, but what – a flock of birds? The creatures in formation moved as one entity, swooping, turning, rising, falling in a hypnotic rhythm. Fred and I bracketed the kids in a tight family huddle. I contemplated Doomsday.

"They're bats," Fred exclaimed, "just like the ones we saw at the animal show -- the fruit bats."

I didn't say so, but goosebumps rose like hackles at my mental image of vampire bats.

Without further discussion, we returned to our march along the waterline. The kids lagged a bit. Dakota complained of hunger. Tina wanted a drink of water. I had nothing to offer them except nervous promises.

Fred whispered to me that he could run ahead and get food and water, but he didn't feel good about leaving us alone. We decided to stick together and try to pick up the pace a little.

I fought bad thoughts and panic that tried to paint horrible pictures in my mind. I tried to focus on distracting the kids and encouraging them to walk faster. I didn't want to think about going on in the dark. At this latitude there was no lingering twilight; night would drop like a Roman shade.

"Lookit, Dad." Dakota's sharp eyes detected something far down the beach.

By squinting I could make out a dock. Civilization at last. We gulped water from the dock owner's garden hose, and the lady of the house gave us some crackers. The man estimated that we had hiked ten miles around the island. That's not far for two fit adults, but what a feat for their offspring!

A few days later, fully recovered from our adventure, we returned to the Joneses in Suva to get ready for a special occasion. Glenn had invited two of his Fijian friends to prepare typical food and demonstrate a popular ceremony. The food, conch ceviche, had incredible depth of flavor and an odd chewy texture. The ritual centered on the drinking of yagona (pronounced yangona and also known as kava in other South Pacific cultures). Under normal circumstances this was a men-only event, but Glenn's friends modified both the drink and the ritual to allow the kids and me to participate. They mixed the yagona in a giant clamshell and dipped out a portion in a polished coconut half shell. The recipe remains a guarded secret, one that I have absolutely no desire to know. Yagona is cloudy like miso soup, smells like old dishwater, and tastes like dirt. At full strength it is a mild narcotic that turns your lips and tongue numb and produces uncontrollable daydreaming. Our watered-down version fell short at mere queasiness.

Glenn's friends also explained the long process involved in the creation of the yagona cups, which involved burying the empty coconut shells in the ground for a year, followed by hours of polishing with a smooth pebble. The finished product shone like fine Japanese laquerware, glossy and flawless.

Glenn drove us down to the waterfront for another surprise. With pride he showed us his boat "The Bilbo Baggins." It reminded me too much of Tom Goff's scow in Monrovia and I declined the invitation for a ride. Tina stuck by me, but Fred and Dakota went merrily motoring out into Suva Bay in the battered Baggins with Captain Glenn for a day of snorkeling.

The next adventure in Glenn's line-up also involved a boat. He had booked a snorkeling trip to Stewart Island on a tour-sized catamaran. At the last minute Tina came down with a fever and I took her to a local doctor instead of joining the guys. The doctor, a woman from India, diagnosed an ear infection and prescribed an antibiotic to clear it up. Tina, Christa, baby Tracy, and I spent a quiet weekend while the boys sailed away.

Our guys had sunny skies, calm seas, favorable winds, and amiable companions – a dream of a tropical cruise. An older lady on the tour fell in love with Dakota and gave him treats and presents. He also received an adorable hand made green palm frond hat from one of the crewmembers. The boys snorkeled in the warm, clear water until their fingers wrinkled like prunes and mask marks engraved their foreheads. Fred and Glenn named the place Hobbit Land for the fantastic variety of marine life – millions of colorful anemones, a kaleidoscope of brilliant fish, and gigantic pillars of brain coral twenty feet tall and six feet wide. The tour included a barbeque of fresh fish caught along the way, conch ceviche, and local vegetables and fruits. Fred said it was the best meal he had ever eaten.

I couldn't think of a way to thank the Joneses properly for our marvelous Fiji vacation. I hoped that someday we would be able to return the favor, little knowing that they would add to our indebtedness many times in the future by inviting us to visit them in other beautiful, exotic, and fascinating places.

The Fletcher

Following our return to Wellington, Fred continued to go to Marathon Clinic meetings. He followed the Marathon Clinic's suggested twelve-week training program and set the Fletcher Marathon in Rotorua as his goal. By increasing his mileage at a steady rate until he reached a peak of seventy-three miles per week, he averaged sixty miles per week for the ten weeks prior to the race.

The marathon took place on Dakota's eighth birthday and ten days before Fred's thirty-seventh birthday, giving the event even more significance. To celebrate Fred's marathon and the two birthdays we hired a guide for a fishing trip on the lake, where each of us caught a big rainbow trout, fun to catch and good to eat. The guide told us that rainbow trout were imported from California as fingerlings and stocked the major lakes in New Zealand. Given perfect conditions and lacking predators, they reproduced in great numbers and grew to tremendous size – some as large as salmon.

On the big day, May 2, 1981, Fred ran his race like a gazelle. Friends from the marathon clinic, Sue and Geoff Kirkham, drove the kids and me to various mile markers so we could see Daddy at critical stages. Every time we saw him, he looked strong, fresh, and happy. About two and a half hours after the start, Geoff suggested that we find a good spot near the finish line. We watched the front-runners come in for half an hour, and Geoff told me that we might see Fred any minute. I turned to tell Dakota and Tina, but I couldn't see Dakota. Before I could get nervous, he appeared out of the crowd, carrying a cold Foster's beer that he had fetched from our cooler to give to his dad at the end of the race. One of Fred's most indelible memories is that of Dakota's tear-streaked yet proud expression as he presented the best prize in the world.

Our ecstatic man finished the Fletcher Marathon in 3 hours, 7 minutes and 10 seconds, a flying pace of seven minutes per mile. He came in 469th of 2494 finishers. As far as we know, he was the only one awarded with a beer. The first runner finished in 2:17:28 and the last crossed the line in 6:26:22, every single one a winner from the fastest to the slowest.

The day after the marathon we toured around the town and nearby area. Rotorua's large Maori population supported several cultural centers, called Marae, where we saw excellent examples of Maori weaving, tattoo patterns, and woodcarving.

Whakarewarewa, also known as the Thermal Village, greeted visitors with a hand painted sign: "Nau mai, haere mai, whakatau mai." Welcome, come in, make yourself at home. The surrounding landscape of erupting geothermal activity created a fantasy world. Geysers spouted high columns of steaming hot water and mud pools burbled like chocolate pudding at full rolling boil. I chuckled when I heard the kiwi pronunciation of the word geyser – it sounded exactly the same as our slang term for old man – geezer.

Tina, dedicated fan of lamb chops, loved the sheep exhibit in Rotorua's Agrodome. I expected her to become a vegetarian after petting the kind of sheep that makes the best chops, but either she didn't make the connection or it didn't bother her -- she didn't eschew meat until she reached the ripe old age of nineteen.

Dakota enjoyed everything about Rotorua, and the fact is Dakota had fun wherever he was. If he ever felt bored, he fell back on his math workbooks and his ever-growing ball of finger-knitting (a skill he learned at Redwood School).

Birth of Marathon Mom

Fred's marathon excitement tipped the scales for me. I had been running a bit and the training effect surprised me. Within five months of my first agonizing mile, I was able to run five miles three times a week. Two months after my fortieth birthday I ran ten miles for the first time and I joined the Marathon Clinic three months after that, still denying any possibility that I would ever consider running the daunting distance of 26.2 miles, but enjoying new friendships and shared experiences with the other runners.

When I felt the thrill of seeing Fred and the other runners cross the finish line at the Fletcher, I too caught the bug. With the encouragement of Fred and my friends, especially Sue Vaughan, Betty Hitchcock, and Katie Bowcutt, I set my sights on the Mannings Marathon in Hamilton in October.

An Extra Move

Our brains churning with ambitious marathon plans, Fred and I inquired about an extension of our two-year assignment in Wellington. Fred asked for two additional years with a home leave in the middle. State Department vetoed that but made a counter offer of a straight three-year assignment. That meant we would not see family for three years unless some of them came to visit us (not likely because of the distance and expense). Staying in New Zealand seemed worth the price, so Fred accepted the terms.

On the downside of this deal lay the two-year lease on our house. The Housing Officer negotiated with the landlord to no avail – we had to move at the end of the lease.

In a stroke of lucky timing, a local man received a New Zealand government assignment to serve in London and he contacted our embassy housing office to offer a lease on his Tawa home. We moved from Oriel Ave to Pembroke Street, a few blocks closer to Redwood School and downtown Tawa. Our new home won me over with its level yard, downstairs playroom, living room fireplace, and best of all -- a central heating system.

Dakota and Tina saw their wish reflected in the big screen of the color television that the landlord left behind for us. I drew up a chart, the first of many, to record points earned by chores and redeemed for TV viewing. I listed the eligible programs such as Cattle Car Plastic Cup (Battlestar Galactica) and The Flukes of Gizzard (The Dukes of Hazard). My children acted like there was nothing funny about my silly names for their beloved programs. But they did their chores without (many) reminders and enjoyed their TV rewards.

The new house had other appealing features. The garage provided good space for my pottery equipment, as well as a cave-like storage area that became a clubhouse for Dakota and his pals. Upstairs, the dining space nestled between kitchen and living room in an alcove with east-facing windows, a warm inviting spot for morning coffee. Tina claimed the hall closet as her domain. Not a traditional closet, it was more like an afterthought. The door opened about a foot and a half above the hall floor and the space inside measured three feet wide by eight feet long. Without shelves or a clothes bar, I couldn't imagine what I would store there besides perhaps luggage or maybe trunks of off-season clothes. It didn't matter what I thought anyway, the closet was destined to be Tina's playhouse. She decorated it with pictures and wall hangings, doll accessories, and floor pillows. Tina's playhouse provided the backdrop for many hours of imaginative games, and once it was the setting for the following drama.

Most Sundays, Fred and I hired fourteen-year-old Tracy Tock, from the old neighborhood, to baby-sit while we spent the morning at Marathon Clinic. On one particular Sunday, Tracy agreed to watch our two, ages eight and seven, plus Tina's classmate Amanda who had spent the night.

Fred and I returned from Marathon Clinic and opened the door to unnatural silence. Tracy and the children sat stiffly on the couch wearing worried faces.

Amanda sobbed and sniffled. "I just want to go home."

We turned to Tracy for an explanation, but she said, "I think Dakota should tell you what happened."

All eyes focused on Dakota. Dakota looked like someone on the way to the guillotine. He stammered at first and then the story took over and words tumbled out as fast as his lips could move.

"It was meant to be a joke," he said.

He thought it would be funny to hide in Tina's playhouse (the hall closet) and jump out to surprise Fred and me when we got home from

Marathon Clinic. When he outlined his plan to the other kids, Tina pointed out that they shouldn't close the door because it couldn't be opened from the inside. Dakota had a solution to that problem, but the other kids didn't think it would work. He convinced them to get into the closet with him for a demonstration. First, he tied a long string around the handle on the outside of the door. Then he ran the length of string under the door, stepped inside the closet with the others, and shut the door. Tina's friend Amanda screamed in the darkness and Dakota flicked the wall switch to turn on the overhead bulb.

At this point in the narrative, Amanda and Dakota gave each other mutual mean looks. Dakota continued his story.

"I pulled on the string to make the handle go down and open the latch, but the door didn't open. I pulled harder and the string slid off."

Amanda glared at Dakota. "We were trapped and --"

Tracy interrupted. "I tried to get the kids to calm down and play a game while we waited for you to come home, but they were too frightened after Dakota told us that we might run out of air in there. Then the phone rang and rang and Amanda started screaming and crying, 'Hello? Hello? Help! Help!' I'm afraid I panicked a bit myself."

Dakota stood up. "I did what I had to do. You can see for yourselves."

We trooped out of the living room and down the hall to the playhouse door. A long jagged gash ran from the top of the door down to the handle.

Dakota picked up the wooden decoupage wall plaque that lay discarded on the floor. "I used this to break through. The first hole I made was too high and I couldn't reach the handle, so I had to keep chopping… am I in terrible trouble?" His big brown eyes glistened and his lower lip trembled.

Fred laughed and I wrapped my arms around our boy. "No, you're not in trouble at all."

The Mannings

Fred and I continued our preoccupation with marathons. To be able to run a marathon in October, I had to start training in late July. Fred planned to run the Mannings Marathon in Hamilton too, so our kids heard nothing but marathon talk for the next twelve weeks. I did many long training runs (18-20 miles each) with my friend Sue and Fred ran several 20-milers with his friend Ian. We all stayed healthy and injury-free, not always possible during the grueling marathon training schedule.

The race was scheduled for Saturday, October 17, 1981, but Fred and I packed gear and kids into our blue station wagon on the Tuesday before. We wanted to allow plenty of time to get settled, get acquainted with the racecourse, and work out our sleeping arrangements – but the main reason for getting there early was probably anxiety. Fred wanted to break three hours and hoped to finish under 2:50, and it was my first marathon….

We made the easy drive in eight hours, including a pleasant half hour lunch break at a big playground in Wanganui. Since we had an early start at 7:30 am, we arrived in Hamilton with time to spare for a thirty-minute jog in the light rain that had developed after the fine, sunny morning. Fred and I went together, talking about our hopes for the race and remarking that the windless, mild weather would be very good for the marathon. We jogged through the Hamilton Gardens, a half-developed public space, and then faced the entrance to a cemetery. I hesitated, not wanting to offend any mourners who might be there, but Fred said he was feeling positive vibrations and felt it was a good thing to do.

Wednesday was a gorgeous sunny day, warm with no wind, the best of springtime in New Zealand. We had a run of about 5 ½ miles together, near the lake and along the river. Later on we took the kids to the zoo, which was more like a menagerie. The animals, with the exception of two lions and a jaguar, could be hand-fed. Dakota and Tina enjoyed feeding the goats and donkeys especially. There were deer, ponies, pigs, rabbits, guinea pigs, kangaroos, wallabies, llamas, exotic birds and many peacocks.

Sue, Geoff and their daughter Nicole arrived by plane Thursday morning; we met them at the airport. The day turned cloudy and windy, making us more nervous about possible weather conditions on Saturday. Sue was at least as nervous and apprehensive as I was, even though this was her second marathon. We went over and over our plans for pacing. During training I had worked out splits (elapsed time at selected distance markers) for 4:12 and even had thoughts of 4:09, but finally I settled for 4:15 with hopes of finishing under 4 ½ hours if I faded over the last 10K. I wasn't sure whether splits served an actual function or fit into the category of superstitious ritual; I just followed the example of the more experienced runners.

All of us went to the lake to feed the swans and ducks and play at the playground. We had a "last ice cream" and then went back to the motel to welcome Sue's mom Judy who had just arrived after a visit to one of her sons in a nearby town.

Our main concerns on Friday were worries about Saturday's weather and fears of eating too much during the day. Geoff, Judy, Sue, Nicole and our family spent a few hours at the zoo visiting our favorite animals. Everyone wanted an early dinner and an early night before the big day. The last news report we heard before bedtime predicted "unsettled weather."

The day began with rain. The temperature was about 12 C (a little less than 54 F) and there was no wind. Perfect marathon weather. I felt nervous but not excited. We left the kids with Judy and parked near the start. We walked to the stadium for one last pee and to say howdy to any Wellington folks we might see. Sue and I had our drink bottles close at hand for the last twenty minutes before starting. Fred found his buddy John Weatherly, and it was time to go to our starting places. I lined up just in front of the 4-hour-plus sign. Rain drizzled and I felt cold, even with a turtleneck under my Marathon Clinic singlet.

Suddenly the crowd of runners surged forward for a short distance. Then the starting gun went off and we continued forward at a walk for a few seconds. Very quickly we were off, jogging in a pack that soon spread out. My 1K time was 6:42, slower than I should be running, but the pace felt comfortable, so I didn't speed up.

The first 5K breezed by. Time called at 5K was 30:31, still a bit behind my splits, but I thought 10K would tell the tale, so I didn't try to speed up. Ten K was gone in 59 minutes, a bit faster than I had planned. Geoff, under his umbrella, looked pleased with my time and that gave me a boost. At this point I felt a distinct lack of enthusiasm and figured I wouldn't have an especially good run. Before the 15K mark I detoured for a pee in the trees.

At 15K the time was 1:30:31, which I reckoned was right on the dot. I wasn't carrying my splits written on anything, only in my head, and so far my brain seemed to be working okay. Someone asked me how I felt and I realized that I was feeling good.

Marathon Clinic supporters cheered from the roadside and I appreciated their encouragement. It was also really inspiring to see both faster and slower runners on the Tramway Road section and also on the East Street loop. I saw everybody at least twice because of the unique layout of the racecourse.

Geoff gave me another high sign at 20K to indicate I was still on my splits. My legs felt all right, but I wished I were beginning the last lap instead of only the third.

The 25K time call put me about one minute behind my predicted goal. At this point I thought I should slow up further in order to save some energy for the last lap. It was very evident that the last lap would be the test. My spirits lifted at the sight of Geoff at the 30K mark even though my legs had gone cold and crampy.

An Auckland YMCA lady named Eunice was my companion at this stage. She stopped to walk twice and managed to catch up with me each time. I asked her if it helped to walk and she said she thought it might, except it was very hard to get going again. My watch read three hours and thirty-five minutes: *Right, now run for just five more minutes and then maybe walk a bit.*

Sue appeared just before I entered the farm area and she said her legs were "gone." On the corner I saw a sign that proclaimed "Survivors Prosecuted." Then I was nearly knocked down by two guys on a motorcycle. I guessed they might have been race officials retrieving signs because the 35K sign was gone when I got there. I walked twice in the farm section, once before and once after the drink station. Then I shuffled and plodded the rest of the way, leaving Eunice behind.

As I passed, a spectator shouted that we were 3K from the finish. My watch read 4:08 and I figured I could still break 4:30 if I kept on jogging. On that last lap, I probably passed six people and maybe four passed me. There was no thrill in passing as I could imagine myself in the same sorry state at any minute. My legs hurt too much and I felt cranky and betrayed by my body, although my breathing was fine throughout and my upper body didn't tire.

The last bit I followed a man and his young son. Aid stations had been abandoned and cars were being released from the parking lot. It was hard work dodging pedestrians, cars, and breathing exhaust fumes.

At last I rounded the corner to enter the stadium. And there were my guys – Fred wrapped in his finisher's Army blanket (he finished in two hours forty-four minutes), Tina and Dakota with beach towels over their heads (raincoats in the closet back at the motel) and mud squishing between their bare toes. Tina seemed a bit shocked. Dakota looked me over carefully and then ran around the track with me. My most lasting memory of the marathon – Dakota jogging along through the muddy grass with his wet towel flapping in the breeze. The clock read 4:28:00 when I crossed the finish line.

So I wrapped up in my own scratchy, mothball smelly Army blanket, congratulated my fellow finishers, and collected my hard-earned t-shirt. Geoff kindly offered to drive us to the motel, so we hobbled back to the car. I had to manually lift each leg over the two-foot-high parking barrier. My leg pain lasted until we went to the spa-pool about forty-five minutes later.

I was surprised to have no dehydration headache later in the afternoon and very little muscle stiffness the following day. After a 15-minute recovery run in the morning, there was no soreness at all. A feeling of strength and accomplishment lasted for weeks after the marathon.

Hitting the Wall

All marathon runners fear the specter of "the wall." When a long distance runner reaches the limits of his endurance on a particular day, he stops short, as suddenly as if he hit a brick wall. I watched Fred encounter the infamous wall about 500 meters from the finish line of the DB Country Marathon in Masterton, barely one month after his triumph in Hamilton. One minute he was running and the next minute his long, powerful stride shrank to a weak wobble. Dakota ran out to him and had to slow to a jog to stay at Dad's side the rest of the way to the finish line. As I helped wrap a blanket around Fred's shoulders, I felt tremors in his muscles and cold sweat on his skin. His gray-green pallor set off an alarm in my heart.

Rest and hydration brought Fred back from the wall. He surprised everyone with his quick recovery. With the clarity of hindsight, he realized that he hadn't drunk enough water to sustain such vigorous exercise on an unusually warm day.

After completing that race, Fred had three marathons to his credit, and my former not-particularly-athletic self had transformed into a real runner, not just an ordinary jogger, but a real honest-to-goodness marathoner. I ran every day, participated in fun runs, and encouraged my two kids to join in. I could have rested on my laurels. Instead, I typed up a training program for the City of Wellington Marathon scheduled for January 1982. The timing seemed right and I liked the familiar scenic route that made two laps of Wellington's Eastern Bays.

15

Fleet footed Fred

1982

The Wellington

I dove into my training program for the City of Wellington Marathon, increased the length of my runs, and dreamed of breaking four hours. I counted on my newly created reward for 20-milers – a quart of diced fruit (banana, apple, orange, grapes, strawberries, kiwi, and tamarillo) topped with a pint of yogurt and sprinkled with crunchy granola. I burned over

1600 calories on a 20-mile run and gloried in the fact that marathon training is one time in a woman's life when she doesn't have to worry about gaining weight.

Several days before the marathon the weather turned nasty –winds gusting to 80 mph, blowing roofs off. Weather reports predicted more rain for the day of the race. Morning dawned crummy, windy, cloudy, but by race time, 8:30 am, it had cleared and become a fine day, though still a bit too windy for good running. Fred had to go to work at 5:30 am, so I got a ride to the start of the race with friends and dropped Dakota and Tina off at another friend's house.

Since the predictions promised better weather, Fred showed up to run the marathon too, although he hadn't trained for it specifically and had felt some burnout after hitting the wall during the Masterton race in November. He got a good start at a pace set by one of his buddies.

One of my friends from Marathon Clinic, Mari Maxwell, ran with me the first half hour to make sure I didn't go out too fast. And then Geoff, over six feet tall and broad-shouldered, ran just in front of me to block the wind. I finished the first half in 2:03, exactly to plan, although not in tune with my desire to finish under four hours. I ran well until about 25K, when I started to feel uncomfortable. I felt hot and then cold and hot again and my legs began to hurt. A hill at 30K slowed me down. Two women from Marathon Clinic ran with me at that stage, trying to help but not knowing what to do.

After the hill, I was joined by two more friends who meant to protect me through the windy section. I wanted to quit, but they encouraged me to go to the next drink station before deciding. So I struggled on, legs hurting more and more. It felt as though my calf and thigh muscles were wrapped in shards of broken glass that gouged and tore with every step. Meanwhile another friend drove her van around offering drinks of water and wet sponges just when I seemed to need them the most. When I passed 35K I really wanted to stop, but I hated to disappoint all those loyal supporters. I forged on, legs screaming for relief.

When I had run four hours and couldn't take it anymore, I stopped, with "only" about 4K (2.4 miles) to go. Another friend was there with a car, so I had a ride, thank goodness. We also picked up Mari, who had run out from the finish line to meet me. In the end, I crossed the finish line at 4:13, exactly the time I had planned, only by car instead of on foot. It was a great day, in spite of not finishing, because I was so impressed by the support and comradeship of our club members. My legs recovered after a couple of hours of rest, no damage done…but I swore off marathons.

"I never have to do that again," I said.

Despite his early morning call to work and a late start, Fred finished the marathon in thirty-second place in a time of 3 hours 5 minutes and 31 seconds. He, more than Bruce Springsteen, was the guy that was "Born to Run."

A Contagious Addiction

Once we heard about it, we had to experience the crazy Round the Bays Fun Run in Auckland. Advertised as the biggest fun run in the country, the event attracted an estimated 80,000 participants, a new world record for a running event. I saved the Auckland Star newspaper for the photo – two full pages -- a panoramic view of a bobbing sea of humanity. The starting line itself stretched for over a mile. Fred and I didn't even try to stay together. We agreed that the best strategy was to go with the flow.

At first I felt like one cell of an enormous organism. Not being a brain cell, I could not choose the direction or speed of movement but had to surrender to the motion of the others. I couldn't see my feet and I hoped I wouldn't trip. Shoulder to shoulder I jostled along with the other cheerful cells.

The organism divided into many parts as some of the runners sped up and others slowed to a walk. I began to distinguish individuals – a dad pushing a pram, a military group dressed in combat gear and counting cadence, a wheelchair athlete, someone in a bear costume, people of all shapes, sizes and levels of fitness, everybody wearing smiles.

The race ended at a vast open space in a city park, where running clubs from all over the country had set up tents, picnic tables and bar-beques. Beer flowed, music blared, and the party went on into the night.

We came back home more obsessed with running. Fred and I devoured our monthly running magazines and digested training tips, profiles of famous runners, nutrition advice, and other useful information about the sport. Running was addictive, the magazines said, a positive addiction because of the health benefits. I agreed. Running was contagious too. At least it seemed that way in the case of our kids.

I thought Dakota and Tina would be sick of running after hearing Fred and me talk endlessly about it, but they surprised me. They said they wanted to come with me on a training run. I didn't expect them to last a mile – Tina was seven and Dakota eight – but they ran two miles. Soon they started participating with Fred and me in fun runs – 6K (3.84) miles at the Radio Windy Basin to Bay Run for Fun, 5K (3.1 miles) at another Wellington event.

Dakota's interest grew ever stronger and he increased his mileage to 7K (4.34 miles) at the Petone Community Run, and 8.5K (5.27 miles) at the Queen's Wharf to Miramar Run. His reached his peak at the Fresh Up 10K (6.2 miles) on May 8, 1982, six days after his ninth birthday. He was the youngest runner to finish the race and his name was announced on the Wellington radio sportscast. About that time, in a kind of rite of passage, Dakota decided to have his ear pierced, like the teen boys were doing in those days. I brought him to the chemist's shop (drug store) where sterile ear piercing was done for the price of the earring, a gold ball stud.

Port Moresby Mystery

In the midst of our marathon mania, bid list time rolled around again. I scrounged a big piece of paper from the kids' arts and crafts drawer and drew ruled lines for a new post selection chart. Fred brought home the open assignments telegram and we set up a command center on the dining room table. I labeled the columns: Job (to rate the size of Fred's section and whether the position matched his rank), School, Housing, Climate, Differential, Language (if an assignment included language training, we considered that a definite plus), and Appeal (the most subjective category).

Fred went to the Personnel Office library and checked out official post reports in batches of five. Once we had read all the post reports and entered our ratings on the chart, I tallied the results and made a rank order list. We pored over the list, made a few adjustments based on gut-level judgments, and finalized it.

The Seychelles topped the list, followed by Papua New Guinea and Somalia. Fred had heard that a Seychelles posting had the reputation of being a plum assignment, a reward to someone who knew somebody in the Good Old Boys network. But it didn't hurt to put it first on our list.

The anxiously awaited cable came. Our new home: Port Moresby, Papua New Guinea. We celebrated with champagne.

A week later, another cable came. Fred's assignment to Port Moresby had been broken. The reason? Fred's career counselor claimed that the powers in Main State had decreed that an employee could not serve consecutive tours in the same geographical area (in those days, State Department divided the world into sectors: Europe, Africa, Latin America, Asia, Middle East, and Pacific Rim). Bull Roar. We knew of several examples that ran contrary to this alleged policy. Fred chalked it up to the Good Old Boys in action and we returned to our holding pattern to await re-assignment.

What a coincidence that the assignment cable arrived on the same day as the National Geographic Magazine that featured an article on Somalia, third choice on Fred's bid list, and our new home-to-be. Our first impressions of Mogadishu started with the photographs in that issue of National Geographic.

The Nike-City of Christchurch International

In the meantime, the successful completion of several fun runs renewed my interest in marathons. I brushed the dust off my training program and set my sights on June and the Nike-City of Christchurch International marathon.

For Fred and me, this was the last chance to run a marathon before leaving New Zealand; in fact, since we would be spending the next two years in Somalia, this could be the last marathon opportunity for quite a long time.

My training for this one went well. I put in six runs of twenty miles or more and another seven runs of two hours or more. Also, I ran a fast half-marathon (2:00:45) on a hilly course just before starting the training program, and I finished a 10K race in 48:38 halfway through my training. I had a cold for about two weeks (immediately after speed-work on the heels of a 35K run, which sounds suspiciously like over-training). Luckily I managed to miss only two days of running while I was ill. Toward the end of the big mileage weeks, my shins started to hurt, painful while not running and for the first half hour of a run. I iced them, swallowed extra vitamin E capsules, stretched carefully, and finally cut my running down to a bare minimum. Two weeks and two days before the marathon, I ran my last 20-miler and after that ran only 80K total, and 60K of that mostly very slow jogging.

This time I concentrated on mental preparation as well as doing as many 20+ milers as I could. By race day I felt mentally prepared to run for 4 ½ hours and had calculated my "collapse point" (3 times average daily mileage over eight weeks) at 26.5 miles. My hocuspocus math gave me confidence in my legs' ability to carry me 0.3 miles past the finish line. If my legs didn't fail me and the weather was reasonable, I calculated I could finish in about 4:20 to 4:25.

The City of Christchurch course was as beautiful as any could be. Starting and ending at the Queen Elizabeth II Stadium (site of the 1974 Commonwealth Games), it followed the River Avon, cut through Hagley Park on a cycle path, went out to the airport, and returned by reverse route.

The weather turned out to be fairly decent: 4 – 8 degrees C (about 40 F), mostly cloudy with intermittent rain, and a light southerly wind (behind us coming home). I wore maximum clothes for running: tights, shorts, long sleeved turtleneck, singlet, rain jacket, hat and gloves – and I was comfortable while others who dressed lightly suffered from the cold.

No one criticized the organization of this marathon. The coordinators provided secure storage for gear, plenty of police and marshals on the route, and the course was well marked. Wheel chair competitors started ten minutes before and half-marathoners ten minutes after the main event.

I jogged in place near the end of the field of 1100 runners and at 10 AM we were off. A slow start, 10:54 for the first mile, but it felt good and relaxed. I spent roughly the first 5K on the lookout for somebody to run with. The leaders of the half-marathon race came zooming past and it was a struggle to keep from speeding on with them. Half-marathoners continued to stream by until we reached their turn-around point at 10.5K.

After chatting with three or four people, I finally found a fellow and a girl running together who seemed to be on my pace. We passed 5K at about 30:50 (my splits called for 31:00), but the girl dropped back because of a stitch in her side. The fellow (an older, 60ish, guy with a Jimmy Durante nose) stayed with me until 15K where I stopped for a drink and he didn't. At 10K we clocked 1:00:40, a bit faster than I had planned, but I figured good company at this stage was worth it.

It must have been 12 or 14K when I started seeing the leaders coming back. Not far behind them was the first woman, a Japanese. I saw Alistair Maxwell, Fred, Geoff, Lottie Thompson, another Wellington Marathon Clinic woman I recognized, and Mari Maxwell. Then, what a great surprise, Ian and Ava Hurndall popped out from the crowd of spectators. Seeing them gave me a great lift and I surged forward. At 16K, my watch read 1:37:57 – very reasonable pacing – and I was feeling invincible.

Just before the halfway mark I caught my Jimmy Durante friend again. He had been joined by a younger fellow who was running his first marathon. We passed the halfway point in 2:08. As we three ran along, talking about running and training, I heard a cheer aimed at me for "The rose between two thorns." Somewhere before 30K the Jimmy Durante guy mentioned a problem with his knee and then faded. I looked for him later but didn't see him again; perhaps he dropped out of the race.

My remaining companion was still running very easily, so I suggested to him that he could speed up after 32K if he still felt fresh. At about 30K he took a loo stop and was able to catch up without any stress. That probably gave him the confidence he needed, because before the 32K mark he poured on the power and gracefully glided ahead.

I was happy to be on my own with no distractions for the last stretch. After 33K I still felt pretty good and started passing people. I noticed toilets beside the road and decided that even though I wasn't desperate to pee, it would be a nice break for my legs. It was a lucky break too, because I discovered my forgotten stash of chewable C tablets. Finding them was worth the minute or two it took to stop. My time at 35K (immediately after the toilet stop) was 3:34. At the "5K to go" sign, I was at 3:48 – giving me a good chance to finish under 4:20.

Ava and Ian appeared again out of nowhere and ran along with me until the stadium was in sight. Ian told me the finishing times of Fred and all the others he could remember. I was really glad to know they had all done well. I think the time called at 40K was 4:04. I thought that would be a disappointing call if you were trying to break four hours. For me it was fine because I had 16 minutes to cover 2.196K.

After Ava and Ian left, I went on passing people; no one seemed to be in real distress, just plodding along. Before entering the stadium I shrugged off my jacket so my race number would be visible. I waved at three silhouettes standing at the top of the stadium, absolutely sure they were Fred, Sue and Geoff. I realized two days later that not one of those three would have felt like climbing all those steps after running 26.2 miles.

Once on the track inside the stadium I picked up the pace and strode out against a chilling wind. Fred and Sue stood there on the sidelines cheering me on (Geoff huddled in a blanket indoors near a heater). Right next to them stood my younger running partner, wrapped in his blanket. We collected my gear and shuffled as fast as we could to the car and then to the spa pool at Sue and Geoff's motel for a nice hot soak.

I puffed up with pride when I thought about my 4:17:15 finish. I beat my 4:20 goal and felt like Queen Kong.

After lunch and a short rest, Fred and I went to the awards party for supper and disco – and we had enough leg power to dance the night away.

It might have been due to the dancing that my legs weren't stiff at all the next day. Left knee, left foot, and all toes were tender and two right toes burned with small but painful blisters – the only battle scars.

Finally the long-sought-after perfect marathon experience was mine. Even though it took three tries to get it right, it was worth it. These New Zealand marathons, three within eight months, polished my character and reinforced my self-confidence in ways that have run deep and true for the rest of my life.

Fond Farewell

The inevitability of leaving New Zealand, perhaps forever, made me sad. It was painful to say goodbye to terrific friends, leave the comforts of home and community, and head out to unknown territory. I know the rest of the family felt conflict too -- sad and reluctant to let go, yet excited to reunite with our family back home and journey on to meet the next adventure.

Fred, itinerary genius, routed us home through Hawaii with a 36-hour layover. He reserved a hotel room on Waikiki Beach where we four made a peaceful tableau, lined up on chaises lounges on the balcony of our hotel room, snoring beneath the sleep masks from our lucky bump up to Business Class.

After my nap I went for a run around Diamond Head, part of the course of the Iron Man Triathlon and Honolulu Marathon, and day-dreamed about my marathons.

We went for an exploration walk and bought souvenirs at tourist shops, blue flowery bikinis for Tina and me, blue flowery Hawaii shirt for Fred, and, Dakota's choice, a t-shirt with a dolphin on it.

When we hit Los Angeles, we went to brother Mike's place. While we were in New Zealand, Mike had won custody of Michael and Mark. He also married his third wife Kathy and they all lived in her house in Huntington Beach. We had a lot of catching up to do, and a visit from our old friend Linda Hall added to the mixture of reminiscences. In the midst of nostalgia, we started making new memories when Fred said he wanted to get his ear pierced. Kathy volunteered to do the deed and all the kids gathered around with gruesome interest. Kathy numbed Fred's earlobe with a frozen carrot, sterilized a hefty sewing needle, and pierced with one swift stroke.

Another day Fred and I took the four children, Dakota (9), Tina (8), Michael (8) and Mark (6) to Disneyland. We got on a boat ride and I reminded the kids that the signs said to keep their hands and arms inside the boat at all times. All four put their hands in their laps, but Michael and Mark stuck their heads outside the boat, in unison as if rehearsed. Their gesture was a perfect example of their attitude toward authority at that time in their lives.

Dakota got a taste of the consequences of flaunting authority several days later in Los Lunas, New Mexico. While Fred and I chatted with my parents and their neighbors, the Morrises, Dakota decided to play with matches. His first experiment with fire set the Morris's haystack ablaze. The Los Lunas Fire Department answered our call and put out the fire, but not before a considerable amount of hay was consumed. That was the worst trouble Dakota had seen in all his young life.

Our visit with Fred's parents turned out to be exciting too. We went camping at Cienega Lake where Tina collected a coffee can full of baby snakes and frogs, and Dakota fished to his heart's content with Granny and Grandpa by his side. Grandpa also showed us a place in the country where Dakota could shoot guns, a .22 rifle and a pistol, the boy's dream come true.

We left New Mexico to head for the Texas Triangle again. At Beth and Dave's in Austin, Fred and I got to show off our running prowess in a challenging 10-mile race called "Run Your A** Off." Later, when we reached Pat and Dick's place in Conroe, the rest of the LaTurner clan joined us for a family reunion, and the usual hilarious hullabaloo erupted. When we weren't diving and splashing in the pool, we cruised around the neighborhood in Pat and Dick's golf cart.

Before we completely partied ourselves out, it was time to hit the road again and move on to Washington DC for a few days with the big bureaucracy before we took off for Somalia.

PART FIVE
SOMALIA SAFARIS

The Sunshine Family

16

True nomads

October 1982

Mogadishu

When we left Washington on that Tuesday afternoon in October 1982 we expected to spend the next two days in Rome – one day for sleep and one day for sightseeing. But at the end of the seven and a half hour flight from New York to Rome, we learned that our hotel reservations were for the previous night, our airline reservations for Mogadishu had us leaving that very night, and there were no hotel vacancies for even a quick nap. Fred phoned the communicator at the embassy in Rome who offered to let us rest at his house, but the distance to his neighborhood precluded that plan.

My head ached and I strained to think of any alternative to ten hours in the airport. I felt like sitting down on the floor and crying. Before I could fall to pieces, Fred remembered the Satellite Hotel in Ostia, where we had stayed on our way home from Cameroon. He called and reserved the only room they had left. There, we napped, had dinner (our cheeky waiter refused to serve us unless Dakota removed his cap) and got ready to take the hotel bus back to the airport for our 11:00 PM flight. The bus was late and by the time we checked in, the only four seats together were in the smoking section. It was hot, stuffy, and fumy for five and a half hours to Addis Ababa and an additional two hours onward to Mogadishu.

I watched my family close their eyes, one after the other, Tina, then Dakota, and finally Fred. I envied their slumber while I squirmed and shifted in futile search of a comfortable position. My head grew heavy and my neck felt thin and brittle. Every time I fell asleep, my falling head jerked me awake. I fantasized about an airline seat equipped with a velvet band to wrap across my weary forehead and tether me to the headrest of my seatback. With interruptions for take-offs, landings, food service, and loudspeaker announcements about seatbelts, Fred and the kids got about three hours of sleep to my one, and not enough for any of us.

My first view of Somalia from the airplane window had the intensity of an acrylic painting -- deep aquamarine water met brilliant white sand reflecting searing sunlight, the sky neon blue and streaked with feathery clouds. As I stepped out of the plane onto the mobile stairway, I brought my hand up to shield my eyes from the blinding light. Dry, clear air replaced the stagnant airplane smaze, and I inhaled with pleasure. I filled my lungs with freshness, such a relief from the second hand smoke that dominated the last eight hours. The air felt charged with ozone and spiced with the perfumes of frankincense and myrrh.

Fred's co-worker Tim and his wife met us at the gate. They explained that they were not allowed to accompany us into the arrival lounge but would meet us outside afterward. The embassy expeditor Hajji Hussein, dressed in a flowing white robe and crocheted skullcap, stepped forward to guide us. We expected him to flash our diplomatic passports and ease our way past the formalities in the manner to which we had become accustomed.

A gray metal door opened into bedlam. Screaming, gesturing, shoving madmen crammed every square foot of floor space in the gymnasium-sized arena. Fred moved close to Hajji Hussein and got a firm grip on Dakota's hand. With Tina in tow, I stepped up behind Fred and wrapped my fingers around the back of his belt. I kept my head down and avoided making eye contact with anyone, especially the wild sixteen-year-old boy soldiers waving their fully loaded AK-47s and shouting unintelligible commands above the din.

Hajji Hussein pushed, shoved, and shouted his way through the mass of bodies. We trailed behind like the tail of a kite. Our destination appeared to be at the center of a siege by hundreds of raving lunatics. Who were these people and what were they doing in this restricted area?

As we inched our way closer to what I assumed was the customs desk, Hajji Hussein turned and gave us an encouraging smile. If he was happy with our progress, that should be good news, I hoped.

When at last the customs official saw and recognized Hajji Hussein, he beckoned us forward, stamped our passports with a flourish and cleared a path to the luggage area, which seemed like a tranquil oasis of bliss compared to the loony bin behind us. Two other embassy employees waited with our bags in hand, holding open the door to our new reality.

Fred reached out to shake hands with Hajji Hussein. Overcome with gratitude, he pulled the Hajji into a brotherly hug. Hajji Hussein's face portrayed a series of emotions from perplexity to embarrassment to shy pride, and a new friendship was born.

Our sponsors waited beside the embassy van and ushered us inside for the trip from the airport to the city. Dakota and Tina, suffering from mild shell-shock and serious sleep-deprivation, climbed into the back row while the adults shared the seats behind the embassy driver.

Mogadishu demanded sunglasses. White flat-roofed buildings and sandy roads amplified the piercing glare to a painful level. Sun-scorched earth beside the road tolerated scraggly thorn bushes and spiny cactus. Bougainvillea brightened a few buildings with splashes of fuchsia and plum. Leafy bushes that looked like giant milkweed swayed in the breeze and flocks of small carmine birds flickered among the few tall trees. The people on the street walked tall, slim, and handsome, dressed in bright cotton garments – simple dresses for women and wrap skirts for men. When they smiled, I noticed their straight, white teeth, remarkably uniform and perfect.

Traffic moved at the pace of donkey carts, the prevailing vehicle. Miniscule puffs of dust rose from each plodding donkey hoof and wafted away on the breeze. In my dazed state, time slowed down to match the donkeys' cadence.

Dakota and Tina rode silently in the back, watching the passing scenery and looking like they might nod off at any moment. Fred and I squeezed each other's hands as we marveled at each exotic sight in our new environment, only half-listening to our sponsors' steady stream of important information about checking in at the embassy, enrolling the kids in school, getting our drivers' licenses....

I did hear them say that none of our air or sea shipments had arrived yet and that we would go into temporary quarters -- an apartment on the compound they called K-7 because of its distance in kilometers from the city's center. The K-7 compound also included the embassy swimming pool and Marine House and lay within walking distance of the school, golf and tennis club, and jogging track.

After I started paying attention, I learned that Fred's office had a small Honda truck to provide transportation for the duty person. And we both heard the terrible news about how difficult/expensive it was going to be to get a battery for our Toyota (shipped without a battery per shipping regulations).

I'm sure Fred was as glad as I was to know that he didn't have to report for work until Saturday, which gave us two full days to complete the check-in process and try to overcome jet lag. Our arrival coincided with the weekend because both the embassy and the American school followed a Saturday through Wednesday schedule, honoring Friday as the Muslim holy day, as was true in Iran, our earlier assignment in a Muslim country.

Jet lag proved to be our most difficult hurdle. The first night, we all woke at midnight when the electric power went off, and we were still awake when the power came back on at seven. We tried not to take naps during the day, hoping that would make us tired enough to sleep through the night. It took a full week for us to recover from the zombie state and get all four bodies on local time after flying through seven time zones.

After that first sleepless week passed into hazy oblivion, we started to build our routines. Dakota and Tina joined their classes, fourth grade and third grade, the year already six weeks along, and both seemed pleased with their teachers and classmates. Fred declared his objective to learn everything about the operation of his office and the workings of the embassy in the shortest possible time. This was his first assignment as boss of the section, so he felt doubly eager to get on top of it. I created my own regimen: up at 5:00 AM for a 30-minute run, get the kids to school by 7:20, do a little yoga and meditation, swim a quarter mile at the pool, take care of some cooking or baking or letter-writing, pick up the kids at 1:00, and spend the rest of the day at the pool with Tina and Dakota and their friends.

During our check in visit to the medical unit, we met the embassy nurse practitioner, Betty Labastida, a convivial sporty-looking woman who told us about a local running group, the Mogadishu Hash, named after the famous Hash House Harriers running and social club. She described the original club, started by six British colonial officers in Kuala Lumpur in 1938, as a drinking club with a running problem. Betty said that the popularity of Hash clubs spread with the running boom in the late 1970s when Hash chapters sprang up on all seven continents.

We accepted Betty's invitation to join her at the next Hash meeting. The Mogadishu bunch included crazy runners from almost every country in the world who met every Sunday afternoon at a different location in the outskirts of Mogadishu for a cross-country run. The organizers encouraged participation by all family members, but Dakota and Tina found it rough going in the loose sand, among thorn bushes, in the heat.

The Hash House Harriers might be proof of the lengths people will go to amuse themselves in a place where there isn't much to do. The

Hash initiation required drinking a large mug of beer (coke for the kids) while the group sang a song. What remained in the mug at the end of the song had to be poured over the initiate's head. Notable Americans in this club were the Ambassador and his wife and the embassy nurse. The Ambassador's wife had to pour a whole beer over her head in punishment for her recommendation that tea should be the post-run drink.

Fred and I enjoyed celebrity status in the Hash, because of our natural charm, I'm sure, but also due to the grapevine intelligence (nurse Betty might have spread the news) that we had shipped twenty-four cases of Australia's best Fosters Beer in our household effects.

In a more orthodox effort to entertain, the Administrative Officer, Fred's immediate supervisor, took us out to dinner at one of the few restaurants in town. Located on a rooftop, the open-air eatery provided a buffet that included roast beef, chicken, rice, okra, eggplant, lasagna, potatoes, fish, and several different casseroles.

Flickering kerosene lanterns added dancing shadows to the intriguing atmosphere. As we filled our plates I wondered what unusual ingredients might have gone into the casserole dishes. Several spicy fragrances wafted about, but I couldn't identify any of them.

I took my first bite from the selection that looked like scrambled eggs.

"Mmmmm. Try these eggs – so tasty. And the texture is creamy as silk."

Fred glanced at my plate and smiled before he lifted a forkful of his own portion to his mouth. He smacked his lips in exaggerated satisfaction.

"I guess you've never eaten scrambled brains before." He chuckled when he saw the expression on my face.

Dakota and Tina laughed too, but I noticed that they pushed their small piles of "scramble" to the far sides of their plates.

Other social events introduced us to the rest of the embassy community, and as I got to know the embassy wives, I realized that almost all of them worked. In the absence of well-trained clerical workers in the local population, the embassy needed the wives to fill in as secretaries, receptionists, typists and file clerks in every office. Morale did seem high for a hardship post – maybe because everybody was gainfully employed rather than sitting bored at home. I felt glad that I didn't need a job to keep me happy.

One of the few unemployed wives took me to the handicraft stalls downtown. Narrow sandy streets meandered among dilapidated buildings that housed the vendors and their wares. I admired the baskets, wood-carvings, leather sandals, carvings in ivory and meerschaum, and many varieties of seashells. The sandals fit my long, narrow feet and cost about $8.00. I bought two hand-woven shopping baskets, one large and one medium, for a little over $4. My companion did the bargaining – I knew the prices would rise when I did the haggling; I had proved my lack of talent years before in Iran and Cameroon.

After our handicraft shopping, we stopped at the embassy annex where the commissary was located. To my shock and surprise, the embassy commissary consisted of one tall metal cabinet containing a five-pound can of US Army cake mix, three bars of Dial soap, and a forlorn roll of multi-flavored Lifesavers. My companion told me that a real commissary would be built and stocked within six months. Now I understood why the embassy had authorized a 5,000-pound shipment of consumables for each family.

Our consumables shipment, still on its way, included detergents, cleaning products, paper products, toiletries, canned goods, fifty pounds of brown rice, breakfast cereals, condiments, staples like sugar and flour and cooking oil, boxed foods like macaroni and cheese, and the infamous twenty-four cases of beer. Certain automotive supplies like motor oil, air filters, and oil filters were on the list provided by the State Department. We stocked up on everything we could think of and made our best guess about the quantity we would need for our two-year assignment. The decision-making process caused laughter at the absurdities and tears over the impossibilities. I did my best. In the end we didn't run out of anything essential, but four years after leaving Somalia we still hadn't used the last of the aluminum foil stash.

Local markets sold fresh fruits and vegetables, but not up to the standards of New Zealand or Cameroon. A Hash friend introduced us to an Italian woman who had a market garden and we filled our baskets with her produce once a week. She grew purple onions, bell peppers, tomatoes, eggplant, and a lot of Swiss chard. We ate Swiss chard daily until we all agreed it would be nice to never see it again.

Some food items came to us via door-to-door sales. I bought eggs that way – even though ten per cent were candidates for an incubator. I couldn't find a more reliable source so I continued to break eggs into a saucer to verify the contents before cooking them. Fred had more success with his purchases from the traveling lobsterman. He traded beer for seafood at the rate of one six-pack for a gunnysack full of live lobster. We ate lobster until we lost the taste for it also.

Somalia's dryness affected everything from food crops to water shortages to lifestyle. Somalia was so dry that it only rained once a week during the rainy season. It was no surprise that almost every species of vegetation bore thorns. Somali nomads must be the toughest people in the world to survive in the most desolate and unforgiving land. To us, it was exotic and starkly beautiful, but we didn't have to struggle for survival.

One Friday night we went to the Golf Club for dinner and watched the rain pour down faster than the sandy soil could absorb it. On the way home we found that rivers flowed in the streets. Fred's office car, the tiny Honda "bread truck," made it through the puddles on our regular homeward route, but muddy water came splooshing in around the doors and wet us to the knees. By next morning, the water had drained away leaving a green tint to the desert where new plants and grasses sprouted after lying dormant for many months. On my run that morning I marveled at the sight of a lone white lily blooming in the center of the jogging path.

After the delivery of our New Zealand airfreight, I started to feel more at home. As I reunited with my own pots and pans, sharp knives, and extra towels after a five-month separation, I had the urge to nest in earnest. I returned the welcome kit borrowed from the embassy warehouse, and anticipated the arrival of the rest of our shipments.

Even though we had been in temporary quarters less than two months, we anxiously awaited our housing assignment too. The embassy's list of available leases included a house that Fred and I agreed was perfect for us, but we had to wait for housing board approval. The house we liked was a new house, so there would be a delay of about three weeks while cabinets were built, air conditioners installed, screens put in, and generator hooked up. That allowed more time for our household effects and car to arrive before our move off the compound.

I was happy with the location of the house -- only about a quarter mile further from the school than K-7 -- but location was a much-discussed topic in the embassy community: whether to be near the school and pool or be near the embassy or be in the section of town that enjoyed the most reliable electricity. Of course it would be best for the kids to be near their friends, but naturally Dakota's best friend and Tina's best friend lived on opposite sides of town. I crossed my fingers in hopes of a timely and favorable housing assignment.

The American school principal, Ron Hubbard, and the vice-principal, Paul Olson, knocked at our apartment door one Saturday morning. The grapevine had told them about my jobless state, and they came to recruit me. I reluctantly agreed to help them out for a few weeks as substitute PE teacher, supervising the swimming program for the whole school as well as a cross-country running unit for each grade. The running classes were easy for me, but I felt out of my depth when it came to swimming instruction. I was glad that the term was ending at that time with races. All I had to do was click the stopwatch, blow my whistle, and make sure nobody drowned.

Home and Away

The housing board approved the new house for us rather than either of the other two new families on the waiting list, and we moved in and were almost unpacked by the beginning of December. The simple cement block three-bedroom house had a wonderful surprise for us, an interior stairway to the roof. We hauled our patio furniture up there and spent many an evening overlooking a buff-colored panorama of one-story flat roofs stretching to the cobalt blue Indian Ocean. Frosty Fosters in hand, Fred and I listened to the menuin's call to prayer echoing behind the shush of feathers as a flock of sacred ibis flew overhead toward the setting sun. We admired the red flag waving over the Turkish Embassy down the block and watched our children drawing chalk pictures on the ochre side of our rooftop water tank.

The large water tank on the roof was designed to collect water delivered by sporadic trickle from the municipal source. Theoretically, enough water would accumulate during the night to meet our needs during the day. The theory did not prove itself in practice; indeed, we ran out of water almost every day. And I couldn't say anything nice about the inability of a gravity-flow shower to rinse shampoo suds from my waist-length hair. After we complained about lack of water for a few months, GSO (embassy general services office) installed a huge fiberglass tank on the ground with a strong electric pump for water pressure, and an embassy truck filled the tank once a week. The main flaw in the new system was its dependence on electricity – in a power outage we had no water unless we cranked up the ear-splitting and neighbor-annoying emergency generator.

Even though I worked full time at the school, I still found time to run every day. I preferred the jogging path around the golf course to running beside the public roadway. Our new friend Betty the embassy nurse and several of the Marines had built the track by hand, grubbing out cactus and acacias with ordinary gardening tools. The path followed the perimeter of the nine-hole sand-green short course and made a loop around the yet-to-be-developed site of the proposed new embassy. Bulldozers had begun preparing the building site and in the process had created a series of high dirt mounds like sand dunes. I ran a weaving route through these dunes to add a quarter mile or so to the 1.75 of the "official" track.

More often than not, I had to stop at least once to pull a thorn out of my shoe. The thorns were long enough to penetrate the sole of a running shoe, go through the sock and make a bloody mess of my foot. One day in the middle of the dunes, as I straightened up after retying my shoe, I saw that I had company. A pack of scrawny feral dogs stood on the rim of the nearest sand pile, staring at me and growling. I turned to resume my run and looked over my shoulder. The dogs advanced. As I picked up speed, they ran faster. I stopped and faced them. They stopped. I tried backing up in baby steps. They crouched and crept toward me, snarling. I grabbed dirt clods and rocks and threw them as fast as I could, screaming like a banshee and lunging toward the dogs. They turned and ran behind the dune.

I walked backwards the rest of the way to the main road, quaking in my trainers and gasping for oxygen to slow my pounding heart. After calming down, I wrote a letter of complaint to GSO. A few weeks later, the Somali police came to get rid of the dogs. First they poisoned the animals, watched them die, and then shot them. Why was I shocked? I didn't expect them to round up the dogs and find homes for them, did I? No, but did they have to double kill them?

Hunter and Homebody

Wild dogs weren't the only predators in Mogadishu. Somalia brought out the hunter in Dakota too. He and his best friend Brian Kellums hunted with slingshots, bows and arrows, and BB guns. They roamed the same undeveloped area where I had encountered those wild dogs. Brian's dad, Bud, was a long-time hunter and fisherman from Arizona, who believed that every boy should learn these manly arts. Brian, two years older than our boy, shared his knowledge with Dakota, who, thanks to his own dad and his grandpa, was not a complete stranger to guns and fishing gear.

Dakota and Brian often brought home their favorite game, dove. Bud taught them how to clean the birds, wrap the breasts (the only part meaty enough to eat) in bacon and charcoal broil them. At the tender ages of nine and eleven, these two hunters developed impressive cooking skills as well.

While Dakota stalked his prey, Tina stayed home, either at our house or at her best friend Kimberley Fuller's place. The girls played school, house, dress-up, and Barbies, on the veranda or on the roof. The kids amused themselves and no one ever complained of boredom. They didn't have TV programs or video games but relied on their own imagination to create entertainment. No one had to worry about rainy day activities – not enough rain to cramp their style.

Dakota and Tina had other friends as well, but Brian and Kimberley were the closest, almost constant, companions. Our families did things together too, like movie nights. The Marines hosted outdoor movies at K-7, and we did have VCRs at home – some of them in the old Beta Max format -- and we traded new videos with other families. We also took day trips to the beach together, and longer trips to explore the reachable parts of Somalia.

17

Transport to adventure

November 1982 – January 1983

Hunting for Hippos

As our short parade of Land Cruisers rolled down the road, the navigator in each vehicle watched for the Kilometer 25 turnoff, a sandy jeep track leading to the Shabelle River, where we hoped to view and photograph a pod of hippopotamuses. In 1982 Somalia had no national game reserves like the famous destinations in Kenya, and wild animals roamed free, protected by the remoteness of their habitat. A colleague at the American Embassy had seen hippos the week before and he gave us directions to the exact spot on the river.

Our caravan included four families in four vehicles: the American school vice-principal and science teacher Paul Olson and his wife Margie who taught second grade; Buddy Kellums, a project manager with USAID (Agency for International Development), and his wife Patti and their children Brian and Heather; Flynn Fuller, also a project manager with AID, and his wife Jo Ellen, first grade teacher, and their daughters Kimberley and Alicia; and us, the LaTurners.

"Look. Mom. Dad. There are those red and blue birds again." Tina's high, clear voice carried in spite of the roaring wind and the rumbling engine of our roofless Land Cruiser.

"What are they called? Oh, lookit! They're swooping right down on the Fullers' truck." Tina bounced up and down as far as her lap belt would allow.

"Carmine Bee-Eaters," Fred answered. "Those iridescent blue heads and brilliant red throats and breasts, wow!"

"But why are they dive-bombing the vehicles?" Dakota asked.

"They feed as they fly," I joined in, "and they're catching insects disturbed by the traffic. The way they follow along, it's like we have our own flashy escort."

"Hang on, everybody," Fred warned, "I have to pull over now. Looks like a military checkpoint."

"Oh great," Tina and Dakota moaned in unison. "We'll never get to the river."

Delays at checkpoints could be short, long, or end the trip altogether, depending on the mood of the guards, or so it seemed to us. An almost endless list of troubles threatened to tear this country apart and the tension at checkpoints made everyone nervous. The armed guards were boys, probably right out of the bush. I wished they had no ammunition for their automatic weapons, but I knew better. We had heard reports of guards shooting each other in cross fire during altercations at other checkpoints. But the situation sounded much more dangerous in the telling than it seemed in the moment. In our experience, safe travel in Somalia required more patience and endurance than courage or bravery.

"All right. We're on our way. That wasn't so bad, was it?" Fred's cheerful outlook returned as soon as the checkpoint was behind us after a mere twenty-minute wait. Our caravan accelerated to cruising speed and we settled back in our seats to enjoy the scenery.

A huge marabou stork held court beside the road jabbing its long cleaver-like bill into the bloated carcass of a hyena. A magnificent creature, the stork, ugly at first glance with its balding, scabby magenta head, fringed with wispy hair-like feathers, and its pendulous pink neck sac; but beautiful in its efficient dedication to cleaning up carrion. I wondered if the ladies of the late nineteenth century realized that the pure white fluffy feathers on their fancy hats came from such a scruffy scavenger.

We stopped to get a closer look. It was a brief stop, partly because the stench brought tears to our eyes and mainly because the stork spread its 10-foot wings and flew away, leaving just the stinky, rotting corpse to examine. Dakota and Brian tormented Tina, Kimberley, Alicia and Heather by threatening to add a few ripe hyena morsels to our picnic basket. The girls' reaction spurred them on, of course. Fred enhanced the macabre mood when he described how the marabou storks pooped on their own legs and feet to protect them from carrion bacteria. The girls started shrieking and the moms decided it was time to hasten our retreat to the Toyotas and get on our way again.

The Kilometer 25 sign was missing, but Dakota's sharp eyes spotted the jeep track. Past the turn, the primitive road wound among trees about two miles to the place Fred's colleague had mapped for us. As our trucks slithered along in the deep sand I remarked on the lush growth of vegetation. Trees and bushes crowded the track and branches scraped a shrill screech along the sides of our vehicles. Rounding a long curve we saw our destination – a clearing among the trees, the perfect place to park and picnic.

While Jo Ellen, Flynn and I brought out the coolers and unfurled our picnic blankets, the rest of the group went off on various missions. Fred and Margie bushwhacked toward the river, hoping to locate the hippos and find a satisfactory observation post. Hippos are dangerous, unpredictable animals. So are their neighbors, the crocodiles. Because our group of children ranged in age from five to eleven years, we needed to take extra safety precautions. Like the animals, kids can be unpredictable at times.

Buddy, a skilled hunter and fisherman, led Dakota and Brian through the trees searching for the fishing pond marked on our hand-drawn map. Patti and Paul organized the girls into a wood-gathering party, as we planned to build a fire to roast hotdogs and later flame up a few marshmallows for S'mores. This rare treat of typical American picnic food came from a U.S. aircraft carrier. When the carrier visited Mogadishu recently, the captain invited embassy families for a tour of the ship and shopping in the ship's store. Without the ship visit, we might have depended on the boys' fishing or settled for PBJ sandwiches.

Fred and Margie's laughter echoed across the clearing before they broke through the underbrush.

"What's so funny?" Jo Ellen and I walked toward them, eager to share the fun.

They were laughing in hysterical fits, neither one could get out more than a word or two at a time.

Fred managed a complete sentence, "Can anyone spare a shirt?" He looked back at Margie and laughter overcame them again.

"What!" Jo Ellen moved closer to Fred, reached out to grab his sleeve, and recoiled. "What happened? Eeeuuw!"

"Oh, God." Margie got a grip on her giggles. "We were searching for the hippos and got startled by a noise in the trees overhead. I looked up and saw a cute little monkey. He chattered at us and dropped some leaves down on our heads. Then he let something else loose. That's monkey poop on Fred's shirt."

Obviously that monkey had plenty of fiber in his diet. A greenish-brown mess covered Fred's shoulder. No one had a shirt to spare, so Fred went topless the rest of the day. He rinsed his shirt in the river but couldn't get rid of the pungent stink.

When we stopped laughing about the monkey incident, Fred reported that he and Margie had not seen any hippos or crocodiles on their scouting expedition. Our map proved we had found the right place, but the hippos must have moved on.

"Hey, Mom." On their way back from the fishing pond, Dakota and

Brian paused by the group of girls. "Seriously, Mom, you need to come over here and see what the girls are doing. Totally gnarly."

The girls were playing near a hollow log on the opposite side of the clearing. I hurried over to see what was going on. All four of them held out their arms to show off their bracelets. Gnarly indeed, those bracelets were tightly coiled giant African millipedes - live giant African millipedes.

"Don't worry, Mrs. LaTurner," Heather, the oldest, spoke up. "Mr. Olson told us all about these millipedes and showed us how to poke them so they'd roll up. He said not to be afraid because they are harmless herbivores. It was my idea to pretend they were bracelets."

"Heather, that is very creative," I said. Or very creepy, I thought. "Allrighty then. How about setting your bracelets free now. It's time for lunch."

Tina grabbed my hand as we walked along. She whispered, "Mom, I have to pee."

"Me too. Let's go behind those bushes."

We had learned about the benefits of wearing a skirt as the Muslim women did for modesty. A skirt also provided more privacy for impromptu pit stops. We found a clear spot in the thicket. Together we lifted skirts, lowered panties, squatted, pulled panties out of the line of fire, and tinkled. As we finished and began readjusting our clothes, I heard Fred calling our names. A sudden eruption of wild cacophony answered his shouts.

Crashing and thrashing and hooting and barking drowned out Fred's voice. I looked at Tina. Tina looked at me. We both looked for Fred.

Fred stood still as a statue. An agitated baboon faced him, pounding his chest, barking and yakking. Long sharp fangs glistened in his wide red mouth. He lunged at Fred in short bursts, threatening again and again. Louder and louder he shrieked and hooted. Tina closed her eyes and covered her ears. I wrapped my arms around her. Fred stood his ground.

The baboon flashed his eyelids at machinegun speed and yawned wide to show his teeth. Fred squared his shoulders and straightened up as tall as a superhero. Baboon and Man locked eyes in a stare down.

I held my breath. The long minute stretched taut until the baboon broke his gaze and pierced the silence with one last loud yak. He leaped sideways and crashed away through the bushes.

Fred ran to us and we dragged each other, trip-stumble-run, to the picnic site, looking behind, feeling baboon eyes on our backs. When we felt safe again among our friends at the picnic area, we tried to figure out what had happened. I thought the baboon objected to us outsiders making "marks" on his territory. Tina believed the baboon saw us as predators and was trying to scare us off. Fred decided the baboon had fallen in love and wanted Tina and me for his harem.

After lunch the group sat around the fire, roasted marshmallows, and reflected on the day. Each one in turn described a favorite experience. Tina was the last to speak. With the wisdom of an eight-year-old she said, "Well, I guess you never know what might happen when you go hunting for hippos."

Tales In and Out of School

When my stint as PE substitute ended, I applied to fill an unexpected vacancy in the school library, left by a British woman whose husband was being transferred out of Somalia in January. The position involved management of the school's library and audiovisual studio. Because of my degree in psychology and six years experience as a social caseworker (before Fred and I married), the School Board added counselor to my title and designated one day a week for that part of my job. My workday lasted one hour longer than the school day, and Dakota and Tina either stayed with me in the library or played with friends on the playground before we all went home together.

The American School Mogadishu (ASM), grades kindergarten through eighth, received support from an annual grant from the U.S. State Department. ASM recruited a set number of teaching couples from the States and provided them transportation and housing. The U.S.-hires while we were there included the principal and his wife (kindergarten teacher), the vice-principal and his wife (second grade teacher), and another couple who taught fourth and fifth grade. The rest

of the staff came from the local ex-pat community, most of them spous-
es of various international agency employees. The student body boasted
United Nations-style diversity with pupils from Finland, Norway, The
Netherlands, Germany, England, Ghana, Nigeria, Sweden, Pakistan,
India, Turkey, Australia, and New Zealand. Instruction followed an
American curriculum and accreditation came from the U.S. Middle
Atlantic States authority.

As librarian/counselor, I had the best job in the whole school, in the
whole world maybe, for me at that time in my life. Four days a week I
reigned in the library. Each class, kindergarten through eighth grade,
came to the library for an hour a week for story time and to check out
books. Individual students could also come at other times at their teacher's discretion, to do research. Everybody wanted to come to the library
at lunch break, to enjoy the air-conditioning as much as the intellectual
ambiance.

None of the classrooms had air-conditioning, nor did the original
audio-visual space, which was a large closet with no windows. The door
closed off more than light, it also shut out the air-conditioning from the
main library unit and any chance of air circulation. The addition of twelve
or fifteen little bodies as a heat source created a sauna. My own body
odor drove me to the principal's office to beg for a bigger AV room. Mr.
Hubbard offered a magnificent alternative. He cleared out a large storage
room and installed an air-conditioning unit. From then on, all AV presen-
tations took place in the splendid official AV studio.

My job description included "repair and maintenance of AV equipment." I learned to handle the basic maintenance part, but 'repair' sounded
like a synonym for 'replace' to me. Our library could afford good books
and good equipment, thanks to the School Board. The library's healthy
budget got an additional vote when the Ambassador appointed Fred to act
as his representative on the board.

The rest of my job description required me to wear the hat of counselor one day a week. The vice-principal sent me a customer once in a
while for a short intervention. I administered a few tests to screen for

learning disabilities. And I led teacher in-service seminars on subjects like classroom discipline, handling disruptions in the classroom, and dealing with bullying.

I loved my little kingdom, the books, and the children, and even the schizophrenic slide projector. I started dreaming about going back to college for a Library Science degree and pursuing a career after the kids entered high school.

Every day at school I saw my own kids' teachers. The teachers praised both Dakota's and Tina's behavior in the classroom and remarked on their ability to catch up after arriving six weeks past the start of the school year. It eased my mind to know that they had the resilience to handle the periodic moves from school to school.

"I have to tell you what Dakota said in class today." Dakota's teacher caught me on the way out of the library. "You know he brought an egg for 'Show and Tell,' right?"

I nodded. That morning I had made scrambled eggs for breakfast. My Home Ec teacher in junior high taught us to break each egg into a saucer first, and Somalia showed me why. The first egg I cracked had a well-developed embryo inside that looked ready to form feathers. That's the egg that Dakota took for science class.

"Well, when his turn came, he got up in front of the class and announced that he had 'chicken genitals' to show. I didn't want to embarrass him, but I almost died trying not to laugh!"

As entertaining as school days could be, I still looked forward to the weekends and our many trips to Shark's Bay. To get there we had to four-wheel drive across the sand dunes on an unmarked, memorized route. Shark's Bay got its name from a large rock formation in the shape of a gigantic shark dorsal fin. To the best of our knowledge, no sharks prowled that beach, although shark attacks were known to occur ten miles away, within the port of Mogadishu.

I learned to body surf at Shark's Bay. The surf wasn't rough, but I wasn't very skillful either. One day, a big wave caught me and drove me to the bottom. Churning water spun me around on the top of my head before

SOMALIA SAFARIS ❧ 203

dropping me on shore like a dead flounder. My hair, which normally hung straight as mop strings to the middle of my back, now tangled worse than Medusa's. When I got home I had to shampoo and rinse a dozen times to get the sand out.

That's when I decided to make an emergency visit to my friend Peggy who had set up a small salon operation in her kitchen. I told her to cut my hair short-short-short and give me a curly-curly-curly perm. I wanted a wash-and-wear hairdo that could defy the perils of body surfing. I got it. But no one in my family could muster up a single compliment for my new hairdo. Dakota cried.

The next morning I met Paul Olson, the vice-principal, on my way to the library from the parking lot.

"Good morning, Ma'am, can I help you?"

None of the teachers recognized me. The children treated me like a substitute. At first it was funny, but as the day wore on I felt a sense of alienation, as if my identity had been stolen and I no longer belonged in my own skin.

Rescue Somali Style

By the end of the week, everybody recognized the new me, and I was eager for a chance to test my hairstyle's seaworthiness. The four of us packed our beach gear and a picnic and got an early start for the beach.

We couldn't have made it to Shark's Bay without the four-wheel drive power of our Toyota Land Cruiser, a used vehicle that we had shipped from our recent home in New Zealand. This model had the short wheelbase and came with custom sheepskin seat covers, chrome wheels, and a removable roof. The Somalis revered the "Lancrooz," and followed our passing with admiring looks.

For several weeks before my haircut, our sturdy Toyota hadn't been running well; the engine had developed a tendency to die at inopportune moments. This time we got half way to Shark's Bay, when, straining to reach the top of a high dune, the engine sputtered and died. Fred coaxed it back to life, but the tires spun a deep hollow in the sand instead of moving us forward. Fred tried a rocking maneuver, forward and back and forward again. The tires dug deeper.

Before I could get seriously worried about our predicament, a lone Somali strode over the top of the dune, equipped with typical Somali gear – a staff and a gourd slung from a shoulder strap – and wearing the traditional cotton wrap skirt and rubber flip-flops. Our visitor indicated that we must help him gather as many rocks and sticks as we could. He showed us how to pile our materials under and around the tires. Finally, with the traction thus supplied, Fred could get the truck unstuck. We offered food and drink to our benefactor, but he wanted nothing more than a few sips of water from the canvas evaporative cooling bag hung on the front of the radiator. Our desert angel left without ceremony and his mirage-like figure disappeared from view among the rolling dunes as if he had never been there at all.

Somali National Character

Naturally, we met far more urban Somalis than nomadic people. We made friends with several Somalis who were employees of the embassy: Fatuma, who operated the snack bar at K-7; Hassan Fido, who was the embassy receptionist and telephone operator; and Hajji Hussein, who guided embassy personnel through the labyrinth of Somali government red tape; all played important roles in our life in Mogadishu.

Fatuma invited us to her home, deep in the maze of Mogadishu's working class sector, humble by any standards, with dirt floor and few comforts. She laid out a feast fit for royalty. She proclaimed our presence an honor, but I wondered if she had decimated her food budget. I knew it could be easy to unwittingly offend Fatuma's relatives who hadn't had as much contact with foreigners, so I went the extra distance and drank raw camels' milk. Its sweetness surprised me. I think they added sugar to cut the overwhelming taste of charcoal -- someone told me that a blazing torch was plunged into the milk in an attempt to pasteurize it. Somalis praised camels' milk as nature's best food and an aid to digestion. One cup gave my system a complete purging, both ends at once, and convinced me that politeness can be hazardous.

Fatuma also brought us her niece, Hawa, when I mentioned that I needed housekeeping help. Hawa, young, inexperienced and shy, swept and mopped and dusted as unobtrusively as the shadow of a genie. I delegated the simple tasks to her while I took charge of the technical jobs like cooking, laundry, and boiling/filtering our drinking water.

Fred supervised Hassan Fido at the embassy. Among his other responsibilities as head of the communications section, Fred managed the telephone system and Hassan Fido carried out the duties of telephone operator and receptionist. Hassan Fido told us about the great oral tradition that carried Somali history forward by word of mouth before their language was first written in the twentieth century. He described the traditional nomadic life and the stigma that sometimes attached to doing work for someone else rather than owning one's own herd of camels, goats, or cows. And it was Hassan Fido who introduced Fred to the chewing of khat leaves, a mild alkaloid-based stimulant and appetite suppressant popular among the poor. Fred said the bitter taste wasn't worth the brief effect, in his opinion.

Hajji Hussein, our other Somali friend, had earned the honorific "Hajjii" by completing a pilgrimage to Mecca several years before. We first met Hajji Hussein in his role as embassy expeditor the day of our arrival in Mogadishu. He helped us time after time throughout our tour, especially when we had to deal with the tangle of Somali bureaucracy. He wielded his magic to acquire our identity cards, driver's licenses, and the permit to allow us to take photos. He translated for us whenever we called on him, and he interpreted the Somali way of life often in stories and anecdotes.

Tina and I learned about one unpleasant Somali habit by direct experience. We were jogging round the Golf Club when a flying rock hit Tina on her arm hard enough to break the skin. I saw a bunch of Somali boys on the other side of the fence. They let loose another volley and we ran faster, dodging the incoming stones. After that I paid more attention to the street kids, and I noticed that they threw rocks at each other all the time.

Run, Fred, Run

On another occasion, Fred also got stoned while running. He chased the perpetrators. One boy fell down and started screaming (in Somali), "Don't kill me, don't kill me!" Fred said he made menacing noises and gestures to scare the kid, at the same time helping him to his feet. A Somali man on the scene who had witnessed the whole episode came over and spoke to Fred in perfect English.

"I am this sorry boy's teacher. I will take him to his father for punishment. He will be beaten, I assure you."

The opposite side of Somali character showed up one day when Fred was running beside the road and passed a Somali man walking in the same direction. As soon as he saw Fred, the man hiked up his skirt and ran along for a couple of miles, keeping up with Fred's fast pace in spite of the flip-flops on his feet, and the cigarette hanging from his grinning lips.

And then there was the time when a donkey cart driver pulled up beside Fred and challenged him to a race. The man claimed that his was the fastest racing donkey in the village. First Fred surged ahead, then the donkey cart. They upped the pace in turns until they reached a full sprint (Fred) and gallop (donkey). Before reaching the point of collapse, they both backed off a bit and agreed to declare a tie. As the donkey cart turned onto a side road, the driver lifted his hand in a comradely wave and beamed a brilliant smile that made Fred feel that he'd won a friend if not the race.

18

Thinking of Mom and home

February 1983

Motherless Child

When Fred was on call, he had to respond at any hour to receive and distribute urgent cables from Washington. The cables might concern government business, but too often the middle-of-the-night call-ins related to notices of family emergencies for Americans employed by any of the many agencies working in Somalia. When a message was tagged "needs immediate action," an automated system triggered an alarm that alerted the Marines to contact the duty communicator. Roused from sleep by a radio call from Marine Post 1, Fred often wondered who had died that night.

He received one of those calls on February 14, 1983. I went back to sleep as soon as he left. Or I thought I slept. I dreamed that I saw my mother standing in the doorway, backlit by the nightlight in the hall. Or I thought I dreamed.

Two hours later, Fred laid his hand on my shoulder with gentle pressure. "I don't know how to tell you…the telegram…your mom passed away."

"I knew it…." My mind's eye held the image of my mother standing in my bedroom doorway, surrounded by a halo of pale yellow light.

Nothing had prepared me for the shock of my mother's sudden death. She hadn't been well, but her illness wasn't supposed to be fatal. She had tried many different kinds of treatments over the years, medical, homeopathic, herbal, you name it, but periodic bloodletting seemed to be the only one that helped. Her malady was polycythemia -- too many red cells in her blood. The hematologist told her that she could expect to live another twenty years if she continued with regular phlebotomies. Typical of mom's way in the world, she didn't discuss her sickness with me or talk about the treatment or how she felt about it. Because everything seemed to be under control, I didn't worry.

Dad told me later that Mom had had a good report from the doctor on Friday and she seemed happy and hopeful for the first time in years. On Sunday morning he slept longer than usual and nudged Mom to tell her they were going to be late for church. Her body was already cold.

At forty-two, I was not ready to be a motherless child. Fred said that I handled the loss of my mother courageously, but I didn't feel brave inside. My relationship with my mom had some gaping holes. Holes that I could no longer hope to fill.

My brother and my father's three sisters flew to Los Lunas right away from Minnesota and Florida. Dad begged me not to come. A winter storm had socked in the whole eastern seaboard and he worried that I would be stranded or worse. I agreed. I didn't feel capable of making the trip. I wanted to hunker down with my husband and children and pull the covers up over all our heads. Wise decision, I think, looking back, even though I had to grieve all over again when we went home for R&R that summer. Thank God Dad had the loving support of family and church; I struggled alone to come to terms with my own issues.

Of course I expected to be sad. I didn't expect to be overcome with paroxysms so fierce they turned my body and my spirit into one wrenching spasm. I remembered the overpowering contractions of childbirth as I suffered the agony of motherdeath. But there was no gain in this pain, only loss. Grief overwhelmed me at odd moments, once in the middle of a ladies' luncheon at the home of the DCM. One second I was talking about the batch of new educational video tapes donated to the school library, and the next second I was sobbing into my napkin. There was no logic in it. Waves of sadness ebbed and flowed in a tide that bore no relationship to my conscious thoughts.

When I thought about my mother, I regretted never telling her that I understood why mothering was a difficult role for her. She had been traumatized at the age of two when a stroke killed her mother. Her only memory of that time was the painful one of being held over the coffin in the parlor and forced to kiss those cold, hard lips. From age two to eleven, she lived in an emotional limbo with her withdrawn father and stoic German maternal grandmother. When she was eleven, her father hired a housekeeper, a "widow" with a one-year-old daughter. Within a year, the housekeeper became Mom's stepmother and Mom lived her adolescence like Cinderella, chastised for leaving dust on light bulbs or forgetting to take the washing down from the clothesline.

I wished I had encouraged my mother to seek help for her depression. As a child I felt responsible for her moodiness, but try as I might, nothing I did made her happy. My childhood, indeed my whole life, was dedicated to being good, to pleasing my mother and taking responsibility for the happiness of everyone around me. I tried to be perfect, as if that could cure all ills. The burden of guilt warped my childhood, fueled my decision to study psychology, and spurred me into therapy in my college years. But I never discussed depression with my mother.

If we had ever had a heart-to-heart, I would have told Mom that I loved her. And I would have praised her intelligence and her accomplishments in business, art, and music. But Mom was gone and I could only mourn her passing and the lost chances to mend our tattered relationship.

I tried running as an antidote, but when a breaker of grief rolled over me during a run, I stopped breathing. Aerobic exercise plus crying equaled a frightening combination as debilitating as an asthma attack.

Mom's appearance in my dreams would have comforted me, but I slept without dreaming. Every morning when I woke into the between time, I felt fine until wakefulness prevailed and reopened an unfathomable void in my chest. I got up and walked my walk and talked my talk, but I was not entirely present in my life. It took me many months to learn that the one real relief for grief is time.

19

Fred and Nancy comb the beach at Shark's Bay

March – September 1983

Beware of Sharks

Grief sapped my energy and I caught every bug that came near. Dakota also suffered a rapid series of colds, one after another, with no time to recover between bouts. The cold symptoms triggered asthma attacks and he had to keep an inhaler close at hand. The last cold settled deep in his lungs.

Nurse Betty's brow furrowed as she concentrated on the sounds coming through her stethoscope. "Hmmm. Pneumonia. Let's get this young man started on antibiotics."

Anxiety squeezed my chest like an anaconda. Would the antibiotic be

212 of VOLUNTARY NOMADS

strong enough or would Dakota need to be flown to a hospital in Nairobi? I drew Betty aside to ask my worried questions. She reassured me and promised that Dakota would feel better in forty-eight hours. I believed Betty's prognosis, but I couldn't sleep. I had to listen to Dakota's every breath. I could hear a difference within twenty-four hours. The antibiotic worked.

After the pneumonia cleared up and the asthma symptoms went away, a painful earache still lingered, and Betty prescribed drops twice daily. Dakota had to lie on his side for half an hour to let the drops penetrate and coat the affected area. I made a cozy place on the couch and brought him some books and magazines. He asked for his trophy shark jaw, recently purchased at the craft market, and I put it on the coffee table where he could see it.

I was in the kitchen making lunch when I heard a sharp cry of pain from the living room. I ran through the dining room and found Dakota beside the couch, hopping on one foot. Blood dripped from his other foot.

"Oh, lord...."

"Sorry, Mom, I needed to pee but when I got up I forgot that I put the shark jaw on the floor...."

"You stepped on it?"

"Yeah – how bad is it?"

I eased him back onto the couch and bent down to examine his foot. *Oh, this needs stitches for sure.*

"I'm going to take you to the med unit. I'll grab some gauze to cover it and we'll get going."

At the medical unit, Dakota winced as Betty cleaned and examined his wound.

"Stitches?" he asked.

"Nope. You almost made hamburger here, kiddo – didn't leave me anything to stitch. It should heal fine, though, if you're careful to follow my directions and keep it clean. Think you can do that?"

Dakota nodded, his expression grave.

"Tell your friends they can call me if they don't believe you were attacked by a shark in your own living room."

Dengue

A few weeks later, I woke before the alarm went off. The clock on the nightstand told me it was nearly time to get up, but I lay staring at the ceiling, mentally organizing my day.

Fred groaned and then whispered in a pitiful voice, "God, I feel awful. My eyes hurt. My bones ache. I'm not sure I can get out of bed."

I put my hand on his forehead and went straight to the medicine cabinet for the thermometer.

"Oh-oh. I'm taking you to the med unit right now – your temperature is 104."

After dropping the kids off at school and letting the principal know I'd be late for work, I drove Fred to the embassy medical unit. Nurse Betty took his temperature, blood pressure, and pulse and made note of all of his symptoms.

"Dengue fever," she said.

"What's that?" Fred said. "Sounds scary."

"It's a mosquito-borne viral illness. Don't worry -- the mild form isn't fatal. I'm not going to kid you – you'll feel pretty darn awful for a couple of weeks, but you will recover."

I asked Betty how she could tell that Fred had the mild form of dengue fever and she replied that the dangerous forms, dengue hemorrhagic fever and dengue shock syndrome, were very rare. She gave us a list of symptoms and danger signs to watch for and told Fred to drink plenty of fluids and take Tylenol to reduce his fever.

Fred spent most of the next two weeks in bed, shivering with chills and moaning with severe bone and muscle pain, curtains closed against the light that stabbed his eyes like hot pokers. We watched for the dire symptoms of more severe disease – bleeding from nose or mouth, bleeding under the skin that gave the appearance of bruising, abdominal pain, frequent vomiting, disorientation – but none of them appeared, and Fred gradually got better.

If the Internet had been available, we would have Googled dengue fever and learned that there were four strains of the virus. We would have been forewarned that Fred could get it again, as he did four years later on the other side of the world. But even the Internet couldn't have told us that Fred would have numerous episodes of similar symptoms in the future, in spite of the fact that dengue fever is not documented to have a chronic form like malaria.

Elmi Abdi Alin

We knew what chronic malaria was like because Elmi, our day guard, suffered from it. He never missed a day of work though. Stalwart Elmi, ancient as he was, greeted us every morning with a snappy salute. He claimed to have served in the Italian Army in World War II. "Mussolini's best machine-gunner," he boasted. Because of his advanced age and poor health, Elmi spent most of his duty-time wrapped in a blanket, asleep in the chair we gave him, his scarred bald head tilted back against the garden wall, lids closed over his rheumy, cataract-clouded eyes.

Elmi worked for us through the embassy contract with a security company to provide guards for embassy-leased property. In a perfect world, Elmi would have already retired on a pension. In his world he was lucky to have a job. He pointed to the deepest scar on his head when he told us that his seniority was due to his heroic defense of American property.

Elmi's gentle charm made allies of Fred and me. We paid attention to his welfare and provided him with extra comforts, clothing, medicine, food, and a bicycle for transportation. He repaid us a thousand-fold with devotion and loyalty.

Elmi smiled like Mona Lisa, lips closed and turned up at the corners. He smiled often, especially while watching Dakota and Tina at play. The day that Fred brought Moses home, Elmi's smile turned to a toothy grin. Moses was a desert tortoise that Fred bought for Dakota at the market. Dakota named him Moses Malone, after the NBA basketball star, and showed Elmi how to feed him hibiscus blooms and watermelon rinds. Moses ate a lot. Moses Malone grew almost big enough to ride. He continued to amuse Elmi, even when his enormous tortoise droppings had to be cleaned up.

Moses might have been the inspiration for Elmi's gift to Tina; it would seem fair for Tina to have a pet if Dakota had one. Elmi brought Tina a black and white kitten that looked exactly like Tweety-Bird's co-star. Tina named him Sylvester and he followed her like a puppy. In fact, he acted more like a dog than a cat. He begged for treats and enjoyed a strong scratch behind the ears. Tina encouraged him to sleep with her, but she complained about his habit of attacking her head and trying to kill her hair in the middle of the night. Sylvester grew fat and fatter. Then one day he gave birth to a litter of seven kitties. Tina had to pick a quick name change and Sylvester became Sylvie.

Charge of the White Rhino

Fully recovered from his bout with dengue fever, Fred came home from work one afternoon and handed me a tan government transmittal envelope, printed on both sides with lines and spaces for the date, the recipient's name and office designation. The last line read, "Date: April 5, 1983 – To: Nancy, Dakota, and Tina – Subject: SURPRISE!" I fumbled with the waxed cord that wound between two closure disks on the flap. Inside were four tickets to Nairobi, Kenya.

"I figured we deserved a get-away vacation during Spring Break."

I answered with a smile, a hug, a kiss and a whooping cheer that brought the kids running to see what was going on.

Fred whetted our appetites with an enticing description of the superb breakfast buffet at the Nairobi Hilton. I could almost taste the pink strawberry milkshakes, sweet golden pineapple, and crusty fresh bread (without the ever-present weevils found in local loaves).

Fred brought out the photos from his TDY in Nairobi five years ago and we talked about all the animals we might see. I looked forward to the chance to reunite with Barbara Koch, the embassy nurse who took such great care of Tina when she had quinsy in Cameroon. Fred had already called Barbara at her new post at the embassy in Kenya and she promised us another treat – a guided tour of Nairobi National Park.

For our trip to Nairobi's game park, Barbara borrowed a Land Rover, a large sturdy four-wheel drive vehicle with bench seats front and rear as well as jump seats in the cargo area. Barbara drove, Fred sat next to her, I shared the back seat with our picnic supplies, and our kids perched on the rear jump seats to take advantage of the great view out the open hatch. We chatted steadily, making up for lost time, while keeping a sharp lookout for animals. Barbara stopped first for a mother monkey sitting in the middle of the road nursing her baby. The monkey watched us watching her. She gave us a bored look after a few minutes and sauntered off into the bush. We moved closer to the river to observe a fat hippo basking in a sunlit pool.

On the next slope, we spotted three giraffes nibbling tender young green leaves from the high branches of an acacia tree. Their nimble blue-black tongues and limber lips slipped around and between the sharp acacia thorns and captured bite after bite of leafy nutrition.

The Land Rover bumped along the two-track road and raised a plume of dust that feathered away in the breeze. The indefinable mixture of odors - something rotting, something blooming, something ripe and edible – symbolized the essence of Africa and made me want to beat my chest like Tarzan.

Over the next hill, a pride of lions lazed in the sun. They sprawled in a circle around the bloody remains of the haunch of a large animal, antelope perhaps. Two cubs growled in mock battle over a bone. The older animals, dozing in postprandial bliss, did not open even one eye to check us out. Barbara pulled off the road and drove around the lions in a detour wide enough to leave them in peace.

"Will we get to see rhinos?" Dakota asked.

"Maybe," Barbara answered. "We're heading for the area where they like to hang out, but there are only five white rhinos in the whole park and they're shy, so I can't say for sure that we'll find them today."

As we reached the summit of the highest of the hills, we caught sight of the skyline of the city of Nairobi. Surrounded by rolling sandy terrain, groves of verdant acacia trees, low growths of gray-green bush, and breeze-ruffled tawny grasses, we gazed across at the striking glint of skyscrapers against a backdrop of cerulean sky.

"Look there!" Barbara stuck her arm out the window and pointed toward the nearest grove of acacias.

A massive rhino ambled into the clearing and began grazing. Barbara put the Land Rover in reverse and brought us closer in a slow, wide arc. With the back of the vehicle facing the rhino, Dakota and Tina had a perfect view through the open hatch.

"That rhino isn't even white." Tina sounded disappointed.

"I know," Barbara said. "I was surprised, too, the first time I saw a white rhino. The name was supposed to be wide, not white. Look at his lips. See how wide they are? The wideness is perfect for gathering big mouths-full of grass."

The rhino went on grazing as if we weren't there discussing his color and his lips.

"Let's see if I can get his attention." Barbara revved the engine once, twice, three times, louder and longer each time.

The rhino raised his head. He snorted. His right front foot pawed the ground. He started trotting toward the Land Rover.

"Oh shit." Barbara jammed the gearshift into first and stomped on the gas. The engine died.

The rhino's trot quickened.

"Go-go-go!" was all I could say.

Barbara cranked the key. The engine coughed and died again.

The rhino's pace accelerated.

The rhino lowered his head.

Tina landed in the seat next to me. I didn't see her coming. She must have flown. Barbara cranked the key again. The engine coughed and start-ed. Barbara trounced the gas pedal and the Land Rover jerked forward.

Dakota froze in the jump seat. He stared at the charging rhino.

The rhino's hooves pounded a dreadful rhythm on the packed earth.

Dust swirled up from the Land Rover's spinning tires and mingled with the cloud raised by the racing rhino hooves. I heard the huff-grunt-huff of the rhino's snorting as he came closer and closer to the back of the truck. The Land Rover picked up speed. The rhino broke into a gallop. "Dakota. Come. Here." I reached back and tried to will Dakota to scramble forward to safety. He did not move. The rhino's charge held him spellbound.

Within inches of our tailgate, for no apparent reason, the rhino turned off to the left. He slowed to a standstill and resumed grazing as if nothing had interrupted his meal. In seconds he disappeared behind the screen of our dust cloud.

Fred and I whooped and hollered while Barbara drove straight for the main park road and the relative safety of the area patrolled by armed rangers.

Dakota at last released his grip on the edge of the jump seat and came back to life. He climbed forward to join Tina and me in the back seat. The rest of us stopped our exclamations and looked at him, waiting to hear his personal eyewitness account.

"You know what?" he used his familiar deliberate delivery that always promised a pithy punch line. "Rhino breath really reeks!"

Anything that followed that experience might suffer in the comparison, but our next stop on this mini-vacation offered more culture than adventure. The Bomas of Kenya presented an extensive living museum that enthralled us with traditional tribal music, dances, and acrobatic shows. The village mock-ups impressed me the most. I wandered through the models, lost in speculation about what daily life was like among the real-life thatched circular dwellings and packed earth yards.

Home Without Mom

Two months later, we set off on another trip. Willie Nelson's "On The Road Again" played in my head as our plane lifted off the runway. See ya later Mogadishu, hello R&R.

I yearned to see my dad even though I dreaded experiencing what home was like without Mom. I was relieved to see how Dad had coped with the loss of his life partner. He still lived with shock, disbelief, and overpowering sadness, but he lived. Mom and Dad had developed a very efficient division of labor during their forty-two years together, and Dad had much to learn about all the things that Mom had taken care of – cooking, cleaning, grocery shopping, and bookkeeping, to name a few. At the time of her death, he knew how to make a peanut butter sandwich, but he didn't know how to write a check.

Dad's three sisters had dealt with Mom's clothes and cosmetics, but Dad wanted me to sort out her papers, jewelry, and craft materials. I needed a box of tissues at my side during the many days it took to go through it all. Mom had never thrown away a single scrap of paper. I found cancelled checks from the 1940s, autograph books from her high school days – a poignant mixture of useless junk and precious treasure. She had no jewelry of any value beyond the sentimental, and I kept it all.

As I went through Mom's extensive collection of craft materials, especially the fabrics, I had many moments of overwhelming nostalgia. Tears flowed and I plucked tissue after tissue to wipe, dab, and clench into a soggy ball.

I picked up a piece of yellow cotton with black scissors printed on it and remembered the oversized pincushion she made of that fabric to attach to her ironing board. I smooth the bright yellow swatch on my knee and traced the stripe of scissors with my finger.

Oh, Mom, why didn't we understand each other? Was I such a difficult child for you to raise? I know I wasn't hyper, or sassy, or naughty, but was I too independent or precocious?

The red and white polka dots of a remnant from my bedroom curtains caught my eye and I laid that piece across my other knee.

Why were you so sad? I tried to please you, but nothing I did made you happy. Nothing I did was ever good enough.

I pictured Mom with her hands in the wide front pocket of her favorite Kelly green apron as I stroked each tiny ladybug in the print on that scrap of fabric.

You told me to be considerate of others, and I learned to put everyone else's happiness ahead of mine. But you still locked yourself in your room and cried for hours. You were broken and I couldn't fix you.

A piece of blue and white checked gingham brought Mom's square-dance dresses to mind. She sewed circle-skirted outfits in every color with matching shirts for my dad so they could twirl away their Saturday nights in style.

I tried so hard to be good! I epitomized the good child, excellent student, valued employee, loyal friend, virtuous wife, capable partner, and devoted mother. But I still felt unworthy. Now that you're gone, I never will earn your approval, will I?

In harmony with my compelling creative urge, I decided to make something from Mom's fabric scraps and buttons. I picked the pieces that held the most memories and put them together in a quilted wall hanging, a tapestry of her life in primary colors. I've kept it with me ever since and it always hangs where I can see and touch it every day.

Dad had another request for me. He asked me to make an urn. He wanted it to be big enough to hold Mom's ashes and his ashes too. When the time came, he wanted my brother and me to scatter their combined ashes on Orono Orchards golf course back in Minnesota where they had played together so many happy times. I made the urn then and there, using the clay, glaze, and kiln available in Mom and Dad's workshop.

Dad announced that he wanted my brother and me to have our inheritance. He suggested deeding his house and 1.5 acres to me with the understanding that he could live out his life in the home and that I would pay Gary half of the appraised value. We all agreed and Dad started the legal process.

While I was busy helping Dad, Tina amused herself as she has always been able to do, and the guys flew to Arizona to play with Buddy and Brian Kellums, who were also home on leave. They fished and shot guns for five days. Buddy had accumulated an inordinate amount of ordnance and I believe they shot it all.

On this R&R of 1983, besides the R's of Rest and Recuperation, we had to Replenish our stock of non-perishable dry goods, such as toiletries, paper products, and cleaning supplies – common items of everyday life not available or very expensive in Mogadishu. I tried to estimate what a year's worth might be and we went shopping at the discount store. We filled two shopping carts with shampoo, bath soap, toothpaste, toothbrushes, dental floss, lotion, aspirin, antacids, cold medicine, tissues, and on and on until we came to the end of my list. At the checkout counter, the clerk did a double take at our overflowing carts and looked the four of us up and down.

"Well, now, you must be the Sunshine Family! Where in the world did you get so tan and why do you need all this stuff?"

Always happy to oblige, Fred told our story to the curious clerk who hung on every word. I thought of us as the Sunshine Family for years afterward.

Tourist Visas No. 1 and 2

On the way back to Mogadishu from R&R, after our usual visits to family in New Mexico and Texas, we met Fred's sister Beth, her husband Dave, and Dave's mother Ileen in New York City. Ileen reserved rooms for us at The Ritz Carlton across from Central Park. We caught a limo from the airport because that was the only vehicle available that could handle our baggage and the four of us. We had the usual suitcases and carry-on bags, plus two sets of golf clubs, and a hand-me-down electric guitar that Uncle Bert had given Dakota.

As we climbed out of the limo in front of the hotel I felt scrutinized like an alien life form. All four of us bronzy tanned people wore comfortable casual clothes, perhaps not quite up to the standard of the Manhattan homeless. Our tattered suitcases sported multiple scars from sadistic baggage handlers, and the top of Fred's golf bag cover was held together with duct tape. Add to this mix the largish guitar case, and you get the picture of a ragged, eccentric mob. The Ritz Carlton did not turn us away, however.

We four shared a room (our preference) that might have served one small person. Filled with our four bodies, our bags, and two beds, there was no room to walk to the closet-sized bathroom. We crawled back and forth across the suitcases, over the golf clubs, around the guitar, and hopped from one bed to the other. Still, it was the Ritz, and each pillow proffered a foil-wrapped chocolate at the head of the turned-down bed.

Ileen took us to a deli for pastrami on rye and to Lindy's for a slice of their famous cheesecake, the ultimate standard for that delicacy, in my opinion. We went off on our own to run in Central Park and visit the Statue of Liberty. It was fun to watch the old gents playing chess outdoors in the park and we enjoyed the music of the street musicians and the scents of ethnic foods flavoring the air.

After two nights at the Ritz we continued our trek back to Mog. Beth and Dave spent a few more days in New York with Ileen before following us. We joked, but it could have been true, that Beth and Dave possessed Tourist Visa No. 1 and Tourist Visa No. 2 issued by the Somali Consulate in 1983.

None of the family had ever come to any of our Foreign Service homes before, and we treated this visit like the momentous occasion it was. We spent several days getting ready for our visitors. Tina moved in with Dakota so Beth and Dave could have her room. Tina's room had a double bed, very comfortable, with a pretty woven wicker headboard and matching dresser and vanity. All tidied up, it made an attractive guest room. I rearranged the patio furniture on the roof while Fred and the kids painted "Welcome Beth and Dave" in big black block letters on the rooftop cistern wall.

On his own time, as a special favor to us, our hero, expeditor Hajji Hussein, escorted our guests through the complicated airport formalities and handed them over to us unscathed. Beth and Dave arrived in the afternoon -- all landings occurred in daylight because the runway lighting system could not be relied upon. Lufthansa experts had advised the Somalis on changes to upgrade their airport and listed the night landing bans as top priority. The Lufthansa advisors also recommended fences to keep cattle from wandering into the path of taxiing aircraft but the Somalis hadn't got around to that yet.

Our brave visitors unpacked and joined us for cocktails on the roof. At bedtime we hugged and kissed and retired to our rooms. Before we were done brushing our teeth, Beth and Dave peeked in our door.

Beth rubbed her arms as Dave spoke. "Um. We hate to complain, but we're not going to be able to sleep in Tina's bed tonight."

Beth grabbed my hand and led me to Tina's room. The problem spoke for itself. The cute rattan headboard was crawling with tiny insects. Fred took a closer look and identified them as baby ticks.

"Frodo," said Fred.

Frodo was Nurse Betty's friend's dog. For the six weeks prior to our R&R we had taken care of him while Betty and her friend went on home leave. Frodo slept with Tina during his visit and apparently left tick off-spring behind. We made other sleeping arrangements that night and Fred made short work of the tick population as soon as possible.

Dave said he'd like to shop for used books and Beth wanted to visit the handicraft stalls to find a painting, so we went downtown. To my surprise, Dave found a street vendor selling second-hand books in English. Beth and I shopped every artist stall and at last picked out camel caravan paintings by the same artist; both of them prime examples of the principle of perspective and true to the desert color palette.

The guys had wandered off while we dithered over our choices. As they walked around the university area they heard music coming from the upper level of a nearby building. They climbed the stairs in the dilapidated old structure and found the Somali version of a garage band. The musicians invited them to sit, provided chairs and hot tea and resumed playing. With an appreciative audience lending encouragement, the musicians found their groove. We couldn't have planned a better treat for long-time fans of live music.

Of course we wanted to show Beth and Dave the time of their lives in Somalia. No visit to Mog could be complete without a trip to Shark's Bay, our favorite secluded sandy beach that ended at the foot of a range of pastel sand dunes. Beth asked if she could try driving the Toyota in four-wheel-drive on the sandy 45-minute cross-country route.

"Go for it," Fred said.

Beth moved the driver's seat forward, tightened the chinstrap on her safari hat, and grabbed the steering wheel at 10 o'clock and 4 o'clock.

"Hang on, everybody!"

Beth let out the clutch inch by inch and the Toyota moved forward. She gave it some gas and picked up speed, keeping pressure on the accelerator in keeping with Fred's caution to avoid bogging down. The Toyota roared onward, charging up one side of a dune and careening down the other side, tipping and swerving.

"What do I do now?" Beth screamed.

"Try the brakes!" Fred shouted.

Fred drove the rest of the way to Shark's Bay, and no one else volunteered to take the controls.

At Shark's Bay we body surfed, snorkeled, explored tide pools, and played in the fountains of the blowholes. The long curve of packed sand at low tide begged for sandcastle building and beach walks. Beth and Dave didn't share our enthusiasm for eating the fresh oysters we pulled from the rock cliffs on the north end of the bay. Maybe they would have if we could have offered them a wedge of lemon.

After seeing how much they enjoyed Shark's Bay, we couldn't wait to take Beth and Dave to Merqa and the Sambusi Beach Hotel. Down the coast south of Mog, Merqa was a frequent weekend destination for our family. The road to Merqa called for low speeds and caution, and the thirty-mile trip took at least ninety minutes. To take care of our excess baggage, Fred and Dave designed and built a roof rack out of a piece of plywood attached to a bicycle rack. With six people and a large cooler stuffed into our small vehicle, the bumpy ride became a challenge in its own right. The back seats were mere benches, equipped with one lap belt each, of no use when two people shared the seat. Dakota squeezed in next to Beth and Tina shared with Dave. They had to hang on as best they could as the bumps and potholes threatened to bounce them from their perches.

We had to take frequent breaks to rest the weary bottoms. At one stop a troop of baboons made an extravagant show of crossing the road from one thicket to another. Using wisdom gained from experience, Tina and I kept our distance from the baboons and picked our potty spot with care.

At last we reached the hotel and checked in. The main hotel had rooms, but we never stayed there, preferring the cabins on the beach. I use the word cabin in the broadest sense. The Sambusi Beach huts were made of cement blocks laid in a circle and roofed with palm thatch forming a peak in the center. Pastel painted plaster covered the exterior walls. The builders left a gap between the walls and the roof to aid air circulation along with the empty doorframe facing seaward and the glassless window across the room, positioned to catch the sea breeze. Each hut had a small entryway and a cubicle that housed a western-style toilet, to be flushed by buckets of seawater that guests hauled across the beach as needed. Once a day, a donkey cart carrying a small water tank delivered one bucket of fresh well water to each unit. Using an empty tin can as a dipper, we washed away salt and sand before going to bed every night.

I had the most wonderful dreams, both nighttime dreams and naptime dreams, on the primitive cots at Sambusi Beach. The cots were made of tightly stretched cowhide, some tufts of hair still attached, with no mattress or springs. I don't know why they were so comfortable. The soft hand-woven cotton sheets drew coolness from the sea air and wrapped me in a smooth cocoon. Before we left Somalia, I bought some of that fabric and sewed a nightgown. It was comfortable enough, but without the gentle caress of an Indian Ocean breeze it didn't inspire the same quality of dreams.

The hotel restaurant's huge dining room echoed with emptiness. Lack of customers doesn't seem like a very good recommendation, but the food was excellent and the service unparalleled. We loved the golden fried calves' liver and succulent sautéed onions for breakfast, and scrumptious spaghetti marinara for dinner. On the day that Dakota caught a fish, the cook turned it into a crispy, rich entrée. Our favorite waiter presented

Tina with a baby desert tortoise and clapped his hands in delight when she said she would name it Mohammed.

Back in Mogadishu, a city without car dealers or auto parts store, Fred enlisted Dave's help to invent a substitute for our Toyota's leaky water pump gasket. Now, Dave is the smartest guy we know, but he is smart like a PhD in statistics is smart, not like an auto mechanic is smart. However he is also the best sport we know (in a tie with Beth, of course) and he agreed to assist in this operation. Fred and Dave set up shop on the dining table. Using the worn gasket as a pattern, they cut a gasket-shaped piece from a thick cardboard government file folder and covered it in layers of duct tape. You may laugh, but the substitute gasket worked until we got a new pump from Nairobi.

A few days before Beth and Dave's departure, Fred's Somali employees invited us to dinner at a place known as the Jungle Restaurant. There was no jungle within hundreds of miles, but the restaurant did claim several acres of acacia forest.

We sat on mats and blankets in the shade of thorn trees and ate with our hands from communal bowls of rice seasoned with cumin, cardamom, cloves, and sage; chunks of roasted goat meat; and bananas. After dinner our Somali hosts gave eloquent speeches about the value of family ties. They presented Beth with a typical Somali dress. Someone plunked a chubby baby in my lap as if I were the child's granny.

As conversations continued, I felt touched by our friends' obvious devotion to Fred. They honored him, and his family as well, for being the best boss they had ever had.

A waiter lit a piece of frankincense in a soapstone burner and I inhaled the pleasant fragrance as I cradled the infant in my arms and let my mind wander. I watched mongooses dart forward from the underbrush in search of scraps from our meal. How lucky we were to have this experience and to be able to share it with Beth and Dave.

We almost didn't let Beth and Dave leave. One thing after another conspired to delay their flight for a full twenty-four hours. Fortunately they had planned a stopover in Nairobi that allowed the extra time to catch their connection to the States. They were our sole visitors in Somalia, the rare breed brave enough and hardy enough and crazy enough to travel across the world to end up in a bed of ticks.

Wreck

A few weeks after Beth and Dave's departure, Dakota and Tina and I drove several miles out of town with handwritten directions and a map. I can't remember where we were going, perhaps to visit a friend from school, but I do recall that I missed the turn and had to backtrack a half-mile or so. Preparing to turn left onto the road I had been looking for, I lowered the signal lever and stuck my arm out the window (a sensible precaution in a land where blinkers either didn't work or were seldom used). When I glanced into the rearview mirror, I saw a car approaching in the far distance, so I moved over as far left as I could. I wanted to give the car behind me enough room to pass on the right. I slowed down, and started to turn. At that instant, the other car came barreling past on the left, nicked my left front fender, and caromed off the left side of the road. The driver overcorrected and sent his vehicle scooting all the way across the pavement where it crashed into a stone fence on the other side.

The accident caused no injuries but it totaled the other car.

Thanks to Fred's insistence that I carry a mobile radio, I had the means to call for help. The embassy security office reported the accident to the police and sent Hajji Hussein to join us at the scene. We all went to police headquarters to complete the accident report. The other driver told his story first. He claimed that I caused the accident by wearing sunglasses. I drew a diagram to illustrate my version and Hajji Hussein translated my statement. Dakota and Tina sat beside me, watching the exchange as if it were a tennis match.

The police captain concluded that I was at fault, not because I wore dark glasses, but because I should have pulled off the road on the right hand side and waited until the road was clear before attempting to turn left. I felt my dander rise, but before I could object, Hajji Hussein reassured me that the captain's judgment had more to do with insurance (I had it, the other driver didn't) than it had to do with my driving skills. Hajji's sage advice saved me from causing trouble with the captain.

We sat like hostages while the captain pecked out his report on an antique typewriter, smudging his mistakes on all six copies misaligned in the machine. He released us only after he had our signatures on each copy of every page.

Merqa Revisited

Since our car escaped damage in the collision it wasn't long before we went out of town again, back to the beach at Merqa. After a quick dip in the ocean, we decided to go for a hike inland. Fred led the way and we four tromped up and down and around the dunes. Dakota and Tina invented a new sport. From the top of the highest dune they dove, flew through the air, then tucked and rolled the rest of the way to the bottom.

From the top of any dune, we could see the ocean on one hand, and rolling sand hills on the other. Fred spotted a sounder of warthogs trotting among the dunes. Holding a finger to his lips, he cautioned us to stand still until the group had disappeared into the distance. With their jaunty upright tails and turned up snouts, warthogs looked comical, but we realized their sharp tusks and unpredictable personalities could be a dangerous combination.

We collected a big sack of shells at Merqa as well as some large bone fragments that appeared to be petrified. The shells were petrified too and much bigger than any living shellfish we had seen in the water here. We added these unexpected treasures to our collection of souvenirs.

20

Sambusi Beach Hotel

October – December 1983

Fueling an Invasion

The clanging slam of our iron gate announced the arrival of someone in a hurry. Ten-year-old Dakota scuttled crab-like down the garden path toward me.

"What's up, Bub?" One look at his odd posture told me that something was wrong. His back bent and twisted; the upper half of his body was hidden from my view. I tried to imagine what had happened in the thirty minutes that passed since he went to his friend's house to make Halloween costumes.

"Me and Tony got a big problem, Mom. Ya hafta help us." Dakota's husky voice trembled.

I took both his hands and turned him to face me. Then I saw what he had tried to conceal: his bright orange American School Mogadishu tee shirt was blotched with black spatters.

"Whoa, is that tar? What have you guys been doing? And where is

Tony? He didn't get burned, did he? Quick, tell me." Dakota flinched and I realized that my grip on his hands had tightened.

"Tony's O.K. He's O.K. Really. He's waiting outside the gate. It's just…he…well…uh… We were throwing rocks into this big puddle of tar by Tony's driveway and…uh…Tony threw this really big one and… uh… I'm gonna go get him and you can see for yourself."

A tearful grimace replaced Tony's usual naughty-boy grin. He flapped his hands at the enormous black blobs covering the front of his polo shirt.

"Mom is gonna k-k-k-kill me! I-wasn't-supposed-to-wear-this-shirt-today-it's new-special-for-my-first-day-at-boarding-school-back-in-the-States-and-Mom-will-tell-Dad-what-I did-oh-God-I-wish-I -could-just-die-now-can-you-please-help-me-Mrs.-LaTurner-please!" He ran out of breath – and words.

"Tony, I am so sorry about your new shirt. Come here, sit down, and let's decide what to do."

Poor Tony. Trouble ruled his life. As school counselor, I knew details. Empathy urged me to help him in any way I could.

"Okay. How about this -- Dakota can loan you a shirt to wear while I try to get rid of the tar. If I'm successful, then there's no more problem and we three can keep this whole thing a secret. If I can't make your shirt look like new again, Dakota and I will go with you to break the news to your Mom and Dad, and I will offer to replace the shirt. Does that sound all right to you?"

Tony nodded and the tension in his shoulders eased. I sent the boys to Dakota's room for clean shirts and asked them to play there while I attacked the tarry mess.

Where would I find a powerful solvent? Mogadishu had no supermarkets or hardware stores and no convenience stores. A search of our storeroom produced nothing better than laundry detergent. That would not cut it. I glanced around the yard and noticed the fuel tank next to our emergency generator. "Daily generator" would have been a better name, due to the frequency and length of power outages, but "emergency generator" was what everybody called it. Wishful thinking?

Diesel fuel should work, shouldn't it? It's worth a try, I thought.

With rubber gloves, an old coffee can full of diesel, and a box of Tide, I headed for the bathroom sink. Full-strength diesel fuel stinks. Mightily. It also dissolves tar. Completely. Now I had stain-free shirts that smelled like a fuel dump. So I filled the basin with hot water and swished the Tide around to make suds. In went the shirts. I squeezed and pummeled and squeezed some more, hoping Tide could eliminate the nasty odor. Then I pulled the plug to drain the wash water. As I reached for the tap to begin rinsing, I felt a tickle on my bare foot. My foot flicked a reflexive kick and I looked down.

Damn cockroach! Even if I could catch up with it, I wasn't about to stomp it with my bare feet. I've always tried to live in peace with Earth's creatures. In fact, before we moved in, I had declined the embassy's offer to spray our house for insects. But cockroaches push me over the edge. The varmint scuttled out of sight; I shuddered and turned back to the basin to rinse the shirts.

Horror! The surface of the sink undulated with movement. Cockroaches swarmed up out of the drain. They crawled over the shirts by the dozen and more followed. I lurched backward, groping for the door handle. Looking down again, I saw cockroaches everywhere. Hundreds of cockroaches scurried in all directions. They covered the bottom of the bathtub. They scrambled across the tiles. Brown ones, black ones, big ones, small ones, hideous tiny white ones. They came from every crack and crevice. They came out from the base of the toilet where those little covers conceal bolts attaching the toilet to the floor. How could they fit through there? God help me; let me wake up from this nightmare.

I ran out as if pursued and grabbed the Embassy communications network radio.

"Eagle One, Eagle One, this is Eagle Twenty, over!"

"This is Eagle One. Go, Eagle Twenty."

The Marine Security Guard who received the call teased me later about the jumble of words that hit his ear that day, but I don't remember being hysterical. Help came right away. A crew of workers sprayed the

232 ᧞ VOLUNTARY NOMADS

house inside and out, flushed the drains, and removed all traces of the disaster.

Although the diesel smell never left Tony's new shirt, his parents accepted the fact with uncharacteristic calm. Happy to be out of trouble, the boys got busy with their costumes and finished in time for the school party that evening. Halloween wasn't as much fun for me; I couldn't stop thinking about the cockroach invasion. And I couldn't shake the creepy sensation that something was crawling up my back.

Travel Mode

The next long weekend that came up – probably Thanksgiving -- a group of embassy folks who enjoyed the same kind of outings got together to plan a camping trip to a beach north of Mogadishu where sea turtles were known to nest. We packed six vehicles full of families, food, and camping gear. A considerable amount of off-road driving took us far from any towns or villages. Fred, by now the acknowledged guru of four-wheeling, demonstrated his skills when the one big RV unit got stuck in the deep sand on the final approach to our campsite.

We were so far from anywhere, I was surprised to find another party had arrived before we did. Their vehicle sat empty and there wasn't a tent in sight or any indication that the owners intended to camp. Dakota pointed to a few dots bobbing offshore, and one of our group suggested that our neighbors were swimming, perhaps hunting sea turtles, either for the tortoise shell or for gourmet soup. Sad to say, that was the case, and the turtle hunters were successful. I'm sure turtle soup is delicious, but witnessing the slaughter of that beautiful animal made me cry. The one poor murdered creature was the only sea turtle we saw on that trip.

But we still had a great time camping. In the evening, we built a grand bonfire and sat around it, singing songs and telling stories. Someone brought out a carton of glow sticks and passed them around. We waved our gleaming batons to the beat of our own music and drew light pictures in the dark. When bedtime came, we smothered the fire with sand. The glow sticks continued to glow, and Fred stuck his into the mound of sand covering the fire. One by one we followed suit, forming a ceremonious procession to the sand mountain and then standing in a circle admiring our faerie lights.

One after another the glow sticks exploded and spewed neon green globs on everyone. We danced about, screaming and laughing, swiping and wiping, in a frenzy to get rid of the green goop that now seemed more like alien toxin than faerie magic.

Most of the group – the ones with the painful hangovers – left the next morning. Our family of four plus Paul and Margie Olson stayed behind to enjoy a day of peaceful bodysurfing and gentle sunburning.

After lunch we headed back toward Mogadishu. About a third of the way home, Paul's old car died. He had prepared for the inevitable by borrowing a towrope ahead of time. With the dead car tethered behind our Toyota, we hit the road again. The same route that had been devoid of traffic on the way out became an obstacle course of half-ton trucks and minibuses crammed with rowdy passengers. We found out later that our trip overlapped with the celebration of Idd ul Adha, the Muslim holiday commemorating the willingness of Abraham to sacrifice his son Ishmail as an act of obedience to God. The faithful were on their way out of town to join in a ritual sacrifice of a cow, goat, or sheep and then distribute the meat among family, friends, and the poor.

Fred maneuvered our tandem vehicles for miles, finding gaps between and among the trucks and minibuses. We were within blocks of home when a taxi sideswiped Paul's car.

Everybody got out to survey the scene for damage. The taxi had too many old dents and scrapes to show any new ones and Paul didn't care about dings on his clunker, so the guys shook hands all around and we got back in our seats.

Before Fred could start the engine, a loud scream brought us out into the street again. A disheveled Somali woman lay on the ground struggling to gather her belongings and stand up. Apparently she had tripped over the towrope while trying to cross between our two vehicles. She was dusty and embarrassed, but not hurt, and we parted ways amicably.

One Thing after Another

I've heard the saying that bad luck comes in threes. How about sets of three? Our spate of misfortune seemed to begin with my first and only visit to the corner tea hut.

Tea huts were common on street corners all over town, residential neighborhoods as well as commercial zones. From a distance our corner tea hut could be mistaken for a wind-blown gargantuan tumbleweed. Its stick and thatch physical construction may have been haphazard, but the social network was tightly woven. Gate guards and domestic employees stopped by every day for a glass of hot, sweet tea and a bit of gossip. Dakota was a frequent patron too; he bought candy there.

"Mom! Come on – I gotta show you something.'" Dakota pulled me by the hand and dragged me out of the house, through the gate, and over to the tea hut.

I followed Dakota into the dim interior, aware of a sudden dampness in my armpits. A dark shape flew at me and dug its claws into my hair and the back of my neck and shoulders. My flailing and screaming only made the thing strengthen its grip. I ran outside. The creature on my back screeched as loud as a demon from hell. Something limber and rough scraped across my calves as I twisted and turned.

"Mom! Mom! Stop!" Dakota couldn't catch up with my spinning flight.

The tea man rescued me. Why was he laughing at my terror? He grabbed the hemp rope that had been slapping my legs and reached toward me with his other hand. My attacker launched itself from my head to the arms of the tea man.

"See? It's only a monkey, geez." Dakota tugged his cap down over his eyes and scuffed his boot in the dirt.

The monkey sneered at my disgrace. I had never felt more foolish.

I slunk home and retreated to the bathroom. I snorted at my reflection in the mirror – red face, wild hair, torn shirt. A shower would fix me up, I thought. But there was no water.

Muttering expletives, I marched outside to check the water pump.

Dead as the proverbial doorknob, this was the sixth water pump to burn out in the nine-month life of our new water system. I was too frustrated to notice any numerological significance of the six and nine.

While we waited for the installation of a new water pump for the house, our car broke down. I cleared the dining room table to make room for another session of gasket making. Fred assured me that the file folder and duct tape replica would keep the car running until we could get a replacement pump from Nairobi, just as Dave's gasket had done the year before. Fine, I thought. What's next?

Next came the Hash event that ran us over, under, around, and through a series of abandoned thorn corrals out in the desert. Maybe they weren't exactly abandoned, but at least there were no occupant animals on that particular day.

Fred and I (the kids opted to visit friends this time) leaped, crawled, hopped, and scrambled over the prickly course, toasting each other with extra beers at the end. We needed pliers to pull the dozens of thorns out of our running shoes. Fred used the tweezers from his Swiss army knife to pull a thorn from his calf. I noticed he limped when we walked to the car.

Over the next few days, Fred's leg hurt more and he was less able to tolerate putting weight on it. I was glad when he finally agreed to go to the medical unit. An antibiotic cured the infection, but a tiny piece of thorn remained as an irritant for months afterward.

Fred was still recuperating when Dakota got hurt. Deep in conversation with his friend Harvey, he leaned back against Harvey's all-terrain vehicle. He didn't realize that the exhaust pipe was still as hot as a branding iron. Off we went to the medical unit to take care of a postcard-sized burn on the back of Dakota's leg.

Either we were having a spell of bad luck, or the world was growing more dangerous. The next major event tipped the scales toward danger in my mind.

It hurt to look at our friend Paul Albers. Bandages, bruises, and stitched wounds made a patchwork of his face, left arm and back. His story came pouring forth and transported us to the scene.

236 ᴄᴏ VOLUNTARY NOMADS

Paul told us it had been an ordinary day – busy as usual, with enough last-minute paperwork to keep him in the embassy for an hour after closing time. He tossed his briefcase into the back seat of his yellow Volkswagen beetle and thought about his wife and two daughters waiting to have dinner with him.

The route was one that Paul traveled often. Even in the dark, he knew the curves, intersections, and landmarks. He had driven down the extension of Via Lenin past the reviewing stand scores of times and he knew about the roadblock manned casually by a few police officers. Paul slowed and coasted through without stopping, as he had done so many times, as we all did at that checkpoint.

A burst of gunfire blasted through the car window, spraying Paul with shards of glass and shrapnel and throwing him prone across the passenger seat. Three more rounds of bullets whizzed above him and riddled the yellow bug with gaping pockmarks.

Paul had failed to notice that national soldiers controlled the roadblock that night instead of local police. When the soldiers saw him driving through the checkpoint without stopping, they followed their standing orders and opened fire. A superior officer intervened and came forward to check Paul's papers. Once he realized that Paul was a diplomat, he arranged emergency transport to the nearest military hospital.

At the hospital, Paul panicked when he saw an unbelievably filthy needle heading his way. He declined the injection and asked to be taken home. His wife called a French physician she knew who came and patched him up. Paul said he felt lucky to be alive.

Within two hours of the incident, the Somali Minister of Defense telephoned the American Ambassador to express his regret. He mentioned that two soldiers were seriously injured in the crossfire. The Ambassador in turn expressed his regret that Paul's failure to stop at the roadblock had resulted in injuries to Somali military personnel. The potential international brouhaha went no further.

An Administrative Circular instructed all embassy personnel: "Do not at any time become complacent about roadblocks, even those you pass daily. Stop, identify yourself, and do not proceed until authorized to do so." Lesson learned.

Mauritius

I begged for a break from bad luck and danger. Christmas vacation was coming up, and Fred and I talked about taking a family trip to Kenya. Then we heard from our old friend Glenn Jones. The Joneses had gone from Fiji to Bonn and then to Port Louis, Mauritius, a tropical island in the Indian Ocean east of Madagascar. Glenn invited us to spend our holidays with him and his family in Port Louis. I could feel a change in our luck on the way.

We flew from Mog to Nairobi to catch our flight to Port Louis with a short stop in Madagascar to take on a few passengers. Too bad our governments weren't talking to each other, or we might have explored that interesting island too.

Glenn, Christa, Tracy (born in New Zealand, almost in Tina's bedroom), and Laurie (born in Bonn fourteen months after Tracy) met us at the airport and made a theatrical fuss about welcoming us. The joke was on Christa's dad who had arrived at the same time from Austria. Why would his family greet apparent strangers with exuberant affection and act like he didn't exist? Herr Bauer had a good sense of humor and he seemed to enjoy Glenn's sometimes-bizarre practical jokes. This one gave him a good long laugh. Glenn hadn't told Christa's Papsch about our visit or us about Herr Bauer, because he didn't want either of us to cancel in deference to the other. We met, we bonded, as Glenn knew we would, and Herr Bauer was Papsch to us from then on.

Glenn and Christa made sure their place felt like home to us. Tracy and Laurie, naked little bodies sticky with mango juice, followed Dakota and Tina everywhere. Dakota turned red with embarrassment, but Tina took charge like a mini-nanny. Laurie and Tracy were adorable, dressed only in their mango juice. They were two and three years old, Tina and Dakota nine and ten, and the four kids got along like cousins.

On our first outing we walked to a nearby volcano crater. Glenn,

Fred, and our two kids skidded down to the bottom and clawed back up to the rim while the rest of us watched. Dakota made sure to verify first that this was not an active volcano. He had developed a respect for volcanoes in New Zealand, home of several active cones.

A visit to the Jones family on a tropical island would not be complete without a hurricane. Unlike our adventurous outing with the Joneses during the Fiji storm in 1981, we stayed indoors for this one as it whirled on a direct course for Port Louis. Glenn closed the hurricane shutters, stocked up on canned goods, batteries, and drinking water. And we weathered the storm. The next morning dawned fresh and clear. Since there was a nationwide power outage, and we would be roughing it anyway, Glenn suggested that we go to the embassy-owned beach house and hang out for a few days.

We rented a Mini Cooper to tour the island and then spent the next few days on our own at the beach house. The lack of electricity (and refrigeration) was the single rough aspect of the comfortable vacation home on a long expanse of white sandy beach. We had to drink warm beer, though, and that's a major sacrifice of creature comfort. When the Joneses joined us on the weekend we kept the same tempo of snorkeling, swimming and warm beverage guzzling. Our entire trip to Mauritius held that high standard of sun, surf, and good company, although the temperature of the drinks improved when the power came back on.

As we waved goodbye to the Joneses, I tried to imagine where we would meet again – it would be someplace interesting for sure.

21

Tina the Ballerina

1984

Developing Talents

During our tour in Somalia, Tina forged a new independence. Once the homebody who stayed within reach of Mom's apron strings, now she ventured out into the world. She went to church with the Fullers. She signed up for after-school French lessons. And she took a ballet class.

Madam Girard, quintessential French lady and a former professional ballerina, offered ballet lessons on the balcony of her home. Her students, the same diverse mixture of nationalities represented at American School Mogadishu, danced with uniform enthusiasm even though the level of talent varied a great deal. Madam announced that the whole class would perform in a recital on the last day of the term. She asked the parents to be sure that their children had proper attire for this special event. She wanted them dressed in pink leotards, pink tights, pink shoes, and pink hair ribbons. For the girls, that is. The lone male dancer could forgo the hair ribbons. There was one exception. La Prima Ballerina, Mademoiselle LaTurner, should wear all white. And her costume should include a tutu.

I didn't expect to run downtown and find a white tutu in the nonexistent Mogadishu Mall. I couldn't find a proper ballet costume in any of our catalogs either. Since there was no residential telephone service and cell phones were a convenience of the future, I had to go to the Embassy to put in an emergency phone call to Aunt Pat, the LaTurner clan's problem-solver and miracle-worker. She sent Uncle Dick to the center of Houston's shopping district and Uncle Dick valiantly brought home the fluffy tutu (and the classic leotard, petite tights, soft leather ballet slippers, and silky white hair ribbons). A month later the package arrived by government pouch, our standard mail delivery method, slow but reliable.

On the day of the recital, the parents sat on the balcony floor, backs braced against the wall of the house, watching prides and joys pirouette and plie across the balcony. Tina the Ballerina danced center stage, a vision of loveliness and grace, her hair gathered into a bun, homage to Madam's classic hairdo.

Tina burst out with new talent in drama too, playing the mother in the school Christmas play. She joined the chorus as well, dancing and singing as a red rooster in the school musical "Rooster Rag," based on the fable "Chanticleer and The Fox." Dakota had the honor of turning the pages for the accompanist.

Dakota could have taken ballet also if he had wanted. But he was too busy with soccer, BMX bike riding, and hunting. Always one to take care of his mom, he added new prey to his list. For my sake, he pumped up his air gun and set himself up at the end of the hall to blast cockroaches to kingdom come. At close range the air gun had enough power to disintegrate the nasty critters. Dakota's practiced aim did not fail. He earned my eternal gratitude.

Nancy's Running Club and Tennis Fame

Many people at ASM and the embassy asked me for fitness tips. News of my marathon experiences made the rounds and gave me credibility. Fred also suggested that my ability to fit into a cute little brown eyelet-trimmed bikini might have influenced a few of the ladies. Either way, I was flattered by the attention. I thought this might be my chance to do some good in the community, so I organized a running club. About twenty people joined and I designed custom fitness programs for each member. Each had his own objective to meet every week, leading up to the long-term goal: a fun run/walk/bike around the jogging track. Some chose walking, some chose running, and several children opted for biking.

My family worked as hard as I did to make the Mogadishu Fun Run a success. They set up an official timing station and water stations along the course. Every participant finished the race, and I believe every finisher felt like a winner.

I played a little tennis in Mog too, very little, compared to what I had done in Yaounde. When the Golf and Tennis Club put on a tournament I gave in to pressure to join the mixed doubles, partnered with the club's top tennis player. Since "mixed" referred to ability as well as to gender, pairing with the best player defined my skill level in those days. My partner, a tall, silent German guy, in his work-a-day life an army colonel acting as advisor to the Somali police, treated me with utmost courtesy. He let me take all the shots on my side of the court, never once poaching, even though he could have returned all the balls I missed. His superior technique and stalwart support raised me to a height far above my usual level.

In the final match for the mixed doubles championship, adrenaline pumped me up and I charged the net. The man on the opposite side returned my partner's backhand shot with a hard line drive that smacked me right in the eyeball, instead of in my racquet, which was not quite in the correct position. That close-up view of lime-green fuzz has remained a vivid memory. I'm sure it hurt, but the pain I recall is from the damage to my ego. At least I didn't quit. I know my partner could have won the match without me, but I soldiered on to earn my trophy. The trophies were chalices made from meerschaum, the date and event lettered in black marker. The lettering washed away the first time I cleaned my trophy, the record as temporary as my triumph.

Nairobi

As a kid growing up in semi-rural Minnesota, I felt drawn to the magic of our big city, Minneapolis. Nairobi attracted me in the same way. Compared to Mogadishu, Nairobi seemed like Paris. It didn't take much of an excuse to jump on the short flight south. Fred and I called it a mini-R&R.

Like most embassy personnel, we took advantage of the embassy's biweekly non-pro courier run and combined business with pleasure. The non-pro courier accompanied the government pouch filled with unclassified bureaucratic paperwork and returned with the same type of bag full of vegetables – the cold climate veggies like broccoli, cauliflower, spinach, and celery – rarely if ever found in Mogadishu.

This time I had a unique excuse to go to Nairobi – a toothache. Our medical unit couldn't recommend a dentist in Mog, so Fred signed us up for the courier run. His go-to guy in the office, Jim Ford, offered to take care of our kids. Dakota and Tina liked Jim – he looked and acted a lot like Santa Claus – and they felt comfortable with Jim's wife Jan and their teenage daughter Mindy. Jim showed me his library of movies and video games and convinced me that the kids wouldn't have time to miss us.

I went to the dentist straight from the airport, suffered through the replacement of a lost filling, and got down to the real business of this trip – having fun with my husband.

Fred booked a tour to Tree Tops, one of the popular game-viewing resorts located several hours from the city, deep in the bush. We hired a car and driver to take us to the designated rendezvous where we joined other tourists for a short bus ride to our resort. Tree Tops did, in fact, roost among the treetops. The bus let us off in a parking area where we were met by several guides carrying rifles. The guides escorted us up a long, elevated boardwalk to the hotel.

The first event on the program was a formal tea, complete with tiny crust-free cucumber sandwiches, diminutive pastel frosted cakes, and champagne. How veddy British indeed. The major-domo gave a short orientation to the Tree Tops experience:

"As you probably know, many of the animals you came to see are most active at night. It is for this reason that we have a buzzer system installed in your rooms. Your guides keep watch all night. When they sight game, they will signal with the buzzer according to the following code: one buzz for hyena, two for water buffalo, three for big cats – could be leopard or lion or cheetah. It goes without saying that complete silence is mandatory, so as to not frighten the animals away. Are there any questions?"

During the day I stayed glued to one spot. Tree Tops had a tunnel leading to a cement bunker very close to a water hole. Salt licks provided an added incentive for the animals. I staked a claim to one of the many slits in the bunker wall for my eye-level window on life around the salt lick (and more or less knee-level to the elephants that congregated there). The same herd came every day. The elephants' social hierarchy was obvious – big mama ruled. The elephants paid a lot of attention to each other, giving gentle forehead bumps and intertwining their trunks. Most of their be-havior looked like mutual affection to me. I watched a young bull loving on big mama and wondered where that might lead. Big mama tolerated the young one's strokes, but didn't reciprocate. After a few minutes, she shoved him away and grunted, then bellowed at him until he ran out of the clearing and into the trees.

A guide explained that this behavior demonstrated a rite of passage in elephant society – young bulls of a certain age are expelled for a period before puberty. They forage for themselves until they are big enough to compete for mating rights. I swear the little bull looked sad and bewil-dered to be shunned from his herd, his family, and his mother. I chided myself for these anthropomorphic thoughts and went back to my window peeping.

Other hotel guests preferred to view the elephants from the balcony where they had unobstructed photo opportunities as well as ready access to

244 の VOLUNTARY NOMADS

the gin tonics at the bar. I overheard two men talking about the elephants. Their conversation made it clear that they were spending the weekend at Tree Tops as mere filler between their arrival in Kenya and the start of their safari in Tanzania where shooting elephants was allowed. They hoped to kill one of these magnificent beasts. I shot mental daggers to their hearts and hurried back to my bunker slot.

The elephants had company at the salt lick. A variety of birds, of course, a pack of hyenas and a herd of water buffalo. The hyenas' behavior struck me as completely random. They trotted back and forth, not too close to the elephants. Did they want salt or water or both? - I couldn't tell. Hyenas' tawny speckled coloring is beautiful, but their slinking posture keeps them from being attractive. The barbed tang of their odor is downright painful too.

The atmosphere of Tree Tops changed in the evening. Gin segued from tonic to vermouth and guests strolled from observation deck to candlelit dining room. Ambiance and alcohol whispered romantic suggestions. Couples drifted to their rooms.

Starting at midnight, the intermittent blasts of the buzzer system dragged us out of bed countless times to peer into the dark and see nothing. Each time we stumbled back down the hall to our room and flopped listlessly on our rack of torture cots, I swore I would not get up again. But I didn't want to risk missing an animal sighting, did I?

In the logical light of day, Fred and I agreed that we had seen enough hyenas and water buffalo. It made sense to respond only to the three-buzzer alert for big cats. That night the signal's insistent squawk woke us many times, but we stayed tucked in, counting the buzzes – one, one-two, but never three.

In spite of my love affair with the elephant family and the marvelous time Fred and I were having together, I was ready to leave Tree Tops when our stay ended. I craved sleep more than anything.

Game Park

Somalia didn't have game parks like Kenya's. In 1984, Somalia was more famous for wretched refugee camps than for anything else. But we heard of a place near Kismayo, the Yamani Safari Camp that was a private enterprise run by an Italian expat. The accommodations sounded interesting, the price was right, and it was a chance to get out of Mog and experience another side of Somalia.

The usual bunch, four LaTurners, four Fullers, and four Kellums (plus cocker spaniel, Sage Brush), formed a caravan of three Land Cruisers and headed south. Fred equipped each vehicle with a mobile radio from his office, and we chatted back and forth during the eight-hour trip

We stopped for lunch outside the town of Kismayo at a surprisingly well-equipped restaurant for such a remote location. The waiter seated us at the biggest table, next to the rail that bordered the veranda, where those of us who faced outward enjoyed a broad view of the savanna. The waiter wrote down our order and cautioned us about the owner's pet ostrich that roamed freely in the restaurant compound. He said the ostrich was very friendly but not good with children.

Our sandwiches came within minutes and we dug in. We had put the kids on the rail side of the table, because they were most interested in food and didn't care about the view. None of them noticed the big black bird trotting in a beeline toward our table. Before anyone could think to shout a warning, the ostrich zoomed its long neck in and snatched Dakota's sandwich. At first Dakota seemed more offended than startled. He stood up as if to chase after his lunch and then sat down abruptly. An unshackled full-grown ostrich can stare down the bravest of sandwich defenders when face-to-face within pecking distance. Dakota was happy to see the manager approach with a replacement for his shanghaied lunch.

We stopped at the Equator to take pictures. The photos remind me that I wore a skirt all the time in Somalia. I even ran in a skirt, a wraparound India print that I wore over my running shorts. The Somalis didn't approve of women in pants -- imagine what they would have thought of a woman in skimpy nylon running gear.

Other than a small monument, there wasn't anything remarkable about the Equator crossing. I straddled the imaginary line and felt colossal.

My first impression of the game park took me back once more to "King Solomon's Mines," my absolute favorite childhood movie. I wanted Stewart Granger to stride out of the main building to welcome us. The actual person couldn't live up to that expectation, even though he was a ruggedly handsome guy in his own right.

An employee showed us to our rooms, in this case, tents. Not ordinary tents, though. These had wood floors and a sturdy foundation. Made of heavy canvas, they stood as solid as a house. The toilet facilities were outside. The shower – I've dreamed ever since of having a shower as magnificent as this one – was also outdoors. Open to the sky and surrounded by a circular stone privacy wall, this phenomenon expanded my bathing-consciousness to the level of bliss. All the elements of equatorial Africa combined to create a sensory, sensual, out-of-body cleansing experience. Birdsong provided mood music and leaf-filtered sunbeams lit the scene. Bubbles of lavender-scented soap tickled my nostrils as a puff of breeze raised thrilling chill bumps on damp flesh. I would have lingered longer but for the need to conserve water.

The manager saw the Kellums's family pet, the cocker Sage Brush, and sighed.

"Be very careful with your puppy, Sir. Cheetahs are quite fond of dog."

I did not like the sound of that at all. Was Sage Brush to be the appetizer, like the sacrificial goat, to lure the cheetah to feast on us inside our tents? Those sturdy tents turned suddenly flimsy in my mind.

The manager moved on to another topic and distracted me out of worry mode. He invited us to take a boat ride. Our group clambered into three wooden fishing boats rowed by hotel fishermen. One guy fished while the other two dove for lobster, and we witnessed the freshness of our dinner-to-be.

Late afternoon on the edge of early evening was the prime time for game watching. Thanks to the luck of the draw, our family got to take the lead jeep with the guide. Fred rode up front, his long telephoto lens sticking out of the window, and the kids and I shared the back seat.

A few minutes down the road the guide slammed on the brakes and cut the engine; our bodies jerked forward and back. About twenty feet ahead a cheetah emerged from the underbrush and glided with regal elegance across the jeep track. Fred focused his telephoto lens and click, whirr, snapped his shot through the open window. The cheetah tensed, turned, and leaped forward into the deep brush. Fred jumped out of the jeep and ran after the cat. We all screamed, guide included, and Dakota the loudest.

"Get back in the car!"

What was he thinking? He told us later that he just wanted to get a good picture of the magnificent cat and wasn't really thinking at all. He had followed the cheetah into the thicket for a few feet before he awoke to where he was. When he turned his head and looked back, he couldn't see our vehicle through the heavy bush. Suddenly afraid, he scrambled backwards as fast as he could and luckily emerged onto the road in front of the jeep.

His children raked him over the coals for hours afterward, and his wife aided and abetted them, while he wore a sheepish grin.

On the day of our departure from Yamani Safari Camp we made a late start, and darkness fell when we were still two hours from Mogadishu. Buddy had taken the lead and set a pace that Flynn and Fred weren't willing to match once daylight was gone. The taillights of Buddy's truck grew smaller, tinier, and disappeared, taking the Kellums family out of sight and out of radio range. The rest of us motored on, Fred's crew in front and Flynn's behind.

We fell into silence, lulled by the hum of the engine in the dark. When the mobile radio crackled to life with incoherent shouting and Jo's panic-filled voice, we startled to attention. Fred made a quick u-turn and sped back toward the Fuller family's truck.

Cries and exclamations rattled the radio speakers. I grabbed our handset and tried to call Jo, but couldn't get through because the other radio was transmitting.

Fred pulled over and parked. He told us to stay inside while he crossed the road to see what had happened. Kimberley's whimpers and Alisa's cries still came over the radio. Whoever held the microphone maintained a death grip on the transmit key.

Fred returned and described a scene of carnage. The Fuller's Land Cruiser had run into a herd of cattle. One cow lay dead and the others milled about the crashed vehicle, mooing frantically. The grief-stricken cowherd, a boy barely in his teens, told Flynn (who spoke Somali) that he had to find his father who was at their nearby camp.

The cowherd's father surveyed the damage and demanded that Flynn pay for the cow -- and her future offspring. Flynn objected. Why should he pay when the accident was clearly the boy's fault? The boy drove the cattle across the road right into Flynn's path. He should have seen the headlights from a long way, while Flynn couldn't see the cows until it was too late to stop. But the man was adamant. Flynn stood firm. To break the stalemate, they agreed to take the matter to the police in the next town, about five miles up the road.

The radiator of Fuller's Toyota now penetrated the engine block, so Fred and Flynn rigged a towrope between our trucks. The cow's owner squeezed in with the Fullers and his son rode with us.

At the police station, the officer in charge examined all of our documents and listened to both sides of the controversy. Our children yawned and sagged in our laps. After a long discussion, the officer concluded that Flynn's diplomatic status earned him the right to return to Mogadishu and complete an insurance claim to cover the cost of repairs to the vehicle and the fair market value of the cow.

The trip back to Mog took most of the remainder of the night at slow towing speed. The kids went to sleep, no problem. My eyes ached from scouring the darkness for creatures in our path. Fred used reserves of strength he didn't know he had to pilot both families safely down the miserable road home.

Farewell to Shark's Bay

Normal life resumed after the Yamani Safari Camp adventure, and the next event on the horizon was Fred's fortieth birthday. Buddy Kellums announced that he had discovered the perfect place for our two families to celebrate. He described a secluded cove a few clicks (slang for kilometers) south of Shark's Bay, and he raved about perfect waves for body surfing, a rock-lined pool for snorkeling and spear fishing, and a grove of palm trees to provide shade for a picnic.

Buddy's oasis was as beautiful as his description. We spread our blankets in the cool shade of rustling palms. Tina and Heather arranged their Barbie dolls and entered their beloved fantasy world. Patti opened her mystery novel to escape into another realm. And the rest of us ran to the water to test our body surfing skills. Every wave broke at the exact spot for a perfect ride onto the smooth sandy beach. We surfed until our muscles cried for mercy.

On the trip back to town, passing Shark's Bay, Fred drew our attention to the unusual number of cars parked on the beach. A few months earlier the trip to Shark's Bay had been simplified by the construction of a real road. The Somali government built a highway to reach a prisoner-of-war camp down the coast from Shark's Bay, but the road passed close enough to the beach to give access to any kind of vehicle, including ordinary passenger cars and motorcycles. Shark's Bay became a popular recreation destination, no longer our private beach. With the shine of adventure removed, our trips there had become less frequent and we hadn't been there in months.

Fred signaled Buddy to stop, and we walked to the beach to see what was going on. People gathered in small groups. There was not a single person in the water. The absence of laughter and happy beach noises left a disturbing void. Buddy approached one of the groups to ask what had happened. He learned that a shark had attacked the teenage son of an Italian diplomat. Two other men yanked the boy from the shark's jaws, but not before the shark had bitten through his leg. Friends had carried the victim to their pickup truck and raced off toward Mogadishu, but the truck spun out in the sand and rolled over, throwing the injured boy out of the truck bed. With the help of bystanders they flipped the truck onto its wheels and went on to the hospital in Mog. We heard later that the victim's family arranged to fly him home to Italy for further treatment, but he died before the plane reached Rome.

In the following weeks we heard another horror story about a family who had invited a friend of their eight-year-old daughter to go to Shark's Bay with them. A shark attacked and killed the daughter's friend, biting her poor little body in half.

I couldn't count the number of times we had played in the water at Shark's Bay without ever worrying about sharks, much less seeing one. I wondered if the new road had brought so many people to the beach that the sharks took notice. Someone told us that the sharks were Zambezi River Sharks that had adopted an alternate migration pattern.

We knew about the danger of sharks on Mogadishu's city beaches. No one from the international community dared to wade in the water near town where aggressive sharks attacked in the shallows (except for the two German men who were killed on the day of their arrival, without getting a chance to hear the warnings). Mogadishu had become a busy port through the destruction of a protective reef. The sharks had unobstructed access to the offal dumped into the harbor by the large-scale meat processing plant located there. Now the sharks had discovered our former paradise and it would never again be the safe playground we had enjoyed so much.

Getting Ready to Go Again

Part of the Foreign Service cycle, the time to submit Fred's bid list, rolled around again. We had a long list of good choices: Port-Au-Prince, Haiti; Alexandria, Egypt; Mombasa, Kenya; Dakar, Senegal; Tunis, Tunisia; Rabat, Morocco; Asuncion, Paraguay; Zagreb, Yugoslavia. But Fred's boss, the DCM, Joe McLaughlan, asked an important question. Joe wanted to know if Fred would be interested in continuing to work for him at his new post, Santo Domingo, Dominican Republic. Fred gave an instant one-word answer. The Dominican Republic assignment satisfied all of our requirements with the added bonus of career-enhancements like ten weeks of Spanish language training, more supervisory duties for Fred, and attaché status as head of section. To top it off, Dakota would be able to continue his close friendship with Joe's son Robbie.

Even with Joe's request on the books, Fred's DR posting was not guaranteed. We still had to chew our fingernails during the long wait until the official telegram arrived.

With the assignment cable in hand, we could start making plans. I brought out the calendar. ASM classes started in August; we would leave Mog in early October; our home leave in Texas and New Mexico would last six weeks; in January Fred had to report to Washington for training, consultation, and Spanish classes; our arrival in Santo Domingo was expected in April. This program looked like fun but maybe not the best plan for school age children.

I didn't want Dakota and Tina to have to change schools four times in one year. I did some research and found out about the Calvert School in Maryland. Calvert School offered home schooling materials with optional teacher support by mail. I signed us up for the whole deal – fifth grade for Tina and sixth grade for Dakota. If successful, my master plan would keep them up-to-date with their studies and able to enter the appropriate grade in Santo Domingo for the final term of the school year.

We asked around and learned that many families faced with the same problems would choose to split up, the wage earner going his way and the spouse and children spending the intervening months in their home of record, until time to show up at the new post when they would reunite. We scoffed at that idea, a practical solution perhaps, but not our style.

I turned my attention from education to logistics. Embassies usually contract with local moving companies to pack employees' household effects. Somalia didn't have moving companies as we know them, so the job reverted back to the employee, or, in most cases, the employee's faithful (or even unfaithful) spouse.

Before I started packing, though, I had to go through the sorting process. Airfreight, sea freight, accompanied baggage, items to discard or give away – our fifth time through the familiar old routine.

At this point I chose to sell my kiln. I hadn't done any pottery in

Somalia, too busy with job, family, and travel. But I hoped to take it up again in the Dominican Republic, making a change from electric firing to gas.

I advertised the kiln in the embassy newsletter. I didn't hold out much hope of selling it, but – what the heck, I had to try.

Fred came home a few days later with a message from a Somali Army Colonel, Commandant of the local barracks, expressing interest in buying the kiln. Fred arranged for Ali, an embassy translator, to take me out to the barracks and help me with my negotiations with the colonel.

Could I have been more anxious? I don't think so. As we drove into the military compound, I felt a desperate urge to run away.

A row of low mud buildings formed a circle around a central court, the parade ground perhaps. Ali asked a couple of idle soldiers to carry the kiln from the embassy truck to a large room in the main building where the colonel waited with a dozen officers ranged along the wall. After introductions were made and tea served, the colonel told me, through Ali's translation, that he wanted his command to be as self-sufficient as possible. He planned to set up a workroom where his men could make all the dishes needed by the outfit.

The colonel asked me to explain how the kiln worked. I couldn't provide a complete demonstration because they lacked a compatible electrical outlet. It surprised me that they had electricity at all. I spoke slowly, pausing after each sentence, so Ali could translate. I outlined the whole pottery-making process and explained what kind of materials, equipment, tools and supplies they would need. The colonel remained silent and nodded often as I spoke.

I felt damp circles widening under my arms and a trickle running down and soaking my waistband. Trapped in the stares of twenty Somali men, I was a foreign object under a microscope. At the end of my presentation, I expected the colonel to thank me for my time and send Ali and me on our way. I wished with all my heart to be elsewhere as soon as possible.

The colonel cleared his throat and, in perfect English, said, "Mrs.

LaTurner, you must state your price and I will pay you in cash for your pottery oven."

And that successful "negotiation" brought me to the packing out phase and another surprise. As soon as GSO delivered the stacks of packing boxes and packing paper, Dakota got to work. He packed all of his possessions the first day.

In his words, "I figure you'll be needing my help with the rest."

I did need his help as well as Fred's and Tina's. Our team effort finished the job on time and resulted in no breakages whatsoever. Can't say the same for all packers, even the professionals.

We sweated as we worked on our packing at home, and the kids and I sweated at school. ASM had no power for three weeks after a backhoe operated by Somali road crew demolished the school's power pole. An emergency generator ran water pumps to keep the bathrooms functional, but the school had no lights, fans, air-conditioning, computers or electric typewriters.

Tina said she didn't miss computer class at all. Fred asked her why.

"I don't think computers are necessary for my chosen profession."

"And what is your chosen profession, Miss?"

"Housewife."

Fred laughed and said he imagined that Tina thought a typical housewife lived in a fine home, had lots of cuddly babies, and told the maid to fix lunch.

As we left Mogadishu, we carried away fond memories of many exciting experiences. But our final adventure in Africa happened during the taxi ride from the Nairobi Hilton to the airport to catch our midnight flight to the States. It was a moonless night, velvet black beyond the reach of the city lights. The hum of the tires and the cozy warmth of the cab almost lulled us to sleep, but the taxi's abrupt stop in the middle of the road bounced us awake. Across the yellow beams of the headlights streamed a parade of phantoms. A herd of wild zebras strolled across the highway, taking no notice of the insignificant intruders in their kingdom. Goodbye, Dark Continent, and thanks for the picturesque farewell salute.

22

Hunter and squirrel pelt

October 1984 – March 1985

In the Good Old USA

We had a two-page plan for our home leave itinerary and we accomplished everything except the deer hunt Dakota had requested. That disappointed Dakota, of course, but it relieved me. My own father came from a hunting family but did not enjoy hunting; I think his attitude rubbed off on me. I considered an eleven-year-old too young to wield a deadly weapon, even an eleven-year old as responsible and mature as Dakota.

When Fred and Grandpa LaTurner offered to take Dakota out into the desert for target practice, I relented and went along – as an observer.

I didn't expect to shoot, but I did want to watch Dakota having fun with his dad and grandpa.

Grandpa took us to a box canyon outside the city limits. Empty shotgun shells and spent cartridges littered the ground, and a variety of used targets leaned at angles against the canyon walls. A shot up washing machine squatted among holey metal real estate signs, perforated coke cans, and broken beer bottles.

The scene carried me back to my dad's brief foray into small game hunting. I was about ten years old and the idea of killing and eating rabbits and squirrels held me in grisly fascination. I remembered a pan-ready squirrel and how it reminded me of a naked human baby lying helpless on its back. Looking back, I realized that Dad was probably exploring a cheap meat source in hard times, rather than engaging in sport. Our family was hungry enough to eat everything he shot.

Because I was interested, Dad taught me how to hold, aim, and shoot his .22 rifle at a paper target tacked on a hay bale. I enjoyed the target practice, but I had no desire to kill. In the years since then, I had developed a strong aversion to hunting and weapons. For several years I didn't even eat meat. Now I felt painful conflict with my son's passion for guns and hunting.

An idea popped into my head. Could I alleviate the conflict by engaging in the activity myself? I didn't try the handguns – the loudness made me nervous -- but I recalled what my dad had taught me about shooting the .22 and decided to take a turn. The pleasure on Dakota's face convinced me that I had made the right decision. He showed me how to make the aluminum cans hop, and laughed with me when I did it too. Then he asked if I wanted to take a shot at a jackrabbit. He was kidding. Wasn't he?

The LaTurner family Christmas reunion at the Bunkhouse in Ruidoso, New Mexico, was the highlight of our home leave. Granny and Grandpa, their five children and spouses, and thirteen grandchildren plus one boyfriend and one dog (Mike's uninvited and unhousebroken black lab puppy) filled every bunk. The bunkhouse had a kitchen, two bathrooms, a fireplace, and two extra long picnic-style tables placed end to end. Granny and Grandpa wielded their special magic to fill the refrigerators with ingredients for every taste, coolers of beer and soft drinks, cases of wine, and the ever-present half-gallons of gin and bourbon. Granny decorated a tree to crown our stack of gifts. We had drawn names and the bunkhouse buzzed with speculation about who had given what to whom.

Some of the family took advantage of the great skiing at Ski Apache while others had hilarious good fun inner tubing. One of the young teenage drivers slid into a ditch on the way back from the slopes and had to be rescued -- no harm done other than slight ego damage.

Beth, Dave, Fred and I couldn't resist the call of the pine forest surrounding the bunkhouse. We jogged and hiked along the trails, blowing clouds of breath in the cold mountain air. A fallen log beckoned us to take a break, and Beth, Fred, and I sat down to enjoy our snacks. I ripped a big crunchy bite out of my apple and watched Dave wander around examining pinecones and rocks and other objects of interest on the forest floor. He bent down to pick something up. "Hey guys, what do you think this is?"

Fred took the first look at the oblong object in Dave's open palm. "Well, that is bear poop, Davey Crockett. Nice and fresh too."

With an instantaneous snap of his wrist, Dave flung his former object of interest as far as possible across the meadow. He wiped his hand back and forth on grass and leaves and up and down on the nearest tree trunk. He scraped at his palm with a stick. Beth handed him a tissue and he scrubbed at the invisible bear poop residue with dedication worthy of Lady Macbeth.

Fred interrupted Dave's compulsive hand wringing. "That bear poop was still warm, you know. Let's get out of here."

Dave was the first to hit the trail.

Back at the bunkhouse, a crowd of cousins surrounded Dakota. Michael and Mark, a year and two years younger than Dakota, stood the closest, glassy-eyed. I peered over the head of the shortest kid to see what the big attraction was.

Dakota held his BB gun in the crook of his left elbow. A dead squirrel dangled from his right hand. My reaction shocked everyone, including me. I wailed and cried. I freaked out, plain and simple. During the next excruciating minute, all eyes were on me. I was consumed with an overwhelming desire to evaporate.

Uncle Dick stepped in with calm assurance. He praised Dakota for his accurate shooting and told him that a good hunter should clean the kill and eat the meat. He showed Dakota how to skin the squirrel, butcher the meat, and dredge the pieces in seasoned flour before frying in hot oil. While the rest of the family watched Dick's demonstration, I fled to the bathroom to reconstruct myself.

Dakota saved the squirrel skin. I always thought he got too much pleasure from tormenting me with that reminder of my embarrassing hysterical outburst. Last time I checked, he still had the awful relic, twenty-six years later.

Part of the family reunion celebrated Christmas and part celebrated the birthdays of Tina and Darrell (the lone boyfriend, high school sweetheart and eventual husband of Pat and Dick's daughter Karen). Darrell was born in December 1964 and Tina in January 1974. They made a cute picture standing side-by-side, tall handsome Darrell and darling petite Tina, blowing out the candles together.

The Bell From Hell

Extra weeks of home leave allowed time for a side trip to Arizona to reunite with the Kellums family who had completed their contract in Somalia and returned to home base in Phoenix.

Fred had a surprise for Buddy that he was excited to deliver. Back in Somalia, Fred and Buddy had repaired the school's water pump and in the re-installation process they had dropped the pump down the well. It took many hours and their combined ingenuity to invent a retrieval device. There was loud shouting and high-kick victory dancing when their contraption pulled the pump into position. The sweaty sunburned duo toasted their success with iced Coors beer and christened their invention "The Bell from Hell."

258 ☙ VOLUNTARY NOMADS

Fred hand-carried "The Bell" from Mogadishu to my dad's workshop and turned it into a lamp for Buddy. The gift was a major surprise and it set the tone for a marvelous visit with our good friends. The combination of nonstop grown-up-partying and kids' energetic games turned the Kellums home into a post-hurricane disaster scene that we laughed about and photographed from every angle.

When we said goodbye to the Kellumses we promised to get together soon and let the LaTurner house take a turn at being wrecked.

Spanish and Other Lessons

Before we were ready for it, the calendar flipped to January and we learned that even the longest imaginable home leave passes far too fast. We set off for Washington DC in our new sand-colored Jeep Cherokee, purchased at the beginning of home leave in Albuquerque. On Tina's actual eleventh birthday, January 9, 1985, in Lexington, Kentucky, she got to choose the motel and the restaurant. She picked Howard Johnson's and Pizza Hut.

Once in Washington, we checked into The Columbia Plaza, a residential hotel up the street from Main State, headquarters of The State Department. The Foreign Service had reserved a block of rooms and suites for personnel in transit. We made our temporary home there, grumbled about the old cranky TV and the cranky old receptionist, and spent most of our time out in the city. We walked down the hill to the Lincoln Memorial, paid a visit to the statue of Albert Einstein, and fed (rather than shot) the squirrels that scampered among the trees along the reflecting pool on the Mall. Fred and I jogged on the paths circling the pool and mall. We watched ice skaters twirling and speeding on the frozen duck pond.

The Columbia Plaza served well on a temporary basis while Fred had business at Main State, but we needed to find someplace else for the ten weeks of Spanish language training. The Foreign Service Lounge, the place to get mail and all sorts of information, had a bulletin board where Fred found a listing of apartments and townhouses for rent. We chose a townhouse located in a neighborhood not far from the Foreign Service Institute in Rosslyn, Virginia, home of the extensive FS language school.

The townhouse gave us more space and seemed more like a home than the Columbia Plaza suite. When I compared it to the dismal apartment we rented on our first trip to DC, I realized how far we had come in ten years. Maybe the basement here was dark and creepy, but it didn't scare me like the first laundry room had.

Fred started his Spanish classes and the kids and I resumed their Calvert lessons. Fred had a full-day schedule; eight hours of Spanish instruction and conversation, plus two hours of homework at night. The kids and I had it easy. If Dakota and Tina worked at a steady pace on each day's lesson, they could finish by lunchtime. For PE, they rode their new BMX bikes beside me while I ran five miles. After official schoolwork was done, we often explored the Smithsonian or any of the other museums and historical attractions in the area.

At the end of each unit in the Calvert course, the kids completed a test that I sent to our teacher/advisor for grading. Both Dakota and Tina did flawless work. Tina seemed to enjoy playing school every day and buckled down each morning to get her work done. Dakota did his assignments too, but he didn't see the fun in it. He said he missed being with other kids so much that he wanted to enroll in regular school.

Frances Scott Key Elementary was a few blocks away. The person in charge of admissions told me that they accepted new students at any time. The student body included many children of diplomats whose comings and goings were unpredictable and often sudden. She said that Dakota could start school as soon as he completed a placement test and submitted the results of his most recent health exam.

I think Dakota was happy with his decision. He said he liked his teacher and he didn't ask to return to home schooling. He did complain a bit about one kid in his class though. This kid sounded like a typical schoolyard bully to me. He teased, helped himself to other's desserts, tripped and pushed, ridiculed and tormented smaller, weaker children.

Friday morning of the first week of his Francis Scott Key attendance,

Dakota asked a question at breakfast. "Do you think I could have a friend come over after school today?"

"Great idea! Who are you going to ask?"

"Darisol."

"Darisol? Isn't he the boy that picks on the other kids all the time?"

"Yeah, but he's my friend now."

"How so?"

"Well, yesterday he tried to pick a fight with me, and I just told him I didn't need to fight him to prove anything." Dakota shrugged. "So Darisol said do I want to be friends and I said okay why not."

Darisol came home with Dakota several times after that. He behaved so well I had trouble seeing him as the class bully. Maybe he didn't need to play that part with a real friend who refused to be intimidated.

Darisol was with us the day we hiked to Theodore Roosevelt Island, an 88-acre park in the middle of the Potomac River. Fred was in class, so it must have been a teacher in-service day at Francis Scott Key. At any rate, Dakota and Darisol had the day off and Tina and I made it a holiday too. We planned to walk to the island, hike around it, have our picnic lunch and walk home. According to the map legend, the distance seemed doable.

To get to the island, we had to cross the Theodore Roosevelt Memorial Bridge from Arlington to DC and then a footbridge to the island. Not particularly impressive by car, the Theodore Roosevelt Memorial Bridge is quite thrilling on foot. A strong wind pushed us forward and the backwash of whizzing traffic buffeted against us. Noise, fumes, and wind-chill spurred us on.

What a relief it was to reach the island, a quiet sanctuary where tall trees shielded us from the wind, soft sandy pathways cushioned our feet, and birdsong soothed our ears. Dakota, Darisol and Tina scrounged walking sticks from the forest edge and we marched on.

We wound our way through the complex system of nature trails commemorating Roosevelt's life-long support of conservation. At one-thirty we picnicked on a bench at the foot of the grand Roosevelt Memorial located on the north side of the island in the center of the widest part. The memorial featured a heroic statue of TR, mounted on a horse, of course.

After lunch we resumed our winding course among the tall trees, heading back toward the bridges at the southern end of the island. In an hour or so, we arrived, not at the footbridge, but back at the TR Memorial. Oops. There was nothing to do but try again.

Our second attempt brought us to the footbridge, thank goodness. But the sun had dropped to a lower angle and clouds had blown in to block its warmth. The wind was behind us on the footbridge, a momentary advantage, but it would be in our faces all the way across the long span of the big bridge. I whipped out my wallet to see if I had enough cash for cab fare. Yes, if I scrooged the tip.

Fortune smiled on my weary bone-chilled troop – an empty taxi was going our way. Whines turned to cheers and the kids told the cab driver all about their adventure. He didn't seem to mind that his tip was so small.

While the kids and I carried on in our carefree way, Fred toiled with his Spanish studies. He said he liked the classes, but he hated the homework. Why would he want to barricade himself in the bedroom with the tape recorder when he could be drinking beer and watching TV?

I borrowed the FSI tapes to keep up with Fred's class. I remember one lesson in particular. The system required listening to phrases and then repeating them. The phrase that stuck in my brain sounded like, "blah bleh BLAI blah bloh bloh BLEH," in rapid fire like an automatic weapon. The tape recorder didn't have a slow function, so I had to listen to that phrase over and over and over to make sense of it. If it had been taken out of context, I would never have figured it out. This phrase, however, was the answer to a previous question, and the context gave good clues. At last, I heard the words and understood. "La que baila con Jose" -- she who dances with Jose. Nonsense became sense and the world turned right side up again.

When Fred's class went to an Argentinean restaurant for lunch to practice their developing conversational skills, I went too, and I left the kids with the next-door neighbor, Mrs. Roland, for a couple of hours. A

widow in her seventies, Mrs. Roland lived alone and always seemed eager
to talk when we bumped into each other out front or happened to be in
our back yards at the same time. She entertained our kids with milk and
cookies and stories of the past.

One story in particular fascinated them. Mrs. R. told about the original owners of the attached town home, the one we were renting. She said
that they were a retired couple that lived there for several years. When the
old man died, his wife couldn't get over her sadness. She stopped talking
to her friends; she never went out of the house. Mrs. R., who was several
years younger, tried to check on her every day and urge her to eat. But
shortly after the old man's death, Mrs. R's daughter in Maryland had a
new baby, and Mrs. R. went to help her for a couple of weeks.

As soon as she got home from her trip to Maryland, Mrs. R. knocked
on the neighbor's door. Her knocks pushed the unlatched door open. She
stepped inside and called her neighbor's name. No answer. She searched
all through the silent house.

The basement was dark and scary and the clanking, growling furnace
startled her. Dakota and Tina understood that – our old furnace spooked
them too.

Mrs. R. continued her story, recalling how she hurried upstairs to the
second floor and searched the bedroom and the closet. Then she noticed
that the door to the attic gaped open. She felt her way inside and patted
along the wall to find the light switch. The single bulb cast eerie shadows. The biggest shadow told her everything she needed to know, and she
turned and ran to the telephone.

Now that they knew that the woman who lived in our townhouse
had hung herself in the attic, Dakota and Tina added a new ritual to their
bedtime routine. They insisted that Daddy check the attic every night and
secure the door by pushing the heaviest chest of drawers tight against it.

In the daylight, nighttime fears forgotten, Dakota thought about his
savings. His own money, earned bagging groceries at the commissary in
Mogadishu, sang siren songs of treasures to be bought. On the way home
from school, he walked past a pawnshop. In the window he saw what he

wanted, a real drum set. He begged Fred to go with him to look at it. The price was right.

Fred helped him set up in the basement, and we lived with the beat of our own drummer. Over the years, the drum kit changed, grew, and evolved, as did the drummer and his family.

From January to April we savored our brief taste of life in the U.S. My brother Gary and his wife Pam and three-year-old son Patrick visited us. So did Beth, Dave, and Ronnie. Ron was on vacation from military school and he showed off his uniform and the moves of "Present Arms."

We visited back and forth with the Ekstroms (Cameroon) in Reston, Virginia, and the Goffs (Iran) in Manassas, Virginia. The Ekstroms introduced us to their favorite sushi restaurant, which became our favorite as well. And the Goffs took us to the Ringling Brothers circus.

Fred made one quick trip back to New Mexico when his dad suffered a heart attack. All five siblings stayed at the hospital until they were sure their dad was sure to recover. Then they took their mom home and discussed ordering a carry out dinner.

Mike suggested Kentucky Fried Chicken.

Fred said, "No, Nancy hates Kentucky Fried Chicken."

Pat, Beth, Laura and Mike laughed.

Beth put her arm around Fred. "But Nancy isn't here now, is she?"

PART SIX

DOMINICAN REPUBLIC DRAMAS

Our son the windsurfer

23

Nancy and Tina, moped tourists in Puerto Plata

April 1985

Welcome

After Fred returned from New Mexico and completed his language training, we packed up our airfreight and surrendered it as well as our car to the shipping experts. It was time to take flight to our new destination.

The 3-1/2 hour layover in the Miami airport served as a warm-up for total immersion in the language and my ears and brain buzzed with Spanish phrases. Our flight from Miami to Santo Domingo was blissfully short at one hour and forty-one minutes, just time enough for the ascent to cruising altitude, a quick meal service, and hurried preparation for landing.

I don't know if it's still true, but in April of 1985, the Santo Domingo arrival lounge offered a unique welcoming party. A group of four rum company representatives greeted us and offered free samples of their wares – large cups of rum and coke -- the perfect introduction to a fun-loving land of party-all-the-time. Merengue music throbbed in the background and my feet moved to the irresistible beat.

Our sponsors, Bill and Maggie, waited with transportation to temporary quarters and we started the picturesque drive along a palm-tree-lined boulevard. A short distance from the airport our van swerved to the curb and stopped.

Bill pointed to the nearby roadside stand. "Maggie and I always stop here," he said.

Faded blue letters on a driftwood sign read, "Coco Frio." We followed Bill and Maggie's lead and rolled down our windows. The smiling vendor pulled fresh coconuts from an ice-filled 50-gallon drum. He whacked off the top of each coconut, inserted a straw, and gave one to each of us. I sipped and held the thin liquid in my mouth to get the full taste of it. The pleasant flavor, neither sweet nor sour, left my tongue feeling clean. The coconut milk satisfied my thirst and soothed my throat. And it blended well with the rum already in my tummy.

Our temporary quarters occupied the entire third floor of a five-story apartment building a mere two blocks from the embassy. Polished terrazzo floors and a modern kitchen gave the place an air of luxury and standard embassy furnishings made us feel at home. We chose our bedrooms, inspected the bathrooms, and spread our belongings out to personalize the space.

The humid air, heavy with cloying tropical odors, brought back a sensory memory of our arrival in Cameroon eight years before. As I opened a window to catch the ocean breeze, the whirr of city traffic reminded me that this country was more sophisticated than the land of jungle drums.

We spent the first week checking into the embassy, obtaining our ID's and driver's licenses, registering the kids at Carol Morgan School, and getting acquainted with people and places – standard operating procedure, same as our previous four posts. I paced the floor, waiting for the results of Dakota's and Tina's placement tests. We celebrated with an ice cream toast when their scores proved that our year of home schooling had kept them at grade level.

One of the guys in Fred's office, Larry, was dating an embassy colleague who had a daughter about Tina's age. Tina and Pamela made friends the first time they met, and Pamela invited Tina to go with her to camp the next week. I knew Tina wouldn't want to go. She had never been away from home for more than one night at a time and this camp lasted a whole week. Pamela was the only person Tina knew in this new country other than our family and she didn't know her very well at all.

But Tina did want to go. What was she thinking? We gave our permission. What were we thinking?

Tina went to camp. She stuck it out, although she didn't have much choice in those circumstances -- no cell phones and no phone service at the camp itself to allow her to let us know she had changed her mind. When she came home she said she had been very sad and homesick and cried herself to sleep every night, but she did enjoy horseback riding and swimming and making handicrafts. She brought home the felt banner she had made. It said "God Loves You." No one had told us that this was a church camp. Nor had Pamela's mother revealed that she sent the girls to camp, a two-hour trip, by themselves in a publico (taxi). I still shudder when I think of everything that could have gone wrong. But it all turned out fine.

Tina and Pamela weren't in the same class at school, though, so their friendship waned when classes resumed after Easter break. Tina made new friends and soon had a busy social life. Dakota too. He had a built-in friend in Robbie McLaughlan (from Somalia) and Robbie's friends became his friends too.

It was not a bad thing to be the newcomer at an international school. Students came and went so often that cliques couldn't solidify. Social groups still existed, of course, but they were more flexible and less exclusive. Most of the students had to be the new kid often enough that they were much more sympathetic to newcomers.

Dark Clouds

I didn't see the dark clouds gathering on the horizon, and I didn't notice any other signs of imminent stormy weather. Even the barometric pressure seemed normal that Sunday afternoon in May when the tempest struck.

"I want a divorce," Fred announced. He stood on the opposite side of the kitchen table, his hands gripping the top rail of the chair he usually sat in at breakfast time.

"What?" My brain refused to process. I searched Fred's face for clues but I read no emotion there. His blue eyes were steely, almost gray. His lips were closed, dry, tense.

"What…." I brushed imaginary crumbs and smoothed nonexistent wrinkles from the pink embassy-issued tablecloth.

I felt vague and two-dimensional, like a figure in a Monet painting, as Fred pronounced the death sentence on our marriage. He said he wanted more out of life – more excitement, more adventure, and more passion. He declared that he wasn't in love with me anymore. He repeated that he wanted a divorce.

My next thought rocketed through my lips before good sense could censor it. "You're having a mid-life crisis!"

"Bullshit!" Fred slammed the door behind him and left me with the echo of his last word.

My head filled with broken images that swirled around in an emotional tornado. I cowered in a corner of rejection, filled with despair. Then I soared high on a wave of rage, screaming threats of revenge. And finally, I steadied myself to face the crisis.

What about our relationship? Fred had always bragged about how well we got along compared to most couples we knew. We had created our life in the Foreign Service as a team and we shared goals and ideals. We cherished our plans for an active life after early retirement. *Does he really want to throw that away?*

What about our family? We agreed from the beginning that family life came first. *Can he turn his back on all of us?*

Passion! Excitement! Adventure! Over the past eighteen years of marriage, our life had seemed well endowed with all of these. *What is he looking for?*

When Fred returned, I asked my questions and beseeched him to think and reflect on the consequences of divorce. I begged him to remember our goals and ideals, and I urged him to consider the children. I proposed separate vacations so he could find excitement and adventure on his own. I suggested counseling.

After a long and grueling discussion, I asked him to give our marriage a chance. He seemed reluctant, but he agreed. We stepped off the cliff together, not holding hands this time, but still heading in the same general direction, I thought.

We scheduled "dates" to invigorate the flagging passion in our relationship. Fred signed up for scuba classes to bring additional excitement and adventure into his life. And we worked at communicating our needs to each other.

I told Fred that I planned to send for information about master's degree programs in library science in the States. If our marriage ended in divorce, I intended to be prepared for life on my own. I thought that a university in Miami might be a good choice. If Fred extended his tour in the Dominican Republic, we would be close enough for the kids to spend vacations and holidays with him. I told him that Dakota and Tina would live with me, no matter what. Fred looked surprised, as if he hadn't given much thought to how the final details of a divorce might play out. He said he would finance my studies if that were the direction we took. I heard a hint of new respect in his voice.

The atmosphere of our relationship reminded me of two dogs circling each other, growling but wagging their tails. The standoff could end in a snarling fight or a playful romp. On any given day, I didn't know what to expect.

A Family Needs a Home

The search for a house provided a welcome distraction from the turmoil in my head and heart. I checked the housing unit's list of available properties and signed up to tour the various options.

Our housing was furnished by the embassy, but instead of a pre-paid lease, Fred received a fixed amount of money each month as a housing allowance. We hoped to stretch that amount to cover both rent and utilities.

I started with the places within our price range. Almost all of those were apartments or houses that were too small or didn't have a yard to accommodate the pets we had promised to get. At that point Fred and I realized we would have to go out of pocket for utilities.

That's when I fell in love with the house on San Geraldino. Fred didn't quite fall in love with it. He calculated the bottom line and saw that his housing allowance wouldn't cover all of the $850 monthly rent or any of the utilities. Then he checked out the other properties and gave in to my desire for this house.

I admired the beauty of the hand-carved woodwork and the ornate plaster mouldings. Maybe the floor plan didn't have the most sensible layout, but I thought it was interesting. Each of three bedrooms had its own bath, but the fourth bedroom had none. The fourth bath was part of the pool changing-room suite in the backyard. The landlord said he had built this house for his wife and promised her a pool, but under the thin layer of soil he found solid coral rock, impossible to dig deep enough to make a swimming pool. The outbuilding for the changing-room/bath stood empty, unused except for storage.

The rest of the house felt open, airy and spacious, but the rooms other than the kitchen didn't demonstrate a clear purpose. The front door opened on an unfurnished room-sized space – like a foyer, only bigger. To the left lay a room we started to refer to as the front room, because of its position at the front of the house. Through an archway, between the front room and the kitchen, was a room that might logically serve as the dining room. Next to the dining room, a large open space connected to the foyer. I dubbed that area the library, because it had a built-in bookshelf. And the library led to a hallway past the bedrooms on the one hand and to another living room/family room on the other. The family room had three solid walls; the fourth side opened onto the covered patio and the back yard and could be closed off for night security with a metal accordion grate.

Behind the kitchen, in an unattached building, we found the maid's quarters, occupied by Juanita, who had been employed by the previous occupants and agreed to stay on with us. Fred's mother, who has always been known as Nita, was born Juanita. And Tina, named for her grandmother, carries the name Juanita on her birth certificate. We made a few bad jokes about Las Tres Juanitas and how they might be related to The Three Stooges. Later, our lame jokes went through a brief revival with the release of the movie The Three Amigos.

Of all the rooms in the house, the master suite attracted me the most. I loved the luxurious cedar-lined walk in closet, the marble double-sink vanity, and the oversized garden tub. It would have been a perfect sanctuary but for the incessant barking of the neighbor's dogs that were penned right outside the window. Those were the same neighbors who had the gall to make grumpy remarks about the noise of our generator during city power outages. Sometimes in the middle of a sleepless night, I fantasized about slipping those dogs a fatal tidbit.

Because our house was on the school bus route, I signed our kids up. Unfortunately, they had to be first on at 6:30 AM and last off at 3:00 PM. Dakota and Tina didn't mind, in fact, they said they enjoyed the extra time with their friends. The bus looked like a rickety bucket of bolts to me. The tropical climate had taken a serious toll on the floorboards, leaving several gaps where the kids could watch the roadway flashing by. The weather didn't aid the engine or tires either, and the bus provided less than reliable service. Still, the kids didn't complain.

Active Life

By the time we moved from temporary quarters into our home, Dakota and Tina had already settled into school and their social lives continued to develop quickly. Carol Morgan School had a well-established music program; Dakota started off with guitar lessons, a prerequisite to percussion, and Tina joined the choir.

Fred and I sought out the running community. We participated in the fun runs held once a month or so and I always placed second or third in my age group. Fred took the spotlight as the winner in the highly competitive Masters category (men over 40). Our new-found fame led to an invitation to join the Amigos del Maratón, a group that worked to promote the sport of running by organizing events and convincing local businesses to sponsor races. The founding members of the club, Hortensia, Fernando, and Adrian, befriended us and invited us to social occasions as well as the sporting events.

Life went on in an outwardly normal way although I was aware of the uncomfortable distance between Fred and me. Our efforts to heal our relationship waned as we dealt with an onslaught of interruptions – like the series of water outages caused by Juanita's running toilet -- and the fractious animal population at our house.

It was true that Fred and I had promised the kids they could have pets, although we had not anticipated inheriting a cat and a bird from the previous tenants. When we agreed to keep the cat, we didn't know she was pregnant. Of course we had no idea that the parakeet hated people. And when we let a departing family talk us into taking their pet hen, we didn't realize that the creature was accustomed to living in the house but had never been introduced to any concept of toilet hygiene.

The parakeet's name was Candy, but she was far from sweet. She attacked any hand that tried to feed her. Fred took pity on her, tried without success to teach her to fly so she could go free, and, as a last resort, installed her cage in his office at the embassy. Once in a while her midnight flutterings would set off the motion sensor alarms, and Fred had to go to the embassy to turn it off. It's a wonder he didn't get busted for having an animal in "the box," as his secure office area was called. For reasons known only to Fred, he stuck by that crazy bird (he renamed her Linda Paloma) until she died of natural (we assume) causes.

The hen, Peck-Peck, did not make the grade as a pet either. Her name when spoken by her original owners sounded affectionate. In real life, her name was definitive. She pecked the cat, she pecked the kids, she pecked

Juanita and she pecked Fred and me. Juanita suggested that a stewing pot might be a suitable home for Peck-Peck and we offered to deliver. I suffered one small pang of guilt when I thought of Juanita's relatives sitting down to dine on chicken stew, but I got over it as soon as our floors were free of chicken poop.

The resident cat birthed her litter and we made a deal with Tina to keep two kittens and find homes for the rest, including the mother cat that had not been friendly with any of us. Tina chose one ginger and one multi-colored kitty. After a couple of weeks she gave the ginger one, all claws and feistiness, to Dakota's friend Robbie who appreciated its aggressive personality.

Little Motley, the multi-colored one, was very sweet, good-natured and affectionate. But the neighbor's horrible dogs made sure she had a short life. After the dog attack we brought her to the vet who didn't find any external injuries. Nevertheless, Tina woke the next morning to find her kitty stiff and cold.

In an attempt to cheer Tina, Fred brought home two hamsters from the pet store at Plaza Naco, the local shopping mall. Tina named the happy couple Beth and Dave. She thought it might bring good luck to the human Aunt Beth and Uncle Dave who were hoping for a baby of their own at the time.

The hamster version of Beth and Dave wasted no time on hope. A litter of eight pups popped into our lives.

Several months later, Tina merely shrugged when I told her the hamster experiment had to end. She admitted she was tired of the racket they made all night, scrabbling round and round on the exercise wheel and gnawing on their nesting material. She wouldn't miss the stink either – or the nasty chore of cage cleaning.

Soon after the departure of the hamster clan, Tina spent a weekend at her friend's family beach house and came home with a coal black orphan kitten named Carbón. The gardener at the beach house had raised the tiny kitty on his few food scraps and fallen mangoes. Carbón became Tina's shadow. He had a unique habit of going to sleep on Tina's lap, sucking on his own teat (which was enlarged as a result). He must have been orphaned at a very young age to learn to find comfort that way.

Dakota still wanted a puppy. Our vet told us about a breeder he knew whose pair of boxers had just produced a litter of ten. He gave me the address and phone number and I called to set up an appointment for Dakota to see the newborns and pick one.

I parked in front of the breeder's house and Dakota rang the bell. No answer. I banged on the door. Silence.

We went home, Dakota sad with disappointment. I fumed with frustration. I assumed the breeder had stood us up. My temper, on a short fuse these days, flared hot. When I called the breeder, I was ready to chew him out, but he answered with a cheery explanation about his address. Because of Santo Domingo's haphazard numbering style, there were two homes, at opposite ends of the street, with the same address, and I had gone to the wrong one. The breeder assured me that he was still ready to keep our appointment if we wanted to return.

Dakota chose the only brindle puppy. I could see the love in his eyes when he looked up at me as he stroked the tiny head. "I'm gonna call him Spike."

A few weeks later, Spike was weaned prematurely when his mother stopped lactating. We brought Spike home and bottle-fed him. At first the adorable little fellow needed extra care to overcome his poor beginning as the runt of his litter. Technically Spike belonged to Dakota, but most of his treatments required adult-level skills. Who better than Mom to fill in? While Dakota and Tina studied at school and Fred worked at the embassy, Spike and I consulted with Dr. Nova.

Between visits to the veterinary clinic, Spike and I stayed at home. I administered the medication for the calcium deficiency that made his legs too weak to hold him up, and I rubbed him with the ointments prescribed for his mangy skin rash. His artistically cropped ears needed daily bandage changes as well. I wiped up his little puddles and other housebreaking mishaps when Dakota wasn't around to perform that chore. Spike also depended on me to protect him from Carbón the cat, big enough to over-power the awkward little puppy.

By the time Spike was six months old, he had outgrown his puppy problems and developed into a healthy dog. At the end of every busy day, when I sank into my rattan rocker, Spike appeared, pushed against my hand to demand a vigorous butt scratch, then plopped down beside me. He rested his plush chin on top of my bare foot and gazed up at me as I stroked his head until he dozed.

One evening after we had assumed our usual positions, Spike jerked awake and jumped up. He sniffed the air in all directions and trotted to the dining room. I followed to see what had aroused him. A gray-brown blur scurried along the wall and froze in the corner. No doubt in my mind, the intruder was a rat, possibly a refugee from the vacant-lot-cum-garbage-dump across the street. I intercepted Spike, swooped him into my arms and scrambled up onto the top of the dining room table.

Spike barked. I screamed. Fred, Dakota, and Tina ran in.

"Let the dog go!" Fred's shout echoed in the high-ceilinged room.

"No, no, the rat might bite." I clutched squirming Spike closer to my chest.

The rat took off, scrabbled for footing on the slick terrazzo floor, and headed straight for Dakota's room. Tina jumped up on the table beside me and buried her face in Spike's shoulder. Fred and Dakota shot us withering looks, strode to the bedroom, and slammed the door.

Muffled thumps, grunts, bangs and thuds sounded across the hall. Spike whined and quivered in my arms as the bedroom door swung open. In one hand Fred brandished Dakota's tennis racket. In the other he clamped the tail of a limp, blood-streaked rat. Beside him, Dakota cocked his baseball bat and mimed a home-run swing. I wished I could apologize to Spike for spoiling his fun, but if Fred and Dakota couldn't understand my motives, how could the dog?

After our hunters disposed of their quarry and embellished their tale a few more times, we calmed down. Spike curled up with his head on my foot as if to say, "No hard feelings, Mom."

Visitors

It was August, but it seemed like we had barely moved into our house, received our household effects, and settled in when Fred's parents announced their plans to visit. I didn't feel ready to host visitors. I wondered if Fred and I could or should hide our problems from his parents. At the same time, I wanted company and something fun to look forward to.

Grandpa was still recovering from a recent heart attack, and I worried about his fitness for travel. He did have his cardiologist's approval, so I knocked on wood for luck and made up the bed in the guestroom. I enlisted the help of the whole family and all of our household help to clean and equip the pool house bathroom for Granny and Grandpa. I set out sweet-smelling soaps, a variety of lotions, fluffy new towels, and a glass carafe filled with bottled water for tooth brushing. I made a mental note to show Granny and Grandpa our cistern that collected city water as it flowed sporadically through the system. When they saw the cockroaches that lived in the cistern, I knew they would understand the need to use bottled water for cooking, drinking, and tooth brushing.

Granny and Grandpa came for three weeks and we had fun, even though we didn't know all of the best touring spots yet. We took them to Playa Royale, a posh beach resort and to Boca Chica, the workingman's beach. Granny and Grandpa were always ready for any kind of adventure and they definitely knew how to have a good time. Inconveniences that might have spoiled the visit for ordinary folks didn't faze our guests. They were, after all, LaTurners.

A sudden tropical rainstorm caught us by surprise one afternoon. Granny, stranded in the outside bathroom, made a run for the house. She pranced around the family room laughing about the squelching noises coming from her cute little white leather Keds. When she went to the guestroom to dry off and change clothes, she brought us running with a shrill screech. The torrent of rain had found a leak in the roof of the guestroom. Water was overflowing Granny's purse that gaped open on the dresser. She giggled as she spread out the contents of her wallet and cosmetics case on the bed to dry. "You didn't tell us we'd be camping out!"

The next afternoon, Granny and Grandpa headed for their bedroom for a nap and found a tarantula in the middle of the bed. They got a good laugh out of that camp-like experience too, once Fred removed the intruder. First the ticks in Beth and Dave's bed in Somalia, now the tarantula in Granny and Grandpa's bed – what were the odds – and why our guests but not us?

When the weather cleared, Fred and I took the folks north to Jarabacoa to see the mountainous part of the country. I suggested that we find a hidden waterfall that I'd heard about. We followed a faint trail through the forest. Although we rested often for Grandpa's sake, he seemed exhausted by the time we found the waterfall. The cascade was as lovely as a bridal veil, but I wondered if the view was worth the cost to Grandpa's heart. Grandpa leaned on Fred as we moved slowly back to the car. He slumped into his seat and let his head fall back onto the headrest.

Fred turned the car onto the road to Santo Domingo and home. Grandpa's eyes closed and I assumed he was asleep.

"Stop!" Grandpa shouted and pointed to a layby beside the highway. *Oh, no, his heart.*

Then I saw what he saw – a roadside stand selling fresh roast pork. I knew Grandpa had been struggling with his new heart-healthy diet. The fragrance of succulence wafting through the open window must have lit a strobe light in his pleasure center. Grandpa devoured his forbidden treat straight from the package and licked the grease from his fingers when he was done. He smiled all the way home.

Work

After Granny and Grandpa left, I started an earnest search for work. With the wonderful American School Mogadishu library job behind me, I hoped to get another library job in Santo Domingo. The Carol Morgan library was already staffed with long-term employees, but the other English-speaking secondary school in town, American School of Santo Domingo, published an ad for director of their new library.

I came home from my interview with mixed feelings. I knew I had made a good impression, but I wasn't sure of my own opinion of the school and its leader. The library was in the planning stages and both the space and the budget seemed skimpy to me. The salary they offered didn't impress me either. My main worry, however, was the abrasive personality of the director of the school. I had serious doubts about being able to work with the man. By the time the official letter arrived, I had made up my mind and felt a sense of relief when I turned down the offer.

There were no jobs available at the embassy, so I responded to an advertisement that had been sent to the Community Liaison Office (CLO) newsletter. That's how I became a Research Associate for Runzheimer International.

In the beginning, I liked the work, which involved gathering cost-of-living data. Runzheimer provided the collected information to various corporations around the world that contemplated establishing a presence in Santo Domingo. Over the next several months I gathered the basic data to establish a cost-of-living baseline, and that was very interesting to me. But after the baseline was established the job dwindled to tedious quarterly updates. I started looking for different employment.

I had worked my way through college with part-time office jobs and I had developed good skills. So I asked the Personnel Officer at the Embassy what they did when secretaries went on vacation. She said they brought in TDY secretaries for the American positions (Ambassador's and DCM's secretaries), but they didn't have a system for the local hires and considered it a problem. I offered myself as a floating substitute. We worked out a pay scale and I signed a personal services contract.

The first assignment placed me in the chair of the secretary to the chief financial officer of AID. I completed the routine office tasks in short order and had time on my hands. The CFO praised my work every day, but I still felt a need to fill those empty hours and at least look busy and productive. After I tidied the supply storeroom, I tackled the secretary's desk and filing system. Of course I meant to be helpful, but I realized from the look on her face when she returned to work, that I had made a serious territorial blunder. Thanks to her easy-going, relaxed approach to life (and her gratitude that she didn't face a mountain of work) I was forgiven. I learned a valuable lesson about respecting personal office boundaries.

I also learned something else on that job: Dominicans had a unique philosophy about filing. Contrary to my belief that filed materials should be accessible if needed in the future, Dominicans defined "filed" as "out of sight" and that of course meant, in many cases, "gone forever."

My next assignment followed immediately, thanks to the recommendation of the CFO's secretary. She suggested that I fill in for her sister who worked at APHIS (the Animal and Plant Health Inspection Service of the United States Department of Agriculture).

I worked alone in APHIS. The office comprised two officers, one in charge of plant inspections and one for animal inspections to certify the health of all agricultural products bound for the US. The officers traveled most of the time, returning to Santo Domingo for a day or two to submit reports or attend meetings at the embassy. This time I left the secretary's space just as I had found it.

The next assignment sent me to the Human Resources Division of AID. First I filled in for the secretary. When she returned she recommended me as a substitute for one of the project managers. The projects managed by HRD focused on education and small business development and my new duties involved some of each. I had found something I could get my teeth into at last. These projects disbursed foreign aid money in ways I could endorse, ways that reached and benefited people in need and changed their lives for the better.

The boss noticed my enthusiasm. When my predecessor returned from vacation, the boss informed her that her contract would not be renewed. And I had a brief introduction to the world of government contract negotiation. I was lucky to have a friend who could guide me through the process and help me land a decent contract.

In governmentese, my title was Program Analyst and Deputy Division Chief. In real life, I managed several specific projects – a $5.5 million initiative that granted college scholarships to gifted graduates of Dominican high schools, a $250,000 fund that provided English language training and educational counseling to Dominican applicants to U.S. universities, and two smaller projects that dealt with radio education for remote areas and technical/vocational education to combat unemployment.

This was demanding work but rewarding as well. I continued with language classes and my fluency improved as I conducted business in Spanish every day. I met the challenges of my job and recognized what a boost success gave to my self-esteem.

I hoped my improved confidence would carry over into my relationship with Fred. I didn't notice that my uncompleted graduate school applications migrated to the bottom of my to-do pile.

Salinas

Fred and I slid from cold war to détente. We still circled each other like rival dogs, but there seemed to be less snarling and more tail wagging.

We agreed that we should find more time to spend together, as a couple and as a family. Fred had pursued his interest in scuba diving, and he played golf and tennis several times a week. He did those things without the kids and me.

The question was what could we do besides our dinner dates? Snorkeling appealed to both of us, but at first we had trouble finding a satisfactory location. None of the local beaches seemed to have any underwater features to attract the population of colorful fish we liked to see. At long last, one of my Dominican friends at work, Sonja, told me about El Derrumbao (the landslide) located near the town of Salinas.

The trip to Salinas was a bit of an expedition, doable in a day, but requiring advance preparations and a couple of hours by car. The road went past the Dominican Naval Base and through the village of Salinas. We had to bring everything we would need – sports equipment, shade, food, water – as the beach area was not developed in any way. We made it a family outing and added Dakota's windsurfing equipment to our gear.

We had to drive slowly through the village where pigs of all sizes wandered everywhere. Little naked brown children scampered among the strolling pig population, flashing their golden blonde curls (mementoes of visiting European sailors perhaps?). At the end of the village the road dwindled to tire tracks in the deep sand and there Fred shifted into four-wheel drive to take us past the extensive salt evaporation beds that give the town its name (Salinas means salt-pits or salt-mines).

On the windward side we unloaded Dakota's gear and helped him get set up. He connected with his windsurfing buddies and Fred, Tina, and I crossed to the leeward side of the peninsula to find our snorkeling spot.

The sand at Salinas was black, the darkest I had ever seen anywhere in the world. This beach was not famous for being hospitable. No shade. Lots of stickery, thorny plants. Plenty of spiny sea urchins in the shallows. But the underwater world made up for the discomforts. El Derrumbao ran about a quarter mile parallel to the beach and a few meters off shore. The water at the edge of the shelf measured less than four feet deep and reached fifteen feet at the deepest part. Live coral offered the main attraction for the many species of fish. The fish weren't big, none larger than my hand, but they were plentiful and beautiful in shallow water as clear as an aquarium.

With my face submerged and the sound of my own breath whooshing through the snorkel, I left the surface world behind. Elegant purple fans of coral waved in the current as if blown by a breeze. Schools of fish swirled past my mask, fish in brilliant hues and somber shades, transparent fish as clear as jellyfish. I floated in weightless freedom and became a part of this fairyland, safe from the tensions on land.

I stayed in the water until a chill reminded me I was not a real fish. When I looked landward to spot our beach umbrellas, I saw pigs. Big pigs. Why were they on the beach? Were they grazing on the sparse grasses? I didn't know whether pigs grazed or not. Did they also root for shellfish or even, well, roots? Someone in New Zealand had told me a story about pigs that dove for shellfish, but I suspected that pigs could no more dive than fly. The pigs weren't bothering me, so I decided not to bother them.

We left the beach pigs behind in late afternoon, hoping to get home before dark. In the narrow main street of the village of Salinas, we came up behind a slow moving motorcycle. The motorcycle carried two men and a huge hog strapped to the luggage rack. While Fred waited for a chance to pass, I speculated on the destination of the pig. Would it make sense to take a dead but unbutchered animal to market in the heat of the day? Before anyone else could comment, the pig stated his opinion. First a leg jerked. Then his head lifted. And all at once the pig began to squirm and thrash. The motorcycle veered to the side of the rode and the two men jumped off to wrestle the pig back into submission.

We passed and continued on our way, but I craned my neck to keep the pig scene in sight as long as possible. A billow of dust concealed all but an upraised arm, a kicking leg, and a smooth expanse of pig haunch. The episode combined elements of comedy and cruelty, and I wished I knew how it would end. I wondered about the beginning too. At the start of their journey, did the men knock the pig out and expect it to remain unconscious for the whole trip, or did they think the pig was dead when they tied it on the motorcycle? The Great Salinas Pig Saga is destined to remain a fragment with its beginning and end shrouded in mystery.

We made frequent trips to Salinas. Dakota enjoyed the high winds and the companionship of other windsurfers on his side of the peninsula while the rest of us snorkeled and picnicked with our friends less than a mile away on the calm side. Over the next four years, we saw the road improve and the beach become more popular. An entrepreneurial soul erected a ramshackle snack bar and we heard talk of further development plans. For me, a developed Salinas could never maintain the charm of the wild Salinas.

24

Beth and Dave's treasures

1986

Never a Dull Moment

When Beth and Dave called to say they had purchased their tickets to Santo Domingo, I told them to pack their snorkeling gear because we planned to take them to Salinas. Of course, Granny and Grandpa had told Beth and Dave about their visit, so Beth and Dave knew what to expect. Dave said they were willing to go anywhere and do anything as long as we would promise that their bed was free of insects and arachnids.

Besides Salinas and the other places we had taken Granny and Grandpa, we now had a new tourist destination to offer Beth and Dave as soon as they arrived. Fred rented a beach house on the north coast near the town of Cabarete and all six of us crammed into our five-passenger Jeep. Because of the bucket seats in front, four passengers had to squeeze in the backseat, meaning the two on the outside had to perch on one haunch each. We rotated positions (except for driver because Fred was the only one who felt capable of dealing with the narrow road and heavy traffic) to ease our fanny fatigue. Thank goodness we had air-conditioning or none of us would have survived.

After a day of swimming, snorkeling, and beachcombing, we lazed on the covered deck of the Cabarete beach house in the shade, admiring Beth and Dave's collection of sand dollars spread out on the picnic table and watching Dakota speed across the horizon on his windsurfer. Beth and I were discussing dinner plans when Beth's face paled in a sickly white ring around her lips. She dashed to the bathroom. Retching sounds and moaning followed. My stomach lurched. I fought down the roiling urge to puke. Beth's method worked – she vomited and felt better faster. I delayed the throwing-up part and spent the next few hours wishing for death.

While Beth and I commiserated with each other, Fred and Dave took the kids to Sosua for yummy, greasy tacos at PJ's. Just the thought of chili-tinted grease running down their elbows bent me over the toilet bowl for another session of upchucks.

Beth and I knew exactly what to blame for our food poisoning misery. The night before leaving Santo Domingo for the north coast, we had gone out to dinner at Vesuvio's, a popular restaurant on the Malecón. Beth and I shared a salad. After we recovered, we renamed Caesar Salad as Seizure Salad, and so it has remained in our lexicon ever since.

Back home in Santo Domingo, Beth and Dave were spared a repeat of Granny and Grandpa's episodes of leaky roof and tarantula encounter. Beth, however, had a near death experience in the family room. She and Tina had been sitting on the couch having an aunt/niece chat. One second after they rose to go to the kitchen for a snack, a huge chunk of decorative plaster fell from the ceiling and landed on the exact spot where Beth had been sitting. In light of our track record, I wondered if I should get additional insurance coverage when we had houseguests.

Ever the good sports, Beth and Dave joined Fred and me at a running event organized by our club, Amigos del Maratón. We ran 10K (6.2 miles) in the heat of the day with two hundred other sweaty aficionados. Fred surged ahead like a hare with the leaders while Beth, Dave, and I plodded together in the middle of the pack. We three tortoises hoped to finish the race without getting lost on the confusing course that followed a winding route through suburban neighborhoods. The police department didn't close the streets to vehicles, but they did post patrolmen at the busiest intersections to control traffic and also to direct the runners. If we were lucky, the officers would still be on duty when we came by at least twenty minutes behind the leaders.

A few scattered bystanders cheered us on, and one guy tossed his bucket of car-washing water at us – to cool us off, I guess. We dodged the nasty shower as best we could. Dave said he was happy we didn't have to drink it.

Fred finished the race in 38 minutes and waited for us at the finish line when we crossed at 55:56. Giddy with runner's high, we jabbered and joked our way to the car. We piled in and got on our way, daydreaming about ice-cold drinks and muscle-soothing showers.

Fred and I hadn't taken the Dominican election campaigns into account. Traffic snarled to a standstill in front of a noisy political demonstration. Pulsating music blared from live bands playing on flatbed trucks. Banners waved, demonstrators shouted slogans and shook their fists in the air. Demonstrations like this had been known to last all night. I clamped my jaw to silence my worry that we were trapped for the duration of the rally.

The bands played ever louder in a relentless duel of cacophony and the racket attracted a larger crowd. Men with paint buckets brushed their political party's colors on tree trunks and light poles. Others plastered signs and slogans and photos of the candidates on every available surface. I tried to rub away the tension that crept up the back of my neck toward a full-blown headache.

Then, in a flash of genius, Fred conceived and achieved our escape.

He gunned the engine, jumped the curb, and pressed forward along the sidewalk to the next side street, honking at pedestrians to make way. I held my breath until we were in the clear and speeding down Expreso 27 de Febrero toward home.

As we roared along the highway, I relished a twisted pleasure in Beth and Dave's shocked reaction to Fred's story of the previous month's shoot-out at the Concorde Hotel. In the middle of a political rally, the opposition opened fire on the speakers' dais. Pistols sprouted all around the room and returned fire. An official headcount of deaths and injuries hadn't been released, but rumor raised the number daily. The hotel had to close for extensive repairs to the banquet hall.

"Sounds like everybody in Santo Domingo carries a gun." Dave looked worried.

I couldn't wait to deliver the punch line. "Just listen to the Dominican definition of macho --I heard this from a friend at work."

Beth and Dave both turned to look at me.

"In the Dominican Republic you're not a real man until you have a mistress, a green card, and a pistol."

Pain

It was inevitable; Beth and Dave had to leave. I dreaded their departure, not only because I would miss them, but also because I knew what came next on my calendar. A dentalphobe since early childhood, I cringed at the thought of my scheduled treatment for periodontal problems.

The dentist, a devastatingly handsome, charming, and sadistic young man, showed me no mercy. He carved deep furrows in my gums, one quarter of my mouth at each session, and sent me home with mere over-the-counter painkillers. When the Novocain wore off, I wished the dentist had slit my throat instead of my gums. Pain dominated my life for the rest of the month. Even lukewarm liquids abused my ravaged mouth; the idea of chewing solid food made me feel faint. I had trouble sleeping. I wanted to run away from my own body.

The world didn't stop though. I went to work and life's details continued to demand my attention. I hated to think about causing pain for anyone else, but I took Tina to the orthodontist for braces. Fred objected. In his opinion, braces belonged to movie stars or the upper class. That raised my hackles; my parents' identical attitude left me with crooked teeth I hid behind a closed-lip smile.

I didn't want to start a fight, but I had to take a stand for Tina's sake so I argued that Tina didn't just want braces -- she needed them to correct her bite as well as straighten her teeth. Fred gave in although I sensed he might not be completely convinced that orthodontia was anything but vanity.

I was thinking about pleasure rather than pain when I booked a long weekend for our family at Club Med. A group of embassy folks planned to gather there to enjoy the many activities provided at this all-inclusive resort.

Dakota and Tina found their friends and made a beeline to the sports activities led by the Club Med G.O.s (Gracious Organizers). Dakota and his buddies headed straight for the windsurfing beach; Tina's bunch homed in on the archery field. Fred and I went sailing for an hour before we parted ways. I wanted to try aerobics. Fred had his eye on the juggling class.

I found out later why the juggling class appealed to Fred. The G.O. was a curvaceous young French cutie whose string bikini had no top half. Impossible as it might have seemed, somehow the whole class, including Fred, did learn to juggle.

The aerobics class pumped me up. I jumped and kicked and hopped around with the best of them. Cardiovascular conditioning from years of running gave me a huge endurance advantage. Lacking proper shoes, I pranced barefoot on the hardwood stage like a Martha Graham clone. There was no logical reason not to do two classes back-to-back, so I did, and finished the second one wanting more.

With our friends at dinner, an all-you-can-eat sumptuous buffet prepared by a team of French chefs, we all babbled our enthusiasm about the Club Med activities, classes, and food. I sipped a plummy young cabernet and made multiple forays to the bread and cheese bar. Crusty, butter-infused garlic bread sang a harmonious duet with ambrosia-rimmed, creamy Camembert.

Constant refills of beer mugs and wine glasses energized the atmosphere and the party gathered steam. Everybody agreed that the post-dinner show in the auditorium should crown our evening.

Guests filled the tiers of wooden bench seats and excited chatter all but drowned out the piped-in background music. Then the lights dimmed and the Master of Ceremonies stepped out onto center stage.

"Okay everybody – it's time for Crazy Signs!"

All of the guests stood up to mimic the moves of the G.O.s as they demonstrated Club Med's signature communal dance. A wild combination of the Hokey Pokey and the Macarena, Crazy Signs drove us insane as we stumbled through the complicated series of waves, claps, stomps, kicks, twists, turns, bends, and shouts. It also broke the ice and set us up for the next act: the Couples' Contest.

Our M.C. called for three couples to volunteer as contestants. The row of embassy people behind Fred and me yelled and whistled while the M.C. chose the first two couples. We didn't know the conspirators in back of us were pointing and gesturing as well as hollering.

Couple Number 3? Fred and Nancy.

A bronze Adonis G.O. guided me to a chair and handed me a heart-shaped scrap of cloth and a threaded needle. He wrapped a red silk scarf around my eyes and then pushed Fred over my knees so that Fred's rear faced the audience. At the M.C.'s signal, we female halves of the three chump couples revealed our total lack of skill at blind-appliqué. The guys yelped when stuck, and the audience cheered. The sadism applause meter gave second place to Fred and me for that event.

Humiliation escalated with the break-dancing contest. Fred got down on the floor and tried to spin around on his back. I blushed ten degrees of flame red while I tripped over my tangled moon walking feet. Couple Number 3 sagged to third place.

I wasn't overjoyed to see the blindfold coming my way again. But this time I carried the victory and won first place for wrapping Fred like a mummy in toilet paper.

Then Fred shook and shimmied in a grass skirt for second place in the hula dance competition.

My face ached from the self-conscious grin stretched from cheek to cheek. What could possibly come next?

Balloons. Each patsy girl had to run the full length of the stage and plop down on a balloon in her guy's lap. I ran as fast as I could and pounced with all my might. I bounced. The other couples' bursting balloons popped and banged like fireworks. The audience roared. The M.C. insisted that I try again. I sprinted across the stage and plunked harder. I ricocheted higher. Same result on my third try. Oh, the shame of it.

At the end of the Couples Contest, the M.C. awarded second place to Couple Number 3 and gave free drinks to all the contestants. For future show-nights at Club Med, Fred and I took care to sit behind our friends, not in front of them.

Early the next morning I woke with a headache – no surprise after a cabernet overdose. When I got out of bed, I staggered and almost fell. Shooting pains jabbed up and down my shins and calves like poison darts launched by a battalion of pygmies. This was a double-aerobics-barefoot-on-hardwood hangover that lasted a full week. But even though I hobbled around like a nonagenarian, I was eager to join the aerobics class at the embassy led by Mary Kay, an embassy political officer and soon to be my best friend.

Pleasure

I needed some pleasure to balance the pain of dental work and sore legs, so I focused on R&R plans. Fred's request for a tour extension had been approved and that meant we would have an R&R that summer of 1986, a home leave with return to post in 1987, a second R&R in 1988, and home leave in 1989 before the next assignment to another country.

Fred had accumulated four weeks of leave time, but I had only two. My boss approved my application for two additional weeks of leave without pay. We could have spent our vacation anywhere, but family ties tugged at our hearts and we split our time among three households – one week with Fred's sister Laura and family in La Porte, TX; one week with Beth and Dave in Austin; and two weeks with my dad in Los Lunas, NM.

I hoped that two weeks with my dad would give us a chance to get acquainted with his new wife. New wife. The concept still seemed alien, although Dad's surprise phone call had announced his marriage a month ago, three years after Mom's death.

Dad had called to tell us that he and Bea met when he started doing yard work for widows and single elderly women from his church. Bea repaid him with brownies and cheery conversation. He basked in her aura of optimism.

Dad proposed, but Bea couldn't agree to a public wedding. They had to elope in secret because Bea's roommate Edith was dying of cancer and Bea couldn't bear to leave her long-time friend at that critical time. Dad and Bea made a day trip to Las Cruces, NM, found a justice of the peace to pronounce them man and wife, and returned to Los Lunas -- to live apart, Dad in his home and Bea in the house that she shared with Edith.

When I met Bea during our R&R visit, I understood Dad's attraction to her. She was thoughtful, kind, warm, generous, and funny. And she adored Dad. Her look of love was unmistakable.

Early one morning at Dad's place, Fred and I came upon Dad and Bea in a private moment – a kiss sizzling with passion and an embrace radiating desire. We shared a silent high-five and retreated, unnoticed by the lovers. I wept tears of joy to see my father living with gusto at age seventy.

More Pain

Near the end of R&R, Dad's sister Corky called from Florida with bad news. My aunt Vida had died. The loss hit me with the force of a tsunami. Vida had been my second mother – the one who lavished me with an inexhaustible supply of unconditional love. She formed the keel of my emotional life – without her would I capsize and sink?

We left New Mexico ahead of schedule to allow a few days in Pompano Beach, Florida, so I could attend Vida's memorial service and spend some time with my other aunts, Corky (Cora), Beets (Berniece), and Betty (Zelda). All of my aunts had done volunteer work at the county hospital and the whole cadre of Pink Ladies attended Vida's memorial. Vida had no husband or children and it warmed my heart to see so many pews filled with her friends and colleagues.

Corky and Beets, who had shared a home with Vida for twenty-five years, gave me the coverlet that Vida had made from a quilt pieced by my grandmother. I embraced the soft cotton treasure and stroked the tiny white stitches, picturing Vida at the quilting frame smiling over her labor of love. When Corky and Beets gave me Vida's set of sterling silver, I broke down again. The whole family knew how much I admired Vida's Royal Danish silverware and how much I would miss Vida's love.

The trip back to Santo Domingo passed like a midnight journey through fog. I spent the next few months in a distant frame of mind, not paying close attention to the events and people around me. Until one evening in November.

On that November night, Fred and I went out to meet friends that I will call Don and Gloria during this telling of the story. We went to Vesuvio's for the lobster thermidor (no seizure salad this time). When Fred and I arrived at the restaurant we found Don and Gloria already seated in the outdoor café.

Vesuvio's location on the Malecón provided tangy sea air and a front row seat for the evening promenade of eccentric characters. I sat down opposite Don. His easy, avuncular style always put me at ease. Gloria was something else altogether. Eight years younger than I, Gloria flaunted her youth. She always showed an intimidating abundance of cleavage and she radiated a disturbing primal heat. I wished I could control the urge to fidget and babble in Gloria's company.

A couple of cocktails smoothed my rough edges and strolling musicians stole my attention from Gloria's allure. When the waiter served our food, my appetite revived and I dug into my portion of Vesuvio's delectable lobster. Licking the last trace of rich wine sauce from the corner of my mouth, I leaned back and sighed.

"There is nothing tastier on the face of the earth. I …"

From that semi-reclining position, my line of sight went below the edge of the starched white tablecloth. Time froze. My eyes found Gloria's face. Gloria stared at me with half-hooded eyes and a feral smile. I gaped at Don. His gaze swept the room for signs of the waiter. I glared at Fred. His eyes blazed straight at Gloria. I forced myself to peek below the table again. Fred's lascivious hand snaked between Gloria's bewitching knees and his feet entwined with hers in an unchaste game of footsie.

I stuttered out words that had a will of their own and continued speaking as if no time had elapsed. "…I…I'm sorry, I have to go home right now. I have a terrible headache."

The table recoiled from the hasty withdrawal of Fred's hand. He lurched to his feet, rubbed his scraped knuckles. "Okay. . . Uh. . . Sure. . . Here, Don, this should cover our share." Fred dropped a crumpled wad of pesos in the middle of the table and followed me to the car.

I managed to contain my fury until Fred fastened his seat belt. "So! Excitement? Passion? Now I see…you bastard. You liar. God damn you to Hell!"

Fred remained silent throughout my tirade. I fumed and snarled all the way home. "You can spend the rest of the night in the guestroom. And I will move to a hotel in the morning. I'll tell the kids. You…you just shut up and stay out of my way."

Fred's face froze in a blank look of shock and he retreated to the guestroom, closing the door behind him with an almost inaudible click.

I thrashed through the night pursued by demons. At dawn I went for a run to clear my head. By the time I got back, Fred had left for work. He didn't leave a note. I convinced myself I didn't care. After packing my suitcase, I explained to Dakota and Tina that I needed to spend some time away to get a better perspective on a disagreement with their dad.

"Don't worry. Everything's going to be fine. I'll be at the Concorde for a few days. I'll call you every night. And you call me at work whenever you want to. Don't tell Dad where I am, though, please? I really need you to keep that secret for now. Just for a little while."

Both Dakota and Tina spread their arms for a group hug. Tina whispered, "Mom, do what you need to do and don't worry about us."

Dakota hugged again. "I love you, Mom. Come home soon, okay?"

My babies. Twelve and thirteen, but still my babies. So solid and yet so vulnerable. I will not let this craziness hurt them.

Reality Check

In spite of lying alone in a strange bed in a strange place, I slept long and hard, and woke with a purpose. An obsessive list-maker and life-long journal writer, I opened to a fresh page in my notebook and started to scribble my thoughts and feelings in a rapid stream of consciousness. I wrote all morning until time to meet my friend Mary Kay for a Sunday afternoon jog in the botanic gardens.

Mary Kay wasted no time with preliminaries. "What's wrong? I don't care whether you start at the beginning, middle, or wherever, as long as you tell me everything."

I let the whole story pour forth, words spilling like an avalanche tumbling and rolling, colliding and crashing, until only sobs remained.

Mary Kay led me to a bench beside the path. "Gloria. That witch."

I leaned into Mary Kay's hug and felt her voice rise.

"When I worked with Don before… in Costa Rica…that was a little over six years ago…I saw her in action. Truth is…Gloria broke up Don's first marriage."

I looked up through tear-blur to see Mary Kay's scornful expression.

"Yeah, it was ugly and the scandal almost ruined his career. And the bitch has the brass to cheat on him."

I sat up straight and blew my nose. "I made a mistake. I've got to go home and defend my family. I will not let Gloria take Fred away from us."

"Mmm, I don't know . . . no offense, but Gloria is not the type to trade down. Don is the perfect meal ticket after all."

My questioning look urged Mary Kay to continue.

"See, he'll inherit his mother's Cincinnati department store fortune, plus his diplomatic career provides connections in high places, and don't forget he has legally adopted her children. Need I go on?"

I shrugged, not quite convinced where Mary Kay's argument would take me.

Mary Kay interpreted my shrug as assent and continued. "Sure, Fred is charming, handsome and sexy, but he is, after all, a lowly communicator with no political connections and a mediocre future. Sorry to sound so harsh, but I think you need a reality check before you make any major moves."

I stopped sniffling and managed a rueful smile. "You're quite the master of tough love, aren't you? Thanks for being straight with me."

Hope

Stepping off the elevator in the Hotel Concorde, I dreaded entering my cold, dark room. *Never mind, I'll turn on all the lights, give Tina a call and find out what's happening at home.* I turned the key, pushed the door open…and came face to face with Fred. The earnest expression in his tear-glazed blue eyes touched a tender spot in my heart.

"Nanny, Honey, please come home. I've been an awful fool, an idiot. Please come home and I promise I'll make it up to you." He held out both hands, palms up in supplication.

I stepped forward and clasped his hands. "Let's go home."

No Pain, No Gain

Fred and I tried to work out our problems, but we made no headway. I couldn't get past the pain of betrayal. He seemed preoccupied, distracted.

When our nineteenth anniversary came up, we slid into a tacit agreement to ignore it. But Tina surprised us with a gift and a card. Her personal note on the traditional anniversary card said, "Remember why you got married in the first place…Love, Tina."

My vision blurred with tears as I tore the gift paper and opened the box. Inside, a Lladró porcelain figurine lay in a bed of white tissue paper.

The elegant bride and groom in formal nuptial attire gazed up at me with enigmatic expressions. Was the bride sympathetic to my plight or did her face convey a hint of accusation? Had I lost sight of why I married Fred? I did feel wrong as well as wronged and my heart curled into a tiny ball of hurt wrapped in anger and capped with guilt.

I held Tina in a long hug and wished for an escape route out of the purgatory of my marriage.

25

Dakota the Scout and proud parents

1987

Scouts

Fred and I moved around each other with caution and maintained our relationship in limbo. We focused our attention on Dakota and Tina's scouting activities. Both the Girl Scout and Boy Scout troops sponsored activities almost every weekend and our lives filled up with preparations for ten-mile hikes and camping trips.

The scout leaders invited parents to participate in a few of the scouts' camping trips and some of the longer hikes. Our whole family went on the camping expedition to Saona Island.

A Dominican naval vessel carried us out to sea. I stood at the rail and drank in the fresh sea air, keeping my eye on the horizon and watching for signs of the island. At first it looked like a tiny bump. The hump grew as we approached and it appeared to sprout fronds like a chia pet when we came closer.

I expected the ship to deliver us to the beach where we would set up our tents in the forest of coconut palms. But no, our captain cut the engines and dropped anchor in deep water several hundred meters off shore.

I felt my heart rate rise as a small motorboat putt-putted toward us. I didn't want to believe that such a feeble scow was meant to be our ferry. We had twenty people and an enormous pile of camping gear to convey across an expanse of water that seemed to widen as we waited. How many trips? Who would go first?

The prospect of transfer from naval vessel to lowly tub terrified me. The waves were too high. The ship lurched one way as the scow sloughed in the opposite direction. To step across the gap required some of the same skills as tightrope walking. I gasped as each scout made the leap. When my turn came, I held my breath and threw myself across the void. I stumbled and flopped like a flounder into the Scout Master's lap. Everyone laughed at my graceless landing so I hammed it up a bit, high on adrenaline and the thrill of landing in the boat instead of in the ocean.

On shore, the leaders told us that the main danger on this expedition was falling coconuts. They shocked and amazed us with terrible tales about legendary fatal head conkings. I kept a wary eye on the fruit hanging high above us, although I wasn't sure if the warnings were serious or tongue-in-cheek. All of the scouting activities went on as planned, and no one in our party got bonked.

Only a month after that successful scouting adventure on Saona Island, I felt inspired to assist the Girl Scout leader with a beach camping trip. We drove out of Santo Domingo with two vanloads of girls and gear and found a perfect spot near the town of Bayahibe. The scouts pitched their tents and made a fire ring for the evening's campfire. Then I suggested a hike on the beach.

We flipped a coin. Heads, we go north; tails, to the south. The twenty-five centavo piece landed heads up. About fifteen minutes up the beach from our campsite, we found a long, shallow tide pool that begged to be explored. As the girls poked sea urchins and chased tiny tropical fish and combative crabs, I climbed a rocky outcrop to see what lay beyond.

I took one look and spun around at once. The beach beyond the rock barrier was crowded with people. Naked people. Unclothed male human beings. Birthday-suited men demonstrating mutual affection.

I clambered down the rocks and quietly urged my charges to return to camp to begin dinner preparations.

When we went beach combing the following day, I led the way without a coin toss. We headed south.

Skewered

Between camping trips and other scouting events, we carried out our normal workaday/school day lives. One afternoon a phone call broke the rhythm of our humdrum days.

Fred answered the call at his desk at work. The nurse at the Medical Unit said, "The doctor wants you to come right away. Your son is here with a piece of metal in his arm."

Fred called me and we both hurried to the Medical Unit.

Sure enough, Dakota lay on the examining table with a long, thin piece of metal protruding from his wrist, the doctor standing next to him, examining x-rays.

The doctor scratched his head, "I can't imagine how, but apparently this thing went in without damaging any bones. Damn lucky."

Fred held Dakota's shoulders down as the doctor grasped the metal and pulled it straight out. Dakota, already numbed and sedated, chuckled, shook his head, and started to tell us what had happened.

He had gone home from school with his friend Shane and they were hanging out on the patio by the pool. Dakota called his girl friend and was talking on the phone while Shane messed around with the barbeque utensils, just killing time. Shane picked up a kabob skewer and began swinging it around by its leather thong. As the skewer swung faster and faster it made a fascinating loud humming sound. Dakota turned his shoulders away from the noise, shifting the receiver to the opposite ear, which brought his forearm across his upper chest and throat. Just then, the leather thong snapped. The metal missile whizzed across the patio and speared Dakota's wrist. If he hadn't been holding the phone in that odd position, the rod's sharp point would have gone right into his neck.

After the doctor cleaned and dressed the wound, we shepherded Dakota to our car. But Dakota refused to go straight home. He said he was worried about Shane. He insisted that we go to Shane's house first, so Shane could see for himself that Dakota was okay. And Dakota was all right. The wound healed and left only a tiny scar to remind him of his freak accident.

Hysteria

One day at work my secretary put another odd and unexpected call through to my office. "It's your landlord. He says it's an emergency."

Oh dear, my thoughts went straight to collapsed roof or plumbing flood.

"Señora LaTurner, please send the Embassy ambulance at once – Juanita has collapsed and she is struggling to breathe."

It took a few minutes to convince him that the embassy did not have an emergency service and that he would have to call a private ambulance to have our housekeeper Juanita transported to a clinic for treatment. I assured him that I would pay the costs and further that I would meet him at the house in five minutes.

I arrived just seconds before the ambulance. The EMT's and I witnessed the scene together. Juanita reclined on the front room sofa, her upper body resting on a pile of pillows. The flustered landlord stood at her side, patting her hand and murmuring. Our gardener and his helper hovered nearby, wringing their hands and ogling Juanita's heaving bosom that threatened to burst free of her loosened bodice as she gasped for breath.

"I cannot see. Dios Mio, I am blind."

The landlord surrendered his guardianship and let the paramedics take over. They whisked Juanita to the ambulance and I followed in my car. Fred met me at the clinic and we sat down in the waiting room while the emergency medical staff attended to Juanita.

Over the past several months I had observed a hierarchy in the Dominican health care system. A few doctors and clinics catered to wealthy Dominicans and foreigners; a second tier of doctors and clinics served the middle class; and, at the lowest level of services, the government provided health care for the poor. We were sitting in the clinic recommended to us as embassy employees.

We didn't have long to wait. Dr. Abreu, clinical director, appeared in the doorway to the waiting room. "Follow me," he said. "I want you to see this."

He led us down the corridor to a room where Juanita lay on a hospital bed, hooked up to the usual apparatus: IV, oxygen, and blood pressure cuff. Dr. Abreu motioned for us to stand at the foot of the bed, while he approached the head.

He spoke to Juanita in a low, soothing voice, in Spanish of course. "Juanita, this is Dr. Abreu speaking to you. I am here to help you. I know that you are unable to see. I can bring back your sight. I will place my hand across your eyes like this…." He covered her eyes with his hand and held it there. "When I remove my hand, you will be able to see. Do you understand?" Juanita nodded. With drama worthy of a magician, Dr. Abreu flourished his hand away. "Juanita, open your eyes and see!"

Juanita opened her eyes and focused on us standing at the foot of her bed. She turned her head and gazed at the doctor. She wept and sobbed and gave thanks to God and to her hero.

The doctor escorted us back to the waiting room and told us he would release Juanita right away. "You see, hysteria is very common among Dominican women of a certain age. We treat it often. I suggest that you give her a few days of rest and then talk to her about what stress in her life might have brought this on."

A few days later I psyched myself up to broach the subject. Juanita spilled out her worries with no coaxing from me. She talked about her two children who were being raised by her mother in the rural north where she herself had grown up. The father of her children was abusive and she had left him long ago. Several months ago, she met an older man who wanted to marry her. This man had his own business, his own home, and could offer her some comforts and a lifestyle she had never known before. However, he was a widower with grown children and he made it very clear to Juanita that he wanted no more offspring. Juanita had become hysterical with worry that she would get pregnant and ruin the possibility of a secure future.

I asked her if she had thought about having an operation. She said she wished for that but had no idea how to do it.

After a short discussion, Fred and I decided to consult Dr. Abreu. He told us that Juanita could have her tubes tied at the government hospital for free, but he cautioned that the conditions there were deplorable. On the other hand, we could arrange for the surgery at his clinic for $300. That seemed like a decent price for giving Juanita peace of mind and helping her improve her life.

Juanita had her operation, recuperated at our house, and moved to La Romana where she got married and started her new life. Before she left, she introduced us to a young woman who could take her place in our household. It seemed like perfect timing, because we were getting ready to move. Our landlord's wife wanted to reclaim our house at the end of our two-year lease. Since Fred had requested, and received, a two-year extension of his tour, we would get to start again like a new assignment, back to square one with a new home and new household help right after home leave.

Wake-up Call

I had no trouble finding another house. The day I started my search, the perfect place showed up on the embassy lease list. I didn't like the idea of a mid-tour move, but what could I do? At least the timing worked in my favor: we had several weeks to get everything packed and GSO would move all of our stuff to the new house while we were on home leave.

I set about the familiar task of sorting, organizing, and boxing up our household. Many evenings I settled into a meditative state and stayed up late performing the repetitive motions of packing. One particular evening I lost all sense of time and worked into the midnight hours. The house lay quiet. All bedrooms were dark, doors shut.

I yawned and shuffled down the long hall past Dakota's room, the guestroom, and Tina's room. Before I reached the master bedroom door, I heard Fred's voice coming from the other side. Muffled words failed to convey their meaning, but the urgency of raw emotion resonated through the wood. My heart rose, then fell and hardened into an icicle as sharp and brittle as those that clung to the eaves of my Minnesota childhood home.

I swung the door wide open and stood silent in the pool of light. An involuntary spasm pulled Fred upright as he hung up the phone. "What are you doing up so late?" he said.

"Did you call her or did she call you? Don't bother with denial - guilt is written all over your face."

I swept up a bundle of nightgown-pillow-robe and stomped to the guestroom, robe sash trailing behind as wretched as a flag of surrender. The door slammed with teeth-jarring finality. The lock clicked like a sarcastic tsk. And I sat on the bed, clutching my bundle, alone with my horrible thoughts.

Images invaded my brain. Pictures of Fred and Gloria, hot and frenzied, Fred's face buried between Gloria's enormous breasts, Gloria's red lacquered claws raking Fred's back. I sobbed. My fists pounded the pillow. I thrashed to my back and felt tears flood my ears. Finally I slept in that land of nightmares where I shouted for help but no sound came out of my swollen throat.

In the morning the shrill ring of the house phone broke into my nightmare marathon. I grabbed the bedside extension and answered without bothering to speculate about the identity of the caller.

"Hi, Nancy? It's Gloria. I was wondering if you might be free for lunch today?"

Trade Off

Seated across from Gloria on the balcony of Il Cappuccino Italian

Restaurant, I poked at the slabs of mozzarella in my Caprese salad and imagined fantastic ways for my nemesis to die while I waited for her to come to the point. So far, she had rambled on about the benefits of life with Don. What a stimulating intellect, generous provider, great father, blah, blah, blah.

"So you see, it's not Don's fault. I have needs -- needs that Don doesn't satisfy. I decided to make a trade when I married him. Life is made up of tradeoffs, you know. Don lacks the fire and passion of the Freds of the world, but he provides everything else I want for my children and myself. As long as I stay discreet and avoid complications, I can do what I want and still keep Don. I can assure you, I am very good at avoiding complications."

Arrogant bitch. So she's done with Fred. Was she was explaining her trade-off theory to him on the phone last night? Was he begging her not to dump him?

My hard icicle heart kept me cool and collected. I said nothing, gave nothing away. We parted on friendly terms and never returned to the subject again, although our families socialized frequently throughout the rest of our stay in the Dominican Republic. Our meeting had declared an unspoken armistice, final and binding.

Healing

I didn't tell Fred about my encounter with Gloria. I did tell him it was time we sought help to repair the wreckage of our marriage. We called Beth to ask her to find a counselor among her colleagues -- social workers and psychologists in Austin -- and she set us up with appointments during our home leave. The power of those marriage-counseling sessions turned the tide for us. Our therapist, Ardyth, guided us back to the basics of our relationship and the realization that we both wanted to stay together. Our work began then in earnest toward the rehabilitation of our relationship. Even though we were on home leave and in vacation/party mode, we stayed on track and practiced our newfound communication skills. And we had as much fun as ever, maybe more.

A couple of days before the end of home leave, Fred and I joined

Dave at his aerobics class at the fitness center. I found a spot in the back row where I could see all of the participants and follow the unfamiliar choreography. I noticed an opening in the wall behind me. It looked like a doorway from Alice in Wonderland – one that required a sip from the bottle marked "Drink Me." I bent down for a quick peek and saw an empty room similar to the aerobics space we were in.

The music amped up and the class started. Thirty jumping feet pounded to the lively beat. After the fourth repetition of the routine, I caught on and found my groove. I jumped and turned, kicked and lunged. In the background I heard some thumps from the room behind and assumed that another aerobics class was about to begin. I jumped and turned, kicked and lunged, and jumped again. But when I landed, the floor slid away and my ankle turned and popped. I glanced down and watched a ball skitter across the polished wood floor back through the Alice in Wonderland door into the basketball game going on in the room behind us.

Funny, my ankle didn't hurt at all. I went on hopping, jumping, and dancing until the class ended forty minutes later.

In the locker room, I sat down to change my shoes and pull on some sweat pants. When I stood up, I had to sit right back down. The pain in my ankle brought tears to my eyes.

X-rays at the urgent care clinic showed that no bones were broken, but the doctor urged me to keep weight off my ankle for at least a week.

"Think of it like this: if you try to glue two pieces of wood together and you keep pulling the pieces apart to test the bond, what will happen?"

"The two pieces will never stick together?"

"Exactly. The healing of your ankle sprain is the same. Here's a prescription for crutches. If you keep from bearing weight on that ankle for a week, it will heal just fine. If you test it, it'll give you trouble."

So I finished the last few days of home leave on crutches and I used them throughout the trip back to the Dominican Republic. I suffered with those clumsy wooden crutches faithfully for a full week. And my ankle did heal permanently, just as the doctor said it would.

Mosquitoes and Prostitutes

On crutches at first and then limping around, I was slow to unpack and arrange our belongings in the new house. Like every move in history, this one had advantages and disadvantages. The location brought us closer to the school but farther from the embassy. The house had four bedrooms and two baths, one of them in the master bedroom, meaning Dakota and Tina had to share with each other and with guests. The backyard had avocado and mango trees, but no coconut palm, grapefruit or chinola (passionfruit) vines. The differences didn't keep us from settling in. Our family knew how to adapt. Practice makes perfect after all.

The first power outage in the new house pointed out a definite downside. The master bedroom occupied the front southeast corner of the house and a semi-circular driveway was all that separated the building from the street. With electricity, the steady hum of the window-mounted air-conditioner muffled any noise coming from outside and the cool air kept the mosquitoes dormant. In the quiet of the first night without power, we opened our windows in hopes of a breeze, thereby letting in all the sounds we had missed hearing before.

A swarm of bloodthirsty mosquitoes discovered me and I slapped my head and ears hoping for a kill. Shouts and giggles drew my attention to the open window where I looked out upon a bus stop. Or whore stop in this case. Customers were plentiful and their raucous negotiations made sleep impossible. Fred sprang into action. He abandoned his good neighbor policy and marched to the backyard to start the generator. Ah, the blissful white noise of air-conditioning drowned the bothersome haggling on the street and chill air drove the aggravating insects to their hiding places.

School for Spike

At our new home Spike spent his outside time on the side of the house where he could peer between the wrought iron fence rails and watch cars and people passing by. I always looked for his shiny black nose peeping through the fence as I turned the last corner toward home.

One day I came home early and caught a group of shoeshine boys teasing Spike through the openings in the fence. They poked him with sticks and made a terrible racket banging on the iron posts. Spike's body shook from the frenzy of his growls and snarls. The boys ran away when they saw me. Our residential street wasn't a regular route for limpia botas, so I didn't expect them to come back.

But Spike's behavior deteriorated over the next several weeks. The sight and smell of young boys triggered insanity. He snarled and lunged at the fence when any youngsters passed. The mere presence of pre-pubescent strangers drove him crazy, although he couldn't have been more loving and gentle with immediate family. I consulted our vet and he suggested obedience training with a strong socialization component. We held a family meeting and agreed to send Spike to the vet's kennel for a six-week course.

I think I missed Spike the most during his absence. Dakota had discovered girls and windsurfing and had little time for his homework much less for his dog. Tina preferred to hang out with her girl friends. And preparations for a VIP visit kept Fred late at the office every day. I wondered if Spike felt as lonely at the kennel as I did at home.

When Spike graduated, we celebrated with hot dogs and ice cream for all. We gathered on the front verandah and entertained each other by putting Spike through his paces. He spent more than an hour off the leash, playing fetch and showing off his obedience to commands. Then, without warning, he leaped the three-foot front wall and raced down the street after an innocent passer-by – a boy, of course. Fred, who held the local 10K record for runners over forty, sprinted after Spike and grabbed his collar just seconds after he knocked his quarry to the ground. The boy did not wait around for an apology. Fred dragged Spike back home and called another family meeting.

Everyone agreed that continued abuse by the shoeshine boys was to blame for Spike's behavior. We decided to prevent further torture by erecting a barrier to keep Spike out of the street-side yard. We vowed to keep him on a short leash in public and to exile him to the backyard if we had guests with children.

Around this time we made some changes to our family constellation that helped Spike with his socialization. We added a driver to our staff of employees. Rafael, a small dignified gentleman, was a true gem. He drove the kids to school first, then picked Fred and me up to take us to our offices. During the day he took care of car maintenance, did the grocery shopping and ran errands as needed. And he spent his free time playing with Spike.

Raphael also recommended his cousin Marianela to us. The woman I had hired after Juanita left for her new life did not work out. She was slow, sloppy and devoid of personality. I had to fire her. I agonized over it. I worried about it. At last I did it, and it was so much easier than I thought it would be. The poor girl seemed relieved to be let go. She packed up her belongings and vanished without a peep.

Marianela shined as brightly as Raphael. She whipped through the housework and asked for more. She wanted to cook for us too, but she couldn't control her heavy-handed use of salt or her dedication to over-cooking vegetables. I told her I preferred to prepare our main meal, so she consoled herself with elaborate after-school "snacks" for the kids. We missed Juanita's delicious meals, but we all doted on Marianela's sunny disposition. She told me many times how grateful she was to be working for us. Her previous experience was with a Dominican family who treated her like a slave. In her opinion, domestic service had three levels: slave -- in the home of wealthy Dominicans; servant -- in the home of ordinary Dominicans; and employee -- in the home of an American family.

A third family addition came out of an earlier loss. Before we left the first house, Tina's cat Carbón had disappeared. He went out one day and never came back. There was a construction site in the vacant lot across the street, and a friend suggested that the workmen might have had Carbón for lunch -- any animal being fair game when food is scarce. We mourned with Tina. We offered to find another kitty, but she refused. She said maybe a puppy would make her feel better.

Coincidentally, Dakota's buddy Scott had a golden retriever who was about to have pups. Tina chose her favorite of the twelve bundles of fuzz and named him Dusty. When she brought him home, Spike acted just like a doting uncle.

Life with two big dogs is never tidy but always full of unconditional love and total devotion. For the untidy parts of dog life, it does help to have a maid, a gardener, and a driver/handyman to take care of the messes. Now I decided that I needed a pet too. Why I chose turtles, I can't say, but I was very happy with my two tiny painted turtles from the pet store at Plaza Naco. Sad for me, Dusty loved them too. In fact, he loved them so much he ate them. The whole family was afraid to tell me, and Marianela tried to take responsibility for leaving the turtle habitat within reach. When all was said and done, my family's tender concern for my feelings made a bigger impression on me than the loss of the turtles.

Finding Fun

The four of us continued our busy lives outside of work and school. We made many trips to the beach together as a family, and we each had our own activities as well, like any family with young teens.

Once Dakota finished the introduction to guitar, he joined the orchestra as a drummer and worked his way up to lead timpanist. The CMS orchestra toured to Curacao and Caracas during Dakota's years with them. His performance on the timpani always gave me a thrill of pride. He took such care to tune his drums and play his part with feeling and authority. And he looked way-cool in his tuxedo.

The highlight of Tina's choir career came when she landed a part in the production of *Oklahoma!* performed at the National Theater. It was an honor for a junior high student to be a part of the chorus in a senior high school production.

Mr. Walker, the director of the orchestra and head of the music department, also directed a choral ensemble of adults in his spare time. I auditioned for him and became a part of the Sacred Music Society. We gave two concerts a year and also participated in the annual CMS Music Festival that hosted choirs and orchestras from all over the Caribbean region. When it came time for the music festival, Dakota, Tina, and I were on stage and Fred supported us in the audience.

Singing with the Sacred Music Society continued a thread of vocal music that had woven throughout my life. Of all the groups I have sung with, the SMS presented the most unique challenges. Many times we had to rehearse by the light of vehicle headlights during the frequent power outages. Once we had to perform our major Christmas concert in candle-light – wonderful for ambiance, not so great if the singers needed to see their music.

Fred found time for tennis and golf several times a week. The Ambassador often called him away from work for a round of golf in the middle of the day. And when he wasn't golfing with either the Ambassador or his friend Jim Ward, he enjoyed fast sets of singles with Peter Brennan on the Ambassador's courts conveniently located on the embassy grounds.

Fred and I ran with the Hash House Harriers most weekends. We also continued to participate in the local fun runs. Fred maintained his fame in the Masters category, taking first place among men over forty. I became the treasurer of Amigos del Maratón and served as part-time spokesper-son for press conferences and other publicity activities. We collected our trophies, Fred's for first place in his age group, mine for third place in my group, and displayed them on the open shelf unit/room divider between the family room and dining room.

We added Casa de Campo to our list of weekend destinations in ad-dition to Club Med and the beach town of Cabarete. Casa de Campo featured a world-class Trent Jones golf course as well as a fancy in-pool bar. Our group of friends shared one of the luxurious rental properties and divided our time between golf, tennis, sunbathing, jogging, playing cards, reading, taking the kids horseback riding, and relaxing and hav-ing fun in general. I'll always remember the time that Robin Rumbarger found a giant bullfrog killed on the road, all flattened and desiccated, named it Frisbee Frog and incorporated it as a landmark for an impromp-tu Hash run. And no one could forget the incident of the floating corpse discovered under the in-pool bar. The body wasn't discovered until the bartenders cleaned up at closing time, so we knew we had shared the water with the deceased that day.

As our Dominican Republic tour sped on, Dakota continued with his windsurfing and drumming and Tina added cheerleading to her activities. Dakota had some difficulties in school and I rode his case pretty hard. One quarter he failed one subject and the next quarter he got an A in that same subject but failed yet another. He did not respond well to my nagging and I decided to bow out. We had a family meeting and I announced my newfound realization that homework and schoolwork belonged to the student, not to the parent. Dakota accepted the responsibility, gratefully I think, and his performance evened out to steady A's and B's. Tina kept up her status as honor student, no matter what else was happening in her life.

Scouting continued to play a major role in our kids' lives. The local troop, led by a Marine colonel, an Eagle Scout himself, offered Cadet scouting, which was co-ed. Both Tina and Dakota got SCUBA certification through the Cadet program, and Tina climbed Pico Duarte with a Cadet group. Dakota at that time had his eye on the Air Force Academy, and he decided that achieving Eagle rank in scouting would benefit his application. He labored over the design of his project as he organized a fun run with proceeds dedicated to a charity. The charity he chose was a home for children with profound disabilities, most of them born with severe defects. I visited the home with him several times. The dire circumstances made us wish we could do more. It was a proud day when Dakota presented the home with a fat envelope of cash for them to spend as needed for food, supplies, or equipment. And another proud day came when Dakota received his rank of Eagle.

Dakota also received the Order of the Arrow. His induction required a survival camping experience. The whole troop went to Boy Scout Camp in Puerto Rico, where Dakota was selected for the Order of the Arrow. The boys swore a secrecy oath, so we don't know all that happened, but Dakota gave us the impression that it was a real adventure. He came home with a new maturity and a sense of pride for having completed the induction and for using his fire-starting skills to save his buddy from hypothermia in the wilderness.

Dakota renewed his early childhood interest in soccer when his scout leader organized an American Embassy team. Most of the team members were adults, officers from the embassy and attached agencies and several Marine Security Guards. The older boy scouts were allowed to train with the team and, if skillful enough, to play in matches against local Dominican teams. The training was tough, led by a Marine Corps colonel, and Dakota complained sometimes. But he stuck with it and improved both his fitness and his soccer skills. It turned out to be great preparation for his years on the high school team.

Cabarete

Although we made many trips to Boca Chica, Playa Royal, Club Med, Casa de Campo, Puerto Plata, and Sosua, our favorite get-away spot was Cabarete. We returned several times to the beach house that Beth and Dave visited, and then we found another that was bigger, newer and nicer, that we often shared with friends.

I liked Cabarete because of the quiet. The beach hadn't yet attracted much attention and we weren't inundated with vendors. The windsurfing community had claimed it as their territory, and that made Dakota happy. Tina always brought a friend with her and asked for nothing more. I loved my schedule at the beach: coffee, jog, breakfast, nap, lunch, beer, nap, watch windsurfers, margarita, dinner, and sweet dreams to the rhythm of a bamboo ceiling fan. The Blue Lagoon Saloon, smack dab on the beach front, became our hangout. They served Fred's ideal combination of icy cold Presidente beer with classic rock and roll on the stereo.

We were sitting at the Blue Lagoon Saloon one afternoon, chatting, sipping our drinks, and gazing at the windsurfers who darted back and forth across the waves like butterflies in a mountain meadow. Fred pointed out a small group of people milling about at the water's edge. Their shouts and agitation portrayed a life or death emergency.

Two men broke from the group and launched a boat. They rowed out about fifty meters. We could see that one of them had a spear gun, which he shot and retrieved several times. After the final shot, the other fellow rowed the boat to shore while the marksman towed his quarry. The crowd closed around and we couldn't see what they had caught. Fred strolled over for a look and jogged back to us.

"Unbelievable. It's a dead body."

As we watched, the crowd hovered for half an hour, until a dented rattletrap pickup truck filled with more people drove out onto the sand. Then the weeping and wailing began. Right there on the beach the mourning women undressed the dead man, cleaned off sand and seaweed, and redressed him in a tuxedo. By the time they had finished their preparations, a black hearse had arrived with a coffin for the drowning victim. As the hearse pulled away, the mourners piled into the back of the pickup and resumed moaning and sobbing.

The word on the beach was that the highly inebriated local guy had been floating on an inner tube. His tube drifted out beyond the reef and somehow he fell out and drowned before anyone noticed his absence – a sobering tale.

On another occasion Fred and I strolled down Cabarete beach toward an exuberant crowd that had gathered there. Hundreds of young men and women, fit and tan, had congregated from all over the world for an international windsurfing competition. A separate, roped-off area had been set aside for the world famous competitors and their gear and equipment. We walked by, as close to the celebrities as we could, and we saw someone we recognized. Right there, in the middle of an animated cluster of windsurfing stars, stood our very own Dakota.

The windsurfing competition itself fizzled due to lack of wind, but Dakota had the time of his life anyway, hobnobbing with his gurus. To keep the competitive atmosphere going, the organizers hired a herd of burros and set up an impromptu racecourse. Windsurfers on burros – only in the Dominican Republic.

Every trip to Cabarete had to include a night out in Sosua for PJ's famously delicious and delectably greasy tacos. The return trip of fifteen miles in the dark had mysterious appeal. At the new moon, the only light came from our headlight beams. One night those beams picked up a giant shadow heading straight for our windshield. We ducked in unison as the huge shape skimmed our roof. In some cultures, a visit from an owl portends death. That's enough to cause a shiver up one's spine when speeding down a deserted bit of narrow road in pitch-blackness.

I can't remember how it started, but we invented a family tradition for that nighttime passage between Sosua and Cabarete. We opened all of the car windows and let loose the loudest primal screams we could muster. It's a great tension reducer but not recommended in populated areas.

Getting to and from Cabarete was not the most fun in the world. The road was narrow, subject to heavy traffic, and never in good repair. Anxious to get to the beach on the way up and eager to get home on the way back, we squirmed with frustration when stuck behind a slow moving, overloaded platano (plantain) truck. Forget passing; a steady stream of traffic in the opposite direction kept that from happening.

On one trip, though, an obstruction became a source of gruesome fascination. The vehicle ahead of us was an ancient battered pickup, sagging in the rear either from broken springs or a heavy load, putt-putting along at ten miles per hour below the speed limit. Fred stayed on the alert for a chance to pass but it seemed like the rare gaps in traffic occurred on a hill or curve with insufficient visibility. I started to beat an irritated tattoo on the dashboard. Then something popped out of the pickup. Fred swerved to miss it. I looked back but could see nothing but a long parade of vehicles behind us. Fred pulled closer to the vehicle in front so we could see what was happening.

The truck carried a load of piglets. They weren't caged or restrained in any way other than overcrowding. Although too small to get out of the pickup bed on their own, they began climbing on top of each other. One after another they mounted the piggy pyramid and jumped off. If pigs have intention, I'm sure theirs was freedom. The result was more like certain death under the wheels of the cars and trucks behind. Fred tried beeping the horn to bring the truck driver's attention to the loss of his investment, but in this land of constant honking he attracted no notice whatsoever. We amused ourselves for the rest of the trip by inventing dialogue between the driver and his passenger when they counted their cargo at the end of the journey.

Cabarete stood out as our favorite destination, but we didn't neglect the other wonderful spots. We all remember Dakota's favorite birthday meal of king crab legs in Puerto Plata. The crabs were a product of a Peace Corps project to bring a new industry to the Dominican economy. They were meant for export and I'm not sure why they were available at this one local restaurant, but I'm grateful for the taste treat, even if it might have been illegal.

Bayahibe comes to mind as another memorable place – the casual ambiance of the sea front restaurant that served the most tender and delicious broiled lobster. Everything tasted better with Presidente beer. Even during long power outages, the Presidente came to the table bien fria (well chilled). Bought from a colmado (local convenience store), an individual beer came wrapped in a small paper bag. The secret, according to Fred, was to keep the beer in the freezer without allowing it to freeze solid and burst the bottle. The result – Presidente slushy, the flagship of Dominican refreshment.

26

Climbers reach the top of Pico Duarte

1988 – 1989

Pico Duarte

Pico Duarte, the highest point in the Dominican Republic, beckoned with promises of adventure. The original instigators of the trip dropped out at the last minute, leaving four eager beavers crazy enough to commit to the expedition. The co-conspirators assumed alternative identities to protect their reputations as respectable citizens: La Doña (me), Mr. Congeniality (Fred), Euell Gibbons (Delbert McCluskey, an experienced AID officer), and Dirk Pathfinder (Adam Namm, a first-tour consular officer).

The explorers prepared for a long weekend of camping and strenuous hiking. In spite of Dirk Pathfinder's sturdy self-image as the epitome of readiness, he forgot his toothbrush and had to borrow one from La Doña before leaving town. After triple-checking their checklists, the intrepid bunch set off for the mountainous world of pine trees and the climb of their lives.

The first leg of their journey took them to Jarabacoa for one night in the candlelit Hotel La Montaña. If it hadn't been so dark, they might have set up bowling pins in the unusually long hallway, but they retired for the night instead. Dirk and Euell went to bed in peace, but La Doña and Mr. Congeniality weren't as lucky.

La Doña, toothbrush (her own) in hand, entered the bathroom and lit a candle on the shelf above the sink. What she saw in the shadowy mirror reflection sent her rushing back to the bedroom, waving her toothbrush wildly above her head.

"Aaack!" she screamed at Mr. Congeniality.

Following the gist of La Doña's posturing, Mr. C. snuck a peek inside the bathroom door where he discovered a family of chartreuse tree frogs secured by their orange suction cup toes to the slick yellow tile of the wall. La Doña peered around his shoulder as he pulled the shower curtain to form a barrier between the frog zone and the area of human occupation.

"That's okay, I really didn't plan to shower anyway." La Doña kept an eye on the shower curtain as she hurried to take care of her most urgent bathroom needs.

As soon as Mr. Congeniality and La Doña cuddled into a comfortable spoon position, electric service resumed. Pupil-constricting light glared down from the single bulb hanging from the high ceiling. The frog family's quack-like croaks echoed in protest.

Before Mr. C. could find the light switch, La Doña spotted a large black something in the nearest corner of the ceiling.

"Hey," she exclaimed. "What's that?"

Mr. C. toddled across the saggy mattress for a closer look. "It's just a bat."

"Just? I can't sleep with that hanging over my head."

Mr. C. jumped down and surveyed the room for potential bat-extraction tools. He grabbed his running shoe and threw it at the bat. He picked up the other shoe and tried again. Pow, the bat fell to the floor and scuttled under the bed.

"Aack!" La Doña pulled knees to chest and scrunched up against the headboard.

Mr. C. jabbed at the bat with his shoe. The bat hissed and retreated further.

"Can't you get that out of here?" A hint of hysteria shrilled in La Doña's squeak.

Valiant Mr. C. thrust shoe into darkness again. This time the bat latched on. With a single mighty swing, Mr. C. launched both shoe and clinging bat out the open window and into the starry night. The bat flew away and the shoe hit the dirt two stories below.

La Doña and Mr. Congeniality laughed themselves to sleep with the quacks of tree frogs croaking in the background.

The next morning, the courageous four reunited for breakfast and the four-wheel trip over a rocky road to Boca del Rio. At the expedition staging area they met their guides who couldn't explain why the pack mules weren't there yet. By the time the pack mules finally showed up, it was 12:30 PM, and the mountain sages pronounced the hour too late in the day to make the whole trip to the top of the mountain.

Dirk Pathfinder laughed in their faces. "Who do you think knows more about this stuff -- yocals who do the mountain twice a week or greenhorn foreigners? If these mountain guides can't even throw a Nerf football spiral, then what kind of athletic advice could they possibly offer?"

Swayed by Dirk's superior reasoning and the promise of a substantial tip, the guides loaded the mules and led the way up the trail.

Euell checked his watch at the 4-kilometer shack. "Four clicks in forty-five minutes. Hey guys, this is going to be easy."

Each of the hearty crew chose a different method to traverse the two-log bridge across a rushing creek. Mr. Congeniality ran. Euell Gibbons strode. Dirk Pathfinder tiptoed. And La Doña inched across on her bottom.

At the 10.5-kilometer checkpoint Dirk slapped a triumphant high-five with Mr. C. "This baby's in the bag – only 7.5 K to go."

Two hours later, the atmosphere on the big climb cooled. The air thinned and so did the patience of the hikers. Euell continued to point out new examples of flora along the trail, but La Doña mumbled under her breath a few words that sounded like, "Shut up, Euell, this is no time for a botany lesson."

Yes, the situation had turned serious. The 15-degree uphill grade went on forever. Leg muscles screamed for relief. The guides insisted that three hours of marching remained, but nightfall was only two hours away. There was no place to pitch a tent on the steep mountainside.

To add to the abject misery of the downtrodden, the clouds released rain. Not enough to soak, just enough to chill. Then, at the very end of twilight, the guides shouted back to the stragglers, "Camp!"

Dirk summed it up. "Thank God, we made it. Now we get to eat and sleep and not die."

Other hikers had reached camp earlier, and our latecomers joined them round the campfire where Bart Grandstander dominated the conversation. Bart had many tales to tell of incredible achievements in white-water rafting, mountain climbing, and photography. Yes, Bart, master outdoorsman who had been everywhere and done everything, waxed eloquent until he bored everyone to sleep.

Next day all hikers trekked to the top. A stroll in the park compared to the climb up to camp. The view alone made yesterday's effort worthwhile.

After an invigorating dip in 45-degree waters of the nearest mountain stream, the campers pursued dinner. Beef stew, chili, and lasagna (all from cans) followed the lead of numerous cans of beer.

That evening Dirk showed the other campers how easy it was to start a raging campfire. All he needed were some dry logs, small pieces of bark and pine needles for kindling, and about half-a-dozen books of matches.

On the way down the mountain Euell shared his knowledge of slimy yellow fungi, lichen, ferns, and several hundred rock types. La Doña, Mr. Congeniality, and Dirk agreed that Euell was more tiresome than their downhill plodding.

Finally the weary trekkers reached the end of the trail. Bodies bathed in the river, clean clothes upon their backs, they collapsed into the chariot that waited to carry them home. Dirk praised the polyester carpeting under foot as well as the vinyl seat below his weary bottom.

"Civilization feels good," Dirk said, and the other three nodded.

Trauma I

On a hot Sunday afternoon a few weeks after my escapade as La Doña, I sat at the typewriter writing a letter while Fred worked in the back yard, thinning out a tangle of vines with his machete. He wore shorts and flip-flops, tossing his shirt aside as soon as he had worked up a sweat. The kids were at the beach with friends and our animals napped in the shade.

A terrible scream shattered the silence and I jumped up to run toward the noise as hideous war cries erupted. By the time I reached the patio, silence reigned again. Fred stood in the far corner of the yard, machete hanging down at his side, a pale look of horror on his face. I saw no blood on Fred, no body at his feet. I could not imagine what had happened. Fred shuddered and began to tell me how a gigantic tarantula had jumped out of the vines onto his bare leg. That's when he screamed. He couldn't remember how he dislodged the spider, maybe with the machete, somehow without cutting himself. The war cries accompanied his frenzied chopping of his assailant. He pointed out the remains, but the pieces were so small I couldn't tell front from back or leg from mouth. In my arachnophobic heart I shared Fred's horror and enjoyed a gruesome jolt of glee over the spider's fate.

Trauma II

"Mom, come see this." Tina called to me from the bathroom. She pointed to a black spot on her hip. "Do I have a tick?"

No, it wasn't a tick. Maybe it was a mole or a blood blister. Tina couldn't remember anything pinching her to make a blood blister. I didn't want to think about why a mole would appear where none had been, black and raised and somewhat irregular around the edges.

We went to the Medical Unit and the nurse sent us to a dermatologist.

The dermatologist said, "Hmmmm. This needs a biopsy. If I were you, I would have it done in Miami."

I called the school principal to request homework for Tina. He said I would have to come to his office to sign something. I sat in his visitor chair feeling a chill that didn't come from air-conditioning. His voice came out low and tight with anger. He left no doubt in my mind that he had some serious issues with embassy parents taking their kids out of school and hurting the Carol Morgan School head count. He threatened to hold Tina back a grade if she missed too much school. I tried not to become defensive, but I think I failed. I believe I told him I didn't care what he did because my highest priority was my child's health. I left some frost of my own in the principal's office that day.

The medevac (medical evacuation) orders sent us to Mt. Sinai Hospital in Miami. The State Department was kind enough to send both parents with the patient. We stayed at the Sofitel Hotel and had strawberries and cream for breakfast. The car rental company happened to be out of economy cars, so we "got stuck with" a red Chrysler LeBaron convertible. While waiting for the results of the biopsy, we toured Monkey Jungle and went mall shopping. I blushed at the memory of my self-righteous speech in the principal's office, but I still worried about the outcome of the biopsy. It turned out negative, thank goodness, and we flew back to Santo Domingo, mole-free and happy.

Trauma III

"Mom." I looked up from my book to see Tina standing in the doorway to our bedroom.

"Mmmm?"

"I took some pills."

These are words no mother wants to hear from her teenage daughter. I'm not sure what happened next. I know I galvanized into readiness with an overwhelming shot of adrenaline. Before I could do anything, Tina ran to the toilet and vomited. She had swallowed perhaps half a bottle of aspirin and several prescription pain pills left over from my periodontal procedures. Not enough to kill her, according to the doctor, but quite enough to cause serious consequences in the form of a medevac, this time to Washington, DC for a psychiatric evaluation.

Dakota seemed happy to stay with his friend Scott while Fred and I accompanied Tina to Washington, but I wonder now how much our son worried and wished he had gone with us instead. It was winter, school holidays, and Dakota flew to California with Scott and his family. Other than his worries, he seemed to have a good time. He enjoyed having sushi with the Schefermans and told the story many times of how they had eaten so much that they were asked to leave the "All You Can Eat" sushi restaurant.

Tina had several sessions with the psychiatrist and his evaluation approved her return to the Dominican Republic provided that she received ongoing counseling. We headed for home and made appointments with Dr. Pacheco, the psychologist recommended by our embassy doctor. Life returned to normal. Tina added both counseling and orthodontia to her schedule.

Poor Tina, this is becoming her chapter, a confirmation that the teen years are indeed tough. Yes, the next trauma incident is hers too.

Trauma IV

Our house had three exits – the front door, the patio door, and the kitchen door that opened toward a separate building that contained the laundry and servant's quarters. Our Agua Cristal watercooler stood next to the kitchen counter beside the door leading outside. One moonless night, Fred got up at about 2:00 AM and went to the cooler for a drink of water. The rattle of the wrought iron security door startled him and he reached for a handy weapon. His fingers closed on the handle of a butcher knife in a wooden rack on the counter. The kitchen door creaked open an inch and he hollered, raised the knife, and lunged. Luck kept him from hacking the intruder into tarantula-sized bits. Good fortune supplied electrical power to the security light that revealed the intruder's identity before the knife came slashing down. Destiny froze Tina in the pool of light, dressed all in black, latchkey still in her hand.

Wakened by Fred's shout, Marianela and I arrived at the same time from opposite directions. We watched as Fred jerked Tina inside the house and planted a swat on her naughty little rear (the one time in her life that Tina ever got spanked by her Daddy).

Such a rough patch for such a sweet girl – teen turmoil added to unrequited love plus uncertainty about her parents' relationship added up to make an unbearably stressful time for Tina. She couldn't help but act out.

Cabo Rojo

I thought it might help the whole family if we took a trip together, but neither Dakota nor Tina wanted to go with us. I could have forced them to go, I suppose, and I thought about it. They might have enjoyed the trip in spite of themselves, but I didn't want to risk a weekend wasted with that special brand of teenage poutiness guaranteed to sour everything. The kids made separate arrangements to spend the weekend with their friends' families; Fred and I pulled our camping gear out of the storage closet.

We joined a group of embassy friends and our flotilla of Land Cruisers four-wheeled over the Baoruco Mountains, through the forest, where we camped, and down the west side of the mountains. We paused at Lake Enriquillo, the largest (209 square miles) lake and the lowest (129 feet below sea level) point in the Caribbean as well as the lowest point on any ocean island. It is one of the few saltwater lakes in the world.

Primitive flat-bottomed wooden boats carried us out to Isla Cabritos, the biggest of four islands, this one famous for caiman and flamingoes. The rank odors of the concentration of crocodilians and the sheer number of prehistoric looking animals both fascinated and repelled me. I was glad to have the experience but happy to leave the stinky, ugly island.

To gain access to the beach at Cabo Rojo, we had to pass through the gates and compound of a small U.S. Military/DEA radar site set up to track drug trafficking from Colombia through this remote area of the Dominican Republic. We had received advance clearance from our good friend, John McFarland, head of the DEA in Santo Domingo, so the soldiers let us through.

The gin-clear water sparkled with the color of swarming fish. I imagined snorkeling through the teeming shoals and feeling the tickle of tiny fins. A fisherman spoke up to caution us not to go in the water. He said sharks would make short work of any and all who dared to swim here. I let my imagination do the snorkeling while I watched from the safety of a sun-warmed rock.

Vertigo

When we got back from Cabo Rojo, I was content to stay at home for a while, but Fred had a better idea. He was keen to go flying with two of his friends, Peter Brennan and David Gardella. They had invited both Fred and me on their flight to the north coast to have lunch at a lobster restaurant. I didn't have much enthusiasm for spending the day in a small plane with the three musketeers, so I suggested that Dakota, with his interest in planes and piloting, might want to tag along instead.

Fred had flown with Peter and Gardella before, once to Haiti and once to Puerto Rico. Those trips were uneventful except for Fred's urgent need to pee long before they landed in Puerto Rico. He held it as long as he could; in final desperation he dumped an aviation map out of its plastic pouch and filled the bag to its brim. When they landed in Puerto Rico, he carried his trash to a receptacle and dropped it in. Security officers leaped into action and interrogated Fred about the nature of his "contraband." Thanks to his diplomatic passport and attaché status, we aren't visiting him in prison.

Dakota welcomed the chance to fly with the big guys and have a lobster lunch at an off-the-beaten-path restaurant. The little plane sailed along and within a couple of hours Gardella spotted landmarks for the small airfield where he intended to land.

Fred tells the story:

"As we headed in the direction of the airstrip, still a few miles away, the weather rapidly deteriorated. Huge cloudbanks blew in and turned our visibility to zero.

"As soon as he recognized the symptoms of complete disorientation, Gardella shouted, 'I've got vertigo!'

"Peter immediately took the controls on his side of the plane and began a steep climb to regain our bearings. We were all desperately straining for landmarks or anything that would give us an idea of where we were.

"Then Dakota shouted, 'I see land…back behind us!'

"The clouds had opened just enough so that Dakota was able to catch a glimpse of the coastline behind us. Without that bit of luck we might have continued on a disastrous course out to sea where we would inevitably run out of fuel.

"Peter turned the aircraft around. As we neared the coast the clouds began to break again and we all saw land to our immense relief.

"We still had a major problem. The storm clouds were so huge we couldn't see enough of the ground to know exactly where we were headed. When Gardella noticed a patch of blue ahead and above our aircraft, he gunned the engine and climbed as quickly as possible into this small clear space. Luck blessed us again. This little blue patch led us through the storm clouds into brilliant sunny skies. Hurray! I was feeling like the worst Dad in the world having exposed my darling son to this horrendous experience. Dakota with his usual unshakable demeanor took it all in stride.

"Had I known what was about to happen next I wouldn't have felt as relieved. As we finally approached the small airfield where Gardella kept his plane, we were all chatting away excitedly about our, to us, near death experience. As we approached the landing a sudden gust of wind lifted the plane off course and shifted us forward. It instantly became obvious that at our rate of speed we would overrun the runway and crash into the huge cement wall that surrounded the airpark.

"As we careened toward the wall Dakota said calmly, 'Well, I guess we're going to die now.'

"I refused to accept this fate and somehow willed the hurtling aircraft to stop – mere inches from the wall.

"Gardella taxied the plane to the parking ramp and we all deplaned in record time. I fell to my knees and literally kissed the ground. At that point I informed my two great buddies that although I loved them dearly

I would never again climb aboard a small plane – and I have not. Nor did Dakota talk further about any plans to enter the Air Force Academy."

Dog Dilemma

Once Fred had received our ongoing assignment, Vienna, and we found out that we would be living in an apartment on one of the embassy compounds, we had to face the dilemma of owning two big dogs. They were big in size, big in personality, and big in their need for space. Neither one behaved well on a leash (in spite of Spike's six-week training course) nor could be called anything close to obedient. My thoughts flew to the future where I pictured myself trying to cope with dog hair, dog boredom, dog barking, dog exercise, and dog feces, not only in the new apartment on a compound shared by many families, but also on a long home leave covering Florida, Texas, New Mexico, Washington, and New Jersey. I shared my worries with Fred and we decided that the dogs needed new homes.

I'm writing this twenty years later and I still feel guilty, although I still feel we made the right decision. It just doesn't seem fair that Dakota and Tina had to give up their beloved pets because it would be inconvenient for me to keep them. They let me off the hook, forgave me, understood the problems; but I haven't been able to forgive myself.

Dusty found a new home with Peter and Lizanne Brennan and their three kids. He became the best family pet imaginable as well as the worst watchdog in history. While Peter and Lizanne were held at gunpoint during a home invasion, Dusty licked the hands of the robbers. But no harm came to anyone, and the Brennans were able to laugh about Dusty's failure as a security guard. They had a similar experience in Venezuela and still laughed about Dusty's lack of guardian instincts.

Spike went to an American colleague who wanted a Boxer. When he was a boy he had to give up his Boxer pup. It seemed fitting that Spike and he should fulfill their mutual need in this way. Still, I cried when we left Spike behind.

At the very end of our days in the Dominican Republic when we were installed in temporary quarters and the dogs had gone to their new homes, Tina and Dakota came down with chicken pox. Not fun anytime, this childhood disease can be rough on teenagers. Our semi-quarantine status put a damper on farewell activities too, so our departure felt a bit anticlimactic after four years of life in one country, the longest our family had lived anywhere.

Unique Home Leave

Home Leave of 1989 stood out as unique, although every home leave was special in its own way. This time we left the country with a huge wad of cash -- $7,000 from the sale of our Land Cruiser. It was obvious that Fred rather enjoyed peeling off Ben Franklins to pay our expenses.

Dakota had just turned sixteen, Tina fifteen. They were leaving many friends and the place they had lived for four years, the longest stretch in their entire lives. Even though this was their lifestyle, and they knew it, the transition wasn't painless. All of the travels and activities of home leave came as a welcome distraction from the pain of saying goodbye to friends.

First stop, Pompano Beach to visit my relatives. My brother Gary's ex-wife Pam and their son Patrick came over from Bradenton and we all went over to cousin Gordy's for a barbeque. We stayed three days in Florida and then moved on to LaPorte to spend a week with Laura and family where Dakota purchased the drum set of his dreams and Tina got an electric guitar and amp (all bought with $100 bills from Fred's bulging pocket). That visit also included a weekend in Galveston that turned out to be a surprise Father's Day gift for Grandpa LaTurner. At that point, we traded our airline tickets for the use of Granny and Grandpa's van.

Next we arrived in Conroe, Texas, at Camp Cox (Aunt Pat and Uncle Dick's home) in River Plantation, known to the locals as R.P. (to us, the initials stood for "Rich People"). After a week of partying, we drove on to Austin and Beth's family. Tina and Dave attended a race-walking clinic together. Beth and baby Zack marched in the Travis Country July 4th parade.

After the July 4th parade, Fred and I pushed Zack around the block in his stroller, still decorated with balloons and crepe paper. Zack stayed very quiet for a long time. When I checked to see if he was asleep, I discovered that he had been busy sucking on one end of the crepe paper streamer. The crepe paper slobber stained his mouth and tongue a brilliant 4th of July blue. Fearing Beth's wrath, we considered running away to South America with Zack, but chose in the end to face the music. Beth laughed at our abject apology for exposing her precious son to unknown toxins.

On our way to New Mexico, our borrowed van developed transmission problems and we had to suffer the final 215 miles from Ft. Stockton, Texas, to Roswell, New Mexico, in the blistering July heat without air-conditioning at forty-five miles per hour. As I recall, I didn't qualify for any awards for patience on that long journey.

My brother Gary flew down to meet us in Los Lunas, New Mexico, and we went together to check out the old place on Los Lentes Road that we still called The Farm. Following Dad's move to Bea's place, the property manager we hired had found renters. The tenants turned out to be deadbeats who couldn't make their monthly payment.

When we surveyed the damage they had done, I felt sick. Horrible stains covered the bathtub. At first I thought it was blood, but a closer look revealed it was iodine or Mercurochrome. Several bashed-in holes in the paneling suggested a frenzied search for a drug stash. Someone had broken into the shed and stolen tools that Dad had stored there. Our dear old place had been violated and we three felt the pain. Later, the property manager made some lame excuse and made me mad enough to complain to the Real Estate Commission. Months later they notified me that, in light of numerous other complaints about this agent, her license had been revoked. I was glad for that tiny bit of justice.

Chris, a neighbor, stepped forward at this time and told us about his long-time interest in the property. He and his wife Lisa offered to clean up the mess. Lisa volunteered to act as property manager and she rented the house to a cousin. Later Chris bought the place from us on a real estate contract and eventually paid it off. When we're in the area these days, since retirement, we drive by, look at the changes in the house and in the neighborhood, and wonder where our life would have gone if we had stayed there rather than joining the Foreign Service. It would have been very different, that's for sure.

While we did our business in Los Lunas, Dakota went to Roswell, his brand new drivers license in hand. He spent about three weeks with Granny and Grandpa. Good old Grandpa, as Roswell County Club Manager, put Dakota to work driving a golf course maintenance truck – a very sweet deal for all concerned.

After our requisite visit to the dentist in Los Lunas, we made tracks for Roswell too. It felt good to reunite with our grown up son. He seemed to be in a pretty good place in his life but not talking much about it. The fact that he ran with us a couple times a week pleased me no end.

Toward the end of July the LaTurner clan gathered for the grand celebration of Granny and Granpa's 50th wedding anniversary. Held at the Roswell Country Club, it was a swingin' festive event. I borrowed a dress from our niece Kathy Cox and felt very special in it – must have been the red belt, my favorite color. It was great to see Granny and Grandpa in the limelight, enjoying the warm regard of family and so many friends.

After the excitement of the party wound down, we trooped back to Los Lunas for a final week with Dad and Bea. The time whizzed by for me but I guess it dragged with boredom for the kids, so isolated with no friends and no cable TV. Dad still used a rotary phone, so it was even a pain in the neck to make long distance calls. And of course he scorned answering machines too.

At the end of the week, we flew straight to Washington DC for three days in civilization at the Columbia Plaza. We managed a pilgrimage to our favorite sushi restaurant, Tachibana, and Dakota spent a day with friends from Dominican Republic days, the Lujans.

Luckily our schedules meshed with the Joneses' and they invited us to spend a week with them at their condo in Ocean City on the Jersey Shore. We rented a car and drove through the beautiful New Jersey countryside, surprised that the whole east coast was not all cement and skyscrapers as we had imagined.

It is impossible to visit the Joneses without having a good time. Glenn showed us how to body skim without a skim board. He demonstrated running to get up speed and then throwing himself onto the hard packed sand and hydroplaning on his stomach on the inch of water at the tail end of a receding wave -- a sport for the most hardy or thick-skinned individuals. He also taught Dakota and Fred all about clamming in the bay. They had a crazy good time, as usual, and we feasted on their catch that evening.

Tracy and Laurie were nine and eight then, and Tracy was feeling down because she couldn't keep up with Laurie's reading ability. Fred had a little talk with her about focusing on her artistic talents and not fretting about the reading. It was an effective pep talk -- I could see the relief on her face. Later she asked Glenn if Fred understood her so well because he was her real dad. She had heard the story of her birth in New Zealand many times, and the part about the doctor assuming Fred was the father stuck in her mind. That sweet little girl's confusion still gives us all a fond chuckle when we reminisce.

The highlight of this trip was our day on the boardwalk. We strolled around, soaked up the local color, and checked out all the stalls. Tina spotted the prizes at the ring toss game.

"Oh, Daddy, win me a bear."

I assumed she was half-joking, but Fred took the bait.

"No problem, Honey." He paid his money and the young woman in the booth handed him three rings. "I'll only be needing one of these." He swaggered up to the counter and exaggerated his throwing stance.

To the total amazement of all concerned, the ring flew straight and plunked down around the neck of one of the bottles. Impossible but true. The attendant had tears in her eyes as she reached up with her long hook to fetch the bear. This was no ordinary bear. Pure white, fluffy, and almost as tall as Tina who claims 5' 2" standing tall.

Glenn died a thousand deaths as his daughters clamored for him to do the same. He confessed that he had misspent his youth in failed attempts to capture such a prize. That day was no different from any other for Glenn, and six rings later he turned away in defeat. Fred never let him forget it. That bear became The Bear, star of many photos captioned with taunts and jibes, torturing Glenn more than twenty years into the future.

When it came time to leave, we had to cram The Bear into the trunk of our rented car on top of the rest of our baggage. Fred made it work, determined as he was to keep the prize in our possession. It was Tina's bear, right? Well, sort of.

Following the visit with the Joneses, we spent two weeks in Warrenton, VA in a Hampton Inn suite. Fred had to complete a course at the training facility there, and the rest of us hung out, reuniting with old friends, jogging on the roads through horse country, and watching a lot of cable TV. Dakota went to Springfield, MA for several days to see Gillian Ward who was visiting Maureen McFall, both close friends of his from Carol Morgan School. We had dinner with the McLaughlins (Somalia and Dominican Republic) and made a trip out to Manassas to see the Goffs (from Tehran days). One day I took Tina, Dakota, and Tina's friend Alex Asselin to King's Dominion amusement park.

Come August, it was time to depart for Vienna. The kids and I left on Tuesday in order to arrive in time for school orientation. Fred moved to a motel, finished his training and consultation, and planned to join us in Vienna on Saturday.

PART SEVEN

AUSTRIA ADVENTURES

Ferris wheel on the Prater

27

Bicycle rest stop in a potato patch

1989

Hell

The kids and I had never traveled without Fred. I suffered from that uneasy feeling of something missing. To add to my discomfort, our two flights were late and later and we had to sit on the runway in New York for three hours due to bad weather somewhere nearby. Ugh. I tried to sleep away the transatlantic flight, but every time the bliss of sleep approached, my flopping head jerked me back to consciousness. At the end of a very long night I blessed our sponsors who met us at the airport. If I had the energy I would have shouted halleluiah when I saw our bags bump through the black rubber flaps onto the carousel. Our gentle sponsors delivered three weary bodies to Apartment 2/3 at 16

Chimanistrasse in the Nineteenth District of Vienna, Austria, our home for the next three years.

Jet lag weighed me down like a lead cape and I dragged through the next few days receiving our airfreight, the embassy welcome kit, and figuring out how to get Dakota and Tina to their school orientation.

Vienna's fabulous public transportation system lay almost at our doorstep with a bus/tram stop less than a block away, on the route that ended at the foot of the hill occupied by the American International School (AIS) campus. Many of the passengers on that route on the day of orientation were the right age to be AIS students. One boy in particular attracted my attention with his animated conversation in the seat ahead of us. That was Sam Torabi, who became one of Dakota's best friends and his future college roommate.

After the kids' introduction to AIS, we looked forward to Fred's arrival on the following day. He had seemed sad about sending us ahead to post, and I thought of a surprise to welcome him home and cheer him up. I stocked the fridge with an assortment of a dozen different Austrian beers and posted a rating sheet on the fridge door.

"What's this?" Fred pointed to my hand-lettered chart.

"Look inside." I swung the fridge door open. "Ta Da!"

Fred's eyes sparkled and he reached for his first tall white and gold can of Zipfer. After finishing the home test of canned beer, Fred switched to bottles and homed in on Gösser as his number one choice in Austrian beers.

We learned that our new home had had a former life as officers' quarters during the American occupation of Vienna following World War II. Our place was formed by the removal of dividing walls between two adjacent two-bedroom apartments. On the ground floor we had two main entrances, two living rooms, two dining rooms, one kitchen, and one laundry room (formerly a kitchen). Two staircases led to the bedrooms, two on each side, and bathrooms, one on each side. We put the kids on one side and us on the other and designated the spare bedroom as guestroom/office. There was a door between the guestroom and Tina's room, but Tina decided to put her dresser against it. She might have been guarding her privacy or merely creating more options for furniture arrangement – she didn't say which.

The apartment had a total of six doors to the outside world – the two main entrances plus glass doors from the kitchen, one dining area, and both living rooms -- and I expected to receive a key ring worthy of a castle's chatelaine. I was surprised and impressed that one key opened all six doors as well as the main gate to the compound. The price tag for duplicate keys for the kids came as a shock. At $20 each, those keys should have been silver-plated.

I dove into German lessons at the embassy and let the personnel office know I was looking for work. Dakota and Tina started school, made friends, and seemed happy. But I noticed that Dakota wrote "Hell" on the top left hand corner of the envelope addressed to his friend from the Dominican Republic. If he did feel banished to Hades, it wasn't long before that feeling faded in the presence of new friends and the experiences available with all of Europe as a playground.

Fred and I made our new friends in the running community. We joined a fun-loving group of English-speaking runners including Tim and Kirsten Fisher (embassy), Elmer and Gretchen Shore (Boeing Aircraft), Mike and Godi Habib (embassy), Janet Auinger (New Yorker married to an Austrian) and Cynthia Reiser (Russian linguist from Texas). On weekends we ran down by the canal, up in the Wienerwald (Vienna Woods), or along the Donau Insel (a recreation area on the island separating the Danube River from the excavated New Danube channel). If our friends weren't available we ran in Turkenschanz, our neighborhood park.

Part of the getting-settled routine for embassy newcomers in Vienna included a shopping trip to the Army Post Exchange (PX) in Nuremberg, Germany. Fred and I stayed in a grand old hotel, once a Nazi SS retreat, now run by our U.S. military, and we took advantage of the many bargains at the PX. Attracted by both the reduced prices and the posh accommodations (Fred's State Department rank snagged the General's suite), we made periodic shopping trips to Nuremberg throughout our Vienna tour. We zoomed with the 100 mph traffic back and forth on the autobahn. When we crossed the border from Germany back into Austria I recognized a sense of returning home.

Within a month of our arrival in Vienna, our household effects came. Thanks to spacious closets and storage areas, our stuff had an easy journey from packing crate to rightful place. As I flattened the last cardboard box and smoothed a second layer of lotion on my paper-chapped hands, I realized that my forty-ninth birthday was only a week away.

Fred treated me to dinner and a concert. Flaky golden vegetable strudel complemented a gently sautéed scallop of pork so beautifully that I was left with no room for dessert.

"Maybe a little chocolate something after the concert?" I patted my full stomach and placed my white damask napkin on the table in surrender.

We walked from the restaurant to the Volksoper (people's opera house) in the crisp autumn air. We had tickets for The Magic Flute and I felt especially excited because of my connection with this operetta, having performed in it in high school. It was doubly thrilling to be in the audience in Mozart's old neighborhood.

The next momentous event was the addition of a kitten to our household. Tina named him Onyx for his shining blackness. He reminded me of Carbón, the cat that disappeared in the Dominican Republic. Onyx was Tina's pet, but he shared his love with all of us. He liked to sit on a lap while the lap owner watched TV. He managed to stealth-creep higher and higher until he draped across the person's chest and nuzzled his face into the crevice where neck and shoulder meet. There he began to sneak frequent sucks on shirt or collar, leaving a wet, wrinkled mess for his hapless host. He loved my merlot (color, not flavor) velour sweats the most.

A few weeks after Onyx joined the family I started my new job in the unclassified computer section of the embassy. Little did I know that I was entering my own version of hell.

I struggled to survive my damnation and in the process I learned a whale of a lot about computers. Most of what I learned pertained to the WANG system, which soon went the way of the dinosaurs, but a good amount of my knowledge could be generalized and wasn't a complete waste of brain cells. The hellish aspects of the job came from the multiple neuroses of my boss, the idiosyncrasies of my coworkers, the frustrating quirks of the equipment, and a backup schedule that required working odd hours. I grew to hate just about everything about the job.

Once I began working full time, I realized that I needed help around the house. One day I herded Dakota and Tina into the laundry room and introduced them to the washer and dryer. Tina stood silent as I started to demonstrate the finer points of washing clothes, but Dakota voiced his opinion in that special teen inflection that turns "Mom" into a two-syllable word.

"Sorry, guys…I miss Marianela too, but we can't afford a maid at Austrian prices."

I turned their attention to the vacuum cleaner and its accessories while explaining that they were now responsible for cleaning their own rooms as well as their shared bathroom. If looks could kill….

The condition of the kids' rooms went downhill until even they couldn't stand living in the mess. They both ran out of clean clothes before asking for a replay of washer/dryer instructions. Without collaboration, Dakota and Tina developed identical methods: they cleaned and washed in one marathon effort and then let the accumulation build to critical mass once more – and repeat.

School and Play

While Fred and I worked, the kids went to classes. Their courses took them further afield than most high school curricula. Dakota's music appreciation class attended concerts and operas in the famous venues of Vienna, the City of Music. His art appreciation class toured Florence, Italy. He attended Model United Nations in The Hague in The Netherlands. Dakota joined the soccer team and played matches in London, England and Frankfurt and Munich in Germany. We were in Munich to see him play in the International Schools Sports Tournament when the Berlin Wall came down in November 1989. A detour to Berlin to see history happening tempted us, but we decided to watch the championship soccer game instead. Dakota's team won.

Tina, as the only varsity girl, ran cross-country in London (where the mud sucked off her shoes and she finished the race in stocking feet). She also went to The Hague for a Speech and Debate competition as a last-minute substitute for Ryan Fisher's partner. She had about thirty minutes notice to pack and catch the train and had to memorize her presentation during the train ride. Tina also attended a drama conference in Rome and a Model UN session in The Hague. Sometimes it seemed that our children were away more than they were at home.

Of course I was glad they had so many opportunities and friends, but again I felt a sense of loss that we weren't doing more things together as a family. I think I must have lived in denial that the process of chicks leaving the nest has to be gradual and not done suddenly on the day they leave for college.

Both Dakota and Tina did well academically too. Dakota had one brief blip when his chemistry teacher took a dislike to him. I offered to speak to the principal about dropping the class, but Dakota said he wanted to stick it out because he knew he would have to learn to deal with people who didn't like him or whom he didn't like. I'm proud to say that he did.

Another of Dakota's interests, music, took a back burner temporarily because AIS had no instrumental music program. We couldn't believe it. Here, in the City of Music, the American school didn't even offer music lessons? After a few months, though, Dakota connected with other musicians and formed a rock band. They played at school dances and school musicals. Our second living room became their practice studio where Dakota set up the gigantic drum set that he bought in Houston, along with his buddies' guitar amplifiers. Those practice sessions rattled our windowpanes.

The sound of just one drummer drumming on that colossal drum set could wake the dead, and our neighbor complained. The neighbor happened to be the unemployed dependent spouse of my boss. Not the best situation. This man I'll call Rex summoned Fred and Dakota to his apartment to hear his emphatic rant about Dakota's inconsiderate disturbance of his tranquility. Dakota offered to restrict his practicing to any time the neighbor would agree to. But Rex, who fancied himself a writer of some importance, explained in an arrogant tone that he wrote according to the schedule of his muse, not by the clock. And furthermore, he resented the rude treatment by Dakota and his friends when they encountered each other at the gate or on the compound. He indicated that he felt the victim of prejudice against his black race.

Dakota placed his hand on Fred's arm, which seemed poised for a punch aimed at the man's nose, and declared a slow, simple truth, "So, maybe you haven't noticed, but I am not exactly lily-white myself."

Our neighbor muttered a few defensive words about color versus culture, and the incident ended. Dakota continued to practice at times that did not disturb the rest of our neighbors. There were no more complaints. We heard later that Rex found a day job.

Meanwhile Tina joined the drama club and became one of the stars of school plays and musicals. Fred and I created a new tradition by attending every performance. We watched her in A Midsummer Night's Dream, Grease (and Dakota played in the band), Life Cycles, West Side Story, and Senior Cabaret. Tina also studied creative writing with Jonathan Carroll (well-known author of fantasy novels) and earned top marks from him.

Tina's choir membership gave me an opportunity too, when adult voices were added for the premier of an oratorio, "Ins Antlitz der Unterdrückung," (In the Face of Oppression) composed by a friend of the American International School choir director. Our group of AIS singers joined several Austrian adult choirs to provide the chorus for a quartet of professionals, and we practiced long and hard, so long and hard that one of the girls in the chorus fainted during dress rehearsal. We sang at the Musikverein, home of the world famous Vienna Philharmonic Orchestra. As we stood on risers on the stage I counted the larger-than-life-size statues that lined the walls of the long gilded hall. Twenty-eight plump golden breasts thrust forward from fourteen voluptuous figures standing guard as if to protect musical excellence. I couldn't imagine an audience member falling asleep in any concert held there.

Whether in or out of school, Tina and Dakota shared some friends and also had friends they didn't share. They spent quite a bit of time socializing in coffee shops and bars. Austrian law allowed wine and beer purchase for anyone over sixteen, so they drank. Austrian law allowed the issue of driver's licenses to applicants over eighteen, so younger teens did not drive. It seemed like a very sensible arrangement to me. The kids got around town by public transportation or by taxi, a mother's dream scenario.

Tina and Dakota and their friends also "quarried." The area they called the quarry was located deep in the Wienerwald (Vienna Woods) above the AIS campus. It had been a popular destination for AIS students for generations, a traditional place for bonfires and beer drinking, philosophizing and romancing, safe from the prying eyes of adults.

Fred and I compared our high school years – his in Roswell, New Mexico, and mine in Long Lake, Minnesota – to our children's and neither of us could comprehend the enormity of the differences. We came from provincial backgrounds and now found ourselves raising citizens of the world. We congratulated each other for providing Dakota and Tina such a marvelous lifestyle.

28

Nancy finds cross-country paradise

1990

A Measure of Leisure

January 1990 marked the beginning of a love affair. Fred and I fell in love with cross-country skiing. We had learned Alpine skiing in Japan and skied Mammoth Mountain while we lived in California and the Alborz Mountains in Iran, but neither of us had ever tried Nordic skiing. When I watched cross-country skiers on TV, I felt my muscles respond and I knew I could do it. Luckily for us, embassy employees could take advantage of the Armed Forces Recreation Center (AFRC) facilities and programs in Garmisch, Germany. We signed up for a week of cross-country ski lessons.

After the first day of lessons with our excellent Czech instructor, we went straight to the PX and bought our own equipment – we were that enthusiastic. But the next morning I had trouble getting out of bed. I had to use both hands to lift my legs over the four-inch lip of the shower stall. Like my experience with aerobics in the Dominican Republic, this was another example of how enthusiasm combined with fitness can lead to trouble. However, a second full day of skiing loosened the stiffness, and an evening sauna toasted away my pain.

We had excellent snow and beautiful sunshine every day, and each outing took us to a different ski course. Garmisch lies in the heart of Bavaria where charming architecture creates a fairy-tale atmosphere. Our package deal included breakfast and dinner in the hotel dining room and the food was superb. We always stopped at a restaurant for lunch where I learned that apfelsaft gespritzt (apple juice with sparkling water) is a better midday beverage than beer for me. Fred stayed loyal to beer, but he didn't suffer from the irresistible urge to nap afterward like I did when I drank it. My favorite lunch, in fact my favorite meal, was potato pancakes with applesauce, made according to the unrivaled German tradition. The combination of crisp, golden potatoes – much like American hash browns -- and smooth, sweet applesauce was my soul food.

At the closing ceremony of our ski week, Fred and I received gold medals (the instructor awarded gold, silver, and bronze to the top men and women achievers) and we made a pact to sign up for the ski package again next year.

As soon as we got home, we pulled out our maps and pinpointed places to go skiing. We started with Nordic centers within a two-hour drive of Vienna, to give us enough time to drive there, ski a couple of hours, and return home before dark.

Even though we were burning with enthusiasm for this new sport, we didn't neglect our running. In fact, we both committed to a 12-week half-marathon training program, in spite of the winter conditions.

Running and racing in Austria offered challenging courses in gorgeous scenery and flawless organization. Unlike Stateside races, the Austrian ones didn't provide commemorative t-shirts, but we learned to live without them. The tradeoff was a huge block party with food, drink, and oompa band music. We ran our favorite half-marathon at Hallstatt, a salt-mining community continuously inhabited since Roman days. Our hotel room faced the mountainside and we heard the gentle song of the trickling stream all night.

Bad Mitterndorf also hosted a fine half-marathon and had a Nordic ski area on top of the mountain. We liked to stay at a game lodge there and partake of wondrous strange foods like deer tongue in horseradish cream, an appetizer to shame all others. The Fishers and Shores usually joined us on these running trips and it was great to have traveling companions with similar interests.

In the spring, I was glad to see Dakota and Fred start playing tennis together regularly on the court on our compound. Fred usually won 6-4 even though Dakota tried his hardest to beat his dad.

Spring weather turned our attention to bicycling too. Fred bought a set of detailed maps of the many bike routes throughout Austria. Once he and I had explored the area in and around Vienna, we put our bikes on the car-rack and ventured into the countryside. We rode much of the time on designated bicycle paths and some of the time on country roads. Outside the city, Austrian drivers seemed less hurried or harried and they gave the utmost consideration to bicyclists; I felt safe. Often we cruised those byways on Sundays and found the quaint little towns virtually deserted. I imagined all the families gathered at Oma's (granny's) house for dinner after Mass. I pictured us as colorful figures on a scenic postcard.

Out in the country, we rode among the hills and valleys, and once we pedaled the perimeter of a potato field. There, in the middle of nowhere, we came upon a small wooden shed with rustic picnic tables outside. Inside the shed, refreshments were sold, including beer and wine. More than just cyclist-friendly, this was cyclist-heavenly.

In May we expected our first visitors. The day before Granny and Grandpa LaTurner were due to arrive, Dakota broke his leg playing indoor soccer. Fred accompanied him through the treatment process and came home full of admiration for the efficiency of the Austrian health care system. Dakota gave Granny and Grandpa the honor of being first to sign his fresh white cast.

Fred and I showed Granny and Grandpa around Vienna, took them to see the operetta *Die Fledermaus* and to the Spanish Riding School for the performance of the Lipizzaner stallions. They took special delight in the location of their seats at these events – box seats at the opera and the Emperor's seats at the Lipizzaner horse show. For reasons of economy, the seats for Fred and me were not as luxurious, and they let us know they enjoyed that contrast too.

Next we drove to Berchtesgaden, Germany. Grandpa was a paratrooper in WWII and we wanted him to experience Hitler's hideaway, the Eagle's Nest. On the way we stopped in Salzburg where Granny shopped for a typical Austrian dress. We also toured Obersalzburg and Hitler's bunkers, a whole city built underground for the Fuhrer's safety.

The Eagle's Nest dominated the whole mountaintop. Hitler's elevator provided room-sized luxury furnished like a sitting room, lined with mirrors and embellished with gilt decorations. Dense fog enveloped the mountain on the day of our visit and I realized the meaning of the phrase "pea soup fog." Fred's Gortex jacket hood had a bright yellow lining, so he was visible up to three feet away and we followed him as our beacon. The fog muffled sound as well as sight in a most ominous way. Dozens of huge black ravens loomed on the edge of the parapet, their feathers fluffed against the chill damp, and I imagined that their caws told the tale of Nazi atrocities. I felt uneasy, claustrophobic, and very relieved to leave at the end of our visit. I waited to hear Grandpa's reaction, but he was lost in his memories of wartime.

Down from the mountain we stayed in another of those picturesque old ex-Nazi hotels like the one Fred and I enjoyed in Nuremberg. This one had a special attraction that excited Grandpa – slot machines. He waited his turn as a woman played the nickel slot over and over. When he grasped the handle, it wasn't long before he hit the jackpot. His nickel-stained hands clutched his precious bag of booty for the rest of the evening. He looked like a little boy flush with Halloween treats. And he paid his entire hotel bill with nickel winnings.

How sad we were to bid farewell to Granny and Grandpa. But we didn't have to wait long for more visitors. In about a month we welcomed our twenty-four-year-old niece Pam Pniak whose visit coincided with Glenn Jones's. Fred, Glenn, Pam, Tina, and I drove to Sopron, Hungary, where we shopped, lunched, and acted silly trying to read and interpret Hungarian signs.

We didn't have a steady stream of visitors in Vienna, but we did have one strange set. An American family that we had met in the Dominican Republic invited themselves to stay with us. They weren't connected to the embassy; we met because our children went to the same school. We agreed to house their two boys, whom Dakota and Tina knew quite well, but we suggested that the parents would be more comfortable in a hotel. The adults could have posed for the Ugly American stereotype poster. I still cringe when I think about Mr. W. waving around his enormous video camera with its bright spotlight ruining the sedate atmosphere in the restaurant at Cobenzl. When Mrs. W. developed a fever and convinced herself that she had "The German Measles," she expected us to provide medical care and acted miffed when we suggested she contact the doctor recommended by their hotel manager.

The W. family's visit brought to mind a couple of my dad's sayings about people who have overstayed their welcome: "Here's your hat, what's your hurry" and "Don't let the door slam your ass on the way out."

Summer activities pushed the W's to a dim corner of memory. Fred and I bicycled a different forty-mile segment of the Danube bike path every weekend. We ran and raced as often as possible. We took Dakota to Neusiedlersee to check out the windsurfing there, but there was no wind that day. The distance from Vienna discouraged frequent trips to the lake anyway, so Dakota decided to sell his windsurf equipment.

Also during this summer of fun we learned that Vienna offered much more than just classical music. Fred finally got to see his beloved Rolling Stones in concert. He went to Santana and Miles Davis concerts as well. And Vienna was the home of the American Institute of Music (AIM) where Dakota wanted to study after high school graduation. He had decided on a career in music and he planned to attend AIM for a year to prepare for college at the Berklee School of Music in Boston.

Get Me Out of Here

Shortly before school began in the fall – Dakota's senior year and Tina's junior year – Dakota came down with a sore throat. He had such a serious case of tonsillitis that the specialist put him in the hospital for intravenous antibiotic treatment.

Poor Dakota lay in a ward of old men with terminal illnesses. Eerie groans floated up from fragile forms huddled under thin white blankets. Caustic smells of antiseptics failed to purify the air. Nurses wafted from bed to bed on rubber soles that squeaked with intermittent cheerless cries.

Dakota peered up at me with an expression like Munch's *Scream*. Tears filled his eyes. "Can't you just get me out of here, Mommy? I want to go home."

It broke my heart to leave him there, but I was convinced he needed the antibiotics.

After visiting hours, a doctor guided Dakota to a treatment room and, without warning or explanation, lanced the abscess on my baby's tonsils. What a horrible experience. Maybe the procedure was medically necessary, but the way it was carried out, without parental permission, without counseling to the patient, just plain made me see red. When the doctor suggested that a tonsillectomy should be the next step, I refused. I got a second opinion from the doctor at the embassy, and liberated Dakota as soon as possible.

Dakota recovered without surgery, never again had tonsillitis, and more than twenty years later he still has his tonsils.

Half Century

Our lovely bicycling excursions over the summer gave me the idea for a birthday trip to celebrate my fiftieth. One of our map packets featured a trail that ran along the Danube and I chose the portion from Passau, Germany to Melk, Austria, a trip that would take three days.

To catch the train to Passau we had to get up at 4:45 AM. We packed our saddlebags the night before and, after some fiddling around, discovered that Fred's bags fit on my bike and vice versa.

We rode our bikes in the early morning darkness with perfect visibility thanks to the bright streetlights. I shivered a little in the wind that made sixty degrees seem chilly.

Traffic on the Gurtel was a little scary. Where could all those people be going at 5:30 in the morning?

Although we purchased our passenger tickets in August, we had to get tickets for the bikes on the day of travel, September 12, my birthday. The man at the ticket window spoke perfect English and handed Fred our tickets as he directed us to take our bicycles up to the platform. Fred assumed that the ticket man meant we should take the escalator along with the regular passengers.

The world switched to slow motion as Fred performed a wild acrobatic routine with his bicycle caught in the escalator's claws. Before the comedy had a chance to turn into a tragedy, a Turkish newspaper vendor stepped in to pull the red emergency ring. The escalator stopped immediately, but the alarm system set off a clamor of bells that centered everyone's attention on Fred's drama. While Fred pulled himself and his bicycle and his baggage together, I stood paralyzed, my view of the world still in shocked slow-mo. An important lesson: bicycles and escalators are best ridden separately.

After that, boarding the train was a snap. This was a special bicycle train with half the cars designed to transport bikes. In typical Austrian fashion, the train got underway right on schedule. As the wheels clickety-clicked along, I watched blue sky replace clouds and improve the outlook for today's forty-four-mile leg of my birthday bike trip.

I removed a layer of clothes. The warmth of the coach and the clack of the wheels made me drowsy, but there was no place for my head – or my legs – just like trying to sleep on an airplane. So I settled for daydreaming about the other passengers. Across from us sprawled two fat guys – also radfahrers (bicyclists). Would we see them later on the trail?

In four hours we arrived in Passau, at the German border. No problem getting our bikes off the train. There were no formalities such as Customs; we just mounted up and rode off.

The well-marked trail brought us past the gothic and baroque architecture of the town of Passau. We turned on the Donau-Radweg (Danube
bicycle path) and pedaled away. Hills – we weren't expecting hills – huff,
puff.

We stopped for lunch at a gasthof. The weather had turned cold
and cloudy, but the restaurant provided a warm and toasty reprieve. We
ordered käsekrainer (sausage stuffed with cheese) with French-fries and
mixed salad – a hearty meal for starving bicyclists.

A few drops of rain fell after lunch, and then the day brightened
again. We stopped often to enjoy beautiful spots where forest met river. It
seemed like a dream. Were we really there, pedaling through such a perfect
postcard scene?

Late in the afternoon we arrived in Aschach, a small town beside the
river. Our home for the night was named "Zur Sonne," (Toward the Sun)
an inn decorated with sun faces rendered in wood and metal. Our tiny
room shared a bathroom across the hall.

A change of clothes turned us into pedestrian tourists and we set out
to search for bier vom fass (beer on tap). Stiegl, the Salzburg brew, waited
for us at a homey little pub. Fred presented me with an extra gift, a gold
bicycle charm, and sang the most beautiful rendition of "Happy Birthday"
ever heard on the banks of the Danube.

We walked through the village and visited a 500-year-old church. A
wreath made of fruits and veggies hung over a big basket of the finest fresh
produce, gracing the altar as a colorful offering. The church posted a photo and an announcement that it had a bicycle-riding priest. Amen to that.

At the end of a delicious trout dinner at our hotel, the beautiful
grandma of the proprietors treated us to a shot of schnapps in honor of
my birthday. Exercise added to beer multiplied by schnapps constituted
the formula for an early bedtime and colorful dreams.

I woke at dawn and watched the sun rise over the Danube. In minutes
I was ready for the typical Austrian breakfast of crunchy hard roll, ham,
salami, cream cheese, jam and a full carafe of coffee.

At the hotel bike stand I checked my tires. Drat, the front one yielded slightly to my squeeze. I made a wish on my new bicycle charm that I would not have flat tires in my immediate future. Fred pumped some air in the soft tire and we found a gas station to top it off before we left town.

The trail veered away from the river and wound through farms and orchards. I praised my many layers of polypropylene and wool that protected me against the brisk midmorning temperature.

When the bike path returned to the Danube we rolled into a fog bank dominated by shades of gray like a 1940s mystery movie.

Passing through Ottensheim I felt the spirits of medieval knights among the noble limestone buildings along the cobblestone streets. We both got so carried away by the perfect beauty of the scene that we forgot to take a snapshot of the picture book village.

At Linz the sun came out. We peeled off two layers and stopped for refreshments. As we rode onward through Linz, I noticed a familiar nasty smell. Was it abattoir or paper mill or sugar beets? I couldn't identify the industry, but I recognized the urgent need to escape the stench. Still, I had to brake and stop to watch a helicopter pass overhead with a huge piece of sculpture in tow. At that angle the sculptured figure appeared to be bigger than the helicopter. I couldn't tell what it represented or where it was going.

We rode along the river on smooth asphalt under sunny skies. Could the ride be "all downhill" as some people said? With very little effort we approached our day's destination in the middle of the afternoon. Oops, a killer hill must be conquered to reach our hotel. After such an easy day I had no excuse, so I geared down as low as I could and powered to the top.

With extra time on our hands, we went for a walk around the village. At the very top of the hill we found a cemetery to investigate. The church, however, was locked -- the first locked church we had ever seen in Austria. Scaffolding and ladders suggested that renovations were going on; perhaps the church had to be locked as a safety precaution.

If I proclaimed Ottensheim the most beautiful town, I had to call Wallsee the most lifeless village on our route. Apparently on Thursdays all shops took the evening off. We commented on a strange lack of welcome.

But a cold beer in the pleasant garden of our hotel made everything all right.

Later we went down the hill, smacking our lips in anticipation of a marvelous fish dinner. But no, the Donau Restaurant had locked doors too. So we trudged back up the hill. The castle might have been interesting, but a sturdy padlock secured its gates. We peeked into the chapel and saw a grim gray monument to fallen soldiers. Was this a Nazi town?

Dinner at our hotel filled us up -- potato soup, pork on a skewer, mixed vegetables, and a crepe for dessert – but it didn't satisfy my desire for fish. We chatted a bit with two Dutch couples on their way (by bicycle tour) to Vienna. Nice folks. The Dutch always amazed me with their ability to speak English with virtually no accent.

A pretty good night's sleep followed (for me) after the mosquito went away (she spent the rest of the night with Fred).

Bells rang wildly at 6:08 AM, again at 6:48 and again at 7:13. Weird. Was the hotel on fire? Was the town on fire? Was this the Wallseeian version of a snooze alarm for sleepyheads? A call to Mass perhaps? I breathed a sigh of relief that emerged as a white plume in the chill air when we left the city limits of that strange town.

On we pedaled, through Weisen, a lovely red-roofed village on a bend of the river. Fred's photos caught the buildings reflected perfectly in the mirror waters of the Danube.

First stop of the day: Freienstein for an apfelsaft gespritzt and a delightful interlude to enjoy the warmth of the sun and contemplate the river as smooth and still as glass.

My bike developed a rattle. Fred put almost all of his tools into play, tightened one stubborn nut in the rear fender, and all was well again.

We made our lazy way – more "downhill" -- along the river, warm in the sun, chilly in the shade, surrounded by beauty so perfect it seemed unreal.

Hunger and Gottsdorf coincided in a lunch stop and we gobbled our tasty Austrian sausages with peasant bread and mustard. Sated and content, I felt a twinge of melancholy that our journey was coming to its end.

We crossed the Danube at Ybbs, then crossed again just before Melk, arriving in the town of Melk before 3:00 PM. After finding the bahnhof (train station) and making arrangements for our bikes, we sipped our beer in the sunshine. Could it really be over this fast?

After a peaceful train ride from Melk to Vienna, our bike trip home from Westbahnhof in the swarm of rush hour mimicked the thrills of Space Mountain at Disneyland. We did survive it unscathed, although I dismounted on wobbly legs at the end of our great adventure. Everybody should be so lucky as to experience a trip like this. Exhilarating, uplifting, full of wonder, it gave me a marvelous fiftieth birthday celebration.

My birthday fun overflowed into the following weekend when I ran a fun run – the Wahringer Volkslauf – with Fred, Tim and Kirsten Fisher, Gretchen and Elmer Shore, Janet Auinger, Cynthia Reiser, and Godi Habib. After the race, Godi and Mike Habib hosted a birthday lunch at their huge mansion (Mike was the DCM then). Tina served the cake and the Shore's kids, Sarah and Andrew, helped me open my gifts. I noticed that multiple birthday parties made the fun last longer and I hatched a plan to celebrate the whole month of September from then on.

29

High School graduate and proud sister

<u>1991</u>

Life Goes On

An eventful year, 1991 started off with "Deadline in the Desert," and moved on to Desert Storm, the Gulf Crisis. I worried that Dakota might be drafted. In those days, eighteen-year-old boys were required to register for the draft, and they did get called up. Dakota registered but did not get called to serve and I am grateful. I admit that all during the Gulf Crisis I had a recurring fantasy about spiriting him to Canada to avoid sending him to war.

Most of the time, though, war didn't enter my thoughts and I devoted my attention to family members. And my family included Onyx the cat. Quite a character, Onyx. And smart too. All of our doors had handles rather than knobs and he figured out how to jump up, pull down the handle, and then paw the door open. He liked to attack Tina's door in the middle of the night so he could come to her bed and wage war with her toes under the blankets. In retaliation, Tina locked her door. Onyx persisted, driving us all crazy with the bang and thump of his repeated assaults on the door handle.

He also wanted to accompany us to the bathroom. I preferred his absence, primarily because he had a habit of exiting before I finished and leaving the door wide open behind him. One day I forgot to lock him out, and, as I sat on the commode, Onyx opened the door, jumped up into the sink beside me, and peed. That gave him a new idea and he started peeing in the bathtubs and all of the sinks, including the kitchen. I had to keep an inch of standing water in the sinks to break him of that nasty habit.

At first, we tried keeping Onyx indoors, but he protested by launching himself from the banister onto the hapless head of whoever sat on the couch below. He convinced us that we would be better off if we turned him loose, so we gave Onyx the freedom to come and go at will through one of the living room windows left open a crack. Several months later he went out one morning and didn't come back. A friend who knew him well told us that she saw his body on the street the morning after his disappearance.

The whole family mourned. And then Silvia, my colleague at work, said that her fiancé, a researcher for a cat food company, had two kittens to give away. These kittens, orphaned at birth, had been raised on the cat food company's formula and were ready to be weaned. Is there a softer touch than the LaTurner family? Tina named the kitten sisters Shadow and Cheyenne.

In February Fred and I made our second trip to Garmisch for the AFRC ski week and had a fabulous time again. Our group of fourteen comprised the intermediate class. During the week of lessons we graduated from blue (moderate difficulty) to black (expert) trails.

Midway through our ski week, I called home to see how the kids were getting along. Tina answered.

"Yeah, great, everything is fine here…. Hey, we have something to tell you."

How many dire circumstances can a mother think of in the miniscule gap between the next question and its answer? It seemed like dozens boiled up from my worry center.

"What's that?" I said, holding the phone between my ear and Fred's.

"Please don't be mad – me and Dakota got tattoos."

Fred snorted a suppressed laugh.

"Cool," I said. *God…Let it be a clean place.* "Tell us about your designs."

I suspect our children were somewhat disappointed by our casual acceptance of their deviant little escapade. Didn't they know that their parents had once been teenagers too?

After Fred and I returned to Vienna, admired the kids' skin art, and slipped back into our daily routines, I received a call from the leader of the aerobics class that met in a community room on the upper compound. She wanted to know if I'd be willing to take over the class while she went on home leave. Why not? I thought. I could get in some good exercise a couple evenings a week and do a good deed at the same time.

The group wasn't as energetic and enthusiastic as the bunch I coached in the Dominican Republic, but I felt good about making a small contribution to the health of the community. And the jumping and kicking helped work off the stress from my hellish job in the embassy's computer center.

For a year and a half, I had endured my work situation while poised like a hawk over the list of job openings. In late February I swooped in to capture a position at the U.S. Mission to the U.N., a dream job that suited me in every way. I worked on contract with Brookhaven National Laboratory. My boss was a nuclear physicist assigned as an advisor/consultant to the United Nations on matters related to nuclear energy. To pay the rent for our office space, so to speak, I also helped the U.S. Mission by scheduling lecturers at the U.N. for various symposia on nuclear issues. And I performed courier duties between the U.S. Mission and the U.N.

across town. I enjoyed those days, riding the subway and tram through the city, and experiencing the energizing bustle and cosmopolitan ambiance at the U.N. building.

My lovely office, with windows and fireplace, was a five-minute walk from home. I wish I could have carried this job with me from post to post. I could have done it forever. How heavenly to enjoy work during the day and know that the job could be left at the office with no hangover at home.

Spring arrived and brought out the yellow daffodils and purple crocuses that I planted in November. My own flowers blooming by the doorstep give an air of permanence to our home and soothed me with a sense of belonging. I got the age-old urge to spring-clean. Is it in our DNA?

The two-story living room windows almost did me in. After one dangerous attempt with an inadequate ladder, I surrendered the window-cleaning job to our compound's caretaker, Herr Sachs. I did, however, wash all of the two-story living room curtains, a Herculean task for this humble Vesta, a never-to-be-forgotten and never-to-be-repeated back-breaking day filled with acres of soggy beige cotton.

Setback

With springtime renewal, a clean house with sparkling windows, and a new job, I relaxed into complacency until the next event shook me up.

"Mom." Dakota's hangdog look foretold bad news on the way. "I got suspended."

I clamped down on a strong urge to interrogate him. I should hear his point of view first.

"Mr. Dawson (high school principal) saw me on the tram with a cigarette behind my ear. I wasn't smoking or anything, but he went ahead and suspended me for two days."

"I'm not sure he has the right to do that. Do you want me to have a talk with him?"

Dakota stared down at his Doc Marten boots. "No, that's okay. But it really sucks I'm off the soccer team too."

I always thought Mr. Dawson was a nice guy, but this changed my mind. Why would he choose such harsh punishment for a small offense committed by one of his most responsible, reliable students? Dakota would miss the final games of his last soccer season in high school – all due to a single unlit cigarette tucked behind his ear. Not fair.

It was not my finest hour, but I went to the principal's office to beg for clemency. My argument that the soccer coach smoked like a foundry had no effect. The principal stood firm on his principles. Was this supposed to teach Dakota a lesson? Or provide an example of zero-tolerance to the student body? Or prove that the principal had absolute power? Not fair.

Congratulations

Dakota went to Turkey on his senior class trip in May and returned mere days before graduation. High school graduation. Where had the time gone? I recalled our photo of not-quite-two-year-old Dakota in Washington, DC, all dressed up in his new Winnie-the-Pooh outfit, ready to fly to Tehran in 1975. Now in 1991 our handsome eighteen-year-old son stood at the beginning of a new path to his own future.

More interested in music than in academics, Dakota decided to stay with us in Vienna for a year of study at the American Institute of Music (AIM). To fill the time between graduation and the start of classes at AIM, he signed up for the summer work program at the embassy. The personnel office did their best to create jobs for teens, gave them a courtesy security clearance based on their parent's background investigation, and paid them to help the gardeners and caretakers or function as security escorts for workmen in unclassified areas of the embassy. Before Dakota got a job through that program, I had a brainstorm: he could do my job while I went on home leave. My boss and the Brookhaven Lab accountants approved the plan.

I wrote glossaries to automate the correspondence that Dakota would have to generate and streamlined the daily routine as much as possible. The story had a perfect ending. Dakota did great work, and I still had a job when I got back. And Dakota survived his two-month bachelor experience as well.

Meanwhile, Tina flew to Washington, DC to spend time with her girlfriend Alex Asselin from Dominican Republic days. Fred and I rode the train to Frankfurt where we could catch a direct flight to Dallas. This was our first time on a night train and our first experience in a sleeping compartment. Novels always describe the wheel clicking rhythm and rocking motion as soothing and dream promoting. But it reminded me of my father pushing on my shoulder to get me up for school, wake up, wake up, wake up, wake up.

In the middle of the night, Fred got up to pee. Being a considerate guy he didn't turn on the light. He groped in the dark to find the floor-level cupboard that held the urinal, a quart-sized vessel with a handle at one end and a spout at the other. After using the urinal, the traveler was supposed to return it to the cupboard where the angle of the shelf would automatically tip the contents (onto the tracks below, I'm guessing).

Fred fumbled the cupboard door open, removed and used the urinal. Bumping and clunking noises followed.

"What the hell?" He flicked on the light. "Damn."

The overhead light glared upon perplexed Fred holding one of his shoes. I watched him pour the contents of his shoe into the urinal. And I giggled. Giggles escalated into belly laughs that disintegrated into hiccupy guffaws. Fred laughed then too, although he didn't seem quite as amused as I was; maybe he wasn't quite as loopy from sleep deprivation.

In Dallas we launched our visit to Fred's sisters who lived within the Texas Triangle, as we called La Porte (Laura), Conroe (Pat), and Austin (Beth). Party, party, party. The Austin segment included a side trip to Port Aransas where I got the second worst sunburn of my life, blistering my calves, during a long walk with Fred up and down the beach.

After our whirlwind tour of the Texas Triangle, we flew to Albuquerque and met up with Tina for our visits to my dad and his wife Bea in Los Lunas and to Fred's parents in Roswell. Tina toured the UNM campus, one of her options for college. She also got her driver's license and practiced driving in my dad's Goldie, a venerable Pontiac sedan. Fred spent the whole vacation feeling sick. We wondered if it might be a recurrence of dengue fever. He felt better by the time we topped off the home leave experience with five days in DC getting physicals and taking care of other business.

When we arrived back in Vienna on that August day, home never looked so good. It would have been perfect if our suitcases had arrived with us, but international travel is not all wine and roses after all. Our bags showed up two days later.

Running and bicycling sweated out the party-hearty residue, but I came down with a terrible cold anyway. I didn't let mere illness keep me from signing up for an embassy-sponsored trip to Budapest, however.

The antiquated underground, the oldest in Europe, drew me like metal to magnet. Glowing tile walls and golden lighting cast a spell that sent me into the heart of Eastern European mystique. I didn't care that neither Fred nor I had any idea where we were going. Our random terminal turned out to be a sunny little suburb called St. Stephens where we bought a pottery vase. Both destination and souvenir seemed mundane compared to my expectant mood of mystery.

Vicissitude

After our trip to Budapest we planned to stick around Vienna, attend the kids' school functions, do some skiing on the local trails, and go to a few concerts. Fred and I discovered "standing room" at the opera – an area designated by velvet ropes where the audience could stand for less than half the price of a seat. Standing room etiquette allowed you to arrive early, tie a scarf on the velvet rope to save your place, and retire to the bar until the performance began.

With such a variety of entertaining activities on tap, why would we need to leave town?

One evening in November I stayed up watching TV after the rest of the family had gone to bed. I didn't hear Tina come down the stairs, and I didn't know she was in the living room until she stroked my hair and slipped in next to me under the lap robe on the couch. I put my arm around her. She snuggled close.

"Mommy…." Tina's voice trailed away in a forlorn sigh. "Mommy, I'm pregnant."

A shot of adrenaline coursed through my nervous system, jolting me out of TV torpor into high readiness alert to protect my young. I fought to slow my racing thoughts and calm my pounding heart. I felt the sobs that punished Tina's slender body, although she made no sound.

"Are you sure?" I lifted Tina's chin so I could look into her eyes.

"Oh, yes, I've used enough test strips to know for sure." One lone tear glistened like a crystal on her cheek.

The crucial question came next. I prayed to sound calm and gentle as I formed the words. "Have you decided what to do?"

Tina nodded.

"Don't worry. Dad and I will stand behind you no matter what your decision is."

"I'm so sorry." Tina's anguish wrenched my heart. "I would have told you sooner, but I couldn't face disappointing you and Dad."

As I wrapped her in my arms to comfort her, I felt my autopilot take over control of my emotions. No matter what Tina decided to do, I would be able to see her through it.

Tina was seventeen, smart and levelheaded. She had given careful consideration to all of the options and in the end chose to terminate the pregnancy.

Because abortion was not permitted in Austria past the earliest weeks of pregnancy, we arranged to go to a clinic in Austin where Tina and I could stay with Aunt Beth and Uncle Dave – a sudden trip to the States that was neither expected nor enjoyed. And all the while I cried inside for being unable to protect my child from this kind of pain, the long lasting emotional hurt from a brief lapse in judgment, the high cost of consequences, the eternal price of irrevocable acts.

And Yet

And yet our lives went on. Within a week, Tina and I returned to Vienna. I helped her put together her college application packets. Fred and I mailed our Christmas cards and carried our boxes of Christmas decorations in from the storeroom.

When Fred and I went to the edge of the Vienna Woods to buy our Christmas tree, the owner of the tree lot sealed the deal with a shot of schnapps, kept in a tub of ice until the time for a holiday toast. The special schnapps, called edelweiss, tasted like dirt from Grandfather's cellar to me. I appreciated the gesture, but after the first tentative sip, I handed my glass to Fred, who, ever the gentleman, finished it off for me.

30

Fred in magical Venice

1992 – 1993

On the Run

The New Year brought Tina's eighteenth birthday and soon after that I announced my commitment to train for the Vienna Marathon. Winter training for a spring marathon: what was I thinking? Fred declined to participate in the marathon madness and he took off for a fun-filled week of skiing at Klagenhurst with his friend Steve Sellers. Unencumbered by a marathoner-in-training, they included a side trip to Venice to experience the joys of authentic Italian Chianti.

During Fred's absence I ground out a sixteen-miler on The Prater (a park for public enjoyment since 1766) on paths that included part of the actual marathon course. My friend Janet joined me on my next long run (eighteen miles on the Donauinsel) and we became training partners for her first marathon and my fourth. A couple of long runs later, we met near Janet's home in Klosterneuburg for a twenty-two mile run. Janet ran low on energy at three hours and I moved out ahead of her. My brain ran low on oxygen a few minutes later and I got lost. I ran the planned distance and then I had to walk an additional thirty minutes searching for our car. I gave myself a rest day after that workout.

Before the first crocuses bloomed, we put Dakota on the train to Frankfurt to audition for a scholarship to Berklee College of Music in Boston. He was a very nervous but brave drummer that day. The scholarship didn't materialize, but he did get a State Department grant and a loan package from Berklee where he would begin studying in the fall, sharing an apartment with a couple of AIS classmates who were attending other universities in Boston.

Not long after his jaunt to Frankfurt, Dakota flew to Norway to visit friends. He got back in time for Tina's starring performance in Senior Cabaret, an AIS tradition as honored as prom.

By the end of April I was ready for the marathon. But I went to bed on marathon eve worried about the weather. A high-pressure system promised unseasonably high temperatures. The day kept that promise and provided a marvelous climate for spectators with glorious sunshine, energetic live music, and beer for sale everywhere. The temperature reached 85 degrees that day, debilitating to this old gal who had trained with heroic diligence in the freezing cold of winter.

I was glad to finish, even in the slow time of 4:49:49, and see loyal Tina standing there, still rubbing sleep from her eyes. I limped across the finish line and leaned on Tina. I couldn't wait to get my shoes off. Hot pavement and sweaty feet had conspired to make my socks bunch up, blistering the bottoms of my feet and aggravating my big toe until it swelled up like a turnip. In the end, three toenails turned purple and died. I called that the Agony. After Janet finished the race we freshened up and went to dinner with a group of friends at Alt Sievering. And that was the Ecstasy.

A week later Fred and I caught the early morning train for a mini-vacation in Venice. We chose the same quaint hotel where Fred had stayed with his friends a couple months earlier. Ochre plaster walls and antique furnishings provided a mellow old-world backdrop. Fred and I exchanged looks of wonderment as we followed the dwarf concierge up the narrow staircase to our floor. The stage was set for romance, mystery, and intrigue.

We strolled to a small neighborhood trattoria where we relaxed in candlelight and enjoyed the best meal of our lives. Baby clams bathed in an unbelievably delicious wine sauce that sent our taste buds to paradise.

After lingering over a second glass of wine, we meandered back to our room, anticipating sweet dreams. But during the night, our hotel lost most of its romanticism. The windows, open in a vain attempt to catch a cooling breeze, overlooked a waterbus stop. Traffic was heavy and mid-night conversations were loud and boisterous.

Well before dawn the next morning, the rest of the romantic air leaked out of our hotel when the fish stall beneath our window opened for business. The musical tones of the fishmonger's patter could have been tolerable, but can anyone luxuriate in bed and relish the smell of dead fish? Ah well, we had plenty of sightseeing to do, so we got up and got going.

At breakfast we learned that sitting down to eat in Italy doubled the bill. A helpful British bystander explained that almost all coffee houses and sandwich shops had a counter where patrons could stand while they ate. He advised us to avoid sitting at a table if we wanted to save money.

We walked what seemed like a hundred miles, seeing all manner of wonderful art and architecture. The pace surprised me. Venetian women in elegant suits and spike heels speed walked everywhere and they gave us lollygagging tourists the evil eye. Window-shopping was definitely un-acceptable in Venice. Fred and I reacted to the censure and focused on museums and churches instead of shop windows.

To get another perspective of the city, we rode the entire route of the main waterbus that circled the city and offered a picturesque view from the water. At lunchtime, we got off at a random stop and wandered the labyrinth of alleyways until we found a café. Sophisticated Venice-wise tourists now, we savored our spinach/mozzarella sandwiches while standing at the narrow street-side counter.

At the end of our dream weekend, we boarded the night train and found our sleeper coach for the return trip to Vienna, arriving at 7:00 AM, two days before the opening night of "Bits and Pieces of Life" starring Tina LaTurner. The drama coach seemed to have chosen this play to showcase Tina's talents. Her proud family basked in the light of her stardom.

Dakota studied and practiced long and hard at AIM. His band, The Junk Funkies, performed at the Rock Inn rock club and also at the huge outdoor music festival, the Donauinselfest. Again, the proud family reveled in fame. Virgin Records offered the boys a contract but they turned it down rather than become a "glam band." Who knows how the opposite choice would have changed their lives?

The summer of '92 brought the peak of my bicycling career. Fred and I went out almost every weekend with the goal of riding as many bike trails as we could. Two of those many rides included surprises that made them stand out from all the others.

The first of those memorable rides wound through fields of poppies in every shade of pink and purple. The hill up to Tröbings castle rebuffed my assault. I huffed and panted, even in the lowest gear. My thighs burned. The steep slope gobbled all my effort and demanded more. My bike barely inched forward. A quarter mile from the castle I had to dismount before I fell off. I walked my bike the rest of the way.

At the top, signs announced a bird of prey show on the castle grounds. We parked our bikes and found a place to sit on the risers at the edge of an open space as large as a football field. The show featured the hunting skills of a wide range of raptors and demonstrated the amazing long-distance vision of falcons and hawks. When an eagle swooped right above our heads, I thrilled to the unforgettable thrum of wind rushing over feathers.

The second extraordinary ride covered the distance from Christa Jones' parents' farm in Mattersburg, Austria over the border and on to

Kapovar, Hungary. Christa's father, Papsch, set a relentless pace on this sixty-mile ride and convinced me he meant to kill us. I felt brutalized even though we had a rest stop at a spa (where Fred and I had to bathe in our bike shorts because Papsch neglected to tell us to bring swim suits) and a leisurely lunch at Papsch's friend's pub. Our host made us welcome, uncomfortably so in my case. I experienced the cliché "he undressed her with his eyes" -- as if my damp spandex bicycle shorts weren't revealing enough. He leered and I blushed. I couldn't have recalled what we ate for lunch, not even immediately after.

The final push to avoid missing the last ferry across Neusiedlersee put me in a mood to murder Papsch (perhaps with some peri-mortem torture thrown in for my own pleasure). Our friend Glenn (Papsch's son-in-law) suffered through this hell ride too and approved my new nickname for Papsch: "Pedal-nazi." Fred's journal entry for that day says it well, "Papsch is an asshole – but we love him."

Tina left for the States in July, stopping off in Washington DC for another visit with her girlfriend Alex Asselin. I headed for Washington myself in August, and Dakota took off for Boston the next day (riding in business class thanks to an upgrade by Fred's pal Steve Sellers). Even though this was a new mode of operation for our family, it seemed natural to be going our separate ways and leaving Fred at home. Each of us had a purpose and an eager desire to accomplish it.

I went to Washington for the oral assessment segment of my recent application to become an official State Department employee. Since I planned to work from now until Fred retired, it made sense to get a job with benefits. My application died on the vine when I answered the question, "Are you willing to serve at a post separate from your husband?" I said, "No," and that was the deal breaker for the State Department.

After my oral assessment folly, I reunited with Tina and we flew to Albuquerque to check her into her dorm at the University of New Mexico where she registered with a major in Theater Arts. Granny and Grandpa LaTurner and Aunt Pat arrived to celebrate with a grand dinner at the Petroleum Club.

I also visited my dad and his wife. Bea and I went to the doctor with Dad to learn about a new chemotherapy treatment for his chronic leukemia. The doctor's words and manner eased my worries somewhat. Not that the new treatment gave us hope for a cure, but rather a chance to slow the cancer's progress. The qualified good news made it easier for me to say goodbye. In only a few short days it was time to get back on a plane and head east.

A quick visit with Dakota in his apartment in Boston showed me a mature and capable young man thriving in his new independence. It soothed this mother's heart to see him in his home. I stored those images in my mind's eye to recall in moments when I felt lonesome for my boy.

Although I missed my kids, I felt excited about Dakota and Tina being at college and experiencing America for the first time on their own. I didn't like being separated when Tina's wisdom teeth had to come out, but Grandpa Pogue and Bea took care of her (they were sweet and kind, but Bea's spaghetti with meat sauce didn't quite make the grade for Tina's post-op meal). Even Thanksgiving without the kids didn't seem too sad. Fred and I used our frequent flyer miles to send them to Austin for the weekend, so at least they were together as well as with extended family. And then they came home for Christmas on the same plane, a happy day. We finished off an active and eventful year still feeling like a family of four.

Dakota had invited his girlfriend from Boston to spend the holidays with him. While he showed Kelly around, Fred, Tina and I went on a cross-country ski trip to St. Martin am Gramming and Schladming Dachstein. We rode a cable gondola and skied on a glacier. When Fred decided to spend a day downhill skiing, Tina and I had a marvelous mother-daughter hike among frozen waterfalls in a fairyland forest.

Empty Nest

Empty nest syndrome hit me the day that Dakota and Tina left together on the same plane to go back to college. It hit hard. My heart shrank into a sharp point of focused pain. My chicks had flown and my nest was empty. That feeling, although mitigated by the passage of many years, still stabs me every time I have to say goodbye to my kids.

But at the time I had to shake it off. I didn't have time for self-pity -- Fred had a new assignment and we were expecting houseguests during pack out.

Although Vienna had been a plum assignment, it was also stress-filled for Fred. Workplace politics chipped away at his immune system and he reacted by catching every virus that came along. He spent three years in a cycle of three weeks sick, three weeks recuperating, three weeks sick. In desperation he started checking the open assignments lists daily, hoping to find a post with an urgent need for someone with his qualifications. None of the choices appealed to us until finally La Paz, Bolivia, popped up. Fred applied and got the assignment. It meant leaving Austria six months early and it meant leaving my cushy job, but we agreed it would be worth the sacrifice if Fred could escape the stress.

Beth, Dave, and four-year-old Zack arrived the same week as our cardboard boxes. We leaned the unformed boxes against the wall and swooped our visitors away on a U.N.-organized ski trip to Admont. We stayed in a medieval castle there. Beth, Dave, and Zack got the biggest, most luxurious room, and Fred and I crammed our bodies and baggage into a turret too small for the most petite Rapunzel. Early morning bag-pipe music provided by one of the guests echoed through the cavernous halls and convinced us we had traveled through time and space.

Unfortunately, Beth, Dave, and Zack brought a Texas virus with them, and Fred and I surrendered to the inevitable three weeks of sniffling and hacking. We weren't the most energetic of hosts, but our guests, enjoying their stage of recovery, went off on their own to explore both Vienna and Bratislava, in spite of snow and cold.

As soon as our guests left we finished organizing our belongings. Thanks to Austrian efficiency our household effects moved from house to container in three days and we took off the following morning, leaving the nest at 19.Chimanistrasse 16/2-3 Wien completely empty.

Transition

Fred commented on the weather to the taxi driver who drove us from Washington DC's National Airport to the Columbia Plaza Hotel near the State Department. "Love this mild weather…unusually balmy for the middle of March."

"Just you wait 'til tomorrow," the cab driver said. "There's a storm on the way."

What a classic understatement. We woke the next morning to a world of white. Newspaper headlines announced the Blizzard of the Century. The District of Columbia looked like an ice sculpture. A human-interest segment on the morning news featured a woman who encouraged everyone to put out birdseed, suet, and water for the birds that were suffering in this natural disaster. A newscaster also called the storm a white hurricane and reported eighteen inches of snow delivered by sixty-nine mile per hour winds creating twelve-foot drifts and closing all the interstate highways in the area.

Fred and I layered on sweaters, jackets, hats, and gloves and waded through knee-deep snow in the middle of deserted, unplowed streets. Down to The Watergate and back, we didn't encounter another single soul.

The snowstorm gave us cause for concern about our new Jeep. We were supposed to pick it up that day and drive out to Warrenton, VA where Fred's eight-week training course was about to begin. Because of the blizzard, the dealership was closed. After several frustrating failed attempts, Fred reached the salesman at his home. He agreed to meet us on Monday at the dealership, open or not, and finalize the sale. Fred would be late to his class, but there was no alternative. He needn't have worried; several other trainees were late too.

Heaps of snow left by snowplows made it difficult to find a place to park near our rented townhome in Warrenton. Those mini-mountains lasted until many weeks of spring weather melted them.

Fred went to class all day every day "on the hill," as the program participants called it. Many times he rode his new mountain bike to the training facility and daydreamed about future rides in the Bolivian Andes. I ran, did some weight work and stretching, piddled with housework and laundry, and worked on cross-stitch embroidery in a southwestern theme of blooming cactus and Native American pottery.

During our time in Warrenton, we enjoyed get-togethers with Norma Goff (now divorced from Tom), John and Deb McFarland, and the Joneses, now living in Virginia where Glenn was assigned to the Dulles Airport Diplomatic Pouch Division. On weekends we enjoyed the warming weather and sampled the surrounding outdoor attractions. We toured Harpers Ferry on one outing and hiked a portion of the Appalachian Trail another day.

Dakota came down from Boston on the train, spent an evening with us and then continued to Charlottesville for a visit with Shane and Gillian Ward. I loved seeing my boy on Mother's Day, and of course I cried when he left.

Because we had our own car, we could drive to New Mexico for our home leave. We had business to attend to, that's for sure. During this home leave, we bought Tina a car (a 1989 Mercury Tracer she named "Sandy"). Before they left for college, we had tried to bribe both our kids with the promise of a car if they would attend the University of New Mexico. The deal for Tina included one year in the dorm before the car purchase and apartment rental.

We bought Sandy in Roswell. It was love at first sight, in spite of the fact that Sandy had a manual transmission and Tina had only driven automatic before. First we bought the car and then she learned to drive it, back and forth in Granny and Grandpa's driveway, and then round and round in the Wool Bowl parking lot. True to her character, when Tina set out to do something, we could count on it getting done.

While Tina practiced driving, Fred and I went house hunting. Our old neighbor Chris had expressed interest in buying our property in Los Lunas, and we figured we could make a deal with him and then get a cozy little house in Roswell for our retirement home.

Although we hadn't made our final decision, retirement could very well be right around the corner. It could come as soon as the end of our tour in La Paz three years hence. I felt an urgent need to have a home waiting for us. That gave us three weeks to sell and buy real estate. And we also went to the dentist and enjoyed a visit from my brother Gary and his wife Nancy, which included a hike on the Pino Trail in Albuquerque. Then we found an apartment for Tina and moved her in.

Our whirlwind of frenzied activity was spiced with interminable nervous waiting for closing dates, title searches, and bank loans. We did it all and left town as the owners of a sweet little two-bedroom cottage at 1212 West Seventh Street in Roswell, New Mexico.

The next week brought us to Austin for a couple of days with Beth and Dave, on to LaPorte to visit Laura, Bert, Erik, Eliot, and Ethan, a day with my aunts in Pompano Beach, Florida and on to Miami to turn our car over to the shippers and board our flight to La Paz.

PART EIGHT
BOLIVIA CLIFFHANGERS

Photo by Victoria LeMair
Mt. Illimani towers over all

31

Isla del Sol, Lake Titicaca

1993

Overbooked and Overweight

I believed our many trips back and forth between Miami and Santo Domingo taught me everything I needed to know about the Miami airport. I was wrong about that; departure from Miami to La Paz presented an entirely different experience. The flight to La Paz showed up at midnight on the timetable. I preferred deep restful REM sleep at that hour. My reality gave me rock bottom numbness in a hard plastic airport chair while I watched the clock tick toward midnight and onward far past the promised hour. Overbooking and weight issues caused the delay – the same every night, a jaded fellow passenger told me. Because of the elevation at La Paz airport (13,313 ft.) the flight had strict limits on the combination of passengers, baggage, and fuel or the plane would not be able to take off from La Paz and get to the refueling port of Cochabamba (at a more forgiving 8,390 ft.) for the return flight to Miami.

Officials buzzed around the airline desk, checking and double-checking their lists. Then they asked for volunteers to take tomorrow's flight. No takers. Forty-five minutes later a voice blared out of the public address speakers offering a $500 travel voucher, a free night in a Miami hotel, and a first class seat for the next night's flight. That's when the volunteers crowded the desk. Our plane left the ground an hour and a half late.

First Impressions

As we began our descent to La Paz shortly before 6:00 AM on that Thursday in July 1993, the pilot announced the local temperature: 30 degrees Farenheit. Fred and I mock-shivered at each other; only six hours ago we left sweltering Miami at 92 degrees and 85% humidity. We had flown south of the equator, trading mid-summer for mid-winter in less than five hours. Approaching the airport we saw millions of twinkling lights in the city but only a faint hint of dawn at that hour.

The terminal teemed with passengers, vendors, and officials swarming in spontaneous bursts of hectic activity. I couldn't have guessed which way to go, but a Bolivian expeditor from the embassy appeared out of the maelstrom and guided us methodically through customs formalities. We wormed our way through the congested lobby and eventually escaped into early morning sunshine. Fred's boss and our sponsors waited in the embassy van.

The road from the airport dropped 2,000 feet in a thirty-minute drive that scared me with an unnerving combination of hairpin turns and drop-offs without guardrails. With every curve the top-heavy van swayed and my stomach surged. Houses along the way, constructed of bare adobe bricks, clung at death-defying angles to the steep hillsides. I'd read about the thunderous rainy season and wondered why these homes hadn't been washed away.

La Paz lay in a bowl that reminded me of a volcano crater. The surrounding mountains brought Albuquerque's Sandias to mind, but here there were more pink hues and less of the green tints of vegetation.

Traffic lived up to my expectations: drivers in La Paz showed no respect for lanes, stoplights, or rules of any kind that I could see. Of all the elements of cultural expression, driving behavior bewildered me the most. I found it far easier to learn the language of the country than to grasp the driving conventions in most of the places I had driven.

I admired the colonial buildings of the city's center as we sped past. Most of the side streets were paved with stones and some looked as steep as Filbert Street in San Francisco. Our jeep, now on its way from Miami, was the perfect vehicle for this terrain.

The embassy van transported us directly to our house in a neighborhood of tile-roofed villas in the suburb of Achumani. My first impression: elegance. The hardwood parquet floor gleamed with the radiance of sunlight reflected from the polished granite tiles that lined the foyer walls.

As soon as our welcoming party left, Fred and I toured the house. Fred discovered a note from GSO that cautioned us about two wiring systems in operation. The outlets all looked like regular 110-volt receptacles, but some of them were 220. To avoid frying our 110 appliances, Fred used his handy voltmeter to find the 220 outlets and I labeled them with masking tape. In twenty years overseas we had never seen this odd (and potentially costly) arrangement.

Although the flood of sunlight from tall windows and several skylights gave the illusion of warmth, I felt colder inside the house than I had outside. Apparently this elegant home had no insulation and relied on fireplaces for heat.

Following our sponsors' recommendations to ward off altitude sickness, we brewed some herbal tea and made up our bed for a nap. Fred dialed the electric blanket to ten; we finished our tea and snuggled under the covers. A twinge of sadness accompanied my thoughts of Dakota in Boston, Tina in Albuquerque. What were they doing this morning? How did they feel about Mom and Dad living in Bolivia without them?

After waking from our short sleep, we layered up to hike around the neighborhood. Within minutes we peeled down to short sleeves as the high altitude demonstrated its power. Our hike was really a baby step shuffle, the best pace we could manage without becoming breathless, but sweaty exertion nonetheless.

Along the way we saw many women in their native dress – voluminous satin skirts, colorful shawls, and bowler hats set at a jaunty angle. In a vacant lot, we watched a group of women and children feeding their longhaired shaggy donkeys. I imagined Andean flute music in the background.

We walked up the main street of our suburb and identified a hardware store, a French bakery, a supermarket (smaller scale than in the U.S.), one ice cream shop, a drycleaner, a few small restaurants, several other little shops, and a large covered fruit/vegetable market. Practically everything imaginable seemed to be available, including U.S. products (at a high price of course). Fruits and veggies looked good and appeared to be reasonably cheap.

Over the next couple of days our sponsors, Jeannine and Homer, introduced us to neighborhood restaurants and showed us some of the local tourist attractions. We admired the stark beauty of the rock formations at the Valley of the Moon and marveled at the contrast with the green gem of the highest golf course in the world. Fred looked forward to playing the course. Dissatisfied with his long game at sea level, he wanted to experience the machismo of altitude-assisted shots from the tee.

Homer turned onto a short detour through an exclusive neighborhood that radiated the swank of drug money. Bolivia might have qualified as one of the poorest counties in South America, but some of her people appeared to be the wealthiest in the world. Fred invented a new term for the extravagant architecture; he called it Drug Lord Design.

On our first Sunday in La Paz, Fred and I walked to the American School, a distance of about a mile, downhill, which we covered in thirty minutes of baby steps. On our way down we met several Bolivian runners going up. I peeked at them humbly from the corners of my downcast eyes as I shuffled along as meek as a tortoise.

The architecture and landscaping of the American School grounds reminded me of a college campus. We toured the sports facilities – open to us for a small fee -- that included tennis and racquetball courts, Olympic-size pool, steam sauna, weight room, and exercise bicycles. We made a plan to start jogging around the soccer field as soon as we felt able to cope with the altitude.

During the first week at post we completed the embassy check-in procedure (getting photo IDs, Bolivian driver's licenses, setting up a commissary account, etc.) and I began my search for a maid and a gardener for the house and a job for me. We weren't required to have a maid and gardener, but it was the accepted practice. The parquet floor and rose bushes convinced me to conform to the norm.

Our shipment of household effects reached La Paz before we did. All shipments, including our car, came by air due to Bolivia's land-locked location and primitive road conditions. However, clearance through customs had to wait for our actual arrival and the process took two to three weeks. It couldn't happen too soon as far as I was concerned; five months had passed since I last lived with my full complement of belongings.

As I wandered about in my new home, I developed a mental picture of where everything would go. I picked a room for Tina's visits – the one with a petite balcony and a view of the moonscape rocks. The room I chose for Dakota overlooked the rose garden. Downstairs in the atrium, I placed two comfortable chairs beside a planter that held well-established ferns, philodendron, rubber tree, ivy, and papyrus plants. I visualized warm sunshine beaming through the tall window and toasting our backs while we sipped hot coffee and read *New Mexico Magazine* and the *Roswell Daily Record.*

The kitchen challenged me with its limited counter space, most of it occupied by an industrial-sized stainless steel water distiller that ran constantly to provide pure drinking water. What a difference from the old days of boiling and filtering in Cameroon and Somalia. It was easy for me to relinquish counter space to such a luxury.

Economy

I had no trouble finding household help. We still tried to call our staff employees, but the common term in use at the time was servant. The American Embassy in La Paz, like every other embassy in a third world country, kept a servant registry and servants were passed along from one departing family to another arriving family. Within two weeks of our arrival we hired Valentina and Mario.

Valentina, Aymara Indian to the core, dressed always in the native costume, her waist-length braids tied together in back. She came to our house daily rather than living in our maid's quarters, her preference as well as ours, as she had a husband and family and we felt ill at ease with live-in help. We decided to offer Valentina the option of bringing her ten-month-old son Diego to work with her and her obvious gratitude touched me. She taught Diego to refer to us as Tia Grande and Tio Grande. When he got to the toddler stage, Diego liked to greet us when we came home from work and engage us in play with his little cars. It felt like a rehearsal for grandparenthood, and I didn't draw Valentina's attention to the tiny smudgy handprints he left on the woodwork.

Mario, our gardener, came twice a week. He kept the garden in exquisite shape, and he cleaned the car, washed windows, and polished the parquet floor twice a month. The floor polishing reminded me of the famous Karate Kid movie scene – "wax on, wax off." Mario used his feet, though, and his circular motions produced a vigorous yet graceful dance. Mario personified the dependable, faithful retainer. His personality was his undoing, poor guy. In our private conversations Fred and I referred to him as Obsequious Man and we avoided him as much as possible. His forelock-touching ways grated on both of us.

Thinking back, I remember with amazement that Mario asked $60 per month for his services and Valentina received $80. Worth every penny, even considering the excess obsequiousness from Mario.

Regarding our home economy, positive predictions about the embassy's job market came true -- I found a secretarial position in the Narcotic Affairs Section within a month. Although the name sounds sexy, this department did not promote doped-up trysts but rather the business of drug interdiction, a somber and dangerous undertaking. My job entailed only office work, however; no danger for me. The senior secretary in the office, Lisa Fowler, young enough to be my daughter, and an innocent newlywed accompanying her husband on his first overseas assignment, heaved a sigh of relief when I let her know I was not at all jealous of her seniority. We got along great.

Around this time, Dakota put a significant amount of money back into our budget by opting out of college and getting a job. A year at Berklee convinced him he wasn't cut out for the music business. What happened next had been foreshadowed in Vienna where he spent his lunch hour watching cooking shows on the British cable network. In Boston, he found a job in the kitchen of a French restaurant, and the head chef mentored him.

With extra money in the bank, Fred and I chose to pay off the Roswell house as soon as we could. It's funny to me now, how that mortgage loomed so ominously in my mind -- the house only cost $39,500, the price of a good car in today's dollars. But my calculations for early retirement didn't allow for debt, even one that small.

Tina, while all this was going on, managed to live without complaint on only $600 a month – another real boost to our bottom line.

High Altitude Antics

On one of our first outings in Bolivia, we drove to Lake Titicaca, located on the high Altiplano. I fell under its spell. A week later we went back again and explored further, across the narrowest part of the lake on a one-car ferry, and an hour and a half down the road to Copacabana, a religious site for both Catholics and Indians. Offshore an hour and a half by boat lay La Isla del Sol, birthplace of the sun according to Inca legend. Haunting Pan flute melodies played against a background illustrated with llamas and alpacas grazing on grassy hillsides. I absorbed the magic in the air.

Shortly after our trip to Lake Titicaca Fred heard about a group of hardy expats who had formed a hiking club called LEG (Landscape Encounter Group). On our first hike with them we reached 17,600 ft. and had to stop because of a blizzard. Some of the members of the group wanted to press on in extremely dangerous conditions. Their impulsiveness planted some seeds of doubt in my mind about their judgment. Fred and I discussed the situation with another couple new to the group and they agreed. That's how we met Paul and Vicki Willebeek-LeMair who became our best Bolivia buddies and life-long friends.

In that quick first encounter, we learned that Paul also worked at the embassy, was a champion bicycle racer, and lived a few blocks from us. His wife Vicki taught first grade at the American School. Thirty-ish and fifty-ish couples, we made an interesting combination, and we went on to share many adventures.

Cruise

We called one of our excursions with Paul and Vicki "The Amazon Cruise," although that sounds grander than it was. We didn't cruise the actual Amazon. We putt-putted down the Mamore River, a tributary of the Amazon, for three days on a boat not much fancier than Humphrey Bogart's African Queen. To get to the boat, we flew to Trinidad and chartered a bus from there to the river.

As our small plane carried us from 13,000 feet to sea level through the Andes, we passed between snow capped mountain peaks looming higher than our cruising altitude on both sides -- more spectacular than the IMAX movie experience – I hung on to the armrests as if I could keep the plane airborne by myself.

Our embassy CLO (Community Liaison Officer) had organized this trip and chartered our amazing craft. We knew all of the passengers, but we partied the most with Paul and Vicki. The fun started early because of Vicki's fear of flying. She swigged a pre-flight dose of courage and continued to drink, as fast as the attendant could serve her, all the way to Trinidad. Vicki personified life-of-the-party all morning.

The bus we caught at Trinidad kept the fiesta theme going with its splash of colorful decorations typical of the region. The worn-out shock absorbers were equally typical of rural Bolivia. We didn't care. Like a bunch of kids on the way to summer camp, we sang songs (led by our tipsy first-grade teacher of course) and laughed and chattered all the way. The sun shone in a cloudless sky. The tropical humidity brought curls even to my stick-straight hair.

The boat looked sea-worthy to me, but I wondered how our crowd could fit on it. When the door of our cabin opened, I understood. Inside I saw a cot-sized bunk bed. That's it. There was just enough room for one person to stand beside the bed. When Fred and I were both in the room, one of us had to crawl into the bed to allow room for the other to change clothes.

One toilet/shower stall served all passengers. I could tell that the shower used murky river water, so I didn't bother with it. I inferred the same about the toilet and lost the tiny spark of enthusiasm I might have had for swimming in the river. Learning that the river hosted piranhas and crocodiles convinced me to stay dry.

Fred, however, trusted that the captain wouldn't encourage any dangerous activity. He swam in that malignant stew of microorganisms and sharp-toothed predators as did a few others, including Vicki and Paul. He also went crocodile hunting. I kissed Fred goodbye when he left on that excursion, not knowing whether he would return in one piece if at all. He was one of six bold hunters who crept out that night. They beamed a bright light along the shoreline to attract the baby crocs and then kidnapped the unwary beasts with their bare hands. Sport for the hunters brought terror to the crocodile nursery, but the catch-and-release escapade ended happily for all.

The day the rains came, our captain asked for volunteers to catch fish for dinner. I raised my hand. Fred looked surprised, but he volunteered too. An older fellow and his grandson joined us, and we stepped into a flat-bottomed wooden rowboat with a crewmember/guide who supplied us with waterproof slickers and fishing gear.

The guide handed each of us an ordinary cane pole equipped with velve inches of steel leader attached to a barbed hook baited with chunks of raw beef. He demonstrated the proper fishing technique. First he dropped the baited hook into the river. Then he slapped the water's surface vigorously for a few seconds with the tip of his pole, and wham! I flinched as he jerked the fish past me into the boat. The guide cautioned us to fling our hooked fish toward the bow of the boat, away from our feet. Using his deft and heavily scarred hands, he grabbed his fish, stabbed it between the eyes with a short knife, and removed the hook.

A gentle rain kept the swarms of mosquitoes at bay and we merry anglers fished for an hour. We caught over forty piranhas and had them for dinner that night, the smaller ones in a savory soup and the larger ones fried to crisp delectability. We nibbled tiny bites, to savor the flavor and also to pick out the numerous tiny bones.

Fred had befriended the captain, trading manly tales and drinking beer with him as he piloted us down the river, and the captain returned the favor by giving Fred a shellacked piranha skull as a memento. We have displayed it on our mantelpiece ever since, to the grisly fascination of our grandsons.

We went on shore once to visit a village. The people lived a simple life with few possessions. Everyone we met wore a smile; most of the younger ones wore only a smile. The village occupied a clearing in a forest of mango trees. We slipped and skidded on the slick conglomeration of rotted mango fruit and river seepage. The sweet stomach-turning odor and proliferation of flying insects drove us back to the boat within minutes. I might have enjoyed the fresh fish and fruit diet, but still I felt glad that I wasn't born to be a resident of the Amazon jungle, prey to the biting hordes.

The rain continued, sometimes heavy, sometimes light, but always steady. We continued to party, as unstoppable as the falling rain. When we had consumed all the beer on the boat, the captain announced that we had set a record. We didn't see pink elephants then, but we did doubt our eyes when pink dolphins cavorted in the water ahead of us. They were real, the captain assured us – a species of fresh water porpoise in shades of pink darkening to purple – colorful beings rollicking in the bow waves of our boat.

At the end of the cruise we expected to reverse our earlier journey. But the unusual amount of rainfall had created a soupy mess where the road used to be and our bus stayed stranded miles away in Trinidad. We had to settle for the best alternative – our group hired two flatbed trucks whose drivers were willing to brave the conditions. We piled in and scrabbled anxiously for a handhold.

The trucks fishtailed down the road, sliding from one side to the other, swerving too close to the edge of a three-foot drop-off to the ditch that ran beside fields of manioc and maize. I clung to Fred and Fred clutched at a splintery board that jerked back and forth with the movement of our truck. As the trucks sashayed, the mud flew and splattered us from head to toe. I clamped my lips closed and kept my head down, grateful for the shelter provided by the bill of my cap.

I feared for our lives, but neither of the trucks overturned or got permanently stuck. We were a stunned bunch of Yankees who disembarked at the airport. Bystanders' incredulous gazes followed as we scraped mud clods from our bodies and straggled single-file toward the check-in desk.

Acclimated

Before Tina came to La Paz for a three-week visit during her Christmas break, I perked up her room with new linens. I placed a metal patio chair on the small balcony outside her room and imagined her sitting there entranced by the view of wind-sculpted spires of rock.

Fred and I made a list of things we wanted to show Tina during her visit: the Valley of the Moon, the Devil's Molar, historic buildings and the teeming marketplace in downtown La Paz. I fussed and fidgeted, counting the hours until she arrived. I wished Dakota could come too, but he couldn't take enough time off work to make the trip worthwhile.

When we picked Tina up at the airport, I read shock in the expression on her face.

"What's wrong, honey?" I kissed her and put my arm around her.

"Boy, I thought you were exaggerating when you warned me about the altitude, but…." She drew in a gasp of thin altiplano air. "The guy in the seat in front of me dropped like a rock as soon as he stood up to deplane. They had to hook him up to oxygen. And he wasn't even old or anything, prob'ly late twenties."

"How about you…do you feel okay?" Fred asked.

"Um, fine I think. Just a little tired."

Fred moved ahead to make an opening through the dense mob, and we ushered our daughter to our jeep and brought her home.

After our first sightseeing tour on the road to Cota Cota, Tina pointed out that Fred and I had acclimated more than we realized. She used the road we had just traveled as an example.

"You drive these ridiculous roads, la-la-la, as if everything is sane and normal. My life flashed before me the whole time, I swear." Then she begged me to massage the place between her shoulder blades where a hard knot had formed.

Two days later Tina bounced carefree in the back seat as our jeep roared up a rough track as scary as the road to Cota Cota. At our destination she conquered the Devil's Molar, a massive rock formation with a steep trail to the top. Talk about quick acclimation, that's our girl.

32

Tina and Fred conquered the Devil's Molar

1994

Mountain Biking

It's true that our minds and bodies made some adjustment to the altitude and other conditions in Bolivia, but neither Fred nor I ever felt entirely right in La Paz. Fred complained of interrupted sleep; he woke several times each night with a sudden wheeze for more air. I was disappointed that I could barely jog, not run; I relied more on our exercise bicycle and Nordic Track machine to keep fit.

Under Paul's influence Fred pursued mountain biking. They rode in remote places over razor terrain to formidable heights. I admired their level of fitness, but I questioned their sanity -- I'm the type who tends to topple from over-braking.

When they pedaled away on their adventures, I waited at home, my hands busy with the colorful fabrics of a quilting project while my worries conjured a whole spectrum of disasters.

One Sunday afternoon the phone rang and I picked up to hear Paul's voice. "Fred's okay. The doc is stitching him up right now."

I flailed about in my stunned state to come up with a halfway meaningful response. Paul reassured me that Fred was truly fine. He told me that he and Vicki would bring Fred and our car home as soon as the doctor finished.

Paul brought Fred home to me with twenty-four stitches in his arm and leg. A short fall onto sharp rocks cut him as neatly as a butcher's cleaver. He claimed he felt no pain. I worried about that too.

Back in the saddle again, Fred endured many more hard rides, going as high as 18,000 feet, where sunburn blistered his face but the rest of him came home injury free. The ride toward Mt. Illimani, however, was almost his last. On that trek, he fell from a cliff and landed on a narrow shelf ten feet below. Lucky to be alive, he hobbled home with bruised ribs and a bent wheel rim, but no broken bones or bloody wounds. I noticed that his bike rides dwindled after that, both in frequency and intensity.

Fred kept up with the Hash House Harriers though. I couldn't even keep up with the post-run partying. Altitude doubled the effects of alcohol on the average drinker; it quadrupled for me. Not only were the running and the partying too hard, the locations put me off. I tried but could not tolerate the stench of human excrement that polluted the air along the Hash routes.

Oxygen Debt

Our young and energetic friends Paul and Vicki dragged us out of the house almost every weekend. Most of our adventures involved hiking and camping, a lot of that above 15,000 ft. with 21,000 ft. snow-covered peaks surrounding us. When I think back to some of the risks we took, I wonder if our brains functioned at normal capacity or did we suffer from oxygen-deprivation? I don't think we were reckless, but maybe we shouldn't have gone so far afield on our outings with Paul and Vicki. We did have directions or hand-drawn maps of the areas we explored, so we knew someone had been there and returned, and we always had two vehicles. Still....

To get to a glacier that we wanted to see, we followed a narrow slate road high above the glacier's lake. The road was a one-lane shelf hacked into the mountainside about 300 feet above the lake and half way to the peak. The surface provided less traction than a sheet of ball bearings. The drop-off plummeted beside the passenger side of our jeep, a personalized torture for white-knuckled me.

Where the road widened at the edge of the glacier, Fred and Paul parked the trucks and we all got out. My knees buckled at first. I knelt down and made a show of kissing the ground.

"Thank God we can go on around the mountain. I don't ever want to see that road again!"

The glacier, so serene and icy, calmed me down. I walked on it, sat on it, and pried out a sparkling piece of black-speckled white granite for a souvenir. After munching a snack of mixed nuts and dried fruit, we returned to the trucks and motored onward, around the glacier, following a gravel road to the valley beyond.

Around the fourth or fifth curve we reached a spot that presented a full view of the valley and the road ahead. Alas, there was not enough road ahead to take us off the mountain; a landslide had seen to that. There was no other choice; we had to turn back the way we had come. My heart raced. Dread dropped over me and I slumped in my seat.

No, I can't do this.

The scariest and longest thirty minutes of my life stretched out in a time warp. I braced one hand against the dashboard and strangled the handle above the door with the other. With eyes closed I produced a steady stream of moans, curses, and piercing screams as the jeep skittered and lurched on the treacherous shale. Vicki told me later that she did the same. Neither Fred nor Paul shouted, "For God's sake, shut up!' but they would have been justified. On that endless stretch, our drivers steered between the precipice on one side and sheer cliff on the other, shifting scree under the tires, and hysterical women blubbering at their sides. They earned their halos that day.

On another trip with Paul and Vicki, we found a river in our path. Paul insisted on trying to ford it. He believed in the superior performance of his Ford Explorer. When the water deepened in the middle of the river, Paul made a wise decision to turn around. But then his engine stopped and wouldn't start again. Fine-grained, silty river mud packed the entire front end of his Explorer. We clawed, scooped, rinsed and scraped for the next hour, cleaning out as much muck as we could. I held my breath as Paul turned the ignition key. If the truck didn't start we would have to leave it where it stalled, miles from nowhere and farther from anywhere. Both vehicles were packed to the ceiling, so we would have to leave some of our gear in order to make room for Paul and Vicki in our truck. Paul turned the key…and the engine sputtered to life. If we lacked anything on that expedition, I was glad it wasn't luck.

On the next camping trip, we bumped along a two-track trail for hours until we reached the area called Three Lakes in an isolated, uninhabited valley. We hurried to set up our tents before going on a hike. Then we challenged each other to a frisky game of hacky sack. We forgot to allow time to acclimate to 17,000 feet and piercing headaches brought all four of us to a standstill. We tried to sleep off the headaches, but freezing cold kept us awake. Paul built a fire. The fire attracted onlookers. The two boys didn't ask for a handout (common practice in the country), but they squatted down as if they were spectators and we were the live entertainment for the weekend. Our headaches prevented any interesting activity on our part, and our audience departed in a few minutes, dematerializing as quickly as they had materialized out of nowhere.

V.I.P.

Although we didn't always welcome uninvited visitors to our campsites, VIP visits to the embassy had to be greeted with enthusiasm. It was part of the job. Be it Congressional Delegation, Secretary of State, Vice-President, or President, an advance team came to make sure everything was set up according to protocol, and a control room was created to handle all the details during each visit. We had the honor of a visit from Vice-President Al Gore and his wife Tipper in March 1994.

Fred, as head of his office, oversaw all aspects of communications – computer networks, phones, cell phones, and a mobile communications van flown in for the visit. Because of his high security clearance, Fred was charged with the task of driving the communications van off the cargo plane onto the tarmac.

I ran errands in the control room and enjoyed watching the aides from DC try to cope with the strange environment. Fred's reward at the end of the visit was to stand "on the rope" and receive a handshake and personal thank you from Al Gore. This handshake was immortalized in a glossy 8x10 photo that Fred framed and sent to sister Laura, a devoted fan of Mr. Gore.

First Trip Back

Before the end of our first year in Bolivia we flew back to the States, courtesy of the embassy's R&R policy. Empowered by the boundless energy that comes from high altitude training, Fred and I ran full tilt through the Miami airport, from arrival gate to departure gate, carry-on bags banging our sides. "Faster than a speeding bullet, more powerful than a locomotive, able to leap tall buildings at a single bound."

Our greeters at the Albuquerque Sunport included Tina, her boyfriend Roger, Dakota and his girlfriend Kelly. Dakota and Kelly had left Boston to find a cheaper place to live. Dakota accepted our bribe and registered at UNM. We upheld our end of the bargain and bought him a 1985 Izuzu Trooper ($3700 in 1994). The blessings of being together again, the four of us, sent me into a state of bliss. I grinned at Roger and Kelly, imagining them as my in-laws in the not-so-distant future.

We fished at Sandia Lakes and Dakota fried the catfish in Tina's vegetarian kitchen. She allowed it even if it was against her new principles.

Fred celebrated his birthday by getting a tattoo from Tina's friend Jespa. Together they designed a yellow and red zia symbol with blue

392 ℝ VOLUNTARY NOMADS

lettering in the center circle. The lettering, altered to conform to the circular space, looked like an abstract design. A closer look revealed that the letters spelled NANCY. I was proud, flattered, to see my name on my husband's shoulder, but a tiny bit embarrassed too.

On this R&R Fred and I divided our time between Albuquerque, Los Lunas, and Roswell. During our stay in Roswell, we took Granny and Grandpa to Sitting Bull Falls southwest of Carlsbad. We strolled along the paths, mindful of Grandpa's ailing heart. It worried me that he wore black polyester on such a warm day, but he claimed to be comfortable. In the early hours of the following morning he woke with bone-wracking chills. Granny dialed 911 and the ambulance delivered Grandpa to the hospital for a three-day stay. This incident marked the beginning of a serious decline in his health.

The greater LaTurner clan gathered in Roswell for a reunion to dedicate the park bench that we had purchased in honor of Granny and Grandpa. The whole crazy bunch celebrated July 4th at the Roswell Country Club, oohing and aahing at the superb fireworks display.

Back in Albuquerque, Tina and I went to get a chest of drawers out of our storage unit, kept for us by the State Department for the nineteen years since we joined the Foreign Service in 1975. Or maybe not. The manager of the storage facility apologized again and again, but couldn't alter the fact that our possessions were no longer there, and had, in fact, been sold at auction because the State Department had stopped paying the bill. He showed me the paper trail of registered letters and invoices. My heart threatened to stop. Not because we had stored items of great monetary value. No, when we left for Tehran in 1975 we didn't own much of anything. We did, however, store keepsakes of significant sentimental value, personal treasures that we wanted to protect from the wear and tear of hauling around the world. It felt like a serious betrayal of our trust too. The State Department simply stopped paying the bill one day? How could that happen?

Anger followed on the heels of despair and I started a complaint/grievance campaign that eventually won us cash compensation for the estimated value of our lost property. The hard-hearted bureaucrats allowed nothing for emotional trauma, not even a sympathetic "I'm sorry," which would have gone a long way toward easing my pain.

Near the end of R&R, on the way back to Roswell, Fred wanted one more adventure and decided to ride his bike the last seventeen miles. We knew it was hot because we drove with the windows open (the air conditioner in Tina's car wasn't working), but we didn't find out until later that the temperature had reached a record 114 degrees that day. Fred could have brewed tea in his black plastic water bottle. When we arrived at Granny and Grandpa's we noticed Granny's new crop of flowers in outdoor pots. They drooped as limp as a mass of boiled greens.

Even six weeks passes quickly when you're having a good time, and we departed for the Miami airport to face the dreaded chaos. The usual scenario of delay, announcement, and request for volunteers played out. I groaned and cursed and wondered why the airline couldn't find a better way to deal with the two-pronged devil of overbooking and overweight.

Cholita Bus

I returned to my job at NAS and my colleague Lisa took a few well-earned days off. The NAS office occupied the northwest corner of the third floor of an old bank building leased by the embassy. A long wall of windows faced the same direction as the embassy's entrance. One of those windows still bore the scars of a recent demonstration -- cracks in a star-shaped pattern from the impact of a small object, maybe a brick or rock. As the newest member of the staff of the Narcotics Affairs Section (NAS) I sat at the desk in the corner of the reception area. Everything about the office seemed decrepit. Heating pipes exposed their peeling paint and electrical wires drooped in random loops hanging here and there. The air smelled like ancient Incan relics from the downtown black market.

In spite of the rundown physical environment and the serious tone of drug interdiction, my office mates were cheerful and upbeat – when they were there, that is. Since most of the coca-growing and cocaine labs were in the jungle region, the staff traveled often, leaving the director's senior secretary and me to run the office.

Demonstrations flared up in front of the embassy about once a month. I was relieved to learn that the demonstrators marched to protest Bolivian, not American, government policies. However, our embassy was located right across the street from the offices of the Bolivian Labor Department. Normally we had plenty of notice before a scheduled march and our security office closed the embassy for a couple of hours and advised everyone to draw the drapes and stay away from the windows. The demonstrators would gather at the top of the street at noon and chant their way down a dozen blocks to the Labor Office, exploding half-sticks of dynamite and throwing bricks at windows along the way.

One particular demonstration played out in a different way, especially for me. This time we had only a few minutes' warning. And it was late in the day, 4:30 PM, almost quitting time at the embassy. When Security announced that the embassy would be locked down in ten minutes, I reacted without considering the consequences. I shut down my computer, grabbed my purse and sweater, rushed down the stairs and out the door. In the back of my mind I pictured flagging down a trufi (share-taxi) on the next street west of the embassy and arriving home in Achumani in thirty minutes, long before the demonstration hit its peak. But when I reached the next street, which was a major taxi route, there was not a single car as far as I could see in both directions. I learned later that part of that day's protest included a taxi drivers' strike, but having no idea in the moment, I hurried along in a direction that I hoped would take me to another taxi route a safe distance from the demonstration.

I crossed street after street as empty as if a major evacuation had already occurred. I began to perspire. I might have been walking fast enough to break a sweat, but I also felt a sense of impending doom. Maybe I was in serious trouble. Best-case scenario, I faced a ten-mile walk home in the dark. Located so close to the equator, La Paz days and nights were of equal length year round, so the fact that it was summer didn't help me, other than providing survivable evening temperatures.

The end-of-the-world appearance of the streets continued until I reached the Prado, the city's downtown area. Traffic appeared to bustle as usual until I noticed that the assortment of vehicles included neither taxis nor minibuses. I reconciled myself to the prospect of a long hike in inadequate shoes because I am neither brave enough nor foolhardy enough to hitchhike. Anywhere. Not in La Paz, Bolivia, of all places. I turned toward home with determination and strode forward, fantasizing about a miraculous rescue coming before holes appeared in my shoe leather.

A passing shot of color caught my eye. I watched the big yellow bus roll past and discharge a passenger on the corner. I had seen these buses every day but never gave serious consideration to riding one. Their routing system was a complete mystery to me and I couldn't imagine being able to manage the embark/disembark procedure. The Cholita buses, as we called them because of the preponderance of bowler-clad Aymara lady passengers, moved along at about ten miles an hour unless picking up or letting off, when they slowed to five miles an hour, requiring the passengers to scurry alongside.

I noticed the lengthening shadows and shivered at the cold strip of dampness between my shoulder blades. I amped up my courage and made the leap onto the next Cholita bus. I scrambled on board and paid my fare, the equivalent of ten cents. I found a vacant seat near the back and prayed that this bus would take me closer to home. From my vantage point I could watch the other passengers and analyze their arrival/departure techniques.

Most of my companions that day were Aymara Indian women, dressed in their ample layered skirts, carrying who-knows-what-all in their multicolored hand-woven aguayo cloth wraps, bowler hats perched on their heads at a rakish angle. I would have been happy to eavesdrop on conversations, but no one spoke. I tried to relax and enjoy the atmosphere, but whiffs of odd odors kept me on edge. I could detect food smells and sweaty smells, but there was also a nostril-crimping undertone that reeked of waste and rot. I squirmed a bit and estimated how long it would take to travel ten miles at an average speed of 8 miles per hour.

I lost the urge to gag as soon as I recognized the shops of Calacoto. Elizabeth's store, where we shopped often for rugs and souvenirs, never looked as good to me before. If the bus continued on this main street, I would be able to jump off at the corner two blocks from our house. I wondered if Fred knew I was unaccounted for. He might be locked in the embassy still, or he might be home already. In those days without cell phones, we were accustomed to spending considerable time out of communication with each other. I hoped he wasn't worried about me.

As the bus started up the hill toward Achumani, I prepared my exit strategy. Stand up, proceed to the side exit and face the door. Wait for the bus to slow as it approaches the corner by our local butcher shop, hold the pole in a firm grip, and exit running.

I stumbled, flailed to regain my balance and – success! I huffed my sense of relief and crossed the main street at our corner.

Lights glowed in our windows and warmed me with a welcome sense of home. I found Fred in the bedroom changing out of his work clothes into his comfies. He had arrived only minutes before, surprised that I wasn't home, but not worried yet. I enjoyed telling him the tale of my journey. He made me promise that was my only ride on a Cholita bus. When I told my friends, their reaction made me feel as brave as nineteenth century explorer Isabella Bird. Lisa, my office mate, gave me a miniature Cholita bus tree ornament that reminds me every Christmas of my potential for spunk.

Solar Eclipse

I saw my second solar eclipse in La Paz (the first happened in Minnesota in 1954 when I was thirteen). Fred missed it because he had to work the early morning shift, so I joined Paul and Vicki and a group of friends at another friend's penthouse apartment on the twenty-first floor. We shared a potluck breakfast and then put on special lenses to stare at the sun in a cloudless sky. The eclipse started at 7:30 AM and the shadow crept across the sun, reaching its peak at 8:35. As the sun disappeared and left us in an eerie semi-dark, I felt the temperature drop, and thought of stone age people having the same experience and perhaps fearing the end of the world had come.

Blasphemy Road

Paul and Vicki were major players in yet another escapade. They invited Fred and me to join a group of people from the American School on a camping trip in the Andes. Or so we understood. We packed our gear for cold weather camping and got in line in the caravan of four-wheel-drive vehicles. Seven hours and two flat tires (not ours) later, after traveling a road that I described in an impassioned and scathing soliloquy of four-letter words, we arrived.

We set up camp on the level bank of a wide, shallow river and learned that we had descended to 4,800 feet. We stripped off layers and enjoyed the surprise gift of oxygen and balmy tropical weather. It wasn't until the next morning that we realized the swarming tropical fauna had eaten us alive. Sand flea bites covered us like measles and we spent the weekend itching and scratching.

On the way back to La Paz we followed an alternate route that the leaders extolled as a scenic short cut. It took an hour longer than the trip down. Before we got home, our group had so many flat tires that we had no more spares among us and we had to stop to have the last flat repaired. While we waited, I repeated my four-letter-word monologue with added sarcasm.

New Embassy

Luck or destiny caused us to be in Bolivia during the construction of a new embassy office building. Originally our embassy occupied the top floors of an historic bank building in the center of La Paz. The old building should have been condemned. It was falling apart. The wiring, which snaked in spaghetti profusion along the walls, threatened to short out at any moment. The elevator broke down more often than it worked. I always used the stairs, in spite of the breathless climb, rather than risk being stuck for hours in that casket-like cubby.

For me, the move meant leaving work on Friday afternoon at the old office and reporting for work on Monday morning at the new (with a little packing and unpacking thrown in, of course). For Fred, the move required a marathon combination of ingenuity, patience, long hours, and hard work. His responsibilities included the entire computer network and the telephone system. The new systems had to be up and running at the same instant that the old systems shut down. Fred made it happen with the help of his crew and a group of technicians on temporary assignment from Washington, DC.

The new embassy, built from foundation to roof with materials and workmen flown in from the U.S., was designed to be a model of security. The security features, including safeguards against car bombs, complied with the standard for new embassy construction around the world.

The building looked more like a fortress than a center for diplomacy, but we lived in an era dominated by terrorism, so it was good to feel safe. The layout of individual offices demonstrated the lack of communication between designer and user; everyone complained about inconveniences such as a reception desk located at the far rear of the suite of offices rather than at the entrance, oddly placed electrical outlets, absurdly located restrooms, and all manner of irritations both large and small. What could be changed got changed and the rest had to be worked around. Foreign Service folks do know how to adapt.

Good Luck Tradition

Our new embassy had something unique – a llama fetus, blessed by a shaman and buried in the foundation for good luck, in keeping with Bolivian folklore.

Fred liked the Bolivian good luck tradition so much, he decided to adapt it and adopt it. Glenn Jones had sent him the stump of his son Kevin's umbilical cord five years earlier, and Fred had been searching for a worthy place to deposit it. The light bulb lit and Fred decided the perfect spot would be the embassy foundation next to the llama fetus. Dakota and Tina followed the tradition many years later by sending their firstborns' relics (Paeton's foreskin and Brody's umbilicus), which we forwarded to Glenn who cemented them into a giant conch shell and sunk them in the deepest pool at the fabled Fountain of Youth in Florida. May all those so commemorated live long and prosper.

Change

When the new embassy opened I moved into a better job in a different office. Changes in NAS persuaded me to work elsewhere.

First, NAS Director Jim Kissinger left. He had set the tone for a happy, cheerful workplace. He treated all of his employees with fairness. And he also gave great parties. His replacement wasn't as amiable. My office-mate Lisa ended too many days in tears. So she quit and left me in the hot seat. The mean boss didn't make me cry, but he provided plenty of motivation to get me out of there. Thanks in large part to our sponsor Homer I left NAS for a dream job in Homer's section, GSO.

Homer left post soon after hiring me, but his replacement liked my work and set about tailoring the job to suit my skills. He gave me a private office and turned me loose to design databases and spreadsheets for the purchasing section and the motor pool. I had the privilege of working with the marvelous Bolivian employees in the purchasing department as well as plenty of time on my own for the design projects that depended on no one but me.

One aspect of my new job, however, terrified me. In my occasional role as security escort for Bolivian technicians who needed to enter classified areas of the embassy, I had to go places I would never choose willingly. I escorted the electrical engineer who came to work on the electronic controls of the elevator; he needed to go to the roof of the building where the control box was located. He loved the view from up there, but my fear of heights made me queasy and I stayed as far from the edge as I could. Elevator cleaning and maintenance was far worse -- I had to ride on the roof of the elevator cabin while the technicians fiddled and fussed with cables and apparatus and stopped the elevator between floors to test the braking system. During the whole ordeal I clung to a metal support in

.he center of the elevator roof and prayed for deliverance while the techs teased and laughed.

Holiday Cheer

The calendar flipped to December again and we welcomed Tina on her second visit to Bolivia. We swept her away on a camping weekend to Copacabana and a tour of Isla del Sol.

We included a day trip to Chacaltaya, at 17,388 feet the highest ski run in the word. Tina's grip on the doorframe demonstrated her level of enthusiasm for the slick rock road. On foot she scampered up the rocks like a mountain goat and didn't bother paying lip service to the altitude. Only the cold, whipping wind subdued her.

Fred pointed out the interesting lift mechanism at the ski slope. The T-bar connected to a rusted cable that was powered by an old automobile engine. The cable ran through a squeaking rusty pulley at each end. To get a ride to the top of the ski run, the skier had to use a metal hook made of rebar to snag a leather loop attached to the cable. This was no simple task. Those who failed to hook on securely risked serious injury and even death.

When we weren't traipsing around the countryside, Fred, Tina and I spent happy hours curled up on couches in the living room, cozy in the glow of two electric heaters placed for full stereo-radiant effect. We watched movies on cable TV, drank frothy Bolivian beer, and ate our fill of spicy roasted peanuts the size of grapes. During commercials and between movies we pored over our coffee table book. Not the usual oversized hardbound volume of glossy photographs, this was a humble three-ring binder containing Fred's collection of clippings from *New Mexico Magazine*. His favorite feature was the "All in a Day" descriptions of day trips all around the state. We guided Tina through this preview of coming attractions in our retirement years and she shared our enthusiasm for the wonders of New Mexico.

33

Contemplating the future from our perch in the Andes

1995-1996

The Zongo

We sang happy birthday to Tina by the light of twenty-one white household emergency candles stuck into empty beer, wine and champagne bottles. The dining room glowed with good cheer. Tina planted two self-stick gift bows on her cheeks and mugged for the camera. I hoped she understood how happy I was to be with her on her birthday. I knew it was a sacrifice to celebrate such a landmark occasion in the middle of nowhere with her parents instead of at a party in Albuquerque with her friends and I was grateful. My heart told me with certainty to cherish these special times.

Before Tina left for the States, we wanted to take her to the Zongo Valley. Fred and I visited the Zongo frequently, usually with Paul and Vicki, to escape the altitude. Our bodies functioned much better at 8,000 feet than at 12,000. In the valley we could camp and hike and also breathe and stay warm. Bolivia lay close enough to the Equator to create subtropical ecosystems at 8,000 feet, making the Zongo Valley a green Eden lush with banana and citrus trees along the rushing river.

There was only one way into the valley, a narrow gravel road constructed for the hydroelectric plants that harnessed the power of the river. Paul and Fred liked to ride their mountain bikes down the road, leaving Vicki and me to drive the vehicles. Driving was bad enough, why would I want to ride a bicycle too? It was so steep and rocky and scary, I only made it a few yards before I fell over, proving that one can draw blood in a zero mile per hour crash.

Unofficial Travel

Tina had been gone about a month when we decided to pay her a visit in Albuquerque. She had earned a major role in *Road*, a play produced by the Riverside Repertory group. I had been Tina's most devoted fan ever since her first performance in the third grade when she played the role of mother in the Christmas play at American School Mogadishu. Fred and I saw every performance during her grade school and high school acting career. Because of the timing of our transfer to Bolivia, we missed seeing her in *Plough and the Stars*, at the university and we didn't want to miss a performance again.

Road played at the KiMo Theater in downtown Albuquerque. I held a purse full of Kleenex for tears of pride and joy, and I shared them with Fred and Dakota whose eyes glistened as brightly as mine.

We took full advantage of our seventeen-day vacation and the fresh February snow on Sandia Mountain. We cross-country skied and watched Dakota, Roger, and Tina carve the slopes on their snowboards. I cherished the chance to have our nuclear family together again, even for a short period; even if we had to issue a tough-love edict about money. Both Dakota and Tina nodded their solemn understanding that Mom and Dad's retirement budget required financial independence on their part by the end of next year.

Dakota had a U-Haul truck packed for a move to Colorado. His girlfriend Kelly, who was an airline flight attendant, had transferred to Denver and Dakota planned to join her there. He told us he had lost interest in pursuing a business degree and wanted to return to restaurant work. Fred and I offered to help him move by driving his Izuzu so he wouldn't have to tow it behind the U-Haul. A typical March blizzard blasted the I-25 corridor and we suffered some terrifying moments until Dakota showed us how to make the defrosters work. It was worth the ordeal to see my son established in his new digs, set up with an interview for a job in the kitchen of the popular Denver Chop House.

Once again Fred and I flew away, first to Miami to run the overbooked/overweight gauntlet and then on to La Paz. I slumped against the rigid chair back in the Miami departure lounge, oblivious to the flapdoodle in the background. *Bolivia – Oblivion. Oblivion – Bolivia.* It wasn't just a play on words; that pairing touched the essence of how I felt about returning to La Paz and our workday routine.

Hail and High Water

Fred usually went to work an hour earlier than I did, and he drove our car. I hardly ever drove in Bolivia, too nerve-wracking for me, so I either caught a trufi (shared taxi running on a set route) or a minibus (also on a set route). The trufis were five-person sedans but they carried six people. Convention dictated that the last person to board squeezed on top of the gearshift console next to the driver. I dreaded that awkward spot where I struggled to keep my skirt down over my knees as the shifter ran up and down the side of my thigh. More often than not, I chose the minibus instead. At least I could count on having a real seat. The custom for minibuses allowed school children to ride free if they stood in front of a seated passenger. In practice that meant that I could expect a child to stand on my feet and lean back against my knees. I preferred that to the trufi gearshift.

One Wednesday in March I stepped out of the embassy into light rain. I lifted my face to catch a few refreshing drops on my cheeks. Rain didn't usually sprinkle in La Paz. Torrential downpours were more common, accompanied by dazzling lightning and crashes of thunder strong enough to rattle our windows and set off the security alarm. The typical storm caused mudslides that tore houses from their foundations and swept them down the hillsides. This day's rain was remarkably gentle at the onset.

I climbed into my usual minibus for the ride home and swung into a window seat as the coach lurched forward. The bus filled up as unprepared pedestrians scurried to escape the now pelting rain. The atmosphere thickened with odors of damp wool and crowded bodies. By the time we reached the steep, narrow, winding descent to the bottom of the river valley, the windshield wipers could not keep up with the deluge.

My fellow passengers murmured in Aymara rather than Spanish so I couldn't understand a single word.

Are they saying the driver should stop and wait out the storm? Would I be safer on the bus or off the bus? Oh God...slow down!

The bus careened back and forth, on the verge of being out of control. When we swerved closer to the river I caught a glimpse of roiling, churning water approaching flood stage.

Will the current sweep us into the river?

In a scene that flashed across my adrenaline-rushed imagination I wrenched the window open and crawled onto the roof seconds before the bus sank to the bottom of the raging river.

I breathed a shaky sigh of relief when the road veered away from the river's edge. The rain stopped. As we started the ascent into Calacoto, the view out my window glowed white. Snow? But snow was rare in La Paz in winter and this was late summer. I cleared a peephole in the foggy condensation on the window with the heel of my hand. Not snow, it was hail. Golf ball-sized hail covered the ground in a layer six inches deep. Leaves and trash littered the street. Street signs hung askew, battered and bent.

I exited the bus at my corner and tiptoed around and through puddles to cross the main street, trying not to ruin my soft red leather flats. If there was a storm drain at this intersection, it was clogged. A fast-moving river filled my street as deep as the curb. I thought about the ever-present human excrement in the gutters of La Paz. I did not want to wade in that water.

I paced up and down the sidewalk, postponing the inevitable plunge with an impossible wish for rescue. Just as I gave in and reached down to slip off my shoes, Valentina's husband arrived. My hero drove his car through the flood and carried me across the torrent and into our carport.

When the hail melted, water poured like a waterfall from the ceiling in the bedroom we called Dakota's room (although he never occupied it). Bedding, mattresses, and carpet got soaked before we even knew there was a leak. Several inches of water covered the lowest level of the house, including a storage closet in the den where we kept miscellany in cardboard boxes. There aren't many containers less useful than wet cardboard boxes. It took two full days to sort the mess and reorganize.

After the hailstorm I made another imaginary hash mark on my pro and con tally of life in La Paz. The cons column was growing. I had a nightmare about dying in Bolivia. Dark fears of never going home hung like thunderheads on the horizon of my daytime thoughts.

City of Rocks

I refused to surrender to doom and gloom; instead I signed up with LEG (the Landscape Encounter Group) for an excursion to the City of Rocks. Because of the remote location, this trip required preparations as detailed as an expedition -- four-wheel drive transport, equipment for the most primitive camping, and proper gear for a day-long hike that began at dawn.

As Fred and I set up our campsite, we noticed that all members of the group were not equally prepared. One pair of women seemed to have brought only a tent. They circulated among the other campers "borrow-ing" water, food, blankets, cookware, and matches. Fred and I could only shake our heads, give them what we could spare, and wonder how some people managed to survive in the world.

Before we began our long hike to the rock formations, the LEG leader outlined the day. He asked us to stick together as a group until we reached our destination. Then we could wander at will among the rocks and rally at a certain landmark at a specified time for a head count before we started back to camp. The plan emphasized the importance of returning to camp before dark.

Our leader set a reasonable pace to accommodate the least experi-enced hikers. The early morning chill put a bounce in my step in spite of the deep sand of the trail. At lunchtime we picnicked beside a wide pond and watched a flock of flamboyant orange flamingos feed in the shallows.

Not long after lunch we entered a sandstone canyon and wound our way through a maze of corridors. And at last we arrived at the City of Rocks, a red sandstone skyline interspersed with smaller formations shaped like…we all called out, like kids naming clouds, "Elephant," "Camel," "Turtle." Camera shutters whirred and clicked. Fred climbed higher in his quest for a panoramic shot. On the way down, he slipped and fell. He didn't hurt himself, but his butt killed our camera.

As the designated hour approached, a few of us gathered at the rally point. The crazed photographers went on snapping "just one more pic-ture." The leader's best effort resembled an attempt to herd rabbits. Fred and I, camera-less, tried to wait patiently, but checking our watches every five minutes didn't help. We didn't leave the City of Rocks until the last die-hard had run out of film (in the digital age we would have had to wait for all the batteries to die). The leader announced that at this late hour we would have to leave the trail and shortcut across country in order to get back to camp before dark

The day had been hot. We had drunk all of our water. Everyone was tired. The sun was low in the sky. Our leader urged us to walk faster. Children whined. Adults grumbled.

No one remarked on the beauty of the sunset's colors saturating the towering bank of clouds on the horizon. The temperature dropped below my comfort zone. I shuddered to think of being forced to survive a night on the cold, cold ground in pitch-black, moonless, starless darkness. I quickened my pace and glared at the stragglers. I let loose a primal scream of frustration inside my head.

When we came upon a jeep trail, hope surged like a flutter of wings. Maybe we would sleep in our down sleeping bags that night. And then I saw the flicker of lights in the distance. Buildings with lights meant civilization. We approached a cluster of shacks that looked as good as Oz to me. One of the shacks sheltered a bar with thirst-quenching beverages for sale. Salvation. Our leader negotiated a truck ride back to camp and we willingly chipped in to pay the fare (all hikers contributed except for the ill-prepared pair, of course).

More Travel

Uncle Sam paid for our next trip to the States, a legitimate R & R, six weeks at the end of May. We divided our time between Tina in Albuquerque, Dakota in Denver, my folks in Los Lunas, and Fred's parents in Roswell. Glenn Jones and family spent a few days in Roswell too. It was a rare opportunity for Granny and Grandpa to meet our friends -- and obvious from their wide smiles that they enjoyed the visit as much as we did. Roswell's Main Street was torn up at the time for a downtown rejuvenation project, and I convinced Fred to take an old iron water-main cover for Granny's garden. I believe that marked the beginning of my love affair with rusty metal objects and my dream of making art from found objects someday.

On our return from this R&R I dreaded the Miami torture more than ever. The scene dragged on, boring and irritating in its predictability and futility. I rolled my eyes and pantomimed exhaustion, plopping my head against Fred's shoulder.

When the airline officials finally reached the incentive stage, Fred grabbed my arm.

"Let's do it."

We sprang to the head of the line and claimed our reward. The first stage was an overnight honeymoon at the Marriott Hotel. Twenty-four hours later, we luxuriated in first class comfort on the way to La Paz. And we pocketed $500 vouchers for future air travel. We both took an extra day off work and napped the entire day of arrival. Not our usual style but quite satisfying for a change of pace.

Three months later, in October, we found a reason to use our airline vouchers. Again, we made the trek to see Tina in a play. Tina led a cast of university players who performed *The Write Stuff* at schools all over the state of New Mexico. The play aimed at encouraging youngsters to participate in creative writing programs. Tina's lively performance captivated her audience. I wanted to shout, Look, that's my daughter!

Even though both Fred and I suffered throughout this visit with nasty cold symptoms, we made the most of our stay in the States. My dad gave us a scare with a four-day stay in the hospital due to pleurisy, and I was grateful to be able to see him through that. Once his condition stabilized we flew to Roswell for a few days with Fred's folks. Fred's dad was sick too. We faced the fact that neither of our fathers had many years left -- strong motivation to leave the Foreign Service at the end of our Bolivia tour in July 1996, nine months away.

The Big Decision

Tina came for her third Christmas visit and we made our requisite trips to the big market for hand-woven aguayo tablecloths and to Elizabeth's shop for gifts and souvenirs that Tina wanted for her friends. Fred and I had a lovely time during Tina's visit. Tina, not so much. Two days after Christmas she spoke her mind at breakfast.

"The last thing I want to do is to hurt your feelings…."

In the pause that followed I gathered courage to face her next words.

"You know how much I love you guys, but…I want to change to an earlier flight…. I have a life and I want to get back to it."

We put her on the plane on December 30, instead of January 10 as planned. That meant we would be apart on her twenty-second birthday, the first birthday without us in her entire life. I put on a serene front but my insides ripped asunder. Letting go required a strength I wasn't sure I had.

In the car on the way home from the airport, Fred and I blinked our swollen, blurry eyes.

"You know what?" I said. "She's right. I think we should leave early too. I have a life and I want to get on with it."

Until that moment we had dithered about setting our retirement date. We wanted to collect our reward of early retirement and live closer to our families, but we had financial fears. With twenty-five years of service, counting his four years in the Army, Fred's annuity would equal fifty percent of the average of his highest three years' salary. The loss of my income would reduce our total budget to about one third of our current spending power. I thought of a pie chart and visualized a one-third-sized wedge. Small. Less than half.

Still, I had read *Your Money or Your Life* by Vicki Robin and I understood how it was possible to live a fulfilling life on less money. The question we had to ask: how much is enough? Our situation would have been more daunting if we hadn't experienced our quasi-hippie period in the early 70s when we learned to make do with much less. Also in our favor was the state of mind we had maintained over the years, living frugally and saving well.

Fred said he was willing to continue in the Foreign Service as long as I would go along. But I was ready to leave it behind. After years of re-inventing myself at every post while staying within the identity of Fred's wife and Dakota and Tina's mother, a basic instinct prodded me to pursue a deeper knowledge of myself. I needed to explore who else I might be – potter, artist, singer, quilter, marathon runner, who-knows-what -- and I wanted to do it in New Mexico.

I crunched our numbers until there was nothing left to crunch. I prepared three scenarios for retirement in 1996 -- at the end of our tour in July, on Fred's fifty-second birthday in May, and the last day of February (the earliest that the government paperwork could be completed). I showed Fred the figures and made my pitch with conviction.

"According to my math, we can do it in February. If it turns out I'm wrong, I'll get a job in Roswell. I promise."

Fred set the retirement wheels in motion. February 29, 1996 would be our last day at work and on March 1 we would fly home to Roswell.

I made several countdown calendars on colorful construction paper. Fred took zany photos of us displaying our calendars as we marked off the days. Excitement made us goofy. I suggested running laps of our garden to let off steam. Not a very big garden, twenty laps might have equaled a quarter mile. We must have looked as nutty as we were.

We worked diligently on our preparations for pack out, and made a giant pile of give-aways that Valentina and Mario happily divided and carried off. Our car left with its new owner and we received notice of our Roswell telephone number – sure signs that we were about to move on. An amazing round of farewell parties transported us to the last day. Before we left the embassy for the last time, I posted a letter – a symbolic act because this letter enclosed our applications as volunteer archeologists for the USDA Forest Service, one brick in the foundation of the new life ahead of us.

Fred and I talked long into the night. It didn't matter that we would have to get up at 4:00 AM to catch our flight. We had reached our most important milestone and were poised to reap the reward of twenty-one years of service. Our dream of early retirement -- the promise of a fulfilling life of leisure after a stimulating era of work – had buoyed us through all those years and was now about to come true. In this final evening, we retold story after story and marveled at how many unique experiences the Foreign Service lifestyle had given us. From the beginning in our thirties to retirement in our fifties we had changed as people do. But we couldn't measure how our evolution had been affected by the cultures we had experienced or the culture of the Foreign Service itself.

"We should write a book," I suggested, as so many Foreign Service veterans have said.

Fred nodded. "Great idea…but can we think about that tomorrow?"

We both laughed and then yawned. Side by side we climbed the stairs, got ready for bed, and lay awake in the dark.

"I'll be so glad to live in the same time zone as the kids – and see them more than once or twice a year." Spoken like a devoted mother.

"Are you thinking about weddings and grandchildren by any chance?" A father's insights rang true.

I smiled and closed my eyes.

"Yeah and our dads too. I hope we can show them some good times before…" Fred let his sentence trail off. The prognosis was not good for either of our fathers, but at least we would be close for their final days.

I changed the subject to a happier one. "I'm so excited about archeology projects. I wonder when we'll hear from them?"

"How soon do you think we'd be ready to go on a dig?"

"As soon as our stuff is delivered and we can get at our camping gear!"

Finally we would have the chance to explore our own state and our home country, whether on an archeology project or on our own. The possibilities seemed endless.

Our conversation moved on to hobbies and sports that we wanted to pursue. We envisioned the discovery of untapped talents. We wondered about fitting into our new community and what our contributions would be.

"There's a lot of work to be done on the house," Fred said.

"Just think of the furniture and appliances we have to buy."

Fred laughed. "We're going to miss old GSO, aren't we?"

We both opened our eyes before the buzz of the alarm clock. I checked everything at least three times – tickets, passports, purse, and tote bag. I peeked between the front window curtains every five minutes, anxious for the arrival of the embassy car.

The front door closed behind us with a resonating click and I thought of the finality of closing the Foreign Service chapter of our lives. Our flight home would provide a segue to unwritten chapters of our future.

We boarded the plane and Fred raised his hand for a high-five.

"Let's wait until the wheels are up, okay?" My stomach jittered with last minute superstition.

With the grind of the landing gear in the background, we slapped our hands high and then held them low, fingers intertwined. The plane headed north and we watched the sun rise on our right, opening a brand new day for the next adventures of our life's story.

CPSIA information can be obtained at www.ICGtesting.com
Printed in the USA
BVOW030216281111

276954BV00005B/205/P

9 781432 780326